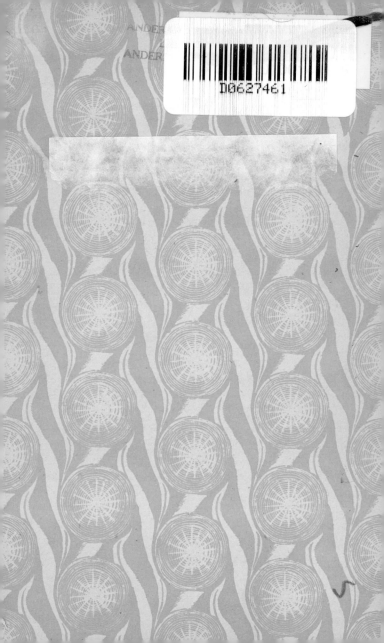

Everyman, I will go with thee, and be thy guide,
In thy most need to go by thy side.

This is No. 931 of Everyman's Library. A list of authors and their works in this series will be found at the end of this volume. The publishers will be pleased to send freely to all applicants a separate, annotated list of the Library.

J. M. DENT & SONS LIMITED
10–13 BEDFORD STREET LONDON W.C.2

E. P. DUTTON & CO. INC.
286–302 FOURTH AVENUE
NEW YORK

EVERYMAN'S LIBRARY
EDITED BY ERNEST RHYS

BIOGRAPHY

THE LETTERS OF GEORGE GORDON
6TH LORD BYRON · SELECTED AND
EDITED BY R. G. HOWARTH, WITH AN
INTRODUCTION BY ANDRÉ MAUROIS

GEORGE GORDON, SIXTH LORD
BYRON, born 22nd January 1788; at
Harrow, 1801–5; at Cambridge, 1805–8;
Eastern tour, 1809–11; death of Mrs. Byron,
meeting with John Murray, and with Thomas
Moore, 1811; marriage, birth of Ada Byron,
1815; separation from Lady Byron, settlement in Italy, 1816; birth of Allegra, 1817;
beginning of association with the Countess
Guiccioli, 1819; death of Allegra, 1822;
departure for Greece, 1823; death at Missolonghi, 19th April 1824.

THE LETTERS OF
LORD BYRON

SELECTED AND EDITED BY
R. G. HOWARTH

LONDON: J. M. DENT & SONS LTD.
NEW YORK: E. P. DUTTON & CO. INC.

INTRODUCTION

BYRON'S fame as a poet, in the last hundred years, has been less disputed on the Continent than in England; but his reputation as a letter-writer, now solidly established in his own country, has scarcely so far crossed the Channel, and this is to be regretted. For the reader whose knowledge of Byron is confined to his poetry has an incomplete and false picture of the man. In *Childe Harold*, in *Lara*, in *Manfred*, Byron projects a romantic, extreme Byron, such as indeed he was in brief moments of violent passion. It is only at the *Don Juan* period that he reveals in his poetry the cynical and cheerful Byron whom his friends knew and loved. The reader of his letters enters into closer and more constant contact with him. It is from his letters and also from the conversations preserved by Moore, Trelawny, Medwin, Lady Byron, and Dr. Kennedy that we can imagine with any sort of probability the man who was, with Napoleon, one of the two most remarkable figures of the nineteenth century.

I

'A writer', says Paul Valéry, 'consoles himself as best he can for any injustice of fate.' In other words, a man experiences the need to create a poetic, an imaginary world, because the world of reality has denied him happiness. In Byron's case, the motives for dissatisfaction are evident from his very childhood. He was born lame and this made him suffer. His mother, proud of her name (she was a Gordon of Gight), was ruined, then deserted by her husband. The child grew up in poverty; at first in an atmosphere of quarrels, later of complaints. This mother, courageous and honest, but wretched and irascible, loved and tortured him at the same time. He was ashamed of her. Because of this shame and his own infirmity he became self-conscious. When chance and the death of a cousin raised him to the peerage, he still retained a naïve, rather too obvious pride which was his revenge for those years of wretchedness.

One important feature: he was brought up in Scotland amongst convinced Calvinists. The doctrine of predestination was preached to him from childhood. It left a deep impression on him. He was told the story of his ancestors. He knew that in both lines of descent they had been terrible, dangerous, and half mad. He thought himself predestined to lead an ardent and guilty life. Nor did it matter that later, under the influence of his irreligious Cambridge friends and the eighteenth-century French sceptics, he was to become a Voltairian deist, then a cynic. Always in his secret heart there lurked a Calvinist who was to judge Don Juan, hope to lead a better life, and despise the too easy women who fell in love with Childe Harold. That the Calvinist survived to the poet's dying day is proved by the conversations with Dr. Kennedy.

Beauty came too late for him to enter the sentimental life with confidence. He was a crippled, fattish, timid young man whom girls made sport of. The first woman he loved, Mary Chaworth, laughed at his love and married another man. The consequence was, that born sentimental and tender, he became unsociable and contemptuous. He had begun life by forming a sublime idea of love and friendship. When men and women disappointed him by their fickleness, he became a misanthrope, or at least he thought he was one. But like the Calvinist, the sentimental survived in him to the end. If you doubt it, study the adventure of Lady Frances Webster, and later Byron's attitude towards Teresa Guiccioli.

To defend himself against sentimentalism, he resorted to a pungent, ironical humour of his own making. It can be perceived already in the letters of his childhood. If Byron describes 'the dowager', his terrible mother, to his sister Augusta, it is in terms which grow more comic with the increasing intensity of his sufferings. At the very moment when he is writing the sombre *Childe Harold*, his letters are gay and simple. Both attitudes are sincere. Poetry serves as a safety valve for his passions. Then, calmed by the poetic explosion, he becomes once more Byron—a humorous, sensible creature.

'If anything was more characteristic of Byron than another, it was his solid common-sense.' The phrase is Disraeli's. It is perfectly true. No being was more capable of perceiving reality without illusions or passion than this most passionate man. When the moment comes to embark for Greece, all his companions utter a thousand heroic stupidities. Byron alone sees the rough, melancholy, and somewhat futile aspect of the adventure.   In action he shows himself a man of action. At Missolonghi, he is the only one who does not lose his head. It is probable that had it not been for his infirmity, he might have been destined for a life of action.   At least that is what he thought himself.

But, incapacitated for action by his bad leg, he fell a prey to ennui.   The danger of a youth spent, like his, in perpetual excitement is that the man who has lived in this state of agitation can never again accustom himself to calm.   'Anything rather than conjugate the terrible verb, "ennuyer."' Here Byron reflects in a marvellous way the spirit of the early nineteenth century, which was so used to the strong emotions of the Revolution and the Napoleonic wars that it had, as Stendhal said, 'a continual thirst for strong emotions'.   There is a remark of Byron's which is very important because it explains a great many of his acts, and nearly all his mistakes. 'The great object of life is sensation—to feel that we exist, even though in pain.   It is this "craving void" which drives us to gaming—to battle, to travel—to intemperate, but keenly felt, pursuits of any description, whose principal attraction is the agitation inseparable from their accomplishment.'

The fear of boredom and the violence of his temperament always drove him to actions of an extreme sort, which he was at the same time impelled to disapprove because of his sentimentalism and his innate respect for the conventions.   This was the cause of the inner conflict that rent his soul.   Had he lived, it is possible, as Harold Nicolson supposes, that he would have gone back to Lady Byron with pleasure, and spent a conventional old age with her and her daughter.   Already at Missolonghi he discovered a very un-Byronic happiness in the moral redemption of sacrifice; but, ever complex, he laughed at his own virtue.   'If I do outlive the campaign, I shall write two poems on the subject—one an epic, and the other a burlesque, in which none shall be spared, and myself least of all. . . .'

When he left England in 1816, Hobhouse, seeing the 'dear fellow' standing on the deck of the ship, had murmured: 'God bless him for a gallant spirit and a kind one'.   These are the right words with which to conclude any portrait of Byron. He was brave, frank, and, though appearances belie it, capable of kindness.   Women complained of him greatly, but it must be allowed that they were more guilty of their misfortunes than he himself. Who can pity a Claire Clairmont? And even a Caroline Lamb? In Paris, when he died, the young men wore a band of crape on their hats, and Jane Welsh wrote to Thomas Carlyle: 'If they had said the sun or the moon had gone out of the heavens, it could not have struck me with the idea of a more awful and dreary blank in the creation than the words: Byron is dead'. For human beings are grateful to men of genius, not for being perfect, but for being great.

II

It would take too long to draw up here a complete list of Byron's correspondents, but it is necessary to indicate the successive groups which they compose.

In his childhood and in his boyhood he wrote to his mother, 'the dowager', to his lawyer Hanson, and to his half-sister, the Hon. Augusta Byron, who soon afterwards became Mrs. Leigh. Then appear the Southwell friends: the charming Elizabeth Pigot, an unassuming confidante, and her brother, John Pigot; and the college friends at Cambridge: Scrope Davies, a likeable buffoon, the sedate Hobhouse, a stern but faithful friend, and the clergyman Hodgson, a man of prudent counsel, rarely listened to.

After the journey to Greece and the publication of *Childe Harold* there come into Byron's life those who were attracted by his new fame. First R. C. Dallas, the officious relative who reads his manuscripts, then fashionable men of letters like Tom Moore and the banker - Mæcenas, Samuel Rogers. To them are added those natural correspondents of a successful author: his publisher, John Murray, his banker and friend, Kinnaird.

Third *entrée* in this 'ballet' of correspondents—the women who loved him: Caroline Lamb, Lady Frances Webster, Lady Oxford, and Annabella Milbanke, whom he baptizes at the time of their first meeting, 'The Princess of Parallelograms'. For so many love affairs he must have a confidante. It is the admirable Lady Melbourne, the most remarkable of Byron's correspondents. She pleased, not perhaps the deeper Byron, the Calvinist and sentimental, but the sarcastic, surface Byron. In prose, he preferred the cynicism of Lady Melbourne to the romanticism of Lady Caroline.

For two years Augusta Leigh, Annabella, and Lady Melbourne became the three centres of his life. Then we have the

marriage, the drama of the separation; and with his residence
in Switzerland appears a fourth group, that of the Shelleys.
The latter's sister-in-law, Claire Clairmont, threw herself at
Byron's head, and introduced him to Shelley. Mary Shelley,
until the end, was to remain on friendly, but somewhat chilly,
terms with Byron. Through the Shelleys, the Shelleys' own
friends found themselves annexed to Byron's life: Medwin,
the Williamses, Trelawny. Leigh Hunt was already known to
Byron, who used to see him in London.

Fifth *entrée*. The Venice group: Teresa Guiccioli and her
incredible husband, her brother Gamba, and the British consul
Hoppner, who becomes, because he is entrusted with Byron's
communications with Claire, and then with his daughter
Allegra, one of the most faithful of the correspondents.

The last group will be composed of those who took a share
in the Greek adventure—the members of the Greek committee
in London, Prince Mavrocordatos, the 'printer colonel' Stanhope, and the banker at Zante, Samuel Barff.

Nothing is more interesting than to see, in the course of a
long correspondence, the successive illumination of the obscure
beings touched by a great destiny in its swift trajectory; just
as in the ray of a passing sunbeam the specks of dust floating
in the transparent air of a room are suddenly lighted up, then,
when the ray has disappeared, become once more invisible.

III

It might be said that there are three sorts of letter-writers:
those who use letters for exposing ideas; those who, having
few facts to relate, turn to marvellous account the minutest
incidents of a rather monotonous life, and adorn any sort
of event with the prestige of form; those, finally, who write
because they cannot do otherwise, and throw their whole
selves, blazing and alive, into their correspondence. Although
there exists, among the greatest letter-writers, a mixture of
these three types, we might say that Taine belongs to the first,
Madame de Sévigné to the second, Byron to the third.

The best-known of Madame de Sévigné's letters are 'literary
pieces'; written to please, destined sometimes for public
reading, skilfully composed like La Bruyère's *Caractères*.
These are not the ones which I like best. Those which best
explain her deserved reputation are the simple letters when
she is writing about anything at all—her visitors, her gardener,

her trees. Byron himself in his letters never writes to produce a literary effect. He writes to give information, to express precise and definite sentiments; and he does it with a direct exactness which is at once the absence of all art and the perfection of art.

Between the prose of the letters and the tone of the poems we find profound similarities. The first is *vigour*. When Byron has formulated a judgment, experienced a desire, conceived a hate, these thoughts *must* spout up. He cannot contain them, nor moderate them. Words underlined mark the force of the outburst. Everything is said, without reserve, without attenuation, savagely. His mother before him wrote like this. The second resemblance is *movement*. One of Byron's letters, like one of his poems, sweeps the reader along in an irresistible onrush. The identity of tone, and, above all, of rhythm between his prose and his verses, is such that sometimes, quite naturally, the letter becomes a poem without the reader being surprised by the change. A good example is the charming letter to Tom Moore on the Venetian carnival.

One could almost say that Byron's prose is more poetic than his poetry. The latter can sometimes incur the reproach of a little too much monotony in the rhythms, a little in-genuousness in the subjects. But his letters, like his journal, exhibit the rather mad poetry of the Elizabethan clowns. In prose, as in verse, he loves phrases with well-marked anti-theses: 'I am losing my relatives and you are adding to the number of yours, but which is best, God knows. . . .' Some-times he captures the very essential music of speech: 'I have hopes, sir—hopes, but she wants me to come to Ravenna. Now this would be all very well for certainties; but for mere hopes . . .' And so certain words recur like rhymes. An irresistible power runs through the phrases. When we see the originals of Byron's letters, difficult to read, imperious, never crossed out, we imagine the prodigious rapidity with which, never stopping, never hesitating, never retouching, this quick, firm pen etched a truthful portrait. It is in the letters, in the journals, in *Don Juan*, and in his delightful 'short lyrics' that the greatest of the English romantics reveals him-self, not far behind Voltaire and Swift, as one of the greatest classic writers.

ANDRÉ MAUROIS.

1933.

BIBLIOGRAPHICAL NOTE

The following is a list of the works of Lord Byron:

Fugitive Pieces, 1806; republished with one omission and several additions as *Poems on Various Occasions*, 1807; a further reissue with omissions and additions, *Hours of Idleness*, 1807; a fourth reissue appeared as *Poems Original and Translated*, 1808. *English Bards and Scotch Reviewers*, 1809; a preliminary copy had been set up under the title of *The British Bards*, and dated 1808; later editions were all added to: second (which first bore Byron's name), 1809; third, 1810; fourth, 1810 (two different fourth editions exist, one dated 1810, and the other 1811); fifth, 1811; the last edition was suppressed and almost entirely destroyed. *Childe Harold's Pilgrimage*, cantos i and ii, 1812; editions containing changes: second, 1812; seventh, 1814; Third Canto, 1816; Fourth Canto, 1818. *The Curse of Minerva*, 1812. *The Waltz*, 1813 (new edition 1821). *The Giaour*, 1813 (seven other editions appeared the same year with additions). *The Bride of Abydos*, 1813 (new editions: second, 1813; fourth, 1813). *The Corsair*, 1814 (new editions: second, 1814; seventh, 1814; ninth, 1815; tenth, 1818). *Ode to Napoleon Buonaparte*, 1814. *Lara* (published with Samuel Rogers's *Jacqueline* in first edition), 1814 (new edition: fifth, 1817). *Hebrew Melodies*, 1815. *Poems on his domestic circumstances*, 1816 (containing *Fare Thee Well*, etc.), *Monody on the Death of Sheridan*, 1816. *The Siege of Corinth* and *Parisina* (published together), 1816. *The Prisoner of Chillon*, etc., 1816. *The Lament of Tasso*, 1817. *Manfred*, 1817. *Beppo*, 1818 (new edition: fifth, 1818). *Don Juan*, Cantos i and ii, 1819 (the full text of cantos i and ii did not appear until the edition of 1833); Cantos iii–v, 1821 (new edition: fifth, 1822); cantos vi–viii, 1823; Cantos ix–xi, 1823; Cantos xii–xiv, 1823; Cantos xv and xvi, 1824; complete work, 1826. *Mazeppa*, 1819. *Sardanapalus, The Two Foscari*, and *Cain*, published together, 1821. *Marino Faliero* and *The Prophecy of Dante*, published together, 1821. *The Age of Bronze*, 1823. *The Island*, 1823. *Werner*, 1823. *The Deformed Transformed*, 1824.

Of his other works, the following appeared in *The Liberal* (1822): 'Heaven and Earth', 'The Blues', 'A Vision of Judgment', 'Morgante Maggiore' (a translation from Luigi Pulci), 'Epigrams on Lord Castlereagh', and a letter to 'My Grandmother's Review'. Posthumous publications were *Hints from Horace* and *The Irish Avatar* (collected edition of 1831). *Imitations and Translations* collected by J. C. Hobhouse (1809) containing nine poems by Byron.

The standard edition of Byron's works is that of which the *Letters and Journals* are edited by Lord Ernle (R. E. Prothero), and the *Poetry* is edited by E. H. Coleridge (thirteen volumes), 1898–1903. The best of the numerous books containing reminiscences and correspondence are: J. C. Hobhouse, *Journey Through Albania*, 1812; R. C. Dallas, *Recollections of the Life of Lord Byron*, 1824; T. Medwin, *Journal of the Conversations of Lord Byron*, 1824; Thomas Moore, *Letters and Journals of Lord Byron*, 1830; T. Kennedy, *Conversations on Religion with Lord Byron*, 1830; Countess Guiccioli, *My Recollections of Lord Byron* (English translation), 1869; E. J. Trelawny, *Recollections of Shelley and Byron*, 1858; Earl of Lovelace, *Astarte*, 1905; E. C. Mayne, *Byron*, 1912; Lord Byron's *Correspondence, Chiefly with Lady Melbourne*, 1922; H. Nicolson, *Byron, the Last Journey*, 1924; André Maurois, *Byron*, 1930; P. Quennell, *Byron*, 1934.

F. W.

EDITOR'S ACKNOWLEDGMENTS

This selection from the whole of the published material was originally issued in the Illustrated Classics series. It has now been revised and slightly reduced, fifty-two of the less important letters being omitted. As before, all letters have been printed in full, except where omissions previously made cannot be supplied. The grateful acknowledgments of the editor are due to Mary, Countess of Lovelace, for permission to include ten letters (namely, Nos. 84, 90, 91, 95, 101, 109, 121, 135, 146, 147) from her edition of the late Earl's *Astarte*; to Sir John Murray for permission to use the text of Lord Ernle's (R. E. Prothero's) edition for many letters, and for leave to include seventeen letters (namely, Nos. 18, 21, 24, 44, 45, 58, 60, 68, 70, 87, 125, 127, 139, 206, 208, 214, 216) from the late Sir John Murray's edition of *Lord Byron's Correspondence*; and to Lord Ernle, whom all editors of Byron's letters must, for the most part, humbly follow.

CONTENTS

CONTENTS

CONTENTS

THE LETTERS OF LORD BYRON

1. TO HIS MOTHER [1]

Nottingham, 13 March, 1799.

DEAR MAMA,

I am very glad to hear you are well. I am so myself, thank God; upon my word I did not expect so long a Letter from you; however I will answer it as well as I can. Mrs. Parkyns and the rest are well and are much obliged to you for the present. Mr. Rogers [2] could attend me every night at a separate hour from the Miss Parkynses, and I am astonished you do not acquiesce in this Scheme which would keep me in Mind of what I have almost entirely forgot. I recommend this to you because, if some plan of this kind is not adopted, I shall be called, or rather branded with the name of a dunce, which you know I could never bear. I beg you will consider this plan seriously and I will lend it all the assistance in my power. I shall be very glad to see the Letter you talk of, and I have time just to say I hope every body is well at Newstead,

And remain, your affectionate Son,

BYRON.

P.S.—Pray let me know when you are to send in the Horses to go to Newstead. May [3] desires her Duty and I also expect an answer by the miller.

2. TO THE HON. AUGUSTA BYRON [4]

Harrow-on-the-Hill,[5] October 25th, 1804.

MY DEAR AUGUSTA,

In compliance with your wishes, as well as gratitude for your affectionate letter, I proceed as soon as possible to answer it; I am glad to hear that *any body* gives a good account of me;

[1] Catherine Gordon of Gight in 1785 became the second wife of Captain John ('Mad Jack') Byron, who died in 1791. She was now at Newstead Abbey, part of her son's inheritance, whilst he remained at Nottingham for the treatment of his misshapen foot.

[2] Dummer Rogers, a teacher.

[3] May Gray, Byron's nurse.

[4] Byron's half-sister, daughter of Captain Byron by his first marriage with the Baroness Conyers. She was brought up by her grandmother, the Countess of Holderness.

[5] Whither Byron had gone in April 1801.

1

but from the quarter you mention, I should imagine it was exaggerated. That you are unhappy, my dear Sister, makes me so also; were it in my power to relieve your sorrows you would soon recover your spirits; as it is, I sympathize better than you yourself expect. But really, after all (pardon me my dear Sister), I feel a little inclined to laugh at you, for love, in my humble opinion, is utter nonsense, a mere jargon of compliments, romance, and deceit; now, for my part, had I fifty mistresses, I should in the course of a fortnight, forget them all, and, if by any chance I ever recollected one, should laugh at it as a dream, and bless my stars, for delivering me from the hands of the little mischievous Blind God. Can't you drive this Cousin [1] of ours out of your pretty little head (for as to *hearts* I think they are out of the question), or if you are so far gone, why don't you give old L'Harpagon (I mean the General [2]) the slip, and take a trip to Scotland, you are now pretty near the Borders. Be sure to Remember me to my formal Guardy Lord Carlisle, [3] whose magisterial presence I have not been into for some years, nor have I any ambition to attain so great an honour. As to your favourite Lady Gertrude, [4] I don't remember her; pray, is she handsome? I dare say she is, for although they are a *disagreeable, formal, stiff* Generation, yet they have by no means plain *persons*, I remember Lady Cawdor was a sweet, pretty woman; pray, does your sentimental Gertrude resemble her? I have heard that the duchess of Rutland was handsome also, but we will say nothing about her temper, as I hate Scandal.

Adieu, my pretty Sister, forgive my levity, write soon, and God bless you.

I remain, your very affectionate Brother,

BYRON.

P.S.—I left my mother at Southwell, [5] some time since, in a monstrous pet with you for not writing. I am sorry to say the old lady and myself don't agree like lambs in a meadow, but I believe it is all my own fault, I am rather too fidgety, which my precise mama objects to, we differ, then argue, and

---

[1] Colonel George Leigh, whom in 1807 she married.

[2] General Charles Leigh, the Colonel's father.

[3] Frederick Howard, Earl of Carlisle, a connection, and from 1799 Byron's guardian.

[4] Carlisle's third daughter. The others were Caroline Isabella, Lady Cawdor; and Elizabeth, Duchess of Rutland.

[5] Mrs. Byron had settled at Burgage Manor, Southwell, near Newstead Abbey.

to my shame be it spoken fall out a *little*, however after a
storm comes a calm; what's become of our aunt the amiable
antiquated Sophia? [1] is she yet in the land of the living, or does
she sing psalms with the *Blessed* in the other world. Adieu.
I am happy enough and Comfortable here. My friends are not
numerous, but select; among them I rank as the principal
Lord Delawarr,[2] who is very amiable and my particular friend;
do you know the family at all? Lady Delawarr is frequently
in town, perhaps you may have seen her; if she resembles her
son she is the most amiable woman in Europe. I have plenty
of acquaintances, but I reckon them as mere Blanks. Adieu,
my dear Augusta.

3. TO HARGREAVES HANSON [3]

Trinity Coll., [Cambridge[4]], Novr. 12th, 1805.

DEAR HARGREAVES,

Return my Thanks to your father for the *Expedition* he has
used in filling my *Cellar*.

He deserves commendation for the *Attention* he paid to my
Request. The Time of 'Oateater's'[5] Journey approaches;
I presume he means to repair his Neglect by Punctuality in
this Respect. However, no *Trinity Ale* will be forthcoming,
till I have broached the promised *Falernum*. College improves
in every thing but Learning. Nobody here seems to look into
an Author, ancient or modern, if they can avoid it. The
Muses, poor Devils, are totally neglected, except by a few
Musty old *Sophs* [6] and *Fellows*, who, however agreeable they
may be to *Minerva*, are perfect Antidotes to the *Graces*. Even I
(great as is my *inclination* for Knowledge) am carried away by
the Tide, having only supped at Home twice since I saw your
father, and have more engagements on my Hands for a week
to come. Still my Tutor and I go on extremely well and for
the first three weeks of my life I have not involved myself in
any Scrape of Consequence.—I have News for you which
I bear with *Christian* Resignation and without any *violent*

[1] Sophia Byron, their father's sister.
[2] George John Sackville West, fifth Earl De La Warr.
[3] Second son of John Hanson, Byron's solicitor. He had left Harrow
in 1804 to enter his father's office.
[4] Byron had gone into residence in the previous month.
[5] His horse.
[6] Sophomores, second-year students.

Transports of *Grief*. My Mother (whose diabolical Temper you well know) has taken it into her *Sagacious* Head to quarrel with me her *dutiful Son*. She has such a Devil of a Disposition, that she cannot be quiet, though there are fourscore miles between us, which I wish were lengthened to 400. The Cause too frivolous to require taking up your time to read or mine to write. At last in answer to a *Furious Epistle* I returned a *Sarcastick* Answer, which so incensed the *Amiable Dowager* that my Letter was sent back without her deigning a Line in the cover. When I next see you, you shall behold her Letter and my Answer, which will amuse you as they both contain fiery Philippics. I must request you will write immediately, that I may be informed when my Servant shall convey 'Oat-eater' from London; the 20th was the appointed; but I wish to hear further from your father. I hope all the family are in a convalescent State. I shall see you at Christmas (if I live) as I propose passing the Vacation, which is only a Month, in London.

Believe me, Mr. Terry, your's Truly,
Byron.

4. TO WILLIAM BANKES [1]

Southwell, March 6, 1807.

Dear Bankes,

Your critique [2] is valuable for many reasons: in the first place, it is the only one in which flattery has borne so slight a part; in the *next*, I am *cloyed* with insipid compliments. I have a better opinion of your judgment and ability than your *feelings*. Accept my most sincere thanks for your kind decision, not less welcome, because totally unexpected. With regard to a more exact estimate, I need not remind you how few of the *best poems*, in our language, will stand the test of *minute* or *verbal* criticism: it can therefore hardly be expected the effusions of a boy (and most of these pieces have been produced at an early period) can derive much merit either from the subject or composition. Many of them were written under great depression of spirits, and during severe indisposition:—hence

[1] William John Bankes, a Trinity contemporary, afterwards a traveller in the East.

[2] His opinion of Byron's second volume of verse, *Poems on Various Occasions*, printed at Newark in 1807.

the gloomy turn of the ideas. We coincide in opinion that the *'poësies érotiques'* are the most exceptionable; they were, however, grateful to the *deities*, on whose altars they were offered—more I seek not.

The portrait of Pomposus [1] was drawn at Harrow, after a *long sitting*; this accounts for the resemblance, or rather the *caricatura*. He is *your* friend, he *never was mine*—for both our sakes I shall be silent on this head. The *collegiate* rhymes are not personal—one of the notes may appear so, but could not be omitted. I have little doubt they will be deservedly abused—a just punishment for my unfilial treatment of so excellent an Alma Mater. I sent you no copy, lest *we* should be placed in the situation of *Gil Blas* and the *Archbishop* of Grenada; [2] though running some hazard from the experiment, I wished your *verdict* to be unbiassed. Had my *'Libellus'* been presented previous to your letter, it would have appeared a species of bribe to purchase compliment. I feel no hesitation in saying, I was more anxious to hear your critique however severe, than the praises of the *million*. On the same day I was honoured with the encomiums of *Mackenzie*,[3] the celebrated author of the *Man of Feeling*. Whether *his* approbation or *yours* elated me most, I cannot decide.

You will receive my *Juvenilia*,—at least all yet published. I have a large volume in manuscript, which may in part appear hereafter; at present I have neither time nor inclination to prepare it for the press. In the spring I shall return to Trinity, to dismantle my rooms, and bid you a final adieu. The *Cam* will not be much increased by my *tears* on the occasion. Your further remarks, however *caustic* or bitter to a palate vitiated with the *sweets of adulation*, will be of service. Johnson has shown us that *no poetry* is perfect; but to correct mine would be an Herculean labour. In fact I never looked beyond the moment of composition, and published merely at the request of my friends. Notwithstanding so much has been said concerning the 'Genus irritabile vatum', we shall never quarrel on the subject—poetic fame is by no means the 'acme' of my wishes.—Adieu. Yours ever,

BYRON.

[1] Dr. George Butler, an unpopular headmaster of Harrow.
[2] In Le Sage's *Gil Blas* the hero is dismissed for making criticisms of the Archbishop's compositions.
[3] Henry Mackenzie (1745–1831) was novelist, playwright, essayist, and political writer.

5. TO ELIZABETH BRIDGET PIGOT [1]

Cambridge, June 30th, 1807.

'Better late than never, Pal,' is a saying of which you know the origin, and as it is applicable on the present occasion, you will excuse its conspicuous place in the front of my epistle. I am almost superannuated here. My old friends (with the exception of a very few) all departed, and I am preparing to follow them, but remain till Monday to be present at 3 *Oratorios*, 2 *Concerts*, a *Fair*, and a *Ball*. I find I am not only *thinner* but *taller* by an inch since my last visit. I was obliged to tell every body my *name*, nobody having the least recollection of my *visage*, or person. Even the hero of *my Cornelian* [2] (who is now sitting *vis-à-vis*, reading a volume of my *Poetics*) passed me in Trinity walks without recognising me in the least, and was thunderstruck at the alteration which had taken place in my countenance, etc., etc. Some say I look *better*, others *worse*, but all agree I am *thinner*,—more I do not require. I have lost 2 lb. in my weight since I left your *cursed*, *detestable*, and *abhorred* abode of *scandal*, where, excepting yourself and John Becher, [3] I care not if the whole race were consigned to the *Pit* of *Acheron*, which I would visit in person rather than contaminate my *sandals* with the polluted dust of Southwell. *Seriously*, unless obliged by the *emptiness* of my purse to revisit Mrs. B., you will see me no more.

On Monday I depart for London. I quit Cambridge with little regret, because our *set* are *vanished*, and my *musical protégé* before mentioned has left the choir, and is stationed in a mercantile house of considerable eminence in the metropolis. You may have heard me observe he is exactly to an hour, 2 years younger than myself. I found him grown considerably, and, as you will suppose, very glad to see his former *Patron*. He is nearly my height, very *thin*, very fair complexion, dark eyes, and light locks. My opinion of his mind you already know;—I hope I shall never have occasion to change it. Every body here conceives me to be an *invalid*. The University at present is very gay, from the fêtes of divers kinds. I supped out last night, but eat (or ate) nothing, sipped a bottle of claret, went to bed at 2 and rose at 8. I have commenced

---

[1] Daughter of a neighbour of Mrs. Byron at Southwell.
[2] Edleston, a Cambridge chorister, whom Byron saved from drowning, had given him a cornelian heart.
[3] The Rev. John Thomas Becher, Byron's literary adviser.

early rising, and find it agrees with me. The Masters and the Fellows all very *polite*, but look a little *askance*—don't much admire *lampoons*—truth always disagreeable.

Write, and tell me how the inhabitants of your *Menagerie* go *on*, and if my publication goes *off* well: do the quadrupeds *growl*? Apropos, my bull-dog is deceased—'Flesh both of cur and man is grass'. Address your answer to Cambridge. If I am gone, it will be forwarded. Sad news just arrived—Russians beat [1]—a bad set, eat nothing but *oil*, consequently must melt before a *hard fire*. I get awkward in my academic habiliments for want of practice. Got up in a window to hear the oratorio at St. Mary's, popped down in the middle of the *Messiah*, tore a *woeful* rent in the back of my best black silk gown, and damaged an egregious pair of breeches. Mem.—never tumble from a church window during service. Adieu, dear * * * *! do not remember me to any body:—to *forget* and be forgotten by the people of Southwell is all I aspire to.

6. TO ELIZABETH BRIDGET PIGOT

London, August 11th, 1807.

On Sunday next I set off for the Highlands. A friend of mine accompanies me in my carriage to Edinburgh. There we shall leave it, and proceed in a *tandem* (a species of open carriage) through the western passes to Inverary, where we shall purchase *shelties*, to enable us to view places inaccessible to *vehicular conveyances*. On the coast we shall hire a vessel, and visit the most remarkable of the Hebrides; and, if we have time and favourable weather, mean to sail as far as Iceland, only 300 miles from the northern extremity of Caledonia, to peep at *Hecla*. This last intention you will keep a secret, as my nice *mamma* would imagine I was on a Voyage of *Discovery*, and raise the accustomed *maternal warwhoop*.

Last week I swam in the Thames from Lambeth through the two bridges, Westminster and Blackfriars, a distance, including the different turns and tracks made on the way, of three miles! You see I am in excellent training in case of a *squall* at sea. I mean to collect all the Erse traditions, poems, etc., etc., and translate, or expand the subject to fill a volume, which may appear next spring under the denomination of

[1] In the Battle of Friedland, 15 June.

'*The Highland Harp*', or some title equally *picturesque*. Of Bosworth Field, one book is finished, another just began. It will be a work of three or four years, and most probably never *conclude*. What would you say to some stanzas on Mount Hecla? they would be written at least with *fire*. How is the immortal Bran? and the Phœnix of canine quadrupeds, Boatswain? I have lately purchased a thorough-bred bull-dog, worthy to be the coadjutor of the aforesaid celestials—his name is *Smut*!—'Bear it, ye breezes, on your *balmy* wings'.

Write to me before I set off, I conjure you, by the fifth rib of your grandfather. Ridge[1] goes on well with the books—I thought that worthy had not done much in the country. In town they have been very successful; Carpenter (Moore's [2] publisher) told me a few days ago they sold all their's immediately, and had several enquiries made since, which, from the books being gone, they could not supply. The Duke of York, the Marchioness of Headfort, the Duchess of Gordon, etc., etc., were among the purchasers; and Crosby says the circulation will be still more extensive in the winter, the summer season being very bad for a sale, as most people are absent from London. However, they have gone off extremely well altogether. I shall pass very near you on my journey through Newark, but cannot approach. Don't tell this to Mrs. B., who supposes I travel a different road. If you have a letter, order it to be left at Ridge's shop, where I shall call, or the post-office, Newark, about six or eight in the evening. If your brother would ride over, I should be devilish glad to see him—he can return the same night, or sup with us and go home the next morning—the Kingston Arms is my inn. Adieu.

Yours ever,

BYRON.

7. TO ELIZABETH BRIDGET PIGOT

Trinity College, Cambridge,[3] October 26th, 1807.

MY DEAR ELIZABETH,

Fatigued with sitting up till four in the morning for the last two days at hazard, I take up my pen to inquire how your highness and the rest of my female acquaintance at the seat of archiepiscopal grandeur go on. I know I deserve a scolding

---

[1] J. Ridge, the Newark publisher.
[2] Thomas Moore (1779–1852), the poet, afterwards one of Byron's intimate friends and his biographer.
[3] He had decided to remain another year.

for my negligence in not writing more frequently; but racing up and down the country for these last three months, how was it possible to fulfil the duties of a correspondent? Fixed at last for six weeks, I write, as *thin* as ever (not having gained an ounce since my reduction), and rather in better humour;— but, after all, Southwell was a detestable residence. Thank St. Dominica, I have done with it: I have been twice within eight miles of it, but could not prevail on myself to *suffocate* in its heavy atmosphere. This place is wretched enough—a villainous chaos of din and drunkenness, nothing but hazard and burgundy, hunting, mathematics, and Newmarket, riot and racing. Yet it is a paradise compared with the eternal dulness of Southwell. Oh! the misery of doing nothing but make *love, enemies,* and *verses.*

Next January (but this is *entre nous only,* and pray let it be so, or my maternal persecutor will be throwing her tomahawk at any of my curious projects) I am going to sea, for four or five months, with my cousin Captain Bettesworth,[1] who commands the *Tartar,* the finest frigate in the navy. I have seen most scenes, and wish to look at a naval life. We are going probably to the Mediterranean, or to the West Indies, or—to the devil; and if there is a possibility of taking me to the latter, Bettesworth will do it; for he has received four and twenty wounds in different places, and at this moment possesses a letter from the late Lord Nelson, stating Bettesworth as the only officer in the navy who had more wounds than himself.

I have got a new friend, the finest in the world, a *tame bear.* When I brought him here, they asked me what I meant to do with him, and my reply was, 'he should *sit for a fellowship*'. Sherard will explain the meaning of the sentence, if it is ambiguous. This answer delighted them not. We have several parties here, and this evening a large assortment of jockies, gamblers, boxers, authors, parsons, and poets, sup with me,— a precious mixture, but they go on well together; and for me, I am a *spice* of every thing, except a jockey; by the bye, I was dismounted again the other day.

Thank your brother in my name for his treatise. I have written 214 pages of a novel,—one poem of 380 lines,[2] to be published (without my name) in a few weeks, with notes,— 560 lines of Bosworth Field, and 250 lines of another poem in

---

[1] George Edmund Byron Bettesworth, connected with Byron through his grandmother.
[2] The first draft of *English Bards, and Scotch Reviewers.*

rhyme, besides half a dozen smaller pieces. The poem to be published is a Satire. *Apropos*, I have been praised to the skies in the *Critical Review*, and abused greatly in another publication. So much the better, they tell me, for the sale of the book; it keeps up controversy, and prevents it being forgotten. Besides, the first men of all ages have had their share, nor do the humblest escape;—so I bear it like a philosopher. It is odd two opposite critiques came out on the same day, and out of five pages of abuse my censor only quotes *two lines* from different poems, in support of his opinion. Now, the proper way to *cut up* is to quote long passages, and make them appear absurd, because simple allegation is no proof. On the other hand, there are seven pages of praise, and more than *my modesty* will allow said on the subject. Adieu.

P.S.—Write, write, write!!!

8. TO ROBERT CHARLES DALLAS [1]

Dorant's [Hotel, Albemarle Street], January 21, 1808.

Sir,

Whenever leisure and inclination permit me the pleasure of a visit, I shall feel truly gratified in a personal acquaintance with one whose mind has been long known to me in his writings.

You are so far correct in your conjecture, that I am a member of the University of Cambridge, where I shall take my degree of A.M. this term; but were reasoning, eloquence, or virtue, the objects of my search, Granta is not their metropolis, nor is the place of her situation an 'El Dorado', far less an Utopia. The intellects of her children are as stagnant as her Cam, and their pursuits limited to the church—not of Christ, but of the nearest benefice.

As to my reading, I believe I may aver, without hyperbole, it has been tolerably extensive in the historical department; so that few nations exist, or have existed, with whose records I am not in some degree acquainted, from Herodotus down to Gibbon. Of the classics I know about as much as most schoolboys after a discipline of thirteen years; of the *Law* of the *Land*, as much as enables me to keep 'within the statute'—to use the poacher's vocabulary. I did study the 'Spirit of Laws', [2] and the Law of Nations; but when I saw the latter violated every

---

[1] An author, whose sister had married Captain George Anson Byron, Byron's uncle.

[2] Montesquieu's *Esprit des Lois*.

month, I gave up my attempts at so useless an accomplishment:
—of geography, I have seen more land on maps that I should
wish to traverse on foot;—of mathematics, enough to give me
the head-ach without clearing the part affected;—of philosophy,
astronomy, and metaphysics, more than I can comprehend;
and of common sense so little, that I mean to leave a Byronian
prize at each of our 'Almæ Matres' for the first discovery,—
though I rather fear that of the longitude will precede it.

I once thought myself a philosopher, and talked nonsense
with great decorum: I defied pain, and preached up equanimity.
For some time this did very well, for no one was in *pain* for
me but my friends, and none lost their patience but my hearers.
At last, a fall from my horse convinced me bodily suffering was
an evil; and the worst of an argument overset my maxims
and my temper at the same moment: so I quitted Zeno for
Aristippus, and conceive that pleasure constitutes the το καλον.

In morality, I prefer Confucius to the Ten Commandments,
and Socrates to St. Paul (though the two latter agree in their
opinion of marriage). In religion, I favour the Catholic emancipation, but do not acknowledge the Pope; and I have refused
to take the sacrament, because I do not think eating bread or
drinking wine from the hand of an earthly vicar will make me
an inheritor of heaven. I hold virtue, in general, or the virtues
severally, to be only in the disposition, each a *feeling*, not a
principle. I believe truth the prime attribute of the Deity,
and death an eternal sleep, at least of the body. You have
here a brief compendium of the sentiments of the *wicked*
George, Lord Byron; [1] and, till I get a new suit, you will perceive
I am badly clothed.

I remain yours, etc.,
BYRON.

9. TO JOHN HANSON [2]

Newstead Abbey, Jan. 15th, 1809.

MY DEAR SIR,

I am much obliged by your kind invitation, but I wish you,
if possible, to be here on the 22nd. [3] Your presence will be of
great service, everything is prepared for your reception exactly
as if I remained, and I think Hargreaves will be gratified by the

---

[1] His great-uncle William, whom he succeeded in the title, was known
as the 'wicked Lord'.

[2] See page 3.   [3] The date of his coming-of-age.

appearance of the place, and the humours of the day. I shall
on the first opportunity pay my respects to your family, and
though I will not trespass on your hospitality on the 22nd,
my obligation is not less for your agreeable offer, which on any
other occasion would be immediately accepted, but I wish you
much to be present at the festivities, and I hope you will add
Charles to the party. Consider, as the Courtier says in the
tragedy of *Tom Thumb* [1]—

> 'This is a day; your Majesties may boast of it,
> And since it never can come o'er, 'tis fit you make the
> most of it'.

I shall take my seat as soon as circumstances will admit.
I have not yet chosen my side in politics, nor shall I hastily
commit myself with professions, or pledge my support to any
men or measures, but though I shall not run headlong into
opposition, I will studiously avoid a connection with ministry.
I cannot say that my opinion is strongly in favour of either
party; on the one side we have the late underlings of Pitt,
possessing all his ill fortune, without his talents; this may
render their failure more excusable, but will not diminish the
public contempt; on the other, we have the ill-assorted fragments of a worn-out minority; Mr. Windham with his coat
twice turned, and my Lord Grenville who perhaps has more
sense than he can make good use of; between the two and the
shuttlecock of both, a Sidmouth, and the general *football* Sir
F. Burdett, kicked at by all, and owned by none.

I shall stand aloof, speak what I think, but not often, nor
too soon. I will preserve my independence, if possible, but
if involved with a party, I will take care not to be the *last* or
least in the ranks. As to *patriotism*, the word is obsolete,
perhaps improperly so, for all men in the Country are patriots,
knowing that their own existence must stand or fall with the
Constitution, yet everybody thinks he could alter it for the
better, and govern a people, who are in fact easily governed,
but always claim the privilege of grumbling. So much for
Politics, of which I at present know little and care less; bye
and bye, I shall use the senatorial privilege of talking, and
indeed in such times, and in such a crew, it must be difficult to
hold one's tongue.

Believe me, etc.,

BYRON.

---

[1] Fielding's *Tom Thumb the Great*, as altered by O'Hara.

10. TO HIS MOTHER

8, St. James's Street, March 6, 1809.

DEAR MOTHER,

My last letter was written under great depression of spirits from poor Falkland's death,[1] who has left without a shilling four children and his wife. I have been endeavouring to assist them, which, God knows, I cannot do as I could wish, from my own embarrassments and the many claims upon me from other quarters.

What you say is all very true: come what may, *Newstead* and I *stand* or fall together. I have now lived on the spot, I have fixed my heart upon it, and no pressure, present or future, shall induce me to barter the last vestige of our inheritance. I have that pride within me which will enable me to support difficulties. I can endure privations; but could I obtain in exchange for Newstead Abbey the first fortune in the country, I would reject the proposition. Set your mind at ease on that score; Mr. Hanson talks like a man of business on the subject,—I feel like a man of honour, and I will not sell Newstead.

I shall get my seat on the return of the affidavits [2] from Carhais, in Cornwall, and will do something in the House soon: I must dash, or it is all over. My Satire must be kept secret for a *month*; after that you may say what you please on the subject. Lord C[arlisle] has used me infamously, and refused to state any particulars of my family to the Chancellor. I have *lashed* him in my *rhymes*, and perhaps his Lordship may regret not being more conciliatory. They tell me it will have a sale; I hope so, for the bookseller has behaved well, as far as publishing well goes.

Believe me, etc.

P.S.—You shall have a mortgage on one of the farms.

11. TO WILLIAM HARNESS [3]

8, St. James's Street, March 18, 1809.

There was no necessity for your excuses: if you have time and inclination to write, 'for what we receive, the Lord make us thankful,'—if I do not hear from you, I console myself with the idea that you are much more agreeably employed.

[1] Charles John Cary, Lord Falkland, was mortally wounded in a duel on the previous day.
[2] Proof of the marriage of his grandfather. Byron took his seat in the House of Lords on 13 March.
[3] A Harrow protégé of Byron's, who became a clergyman and writer.

I send down to you by this post a certain Satire lately published, and in return for the three and sixpence expenditure upon it, only beg that if you should guess the author, you will keep his name secret; at least for the present.   London is full of the Duke's business.[1]   The Commons have been at it these last three nights, and are not yet come to a decision.   I do not know if the affair will be brought before our House, unless in the shape of an impeachment.   If it makes its appearance in a debatable form, I believe I shall be tempted to say something on the subject.—I am glad to hear you like Cambridge: firstly, because, to know that you are happy is pleasant to one who wishes you all possible sublunary enjoyment; and, secondly, I admire the morality of the sentiment.   *Alma Mater* was to me *injusta noverca*: and the old beldam only gave me my M.A. degree[2] because she could not avoid it.—You know what a farce a noble Cantab must perform.

I am going abroad, if possible, in the spring, and before I depart I am collecting the pictures of my most intimate schoolfellows; I have already a few, and shall want yours, or my cabinet will be incomplete.   I have employed one of the first miniature painters[3] of the day to take them, of course at my own expense, as I never allow my acquaintance to incur the least expenditure to gratify a whim of mine.   To mention this may seem indelicate; but when I tell you a friend of ours first refused to sit, under the idea that he was to disburse on the occasion, you will see that it is necessary to state these preliminaries to prevent the recurrence of any similar mistake. I shall see you in time, and will carry you to the *limner*.   It will be a tax on your patience for a week; but pray excuse it, as it is possible the resemblance may be the sole trace I shall be able to preserve of our past friendship and acquaintance.   Just now it seems foolish enough, but in a few years, when some of us are dead, and others are separated by inevitable circumstances, it will be a kind of satisfaction to retain in these images of the living the idea of our former selves, and to contemplate in the resemblances of the dead, all that remains of judgment, feeling, and a host of passions.   But all this will be dull enough for you, and so good night; and to end my chapter, or rather my homily,

Believe me, my dear H., yours most affectionately.

---

[1] An inquiry into charges made against the Duke of York and his mistress.
[2] On 4 July 1808.
[3] George Sanders (1774–1846).

12. TO HIS MOTHER

DEAR MOTHER,   Falmouth, June 22d, 1809.

I am about to sail in a few days; probably before this reaches you. Fletcher [1] begged so hard, that I have continued him in my service. If he does not behave well abroad, I will send him back in a *transport*. I have a German servant (who has been with Mr. Wilbraham in Persia before, and was strongly recommended to me by Dr. Butler of Harrow), Robert and William; they constitute my whole suite. I have letters in plenty:— you shall hear from me at the different ports I touch upon; but you must not be alarmed if my letters miscarry. The Continent is in a fine state—an insurrection has broken out at Paris, and the Austrians are beating Buonaparte—the Tyrolese have risen.

There is a picture of me in oil,[2] to be sent down to Newstead soon.—I wish the Miss Pigots had something better to do than carry my miniatures to Nottingham to copy. Now they have done it, you may ask them to copy the others, which are greater favourites than my own. As to money matters, I am ruined— at least till Rochdale [3] is sold; and if that does not turn out well, I shall enter into the Austrian or Russian service—perhaps the Turkish, if I like their manners. The world is all before me, and I leave England without regret, and without a wish to revisit any thing it contains, except *yourself*, and your present residence.

Believe me, yours ever sincerely.

P.S.—Pray tell Mr. Rushton his son is well, and doing well; so is Murray,[4] indeed better than I ever saw him; he will be back in about a month. I ought to add the leaving Murray to my few regrets, as his age perhaps will prevent my seeing him again. Robert I take with me; I like him, because, like myself, he seems a friendless animal.

13. TO FRANCIS HODGSON [5]

MY DEAR HODGSON,   Falmouth, June 25, 1809.

Before this reaches you, Hobhouse,[6] two officers' wives, three

---

[1] William Fletcher, his valet, the 'staunch yeoman', as Robert Rushton is the 'little page', of Childe Harold's 'Good Night', in Canto 1 of the *Pilgrimage*.

[2] By George Sanders, who painted several portraits of Byron.

[3] His property in Lancashire.

[4] Joe Murray, an old servant, who accompanied him as far as Gibraltar.

[5] The Rev. Francis Hodgson, a prolific poet, whom Byron had met in 1807, when he was a tutor of King's College, Cambridge.

[6] John Cam Hobhouse, afterwards Baron Broughton de Gyfford, who, with Charles Skinner Matthews and Scrope Berdmore Davies, was most closely associated with Byron at Trinity.

children, two waiting-maids, ditto subalterns for the troops, three Portuguese esquires and domestics, in all nineteen souls, will have sailed in the Lisbon packet, with the noble Captain Kidd, a gallant commander as ever smuggled an anker of right Nantz.

We are going to Lisbon first, because the Malta packet has sailed, d' ye see?—from Lisbon to Gibraltar, Malta, Constantinople, and 'all that', as Orator Henley said, when he put the Church, and 'all that', in danger.

This town of Falmouth, as you will partly conjecture, is no great ways from the sea. It is defended on the sea-side by tway castles, St. Maws and Pendennis, extremely well calculated for annoying every body except an enemy. St. Maws is garrisoned by an able-bodied person of fourscore, a widower. He has the whole command and sole management of six most unmanageable pieces of ordnance, admirably adapted for the destruction of Pendennis, a like tower of strength on the opposite side of the Channel. We have seen St. Maws, but Pendennis they will not let us behold, save at a distance, because Hobhouse and I are suspected of having already taken St. Maws by a coup de main.

The town contains many Quakers and salt fish—the oysters have a taste of copper, owing to the soil of a mining country— the women (blessed be the Corporation therefor!) are flogged at the cart's tail when they pick and steal, as happened to one of the fair sex yesterday noon. She was pertinacious in her behaviour, and damned the mayor.

This is all I know of Falmouth. Nothing occurred of note in our way down, except that on Hartford Bridge we changed horses at an inn, where the great * * * * * * * * *, Beckford,[1] sojourned for the night. We tried in vain to see the martyr of prejudice, but could not. What we thought singular, though you perhaps will not, was that Ld Courtney travelled the same night on the same road, only one stage *behind* him.

Hodgson, remember me to the Drury,[2] and remember me to yourself when drunk. I am not worth a sober thought. Look to my satire at Cawthorn's,[3] Cockspur Street, and look to the *Miscellany* [4] of the Hobhouse. It has pleased Providence to

---

[1] William Beckford of Fonthill (1760–1844), author of *Vathek.*

[2] Henry Drury, an assistant master at Harrow.

[3] James Cawthorn, a publisher.

[4] *Imitations and Translations from the Antient and Modern Classics: Together with Original Poems never before published.* It contained nine pieces by Byron, and was published in this year.

interfere in behalf of a suffering public by giving him a sprained wrist, so that he cannot write, and there is a cessation of ink-shed.

I don't know when I can write again, because it depends on that experienced navigator, Captain Kidd, and the 'stormy winds that (don't) blow' at this season. I leave England without regret—I shall return to it without pleasure. I am like Adam, the first convict sentenced to transportation, but I have no Eve, and have eaten no apple but what was sour as a crab;—and thus ends my first chapter.   Adieu.

Yours, etc.

Falmouth Roads, June 30, 1809.

> Huzza! Hodgson, we are going,
>   Our embargo's off at last;
> Favourable breezes blowing
>   Bend the canvass o'er the mast.
> From aloft the signal's streaming,
>   Hark! the farewell gun is fired,
> Women screeching, tars blaspheming,
>   Tell us that our time's expired.
>   Here's a rascal
>   Come to task all,
>   Prying from the Custom-house;
>   Trunks unpacking,
>   Cases cracking,
>   Not a corner for a mouse
> 'Scapes unsearch'd amid the racket,
> Ere we sail on board the Packet.
>
> Now our boatmen quit their mooring,
>   And all hands must ply the oar;
> Baggage from the quay is lowering,
>   We're impatient—push from shore.
> 'Have a care! that case holds liquor—
>   Stop the boat—I'm sick—oh Lord!'
> 'Sick, ma'am, damme, you'll be sicker
>   Ere you've been an hour on board.'
>   Thus are screaming
>   Men and women,
>   Gemmen, ladies, servants, Jacks;
>   Here entangling,
>   All are wrangling,
>   Stuck together close as wax.—

Such the general noise and racket,
Ere we reach the Lisbon Packet.

Now we 've reach'd her, lo! the captain,
   Gallant Kidd, commands the crew;
Passengers their berths are clapt in,
   Some to grumble, some to spew.
'Hey day! call you that a cabin?
   Why 'tis hardly three feet square;
Not enough to stow Queen Mab in—
   Who the deuce can harbour there?'
     'Who, sir? plenty—
     Nobles twenty—
Did at once my vessel fill'—
     'Did they? Jesus,
     How you squeeze us!
Would to God they did so still!
Then I 'd 'scape the heat and racket,
Of the good ship, Lisbon Packet.'

Fletcher! Murray! Bob! where are you?
   Stretch'd along the deck like logs—
Bear a hand, you jolly tar you!
   Here 's a rope's end for the dogs.
Hobhouse muttering fearful curses,
   As the hatchway down he rolls;
Now his breakfast, now his verses,
   Vomits forth—and damns our souls.
     'Here 's a stanza
     On Braganza—
Help!'—'A couplet?'—'No, a cup
     Of warm water.'—
     'What 's the matter?'
'Zounds! my liver 's coming up;
I shall not survive the racket
Of this brutal Lisbon Packet.'

Now at length we 're off for Turkey,
   Lord knows when we shall come back!
Breezes foul and tempests murky
   May unship us in a crack.
But, since life at most a jest is,
   As philosophers allow,

> Still to laugh by far the best is,
>   Then laugh on—as I do now.
>   Laugh at all things,
>   Great and small things,
>   Sick or well, at sea or shore;
>   While we 're quaffing,
>   Let 's have laughing—
> Who the devil cares for more?—
> Some good wine! and who would lack it,
> Ev'n on board the Lisbon Packet?

> BYRON.

14. TO FRANCIS HODGSON

Lisbon, July 16, 1809.

Thus far have we pursued our route, and seen all sorts of marvellous sights, palaces, convents, etc.;—which, being to be heard in my friend Hobhouse's forthcoming Book of Travels, I shall not anticipate by smuggling any account whatsoever to you in a private and clandestine manner. I must just observe, that the village of Cintra in Estremadura is the most beautiful, perhaps, in the world.

I am very happy here, because I loves oranges, and talks bad Latin to the monks, who understand it, as it is like their own,—and I goes into society (with my pocket-pistols), and I swims in the Tagus all across at once, and I rides on an ass or a mule, and swears Portuguese, and have got a diarrhœa and bites from the mosquitoes. But what of that? Comfort must not be expected by folks that go a pleasuring.

When the Portuguese are pertinacious, I say *Carracho!*—the great oath of the grandees, that very well supplies the place of 'Damme',—and, when dissatisfied with my neighbour, I pronounce him *Ambra di merdo*. With these two phrases, and a third, *Avra bouro*, which signifieth 'Get an ass', I am universally understood to be a person of degree and a master of languages. How merrily we lives that travellers be!—if we had food and raiment. But, in sober sadness, any thing is better than England, and I am infinitely amused with my pilgrimage as far as it has gone.

To-morrow we start to ride post near 400 miles as far as Gibraltar, where we embark for Melita and Byzantium. A letter to Malta will find me, or to be forwarded, if I am absent. Pray embrace the Drury and Dwyer, and all the Ephesians you encounter. I am writing with Butler's donative pencil, which makes my bad hand worse. Excuse illegibility.

Hodgson! send me the news, and the deaths and defeats and capital crimes and the misfortunes of one's friends; and let us hear of literary matters, and the controversies and the criticisms. All this will be pleasant—*Suave mari magno*, etc. Talking of that, I have been sea-sick, and sick of the sea. Adieu.

Yours faithfully, etc.

15. TO HIS MOTHER

Gibraltar, August 11th, 1809.

DEAR MOTHER,

I have been so much occupied since my departure from England, that till I could address you at length I have forborne writing altogether. As I have now passed through Portugal, and a considerable part of Spain, and have leisure at this place, I shall endeavour to give you a short detail of my movements.

We sailed from Falmouth on the 2nd of July, reached Lisbon after a very favourable passage of four days and a half, and took up our abode in that city. It has often been described without being worthy of description; for, except the view from the Tagus, which is beautiful, and some fine churches and convents, it contains little but filthy streets, and more filthy inhabitants. To make amends for this, the village of Cintra, about fifteen miles from the capital, is, perhaps in every respect, the most delightful in Europe; it contains beauties of every description, natural and artificial. Palaces and gardens rising in the midst of rocks, cataracts, and precipices; convents on stupendous heights—a distant view of the sea and the Tagus; and, besides (though that is a secondary consideration), is remarkable as the scene of Sir Hew Dalrymple's Convention.[1] It unites in itself all the wildness of the western highlands, with the verdure of the south of France. Near this place, about ten miles to the right, is the palace of Mafra, the boast of Portugal, as it might be of any other country, in point of magnificence without elegance. There is a convent annexed; the monks, who possess large revenues, are courteous enough, and understand Latin, so that we had a long conversation: they have a

---

[1] Sir Hew Whitefoord Dalrymple, the English commander in the Peninsular War, signed the Convention of Cintra on 31 August 1808, at a palace thirt 1 miles away.

large library, and asked me if the *English* had *any books* in their country?

I sent my baggage, and part of the servants, by sea to Gibraltar, and travelled on horseback from Aldea Galhega (the first stage from Lisbon, which is only accessible by water) to Seville (one of the most famous cities in Spain) where the Government called the Junta is now held. The distance to Seville is nearly four hundred miles, and to Cadiz almost ninety farther towards the coast. I had orders from the government, and every possible accommodation on the road, as an English nobleman, in an English uniform, is a very respectable personage in Spain at present. The horses are remarkably good, and the roads (I assure you upon my honour, for you will hardly believe it) very far superior to the best English roads, without the smallest toll or turnpike. You will suppose this when I rode post to Seville, in four days, through this parching country in the midst of summer, without fatigue or annoyance.

Seville is a beautiful town; though the streets are narrow, they are clean. We lodged in the house of two Spanish un-married ladies, who possess *six* houses in Seville, and gave me a curious specimen of Spanish manners. They are women of character, and the eldest a fine woman, the youngest pretty, but not so good a figure as Donna Josepha. The freedom of manner which is general here astonished me not a little; and in the course of further observation I find that reserve is not the characteristic of the Spanish belles, who are, in general, very handsome, with large black eyes, and very fine forms. The eldest honoured your *unworthy* son with very particular attention, embracing him with great tenderness at parting (I was there but three days), after cutting off a lock of his hair, and presenting him with one of her own, about three feet in length, which I send, and beg you will retain till my return. Her last words were, *Adios, tu hermoso! me gusto mucho*—'Adieu, you pretty fellow! you please me much'. She offered a share of her apart-ment, which my *virtue* induced me to decline; she laughed, and said I had some English *amante* (lover), and added that she was going to be married to an officer in the Spanish army.

I left Seville, and rode on to Cadiz, through a beautiful country. At *Xeres*, where the sherry we drink is made, I met a great merchant — a Mr. Gordon of Scotland — who was extremely polite, and favoured me with the inspection of his vaults and cellars, so that I quaffed at the fountain head.

Cadiz, sweet Cadiz, is the most delightful town I ever beheld, very different from our English cities in every respect except cleanliness (and it is as clean as London), but still beautiful, and full of the finest women in Spain, the Cadiz belles being the Lancashire witches of their land. Just as I was introduced and began to like the grandees, I was forced to leave it for this cursed place; but before I return to England I will visit it again. The night before I left it, I sat in the box at the opera with Admiral Cordova's family; he is the commander whom Lord St. Vincent defeated in 1797, and has an aged wife and a fine daughter, Sennorita Cordova. The girl is very pretty, in the Spanish style; in my opinion, by no means inferior to the English in charms, and certainly superior in fascination. Long black hair, dark languishing eyes, *clear* olive complexions, and forms more graceful in motion than can be conceived by an Englishman used to the drowsy, listless air of his country-women, added to the most becoming dress, and, at the same time, the most decent in the world, render a Spanish beauty irresistible.

I beg leave to observe that intrigue here is the business of life; when a woman marries she throws off all restraint, but I believe their conduct is chaste enough before. If you make a proposal, which in England would bring a box on the ear from the meekest of virgins, to a Spanish girl, she thanks you for the honour you intend her, and replies, 'Wait till I am married, and I shall be too happy'. This is literally and strictly true.

Miss Cordova and her little brother understood a little French, and, after regretting my ignorance of the Spanish, she proposed to become my preceptress in that language. I could only reply by a low bow, and express my regret that I quitted Cadiz too soon to permit me to make the progress which would doubtless attend my studies under so charming a directress. I was standing at the back of the box, which resembles our Opera boxes, (the theatre is large and finely decorated, the music admirable,) in the manner which Englishmen generally adopt, for fear of incommoding the ladies in front, when this fair Spaniard dispossessed an old woman (an aunt or a duenna) of her chair, and commanded me to be seated next herself, at a tolerable distance from her mamma. At the close of the performance I withdrew, and was lounging with a party of men in the passage, when, *en passant*, the lady turned round and called me, and I had the honour of attending her to the admiral's mansion. I have an invitation on my return to Cadiz, which I shall accept if I repass through the country on my return from Asia.

I have met Sir John Carr, Knight Errant,[1] at Seville and Cadiz. He is a pleasant man. I like the Spaniards much. You have heard of the battle near Madrid,[2] and in England they would call it a victory—a pretty victory! Two hundred officers and five thousand men killed, all English, and the French in as great force as ever. I should have joined the army, but we have no time to lose before we get up the Mediterranean and Archipelago. I am going over to Africa to-morrow; it is only six miles from this fortress. My next stage is Cagliari in Sardinia, where I shall be presented to His Majesty. I have a most superb uniform as a court dress, indispensable in travelling.

August 13.—I have not yet been to Africa—the wind is contrary—but I dined yesterday at Algesiras, with Lady Westmorland,[3] where I met General Castanos, the celebrated Spanish leader in the late and present war. To-day I dine with him. He has offered me letters to Tetuan in Barbary, for the principal Moors, and I am to have the house for a few days of one of the great men, which was intended for Lady W., whose health will not permit her to cross the Straits.

August 15.—I could not dine with Castanos yesterday, but this afternoon I had that honour. He is pleasant and, for aught I know to the contrary, clever. I cannot go to Barbary. The Malta packet sails to-morrow, and myself in it. Admiral Purvis, with whom I dined at Cadiz, gave me a passage in a frigate to Gibraltar, but we have no ship of war destined for Malta at present. The packets sail fast, and have good accommodations. You shall hear from me on our route.

Joe Murray delivers this; I have sent him and the boy back. Pray show the lad any kindness, as he is my great favourite; I would have taken him on. . . . Say this to his father, who may otherwise think he has behaved ill.

I hope this will find you well. Believe me,

Yours ever sincerely,

BYRON.

P.S. So Lord G——[4] is married to a rustic! Well done! If I wed, I will bring home a Sultana, with half a dozen cities for a dowry, and reconcile you to an Ottoman daughter-in-law, with a bushel of pearls not larger than ostrich eggs, or smaller than walnuts.

[1] 'Jaunting Carr', who published many books of travels.
[2] Talavera, 27–28 July.
[3] Wife of John, Earl of Westmorland.
[4] Lord Grey de Ruthyn, a former tenant of Newstead. He married Anna Maria Kelham, of Ryton-upon-Dunsmore, Warwick.

16. TO HIS MOTHER

Prevesa, November 12, 1809.

MY DEAR MOTHER,

I have now been some time in Turkey: this place is on the coast, but I have traversed the interior of the province of Albania on a visit to the Pacha. I left Malta in the *Spider*, a brig of war, on the 21st of September, and arrived in eight days at Prevesa. I thence have been about 150 miles, as far as Tepaleen, his Highness's country palace, where I staid three days. The name of the Pacha is *Ali*, and he is considered a man of the first abilities: he governs the whole of Albania (the ancient Illyricum), Epirus, and part of Macedonia. His son, Vely Pacha, to whom he has given me letters, governs the Morea, and he has great influence in Egypt; in short, he is one of the most powerful men in the Ottoman empire. When I reached Yanina, the capital, after a journey of three days over the mountains, through a country of the most picturesque beauty, I found that Ali Pacha was with his army in Illyricum, besieging Ibrahim Pacha in the castle of Berat. He had heard that an Englishman of rank was in his dominions, and had left orders in Yanina with the commandant to provide a house, and supply me with every kind of necessary *gratis*; and, though I have been allowed to make presents to the slaves, etc., I have not been permitted to pay for a single article of household consumption.

I rode out on the vizier's horses, and saw the palaces of himself and grandsons: they are splendid, but too much ornamented with silk and gold. I then went over the mountains through Zitza, a village with a Greek monastery (where I slept on my return), in the most beautiful situation (always excepting Cintra, in Portugal) I ever beheld. In nine days I reached Tepaleen. Our journey was much prolonged by the torrents that had fallen from the mountains, and intersected the roads. I shall never forget the singular scene on entering Tepaleen at five in the afternoon, as the sun was going down. It brought to my mind (with some change of *dress*, however) Scott's description of Branksome Castle in his *Lay*,[1] and the feudal system. The Albanians, in their dresses, (the most magnificent in the world, consisting of a long *white kilt*, gold-worked cloak, crimson velvet gold-laced jacket and waistcoat, silver-mounted pistols and daggers,) the Tartars with their high caps, the Turks in their vast pelisses and turbans, the soldiers and black slaves

[1] *The Lay of the Last Minstrel*, Canto 1.

with the horses, the former in groups in an immense large open gallery in front of the palace, the latter placed in a kind of cloister below it, two hundred steeds ready caparisoned to move in a moment, couriers entering or passing out with despatches, the kettle-drums beating, boys calling the hour from the minaret of the mosque, altogether, with the singular appearance of the building itself, formed a new and delightful spectacle to a stranger. I was conducted to a very handsome apartment, and my health inquired after by the vizier's secretary, *à-la-mode Turque*.

The next day I was introduced to Ali Pacha. I was dressed in a full suit of staff uniform, with a very magnificent sabre, etc. The vizier received me in a large room paved with marble; a fountain was playing in the centre; the apartment was surrounded by scarlet ottomans. He received me standing, a wonderful compliment from a Mussulman, and made me sit down on his right hand. I have a Greek interpreter for general use, but a physician of Ali's named Femlario, who understands Latin, acted for me on this occasion. His first question was, why, at so early an age, I left my country?—(the Turks have no idea of travelling for amusement). He then said, the English minister, Captain Leake,[1] had told him I was of a great family, and desired his respects to my mother; which I now, in the name of Ali Pacha, present to you. He said he was certain I was a man of birth, because I had small ears, curling hair, and little white hands, and expressed himself pleased with my appearance and garb. He told me to consider him as a father whilst I was in Turkey, and said he looked on me as his son. Indeed, he treated me like a child, sending me almonds and sugared sherbet, fruit and sweetmeats, twenty times a day. He begged me to visit him often, and at night, when he was at leisure. I then, after coffee and pipes, retired for the first time. I saw him thrice afterwards. It is singular that the Turks, who have no hereditary dignities, and few great families, except the Sultans, pay so much respect to birth; for I found my pedigree more regarded than my title.

His highness is sixty years old, very fat, and not tall, but with a fine face, light blue eyes, and a white beard; his manner is very kind, and at the same time he possesses that dignity which I find universal amongst the Turks. He has the appearance of anything but his real character, for he is a remorseless tyrant, guilty of the most horrible cruelties, very brave, and so good

[1] William Martin Leake, later the author of topographical works.

a general that they call him the Mahometan Buonaparte.
Napoleon has twice offered to make him King of Epirus, but he
prefers the English interest, and abhors the French, as he
himself told me.   He is of so much consequence, that he is much
courted by both, the Albanians being the most warlike subjects
of the Sultan, though Ali is only nominally dependent on the
Porte; he has been a mighty warrior, but is as barbarous as he
is successful, roasting rebels, etc., etc.   Buonaparte sent him a
snuff-box with his picture.   He said the snuff-box was very well,
but the picture he could excuse, as he neither liked it nor the
original.   His ideas of judging of a man's birth from ears,
hands, etc., were curious enough.   To me he was, indeed, a
father, giving me letters, guards, and every possible accommodation.   Our next conversations were of war and travelling,
politics, and England.   He called my Albanian soldier, who
attends me, and told him to protect me at all hazard; his name
is · Viscillie, and, like all the Albanians, he is brave, rigidly
honest, and faithful; but they are cruel, though not treacherous,
and have several vices but no meannesses.   They are, perhaps,
the most beautiful race, in point of countenance, in the world;
their women are sometimes handsome also, but they are treated
like slaves, *beaten*, and, in short, complete beasts of burden;
they plough, dig, and sow.   I found them carrying wood, and
actually repairing the highways.   The men are all soldiers,
and war and the chase their sole occupations.   The women
are the labourers, which after all is no great hardship in so
delightful a climate.   Yesterday, the 11th of November, I
bathed in the sea; to-day is so hot that I am writing in a shady
room of the English consul's, with three doors wide open, no
fire, or even *fireplace*, in the house, except for culinary purposes.

To-day I saw the remains of the town of Actium, near which
Antony lost the world, in a small bay, where two frigates could
hardly manœuvre: a broken wall is the sole remnant.   On
another part of the gulf stand the ruins of Nicopolis, built by
Augustus in honour of his victory.   Last night I was at a
Greek marriage; but this and a thousand things more I have
neither time nor *space* to describe.

I am going to-morrow, with a guard of fifty men, to Patras
in the Morea, and thence to Athens, where I shall winter.
Two days ago I was nearly lost in a Turkish ship of war, owing
to the ignorance of the captain and crew, though the storm was
not violent.   Fletcher yelled after his wife, the Greeks called
on all the saints, the Mussulmans on Alla; the captain burst

into tears and ran below deck, telling us to call on God; the sails were split, the main-yard shivered, the wind blowing fresh, the night setting in, and all our chance was to make Corfu, which is in possession of the French, or (as Fletcher pathetically termed it) 'a watery grave'. I did what I could to console Fletcher, but finding him incorrigible, wrapped myself up in my Albanian capote (an immense cloak), and lay down on deck to wait the worst. I have learnt to philosophise in my travels; and if I had not, complaint was useless. Luckily the wind abated, and only drove us on the coast of Suli, on the main land, where we landed, and proceeded, by the help of the natives, to Prevesa again; but I shall not trust Turkish sailors in future, though the Pacha had ordered one of his own galliots to take me to Patras. I am therefore going as far as Missolonghi by land, and there have only to cross a small gulf to get to Patras.

Fletcher's next epistle will be full of marvels. We were one night lost for nine hours in the mountains in a thunder-storm, and since nearly wrecked. In both cases Fletcher was sorely bewildered, from apprehensions of famine and banditti in the first, and drowning in the second instance. His eyes were a little hurt by the lightning, or crying (I don't know which), but are now recovered. When you write, address to me at Mr. Strané's, English consul, Patras, Morea.

I could tell you I know not how many incidents that I think would amuse you, but they crowd on my mind as much as they would swell my paper, and I can neither arrange them in the one, nor put them down on the other, except in the greatest confusion. I like the Albanians much; they are not all Turks; some tribes are Christians. But their religion makes little difference in their manner or conduct. They are esteemed the best troops in the Turkish service. I lived on my route, two days at once, and three days again, in a barrack at Salora, and never found soldiers so tolerable, though I have been in the garrisons of Gibraltar and Malta, and seen Spanish, French, Sicilian, and British troops in abundance. I have had nothing stolen, and was always welcome to their provision and milk. Not a week ago an Albanian chief, (every village has its chief, who is called Primate,) after helping us out of the Turkish galley in her distress, feeding us, and lodging my suite, consisting of Fletcher, a Greek, two Athenians, a Greek priest, and my companion, Mr. Hobhouse, refused any compensation but a written paper stating that I was well received; and when I pressed him to accept a few sequins, 'No,' he replied; 'I wish you to love me, not to pay me'. These are his words.

It is astonishing how far money goes in this country. While I was in the capital I had nothing to pay by the vizier's order; but since, though I have generally had sixteen horses, and generally six or seven men, the expense has not been *half* as much as staying only three weeks in Malta, though Sir A. Ball,[1] the governor, gave me a house for nothing, and I had only *one servant*. By the by, I expect Hanson to remit regularly; for I am not about to stay in this province for ever. Let him write to me at Mr. Strané's, English consul, Patras. The fact is, the fertility of the plains is wonderful, and specie is scarce, which makes this remarkable cheapness. I am going to Athens, to study modern Greek, which differs much from the ancient, though radically similar. I have no desire to return to England, nor shall I, unless compelled by absolute want, and Hanson's neglect; but I shall not enter into Asia for a year or two, as I have much to see in Greece, and I may perhaps cross into Africa, at least the Egyptian part. Fletcher, like all Englishmen, is very much dissatisfied, though a little reconciled to the Turks by a present of eighty piastres from the vizier, which, if you consider every thing, and the value of specie here, is nearly worth ten guineas English. He has suffered nothing but from cold, heat, and vermin, which those who lie in cottages and cross mountains in a cold country must undergo, and of which I have equally partaken with himself; but he is not valiant, and is afraid of robbers and tempests. I have no one to be remembered to in England, and wish to hear nothing from it, but that you are well, and a letter or two on business from Hanson, whom you may tell to write. I will write when I can, and beg you to believe me,

Your affectionate son,
BYRON.

P.S.—I have some very 'magnifiques' Albanian dresses, the only expensive articles in this country. They cost fifty guineas each, and have so much gold, they would cost in England two hundred.

I have been introduced to Hussein Bey, and Mahmout Pacha, both little boys, grandchildren of Ali, at Yanina; they are totally unlike our lads, have painted complexions like rouged dowagers, large black eyes, and features perfectly regular.

---

[1] Rear-Admiral Sir Alexander John Ball.

They are the prettiest little animals I ever saw, and are broken into the court ceremonies already. The Turkish salute is a slight inclination of the head, with the hand on the breast; intimates always kiss. Mahmout is ten years old, and hopes to see me again; we are friends without understanding each other, like many other folks, though from a different cause. He has given me a letter to his father in the Morea, to whom I have also letters from Ali Pacha.

17. TO HENRY DRURY

Salsette frigate, May 3, 1810.

MY DEAR DRURY,

When I left England, nearly a year ago, you requested me to write to you—I will do so. I have crossed Portugal, traversed the south of Spain, visited Sardinia, Sicily, Malta, and thence passed into Turkey, where I am still wandering. I first landed in Albania, the ancient Epirus, where we penetrated as far as Mount Tomarit—excellently treated by the chief Ali Pacha, —and, after journeying through Illyria, Chaonia, etc., crossed the Gulf of Actium, with a guard of fifty Albanians, and passed the Achelous in our route through Acarnania and Ætolia. We stopped a short time in the Morea, crossed the Gulf of Lepanto, and landed at the foot of Parnassus;—saw all that Delphi retains, and so on to Thebes and Athens, at which last we remained ten weeks.

His Majesty's ship, *Pylades*, brought us to Smyrna;[1] but not before we had topographised Attica, including, of course, Marathon and the Sunian promontory. From Smyrna to the Troad (which we visited when at anchor, for a fortnight, off the tomb of Antilochus) was our next stage; and now we are in the Dardanelles, waiting for a wind to proceed to Constantinople.

This morning I *swam* from *Sestos* to *Abydos*. The immediate distance is not above a mile, but the current renders it hazardous; —so much so that I doubt whether Leander's conjugal affection must not have been a little chilled in his passage to Paradise. I attempted it a week ago, and failed,—owing to the north wind, and the wonderful rapidity of the tide,—though I have been from my childhood a strong swimmer. But, this morning being calmer, I succeeded, and crossed the 'broad Hellespont' in an hour and ten minutes.

[1] Where Byron completed the first two cantos of *Childe Harold's Pilgrimage*.

Well, my dear sir, I have left my home, and seen part of Africa and Asia, and a tolerable portion of Europe. I have been with generals and admirals, princes and pashas, governors and ungovernables,—but I have not time or paper to expatiate. I wish to let you know that I live with a friendly remembrance of you, and a hope to meet you again; and if I do this as shortly as possible, attribute it to any thing but forgetfulness.

Greece, ancient and modern, you know too well to require description. Albania, indeed, I have seen more of than any Englishman (except a Mr. Leake), for it is a country rarely visited, from the savage character of the natives, though abounding in more natural beauties than the classical regions of Greece, —which, however, are still eminently beautiful, particularly Delphi and Cape Colonna in Attica. Yet these are nothing to parts of Illyria and Epirus, where places without a name, and rivers not laid down in maps, may, one day, when more known, be justly esteemed superior subjects, for the pencil and the pen, to the dry ditch of the Ilissus and the bogs of Bœotia.

The Troad is a fine field for conjecture and snipe-shooting, and a good sportsman and an ingenious scholar may exercise their feet and faculties to great advantage upon the spot;—or, if they prefer riding, lose their way (as I did) in a cursed quagmire of the Scamander, who wriggles about as if the Dardan virgins still offered their wonted tribute. The only vestige of Troy, or her destroyers, are the barrows supposed to contain the carcasses of Achilles, Antilochus, Ajax, etc.;—but Mount Ida is still in high feather, though the shepherds are now-a-days not much like Ganymede. But why should I say more of these things? are they not written in the *Boke* of *Gell*? [1] and has not Hobhouse got a journal? I keep none, as I have renounced scribbling.

I see not much difference between ourselves and the Turks, save that we have * * and they have none—that they have long dresses, and we short, and that we talk much, and they little. They are sensible people. Ali Pacha told me he was sure I was a man of rank, because I had *small ears* and *hands*, and *curling hair*. By the by, I speak the Romaic, or modern Greek, tolerably. It does not differ from the ancient dialects so much as you would conceive; but the pronunciation is diametrically opposite. Of verse, except in rhyme, they have no idea.

[1] Sir William Gell (1777–1836), author of many topographical works on Greece, two of which Byron in 1811 reviewed.

I like the Greeks, who are plausible rascals,—with all the Turkish vices, without their courage. However, some are brave, and all are beautiful, very much resembling the busts of Alcibiades;—the women not quite so handsome. I can swear in Turkish; but, except one horrible oath, and 'pimp', and 'bread', and 'water', I have got no great vocabulary in that language. They are extremely polite to strangers of any rank, properly protected; and as I have two servants and two soldiers, we get on with great *éclat*. We have been occasionally in danger of thieves, and once of shipwreck,—but always escaped.

At Malta I fell in love with a married woman,[1] and challenged an aide-de-camp of General * * (a rude fellow, who grinned at something,—I never rightly knew what)—but he explained and apologized, and the lady embarked for Cadiz, and so I escaped murder and crim. con. Of Spain I sent some account to our Hodgson, but have subsequently written to no one, save notes to relations and lawyers, to keep them out of my premises. I mean to give up all connection, on my return, with many of my best friends—as I supposed them—and to snarl all my life. But I hope to have one good-humoured laugh with you, and to embrace Dwyer, and pledge Hodgson, before I commence cynicism.

Tell Dr. Butler I am now writing with the gold pen he gave me before I left England, which is the reason my scrawl is more unintelligible than usual. I have been at Athens, and seen plenty of these reeds for scribbling, some of which he refused to bestow upon me, because topographic Gell had brought them from Attica. But I will not describe,—no—you must be satisfied with simple detail till my return, and then we will unfold the floodgates of colloquy. I am in a thirty-six gun frigate, going up to fetch Bob Adair [2] from Constantinople, who will have the honour to carry this letter.

And so Hobhouse's *boke* [3] is out, with some sentimental singsong of my own to fill up,—and how does it take, eh? and where the devil is the second edition of my Satire,[4] with additions? and my name on the title page? and more lines tagged to the end, with a new exordium and what not, hot from my anvil before I cleared the Channel? The Mediterranean and the Atlantic roll between me and criticism; and the thunders

---

[1] Mrs. Spencer Smith, wife of the British Minister at Stuttgart.
[2] The Ambassador Extraordinary to Turkey.
[3] See p. 16.
[4] Published in October 1809.

of the Hyperborean Review are deafened by the roar of the Hellespont.

Remember me to Claridge,[1] if not translated to college, and present to Hodgson assurances of my high consideration. Now, you will ask, what shall I do next? and I answer, I do not know. I may return in a few months, but I have intents and projects after visiting Constantinople.—Hobhouse, however, will probably be back in September.

On the 2d of July we have left Albion one year—*oblitus meorum obliviscendus et illis*.[2] I was sick of my own country, and not much prepossessed in favour of any other; but I 'drag on my chain' without 'lengthening it at each remove'.[3] I am like the Jolly Miller,[4] caring for nobody, and not cared for. All countries are much the same in my eyes. I smoke, and stare at mountains, and twirl my mustachios very independently. I miss no comforts, and the musquitoes that rack the morbid frame of H. have, luckily for me, little effect on mine, because I live more temperately.

I omitted Ephesus in my catalogue, which I visited during my sojourn at Smyrna; but the Temple has almost perished, and St. Paul need not trouble himself to epistolise the present brood of Ephesians, who have converted a large church built entirely of marble into a mosque, and I don't know that the edifice looks the worse for it.

My paper is full, and my ink ebbing—good afternoon! If you address to me at Malta, the letter will be forwarded wherever I may be. H. greets you; he pines for his poetry,—at least, some tidings of it. I almost forgot to tell you that I am dying for love of three Greek girls at Athens, sisters. I lived in the same house. Teresa, Mariana, and Katinka,[5] are the names of these divinities,—all of them under fifteen.

Your ταπεινοτατος δουλος,[6]

BYRON.

---

[1] John Claridge, a young Harrow friend.
[2] Horace, *Epistles*, i, xi, 9.
[3] Goldsmith, *The Traveller*, 9–10.
[4] In the song by Isaac Bickerstaffe, 1762.
[5] The daughters of Theodora Macri, whose father had been English Vice-Consul. Teresa is the 'Maid of Athens'.
[6] Most humble servant.

18. TO JOHN CAM HOBHOUSE [1]

The Convent, Athens, August 23rd, 1810.

MY DEAR HOBHOUSE,

Lord Sligo's [2] unmanageable brig being remanded to Malta, with a large quantity of vases, amounting in value (according to the depreciation of Fauriel [3]) to one hundred and fifty piastres, I cannot resist the temptation of assailing you in this third letter, which I trust will find you better than your deserts, and no worse than my wishes can make you.

I have girated the Morea, and was presented with a very fine horse (a stallion), and honoured with a number of squeezes and speeches by Velly Pasha, besides a most pressing invitation to meet him at Larissa in his way to the wars.

I returned to Athens by Argos, where I found Lord Sligo with a painter, who has got a fever with sketching at midday, and a dragoman who has actually lied himself into a lockjaw.

I am most auspiciously settled in the Convent, which is more commodious than any tenement I have yet occupied, with room for my *suite*; and it is by no means solitary, seeing there is not only 'il Padre Abbate', but his 'schuola', consisting of six 'Ragazzi', [4] all my most particular allies.

These gentlemen being almost (saving Fauriel and Lusieri [5]) my only associates, it is but proper their character, religion, and morals, should be described.

Of this goodly company three are Catholics, and three are Greeks, which schismatics I have already set a boxing to the great amusement of the Father, who rejoices to see the Catholics conquer.

Their names are Barthelemi, Giuseppè, Nicolo, Zani, and two anonymous, at least in my memory. Of these, Barthelemi is a 'simplice Fanciullo', [6] according to the account of the Father, whose favourite is Giuseppè, who sleeps in the lantern of Demosthenes.

We have nothing but riot from noon to night. The first time I mingled with these sylphs, after about two minutes' reconnoitring, the amiable Signor Barthelemi, without any

[1] Now on his way to England, having parted from Byron at Zea.
[2] Howe Peter Browne, Marquis of Sligo, who had been at Cambridge with Byron, was at Athens in command of a twelve-gun brig.
[3] The French consul. ('Fauvel' is the name given in Byron's printed notes to *Childe Harold*, Canto II.)
[4] Boys.
[5] Battista Lusieri, an Italian artist employed by Lord Elgin to make drawings of the antiquities.
[6] Simple youth.

previous notice, seated himself by me, and after observing by way of compliment that my 'Signoria' was the 'piu bello' of his English acquaintance, saluted me on the left cheek, for which freedom being reproved by Giuseppè, who very properly informed him that I was 'μεγάλος';[1] he told him I was his 'φίλος',[2] and 'by his beard' he would do so again, adding, in reply to the question 'διὰ τὶ ἀσπάσετε?'[3] 'you see he laughs', as in good truth I did heartily.

But my friend, as you may easily imagine, is Nicolo, who, by-the-bye, is my Italian master, and we are already very philosophical. I am his 'Padrone'[4] and his 'amico', and the Lord knows what besides. It is about two hours since, that, after informing me he was most desirous to follow *him* (that is me) over the world, he concluded by telling me it was proper for us not only to live, but 'morire insieme'.[5]

The latter I hope to avoid—as much of the former as he pleases.

I am awakened in the morning by those imps shouting 'Venite abasso',[6] and the friar gravely observes it is 'bisogno bastonare'[7] everybody before the studies can possibly commence.

Besides these lads, my suite,—to which I have added a Tartar and a youth to look after my two new saddle horses,—my suite, I say, are very obstreperous, and drink skinfuls of Zean wine at eight paras the olne daily. Then we have several Albanian women washing in the 'giardino', whose hours of relaxation are spent in running pins into Fletcher's backside.

'*Damnata di mi, if I have seen such a spectaculo in my way from Viterbo.*'

In short, what with the *women*, and the *boys*, and the suite, we are very disorderly. But I am vastly happy and childish, and shall have a world of anecdotes for you and the 'citoyen'.[8]

Intrigue flourishes: the old woman, Theresa's mother, was mad enough to imagine I was going to marry the girl; but I have better amusement. Andreas is fooling with Dudu, as usual, and Mariana has made a conquest of Dervise Tahiri; Vircillie, Fletcher and Sullee, my new Tartar, have each a mistress—'Vive l'Amour'.

I am learning Italian, and this day translated an ode of Horace, 'Exegi monumentum', into that language. I chatter with everybody, good or bad, and tradute prayers out of the mass ritual; but my lessons, though very long, are sadly inter-

---

[1] Great.   [2] Friend.   [3] Why do you salute him?
[4] Patron.   [5] Die together.   [6] Come down.
[7] Perhaps for 'bisogna bastonare,' 'it is necessary to beat.'
[8] C. S. Matthews.

rupted by scamperings, and eating fruit, and peltings and playings; and I am in fact at school again, and make as little improvement now as I did there, my time being wasted in the same way.

However, it is too good to last; I am going to make a second tour of Attica with Lusieri, who is a new ally of mine, and Nicolo goes with me at his own most pressing solicitation, 'per mare per terras'. 'Forse' you may see us in Inghilterra, but 'non so, come, etc.' For the present, good-even, Buona sera a vossignoria. Bacio le mani:[1]—August 24th, 1810.

I am about to take my daily ride to the Piræus, where I swim for an hour despite of the heat; here hath been an Englishman ycleped Watson, who died and is buried in the Tempio of Theseus. I knew him not, but I am told that the surgeon of Lord Sligo's brig slew him with an improper potion, and a cold bath.

Lord Sligo's crew are sadly addicted to liquor. He is in some apprehension of a scrape with the Navy concerning certain mariners of the King's ships.

He himself is now at Argos with his hospital, but intends to winter in Athens. I think he will be sick of it, poor soul, he has all the indecision of your humble servant, without the relish for the ridiculous which makes my life supportable.

I wish you were here to partake of a number of waggeries, which you can hardly find in the gun-room or in Grub Street, but then you are so very crabbed and disagreeable, that when the laugh is over I rejoice in your absence. After all, I do love thee, Hobby, thou hast so many good qualities, and so many bad ones, it is impossible to live with or without thee.

Nine in the Evening.

I have, as usual, swum across the Piræus, the Signor Nicolo also laved, but he makes as bad a hand in the water as L'Abbé Hyacinth at Falmouth; it is a curious thing that the Turks when they bathe wear their lower garments, as your humble servant always doth, but the Greeks not; however, questo giovane è vergognóso.[2]

Lord Sligo's surgeon has assisted very materially the malignant fever now fashionable here; another man *dead* to-day, two men a week, like fighting Bob Acres[3] in the country. Faurel says he is like the surgeon whom the Venetians fitted out against the Turks, with whom they were then at war.

Yours ever,
BYRON.

[1] I kiss your hands.   [2] This young man is bashful.
[3] In Sheridan's *Rivals*.

19. TO FRANCIS HODGSON

Patras, Morea, October 3, 1810.

As I have just escaped from a physician and a fever, which confined me five days to bed, you won't expect much *allegrezza* in the ensuing letter.   In this place there is an indigenous distemper, which when the wind blows from the Gulf of Corinth (as it does five months out of six), attacks great and small, and makes woful work with visitors.   Here be also two physicians, one of whom trusts to his genius (never having studied)—the other to a campaign of eighteen months against the sick of Otranto, which he made in his youth with great effect.

When I was seized with my disorder, I protested against both these assassins;—but what can a helpless, feverish, toasted-and-watered poor wretch do?   In spite of my teeth and tongue, the English consul, my Tartar, Albanians, dragoman, forced a physician upon me, and in three days vomited and glystered me to the last gasp.   In this state I made my epitaph—take it:—

> Youth, Nature, and relenting Jove,
> To keep my lamp *in* strongly strove;
> But Romanelli was so stout,
> He beat all three—and blew it *out*.

But Nature and Jove, being piqued at my doubts, did, in fact, at last, beat Romanelli, and here I am, well but weakly, at your service.

Since I left Constantinople, I have made a tour of the Morea, and visited Vely Pacha, who paid me great honours, and gave me a pretty stallion.   H. is doubtless in England before even the date of this letter:—he bears a despatch from me to your bardship.   He writes to me from Malta, and is desperate of his Miscellany, but has other plots against the public, and requests my journal, if I keep one.   I have none, or he should have it; but I have replied in a consolatory and exhortatory epistle, wherein I do recommend him to turn his hand to prose, which must go down or the Devil's in't at the same time—praying him to abate three and sixpence in the price of his next boke, seeing that half a guinea is a price not to be given for any thing save an opera ticket.

As for England, it is long since I have heard from it.   Every one at all connected with my concerns is asleep, and you are my only correspondent, agents excepted.   I have really no friends in the world; though all my old school companions are gone forth into that world, and walk about there in monstrous disguises, in the garb of guardsmen, lawyers, parsons, fine gentlemen, and such other masquerade dresses. So, I have shaken hands and cut with all these busy people, none of whom write to me. Indeed I asked it not;—and here I am, a poor traveller and heathenish philosopher, who hath perambulated the greatest part of the Levant, and seen a great quantity of very improvable land and sea, and, after all, am no better than when I set out—Lord help me!

I have been out fifteen months this very day, and I believe my concerns will draw me to England soon; but of this I will apprise you regularly from Malta. On all points Hobhouse will inform you, if you are curious as to our adventures. I have seen some old English papers up to the 15th of May. I see the *Lady of the Lake* advertised. Of course it is in his old ballad style, and pretty. After all, Scott is the best of them. The end of all scribblement is to amuse, and he certainly succeeds there. I long to read his new romance.

And how does *Sir Edgar* ?[1] and your friend Bland?[2] I suppose you are involved in some literary squabble. The only way is to despise all brothers of the quill. I suppose you won't allow me to be an author, but I contemn you all, you dogs!—I do.

You don't know Dallas, do you? He had a farce[3] ready for the stage before I left England, and asked me for a prologue, which I promised, but sailed in such a hurry I never penned a couplet. I am afraid to ask after his drama, for fear it should be damned—Lord forgive me for using such a word! but the pit, Sir, you know, the pit—they will do those things in spite of merit. I remember this farce from a curious circumstance. When Drury Lane was burnt to the ground,[4] by which accident Sheridan and his son[5] lost the few remaining shillings they were worth, what doth my friend Dallas do? Why, before the fire was out, he writes a note to Tom Sheridan, the manager of this combustible concern, to inquire whether this farce was not converted into fuel with about two thousand other unactable manuscripts, which of course were in great peril, if not actually consumed. Now was not this characteristic? — the ruling passions of Pope are nothing to it. Whilst the poor distracted

[1] *Sir Edgar, a Tale*, which Hodgson published in this year.
[2] The Rev. Robert Bland, who collaborated with J. Herman Merivale in translations from the Greek Anthology.
[3] *Not at Home*.
[4] In February 1809.
[5] Richard Brinsley Sheridan, the dramatist (1751–1816), and his son Tom (1775–1817).

manager was bewailing the loss of a building only worth 300,000*l.*, together with some twenty thousand pounds of rags and tinsel in the tiring rooms, Bluebeard's elephants,[1] and all that—in comes a note from a scorching author, requiring at his hands two acts and odd scenes of a farce!!

Dear H., remind Drury that I am his well-wisher, and let Scrope Davies [2] be well affected towards me. I look forward to meeting you at Newstead, and renewing our old champagne evenings with all the glee of anticipation. I have written by every opportunity, and expect responses as regular as those of the liturgy, and somewhat longer. As it is impossible for a man in his senses to hope for happy days, let us at least look forward to merry ones, which come nearest to the other in appearance, if not in reality; and in such expectations I remain, etc.

20. TO HIS MOTHER

Athens, January 14, 1811.

MY DEAR MADAM,

I seize an occasion to write as usual, shortly, but frequently, as the arrival of letters, where there exists no regular communication, is, of course, very precarious. I have received, at different intervals, several of yours, but generally six months after date; some sooner, some later, and, though lately tolerably stationary, the delays appear just the same. I have lately made several small tours of some hundred or two miles about the Morea, Attica, etc., as I have finished my grand giro by the Troad, Constantinople, etc., and am returned down again to Athens. I believe I have mentioned to you more than once that I swam (in imitation of Leander, though without his lady) across the Hellespont, from Sestos to Abydos. Of this, and all other particulars, Fletcher, whom I have sent home with papers, etc., will apprize you. I cannot find that he is any loss; being tolerably master of the Italian and modern Greek languages, which last I am also studying with a master, I can order and discourse more than enough for a reasonable man. Besides, the perpetual lamentations after beef and beer, the stupid, bigoted contempt for every thing foreign, and insurmountable incapacity of acquiring even a few words of any language,

---

[1] Wickerwork animals used in George Colman the Younger's *Bluebeard, or Female Curiosity.*

[2] Scrope Berdmore Davies, Fellow of King's College, Cambridge, wit, and gambler.

rendered him, like all other English servants, an incumbrance. I do assure you, the plague of speaking for him, the comforts he required (more than myself by far), the pilaws (a Turkish dish of rice and meat) which he could not eat, the wines which he could not drink, the beds where he could not sleep, and the long list of calamities, such as stumbling horses, want of *tea*!!! etc., which assailed him, would have made a lasting source of laughter to a spectator, and inconvenience to a master. After all, the man is honest enough, and, in Christendom, capable enough; but in Turkey, Lord forgive me! my Albanian soldiers, my Tartars and Janizary, worked for him and us too, as my friend Hobhouse can testify.

It is probable I may steer homewards in spring; but, to enable me to do that, I must have remittances. My own funds would have lasted me very well, but I was obliged to assist a friend, who, I know, will pay me; but, in the mean time, I am out of pocket. At present, I do not care to venture a winter's voyage, even if I were otherwise tired of travelling; but I am so convinced of the advantages of looking at mankind instead of reading about them, and the bitter effects of staying at home with all the narrow prejudices of an islander, that I think there should be a law amongst us, to set our young men abroad, for a term, among the few allies our wars have left us.

Here I see and have conversed with French, Italians, Germans, Danes, Greeks, Turks, Americans, etc., etc., etc.; and without losing sight of my own, I can judge of the countries and manners of others. Where I see the superiority of England (which, by the by, we are a good deal mistaken about in many things), I am pleased, and where I find her inferior, I am at least enlightened. Now, I might have stayed smoked in your towns, or fogged in your country, a century, without being sure of this, and without acquiring any thing more useful or amusing at home. I keep no journal, nor have I any intention of scribbling my travels. I have done with authorship, and if, in my last production, I have convinced the critics or the world I was something more than they took me for, I am satisfied; nor will I hazard *that reputation* by a future effort. It is true I have some others in manuscript, but I leave them for those who come after me; and, if deemed worth publishing, they may serve to prolong my memory when I myself shall cease to remember.

I have a famous Bavarian artist taking some views of Athens, etc., etc., for me. This will be better than scribbling, a disease I hope myself cured of. I hope, on my return, to lead a quiet recluse life, but God knows and does best for us all; at least, so they say, and I have nothing to object, as, on the whole, I have no reason to complain of my lot. I am convinced, however, that men do more harm to themselves than ever the devil could do to them. I trust this will find you well, and as happy as we can be; you will, at least, be pleased to hear I am so, and

Yours ever,

BYRON.

21. TO FRANCIS HODGSON

Athens, January 20th, 1811.

MY DEAR HODGSON,

In most of your letters, that is to say two, the only ones I have received of yours, you complain of my silence. This complaint I presume to be removed by this time, as I have written frequently, but more particularly by H., who is of course long ago landed, and will amply gratify any further curiosity you may have beyond the limits of a letter. I also wrote by the Black John, which however was taken off Algiers with the Capt. Moses Kennedy and several bags of long letters, but especially Hobhouse's intimates have to regret the capture of some enormous packets, which cost him a world of pains at Constantinople, in the Troad and elsewhere, as I can witness, and unless the French Government publish them, I am afraid we have little chance of recovering these inestimable manuscripts. But then to make amends he himself followed close on the heels of his letters (by the bye I fear *heels* of letters is a very incorrect metaphor) and will tell the world all how and about it, unless he also has been boarded and taken off Algiers. Talking of taking, I was nearly taken myself six weeks ago by some Mainote pirates (Lacedemonians and be damned to them) at Cape Colonna, but being well armed, and attended, the varlets were afraid, or they might have bagged us all with a little skirmishing. I am still in Athens making little tours to Marathon, Sunium, the top of Hymettus, and the Morea occasionally to diversify the season. My Grand Giro finished with Constantinople and I shall not (I think) go further Eastward, but I am sure of nothing so little as my own intentions, and if I receive cash and comfortable news from home, I shan't trouble your foggy Island for amusement. I am studying modern Greek with a Master, and my current tongue is Levant Italian, which I gabble perforce. My late dragoman spoke bad Latin, but having dismissed him, I am left to my resources, which consist in tolerably fluent Lingua Franca, middling Romaic (modern Greek) and some variety of Ottoman oaths of great service with a stumbling horse or a stupid servant. I lately sent to England my only remaining Englishman with some papers about money matters, and am left d' ye see all by myself in these outlandish parts, and I don't find it *never* the *worse*, for friends and servants, that is to say fellow countrymen in those capacities, are troublesome fellow travellers. I have a variety of acquaintance, French, Danes, German, Greek, Italian, and Turkish, and have contracted an alliance with Dr. Bronstedt of Copenhagen, a pretty philosopher as you 'd wish to see. Besides I am on good terms with some of my countrymen here, Messrs. Graham and Haygarth, and I have in pay a Bavarian Baron named 'Lynch' (pronounce it *Lynk*) who limns landscapes for the lucre of gain. Here also are Messrs. Fyott, Cockerell and Forster, all of whom I know, and they are all vastly amiable and accomplished. I am living in the Capuchin Convent, Hymettus before me, the Acropolis behind, the Temple of Jove to my right, the Stadium in front, the town to the left; eh, Sir, there 's a situation, there 's your picturesque! nothing like that, Sir, in Lunnun, no not even the Mansion House. And I feed upon Woodcocks and Red Mullet every day, and I have three horses (one a present from the Pasha of the Morea), and I ride to Piræus, and Phalerum, and Munychia, which however don't look quite so magnificent after the harbours of Cadiz, Lisbon, Constantinople, and Gibraltar, not forgetting Malta. I wish to be sure I had a few books, one's own works for instance, any damned nonsense on a long Evening. I had a straggling number of the E[dinburgh] Review given me by a compassionate Capt. of a frigate lately, it contains the reply to the Oxonian pamphlet on the Strabonic controversy, the reviewer seems to be in a perilous passion and heaves out a deal of Slack-jaw as the Sailors call it. You have to direct to Malta, whence my letters are or ought to be forwarded. In two days I shall be twenty-three, and on the 2d above a year and a half out of England. I suppose you and Drury sometimes drink one's health on a speech day, and I trust we shall meet merrily, and make a tour some summer to Wales or Scotland, it will be a great relaxation to me jaunting once more in a Chay. I need not write at length

as Hobby is brimful of remarks, and it would be cruel to curtail
him of a syllable. Tell him I have written to him frequently,
as indeed I have to yourself and also to Drury and others, but
this is a plaguey distance for a 'Single Sheet'.

Yours alway,
BYRON.

22. TO HIS MOTHER

Volage frigate, at sea, June 25, 1811.

DEAR MOTHER,

This letter, which will be forwarded on our arrival at Portsmouth, probably about the 4th of July, is begun about twenty-
three days after our departure from Malta. I have just been
two years (to a day, on the 2d of July) absent from England,
and I return to it with much the same feelings which prevailed
on my departure, viz. indifference; but within that apathy I
certainly do not comprise yourself, as I will prove by every means
in my power. You will be good enough to get my apartments
ready at Newstead; but don't disturb yourself, on any account,
particularly mine, nor consider me in any other light than as a
visitor. I must only inform you that for a long time I have
been restricted to an entire vegetable diet, neither fish nor
flesh coming within my regimen; so I expect a powerful stock
of potatoes, greens, and biscuit; I drink no wine. I have two
servants, middle-aged men, and both Greeks. It is my intention
to proceed first to town, to see Mr. Hanson, and thence to Newstead, on my way to Rochdale. I have only to beg you will not
forget my diet, which it is very necessary for me to observe.
I am well in health, as I have generally been, with the exception
of two agues, both of which I quickly got over.

My plans will so much depend on circumstances, that I shall
not venture to lay down an opinion on the subject. My
prospects are not very promising, but I suppose we shall
wrestle through life like our neighbours; indeed, by Hanson's
last advices, I have some apprehension of finding Newstead
dismantled by Messrs. Brothers,[1] etc., and he seems determined
to force me into selling it, but he will be baffled. I don't suppose I shall be much pestered with visitors; but if I am, you must
receive them, for I am determined to have nobody breaking in
upon my retirement: you know that I never was fond of society,
and I am less so than before. I have brought you a shawl, and

[1] Nottingham upholsterers, who were executing for an unpaid bill.

a quantity of attar of roses, but these I must smuggle, if possible. I trust to find my library in tolerable order.

Fletcher is no doubt arrived. I shall separate the mill from Mr. B * *'s farm, for his son is too gay a deceiver to inherit both, and place Fletcher in it, who has served me faithfully, and whose wife is a good woman; besides, it is necessary to sober young Mr. B * *, or he will people the parish with bastards. In a word, if he had seduced a dairy-maid, he might have found something like an apology; but the girl is his equal, and in high life or low life reparation is made in such circumstances. But I shall not interfere further than (like Bonaparte) by dismembering Mr. B.'s *kingdom*, and erecting part of it into a principality for field-marshal Fletcher! I hope you govern my little *empire* and its sad load of national debt with a wary hand. To drop my metaphor, I beg leave to subscribe myself

Yours ever,
BYRON.

July 14.—This letter was written to be sent from Portsmouth, but, on arriving there, the squadron was ordered to the Nore, from whence I shall forward it. This I have not done before, supposing you might be alarmed by the interval mentioned in the letter being longer than expected between our arrival in port and my appearance at Newstead.

B.

23. TO SCROPE BERDMORE DAVIES

Newstead Abbey, August 7, 1811.

MY DEAREST DAVIES,

Some curse hangs over me and mine. My mother lies a corpse in this house; [1] one of my best friends is drowned in a ditch.[2] What can I say, or think, or do? I received a letter from him the day before yesterday. My dear Scrope, if you can spare a moment, do come down to me—I want a friend. Matthews's last letter was written on *Friday*, —on Saturday he was not. In ability, who was like Matthews? How did we all shrink before him? You do me but justice in saying, I would have risked my paltry existence to have preserved his. This very evening did I mean to write, inviting him, as I invite you, my

[1] Mrs. Byron died suddenly on 1 August, before her son had returned to Newstead.
[2] Charles Skinner Matthews, Fellow of Downing College, Cambridge, was drowned in the Cam.

very dear friend, to visit me. God forgive * * * for his apathy! What will our poor Hobhouse feel! His letters breathe but of Matthews. Come to me, Scrope, I am almost desolate—left almost alone in the world—I had but you, and H., and M., and let me enjoy the survivors whilst I can. Poor M., in his letter of Friday, speaks of his intended contest for Cambridge, and a speedy journey to London. Write or come, but come if you can, or one or both.

Yours ever.

24. TO JOHN CAM HOBHOUSE

Newstead Abbey, August 10th, 1811.

My dear Hobhouse,

From Davies I had already received tidings of the death of Matthews, and from *M. a letter* dated the *day* before his *death*. In that letter he mentions you, and as it was perhaps the last he ever wrote, you will derive a poor consolation from hearing that he spoke of you with that affectionate familiarity, so much more pleasing from those we love, than the highest encomiums of the world.

My dwelling you already know is the house of mourning, and I am really so much bewildered with the different shocks I have sustained, that I can hardly reduce myself to reason by the most frivolous occupations.

My poor friend, J. Wingfield,[1] my mother, and your best friend (and surely not the worst of mine), C. S. M., have disappeared in one little month, since *my return*, and without my seeing *either*, though I have *heard* from *all*.

There is to me something so incomprehensible in death, that I can neither speak nor think on the subject. Indeed, when I looked on the mass of corruption which was the being from whence I sprung, I doubted within myself whether I *was*, or whether she *was not*.

I have lost her who gave me being, and some of those who made that being a blessing. I have neither hopes nor fears beyond the grave, yet if there is within us 'a spark of that Celestial fire',[2] M[atthews] has already 'mingled with the gods'.

In the room where I now write (flanked by the *skulls* you have seen so often) did you and Matthews and myself pass some joyous unprofitable evenings, and here we will drink to his

[1] John Wingfield, who had been at Harrow with Byron, died at Coimbra in May.

[2] Gray's *Elegy*, 46.

memory, which though it cannot reach the dead, will soothe the survivors, and to them only death can be an evil.

I can neither receive nor administer consolation; time will do it for us; in the interim let me see or hear from you, if possible both.

I am very lonely, and should think myself miserable were it not for a kind of hysterical merriment, which I can neither account for nor conquer; but strange as it is, I do laugh, and heartily, wondering at myself while I sustain it.

I have tried reading, and boxing, and swimming, and writing, and rising early, and sitting late, and water, and wine, with a number of ineffectual remedies, and here I am, wretched, but not 'melancholy or gentlemanlike'.[1]

My dear '*Cam of the Cornish*' (Matthews's last expression!!), may man or God give you the happiness which I wish rather than expect you may attain; believe me, none living are more sincerely yours than

BYRON.

25. TO ROBERT CHARLES DALLAS

Newstead, August 21, 1811.

MY DEAR SIR,

Your letter gives me credit for more acute feelings than I possess; for though I feel tolerably miserable, yet I am at the same time subject to a kind of hysterical merriment, or rather laughter without merriment, which I can neither account for nor conquer, and yet I do not feel relieved by it; but an indifferent person would think me in excellent spirits. 'We must forget these things', and have recourse to our old selfish comforts, or rather comfortable selfishness.

I do not think I shall return to London immediately, and shall therefore accept freely what is offered courteously—your mediation between me and Murray.[2] I don't think my name will answer the purpose, and you must be aware that my plaguy Satire will bring the north and south Grub Streets down upon the *Pilgrimage*;—but, nevertheless, if Murray makes a point of it, and you coincide with him, I will do it daringly; so let it be entitled 'By the Author of *English Bards and Scotch Reviewers*'. My remarks on the Romaic, etc., once intended to accompany

---

[1] Jonson, *Every Man in his Humour*, i, iii, 130.
[2] John Murray, of 32 Fleet Street, who was to be Byron's chief publisher and lifelong friend.

the *Hints from Horace*, shall go along with the other, as being indeed more appropriate; also the smaller poems now in my possession, with a few selected from those published in Hobhouse's *Miscellany*. I have found amongst my poor mother's papers all my letters from the East, and one in particular of some length from Albania. From this, if necessary, I can work up a note or two on that subject. As I kept no journal, the letters written on the spot are the best. But of this anon, when we have definitively arranged.

Has Murray shown the work to any one? He may—but I will have no traps for applause. Of course there are little things I would wish to alter, and perhaps the two stanzas of a buffooning cast on London's Sunday are as well left out. I much wish to avoid identifying Childe Harold's character with mine, and that, in sooth, is my second objection to my name appearing in the title-page. When you have made arrangements as to time, size, type, etc., favour me with a reply. I am giving you a universe of trouble, which thanks cannot atone for. I made a kind of prose apology for my scepticism at the head of the MS., which, on recollection, is so much more like an attack than a defence, that, haply, it might better be omitted:—perpend, pronounce. After all, I fear Murray will be in a scrape with the Orthodox; but I cannot help it, though I wish him well through it. As for me, 'I have supped full of criticism', and I don't think that the 'most dismal treatise' will stir and rouse my 'fell of hair' till 'Birnam wood do come to Dunsinane'.

I shall continue to write at intervals, and hope you will pay me in kind. How does Pratt[1] get on, or rather get off, Joe Blacket's posthumous stock? You killed that poor man amongst you, in spite of your Ionian friend[2] and myself, who would have saved him from Pratt, poetry, present poverty, and posthumous oblivion. Cruel patronage! to ruin a man at his calling; but then he is a divine subject for subscription and biography; and Pratt, who makes the most of his dedications, has inscribed the volume to no less than five families of distinction.

I am sorry you don't like Harry White:[3] with a great deal of cant, which in him was sincere (indeed it killed him as you killed Joe Blacket), certes there is poesy and genius. I don't say

---

[1] Samuel Jackson Pratt, miscellaneous writer and patron of the cobbler-poet, Joseph Blacket.

[2] Waller Rodwell Wright, author of *Horæ Ionicæ*.

[3] Henry Kirke White (1785–1806), whose poems appeared in 1803 and 1807.

this on account of my simile and rhymes; but surely he was beyond all the Bloomfields[1] and Blacketts, and their collateral cobblers, whom Lofft[2] and Pratt have or may kidnap from their calling into the service of the trade. You must excuse my flippancy, for I am writing I know not what, to escape from myself. Hobhouse is gone to Ireland. Mr. Davies has been here on his way to Harrowgate.

You did not know Matthews: he was a man of the most astonishing powers, as he sufficiently proved at Cambridge, by carrying off more prizes and fellowships, against the ablest candidates, than any other graduate on record; but a most decided Atheist, indeed noxiously so, for he proclaimed his principles in all societies. I knew him well, and feel a loss not easily to be supplied to myself—to Hobhouse never. Let me hear from you, and believe me,

Always yours,

BYRON.

26. TO FRANCIS HODGSON

Newstead Abbey, August 22, 1811.

You may have heard of the sudden death of my mother, and poor Matthews, which, with that of Wingfield, (of which I was not fully aware till just before I left town, and indeed hardly believed it,) has made a sad chasm in my connections. Indeed the blows followed each other so rapidly that I am yet stupid from the shock; and though I do eat, and drink, and talk, and even laugh, at times, yet I can hardly persuade myself that I am awake, did not every morning convince me mournfully to the contrary.—I shall now wave the subject,—the dead are at rest, and none but the dead can be so.

You will feel for poor Hobhouse,—Matthews was the 'god of his idolatry'[3]; and if intellect could exalt a man above his fellows, no one could refuse him pre-eminence. I knew him most intimately, and valued him proportionably; but I am recurring —so let us talk of life and the living.

If you should feel a disposition to come here, you will find 'beef and a sea-coal fire',[4] and not ungenerous wine. Whether

---

[1] Robert Bloomfield (1766–1823), a shoemaker, author of *The Farmer's Boy*.

[2] Capel Lofft, who had *The Farmer's Boy* published in 1800.

[3] *Romeo and Juliet*, II, ii, 114.

[4]   'Give but an Englishman his whore and ease,
         Beef and a sea-coal fire, he 's yours for ever.'
                              Otway, *Venice Preserved*, II, iii.

Otway's two other requisites for an Englishman or not, I cannot
tell, but probably one of them.—Let me know when I may expect
you, that I may tell you when I go and when return.　I have not
yet been to Lancs. . . . Davies has been here, and has invited
me to Cambridge for a week in October, so that, peradventure,
we may encounter glass to glass.　His gaiety (death cannot mar
it) has done me service; but, after all, ours was a hollow laughter.

You will write to me?　I am solitary, and I never felt solitude
irksome before.　Your anxiety about the critique on * *'s book
is amusing; as it was anonymous, certes it was of little consequence: I wish it had produced a little more confusion, being
a lover of literary malice.　Are you doing nothing? writing
nothing? printing nothing? why not your Satire on Methodism?
the subject (supposing the public to be blind to merit) would do
wonders.　Besides, it would be as well for a destined deacon
to prove his orthodoxy.—It really would give me pleasure to
see you properly appreciated.　I say *really*, as, being an author,
my humanity might be suspected.

Believe me, dear H., yours always.

27. TO JOHN MURRAY

Newstead Abbey, Notts., August 23, 1811.

SIR,

A domestic calamity in the death of a near relation has
hitherto prevented my addressing you on the subject of this
letter.—My friend, Mr. Dallas, has placed in your hands a
manuscript poem written by me in Greece, which he tells me
you do not object to publishing.　But he also informed me in
London that you wished to send the MS. to Mr. Gifford.[1]　Now,
though no one would feel more gratified by the chance of obtaining his observations on a work than myself, there is in such
a proceeding a kind of petition for praise, that neither my pride
—or whatever you please to call it—will admit.　Mr. G. is
not only the first satirist of the day, but editor of one of the
principal Reviews.　As such, he is the last man whose censure
(however eager to avoid it) I would deprecate by clandestine
means.　You will therefore retain the manuscript in your own
care, or, if it must needs be shown, send it to another.　Though
not very patient of censure, I would fain obtain fairly any little
praise my rhymes might deserve, at all events not by extortion,

[1] William Gifford, author of two satires, the *Baviad*, 1794, and the
Mæviad, 1795, and editor of the *Quarterly Review*.

and the humble solicitations of a bandied-about MS. I am sure a little consideration will convince you it would be wrong.

If you determine on publication, I have some smaller poems (never published), a few notes, and a short dissertation on the literature of the modern Greeks (written at Athens), which will come in at the end of the volume.—And, if the present poem should succeed, it is my intention, at some subsequent period, to publish some selections from my first work,—my Satire,—another nearly the same length,[1] and a few other things, with the MS. now in your hands, in two volumes.—But of these hereafter. You will apprize me of your determination.

I am, Sir, your very obedient, humble servant,

BYRON.

28. TO JOHN MURRAY

Newstead Abbey, Notts., Sept. 5, 1811.

SIR,

The time seems to be past when (as Dr. Johnson said) a man was certain to 'hear the truth from his bookseller', for you have paid me so many compliments, that, if I was not the veriest scribbler on earth, I should feel affronted. As I accept your compliments, it is but fair I should give equal or greater credit to your objections, the more so as I believe them to be well founded. With regard to the political and metaphysical parts, I am afraid I can alter nothing; but I have high authority for my Errors in that point, for even the *Æneid* was a *political* poem, and written for a *political* purpose; and as to my unlucky opinions on Subjects of more importance, I am too sincere in them for recantation. On Spanish affairs I have said what I saw, and every day confirms me in that notion of the result formed on the Spot; and I rather think honest John Bull is beginning to come round again to that Sobriety which Massena's retreat had begun to reel from its centre—the usual consequence of *un*usual success. So you perceive I cannot alter the Sentiments; but if there are any alterations in the structure of the versification you would wish to be made, I will tag rhymes and turn stanzas as much as you please. As for the '*Orthodox*', let us hope they will buy, on purpose to abuse—you will forgive the one, if they will do the other. You are aware that any thing from my pen must expect no quarter, on many accounts; and as

[1] *Hints from Horace.*

the present publication is of a nature very different from the former, we must not be sanguine.

You have given me no answer to my question—tell me fairly, did you show the MS. to some of your corps?—I sent an introductory stanza to Mr. Dallas, that it might be forwarded to you; the poem else will open too abruptly. The Stanzas had better be numbered in Roman characters, there is a disquisition on the literature of the modern Greeks, and some smaller poems to come in at the close. These are now at Newstead, but will be sent in time. If Mr. D. has lost the Stanza and note annexed to it, write, and I will send it myself.—You tell me to add two cantos, but I am about to visit my *Collieries* in Lancashire on the 15th instant, which is so *unpoetical* an employment that I need say no more.

I am, sir, your most obedient, etc., etc.,

BYRON.

29. TO ROBERT CHARLES DALLAS

Newstead Abbey, September 7, 1811.

MY DEAR SIR,

As Gifford has been ever my 'Magnus Apollo', any approbation, such as you mention, would, of course, be more welcome than 'all Bokara's vaunted gold, than all the gems of Samarkand'.[1] But I am sorry the MS. was shown to him in such a manner, and had written to Murray to say as much, before I was aware that it was too late.

Your objection to the expression 'central line' I can only meet by saying that, before Childe Harold left England, it was his full intention to traverse Persia, and return by India, which he could not have done without passing the equinoctial.

The other errors you mention, I must correct in the progress through the press. I feel honoured by the wish of such men that the poem should be continued, but to do that I must return to Greece and Asia; I must have a warm sun and a blue sky; I cannot describe scenes so dear to me by a sea-coal fire. I had projected an additional canto when I was in the Troad and Constantinople, and if I saw them again, it would go on; but under existing circumstances and *sensations*, I have neither harp, 'heart, nor voice' to proceed. I feel that *you are all right* as to the metaphysical part; but I also feel that I am sincere, and that if I am only to write '*ad captandum vulgus*', I might as

[1] From Sir W. Jones's translation of a song by Hafiz.

well edit a magazine at once, or spin canzonettas for
Vauxhall.[1] . . .

My work must make its way as well as it can; I know I have
every thing against me, angry poets and prejudices; but if the
poem is a *poem*, it will surmount these obstacles, and if *not*, it
deserves its fate. Your friend's Ode [2] I have read—it is no great
compliment to pronounce it far superior to Smyth's [3] on the
same subject, or to the merits of the new Chancellor. It is
evidently the production of a man of taste, and a poet, though
I should not be willing to say it was fully equal to what might
be expected from the author of '*Horæ Ionicæ*'. I thank you
for it, and that is more than I would do for any other Ode of
the present day.

I am very sensible of your good wishes, and, indeed, I have
need of them. My whole life has been at variance with propriety, not to say decency; my circumstances are become
involved; my friends are dead or estranged, and my existence
a dreary void. In Matthews I have lost my 'guide, philosopher,
and friend' [4]; in Wingfield a friend only, but one whom I could
have wished to have preceded in his long journey.

Matthews was indeed an extraordinary man; it has not
entered into the heart of a stranger to conceive such a man:
there was the stamp of immortality in all he said or did;—
and now what is he? When we see such men pass away and
be no more—men, who seem created to display what the Creator
could make his creatures, gathered into corruption, before the
maturity of minds that might have been the pride of posterity,
what are we to conclude? For my own part, I am bewildered.
To me he was much, to Hobhouse every thing. My poor Hobhouse doted on Matthews. For me, I did not love quite so
much as I honoured him; I was indeed so sensible of his infinite
superiority, that though I did not envy, I stood in awe of it.
He, Hobhouse, Davies, and myself, formed a coterie of our own
at Cambridge and elsewhere. Davies is a wit and man of the
world, and feels as much as such a character can do; but not as
Hobhouse has been affected. Davies, who is not a scribbler,
has always beaten us all in the war of words, and by his col-
loquial powers at once delighted and kept us in order. Hobhouse

---

[1] Vauxhall Gardens, at which music and singing formed part of the
entertainment.
[2] By Waller Rodwell Wright, on the installation of the Duke of Gloucester
as Chancellor of Cambridge University.
[3] W. Smyth's ode was chosen for performance.
[4] Pope, *Essay on Man*, iv, 390.

and myself always had the worst of it with the other two; and even Matthews yielded to the dashing vivacity of Scrope Davies. But I am talking to you of men, or boys, as if you cared about such beings.

I expect mine agent down on the 14th to proceed to Lancashire, where I hear from all quarters that I have a very valuable property in coals, etc. I then intend to accept an invitation to Cambridge in October, and shall, perhaps, run up to town. I have four invitations—to Wales, Dorset, Cambridge, and Chester; but I must be a man of business. I am quite alone, as these long letters sadly testify. I perceive, by referring to your letter, that the Ode is from the author; make my thanks acceptable to him. His Muse is worthy a nobler theme. You will write as usual, I hope. I wish you a good evening, and am,

Yours ever,

Byron.

30. TO THE HON. AUGUSTA LEIGH [1]

Newstead Abbey, Sept. 9th, 1811.

My dear Augusta,

My Rochdale affairs are understood to be settled as far as the Law can settle them, and indeed I am told that the most valuable part is that which was never disputed; but I have never reaped any advantage from them, and God knows if I ever shall. Mr. H.,[2] my agent, is a good man and able, but the most dilatory in the world. I expect him down on the 14th to accompany me to Rochdale, where something will be decided as to selling or working the Collieries. I am Lord of the Manor (a most extensive one), and they want to enclose, which cannot be done without me; but I go there in the worst humour possible and am afraid I shall do or say something not very conciliatory. In short all my affairs are going on as badly as possible, and I have no hopes or plans to better them as I long ago pledged myself never to sell Newstead, which I mean to hold in defiance of the Devil and Man.

I am quite alone and never see strangers without being sick, but I am nevertheless on good terms with my neighbours, for I neither ride or shoot or move over my Garden walls, but I fence and box and swim and run a good deal to keep me in exercise and get me to sleep. Poor Murray [3] is ill again, and one of my Greek servants is ill too, and my valet has got a pestilent cough, so that we are in a peck of troubles; my family Surgeon sent an Emetic this morning for *one* of them, I did not very well

---

[1] At Six Mile Bottom, Newmarket.   [2] John Hanson.   [3] Joe Murray.

know *which*, but I swore *Somebody* should take it, so after a deal of discussion the Greek swallowed it with tears in his eyes, and by the blessing of it, and the *Virgin* whom he invoked to assist *it* and *him*, I suppose he 'll be well to-morrow, if not, *another* shall have the *next*. So your Spouse likes children, *that* is lucky as he will have to bring them up; for my part (since I lost my Newfoundland dog,[1]) I like nobody except his successor a Dutch Mastiff and three land Tortoises brought with me from Greece.

I thank you for your letters and am always glad to hear from you, but if you won't come here before Xmas, I very much fear we shall not meet *here* at all, for I shall be off somewhere or other very soon out of this land of Paper credit (or rather no credit at all, for every body seems on the high road to Bankruptcy), and if I quit it again I shall not be back in a hurry.

However, I shall endeavour to see you somewhere, and make my bow with decorum before I return to the Ottomans, I believe I shall turn Mussulman in the end.

You ask after my health; I am in tolerable leanness, which I promote by exercise and abstinence. I don't know that I have acquired any thing by my travels but a smattering of two languages and a habit of chewing Tobacco.

Yours ever,

B.

31. TO FRANCIS HODGSON

Newstead Abbey, September 13, 1811.

My DEAR HODGSON,

I thank you for your song, or, rather, your two songs,—your new song on love, and your *old song* on *religion*. I admire the *first* sincerely, and in turn call upon you to *admire* the following on Anacreon Moore's new operatic farce,[2] or farcical opera— call it which you will:—

> Good plays are scarce,
> So Moore writes *Farce*;
> Is Fame like his so brittle?
> We knew before
> That '*Little*' 's Moore,
> But now '*tis* Moore that 's *Little*.

[1] Boatswain, buried in the vault, and commemorated by a misanthropical inscription on a monument erected to him in the gardens.
[2] Thomas Moore had won fame by his translation of *Anacreon*, 1800, and *The Poetical Works of the late Thomas Little*, 1801. His farce, *M.P.*, *or The Bluestocking*, was produced at the Lyceum on 9 September, 1811.

I won't dispute with you on the arcana of your new calling; they are Bagatelles like the King of Poland's rosary. One remark, and I have done; the basis of your religion is *injustice*; the *Son* of *God*, the *pure*, the *immaculate*, the *innocent*, is sacrificed for the *Guilty*. This proves *His* heroism; but no more does away *man's* guilt than a schoolboy's volunteering to be flogged for another would exculpate the dunce from negligence, or preserve him from the Rod. You degrade the Creator, in the first place, by making Him a begetter of children; and in the next you convert Him into a Tyrant over an immaculate and injured Being, who is sent into existence to suffer death for the benefit of some millions of Scoundrels, who, after all, seem as likely to be damned as ever. As to miracles, I agree with Hume that it is more probable men should *lie* or be *deceived*, than that things out of the course of Nature should so happen. Mahomet wrought miracles, Brothers [1] the prophet had *proselytes*, and so would Breslaw the conjuror, had he lived in the time of Tiberius.

Besides I trust that God is not a *Jew*, but the God of all Mankind; and as you allow that a virtuous Gentile may be saved, you do away the necessity of being a Jew or a Christian.

I do not believe in any revealed religion, because no religion is revealed: and if it pleases the Church to damn me for not allowing a *nonentity*, I throw myself on the mercy of the '*Great First Cause, least understood*', who must do what is most proper; though I conceive He never made anything to be tortured in another life, whatever it may in this. I will neither read *pro* nor *con*. God would have made His will known without books, considering how very few could read them when Jesus of Nazareth lived, had it been His pleasure to ratify any peculiar mode of worship. As to your immortality, if people are to live, why die? And our carcases, which are to rise again, are they worth raising? I hope, if mine is, that I shall have a better *pair of legs* than I have moved on these two-and-twenty years, or I shall be sadly behind in the squeeze into Paradise. Did you ever read 'Malthus on Population'? If he be right, war and pestilence are our best friends, to save us from being eaten alive, in this 'best of all possible Worlds'.

I will write, read, and think no more; indeed, I do not wish to shock your prejudices by saying all I do think. Let us make the most of life, and leave dreams to Emanuel Swedenborg.

Now to dreams of another genus—Poesies. I like your song

[1] Richard Brothers (1757–1824), who preached that in 1795 he would be revealed as Prince of the Hebrews and ruler of the world.

much; but I will say no more, for fear you should think I wanted to scratch you into approbation of my past, present, or future acrostics. I shall not be at Cambridge before the middle of October; but, when I go, I should certes like to see you there before you are dubbed a deacon. Write to me, and I will rejoin.

Yours ever,

BYRON.

32. TO FRANCIS HODGSON

Newstead Abbey, Sept. 25, 1811.

MY DEAR HODGSON,

I fear that before the latest of October or the first of November, I shall hardly be able to make Cambridge. My everlasting agent puts off his coming like the accomplishment of a prophecy. However, finding me growing serious he hath promised to be here on Thursday, and about Monday we shall remove to Rochdale. I have only to give discharges to the tenantry here (it seems the poor creatures must be raised, though I wish it was not necessary), and arrange the receipt of sums, and the liquidation of some debts, and I shall be ready to enter upon new subjects of vexation. I intend to visit you in Granta, and hope to prevail on you to accompany me here or there or anywhere.

I am plucking up my spirits, and have begun to gather my little sensual comforts together. Lucy is extracted from Warwickshire; some very bad faces have been warned off the premises, and more promising substituted in their stead; the partridges are plentiful, hares fairish, pheasants not quite so good, and the Girls on the Manor * * * *. Just as I had formed a tolerable establishment my travels commenced, and on my return I find all to do over again; my former flock were all scattered; some married, not before it was needful. As I am a great disciplinarian, I have just issued an edict for the abolition of caps; no hair to be cut on any pretext; stays permitted, but not too low before; full uniform always in the evening; Lucinda to be commander—*vice* the present, about to be wedded (*mem.* she is 35 with a flat face and a squeaking voice), of all the makers and unmakers of beds in the household.

My tortoises (all Athenians), my hedgehog, my mastiff and the other live Greek, are all purely. The tortoises lay eggs, and I have hired a hen to hatch them. I am writing notes for *my* quarto (Murray would have it a *quarto*), and Hobhouse is writing text for *his* quarto;[1] if you call on Murray or Cawthorn you will hear news of either. I have attacked De Pauw,[2] Thornton,[3] Lord Elgin,[4] Spain, Portugal, the *Edinburgh Review*,[5] travellers, Painters, Antiquarians, and others, so you see what a dish of Sour Crout Controversy I shall prepare for myself. It would not answer for me to give way, now; as I was forced into bitterness at the beginning, I will go through to the last. *Væ Victis !* If I fall, I shall fall gloriously, fighting against a host.

Felicissima Notte a Voss. Signoria,

B.

33. TO ROBERT CHARLES DALLAS

Newstead Abbey, Oct. 11, 1811.

DEAR SIR,

I have returned from Lancashire, and ascertained that my property there may be made very valuable, but various circumstances very much circumscribe my exertions at present. I shall be in town on business in the beginning of November, and perhaps at Cambridge before the end of this month; but of my movements you shall be regularly apprized. Your objections I have in part done away by alterations, which I hope will suffice; and I have sent two or three additional stanzas for both 'Fyttes'. I have been again shocked with a *death*, and have lost one very dear to me in happier times;[6] but 'I have almost forgot the taste of grief', and 'supped full of horrors'[7] till I have become callous, nor have I a tear left for an event which, five years ago, would have bowed down my head to the earth. It seems as though I were to experience in my youth the greatest misery of age. My friends fall around me, and I shall be left a lonely tree before I am withered. Other men can always take refuge in their families; I have no resource but my own reflections, and they present no prospect here or hereafter,

---

[1] *Travels in Albania.*
[2] Cornelius de Pauw, the Dutch historian, whose *Recherches philosophiques sur les Grecs* appeared in 1787. See *Childe Harold*, Canto II, note 33, part ii.
[3] Thomas Thornton, author of *The Present State of Turkey*, 1807. See note 33, part ii.
[4] Thomas Bruce, Earl of Elgin, had annoyed Byron by his operations in the Parthenon. See note 6.
[5] See note 33, part iii.
[6] Edleston (see page 6) died of consumption in May 1811.
[7] *Macbeth*, v, v, 9, 13.

except the selfish satisfaction of surviving my betters. I am indeed very wretched, and you will excuse my saying so, as you know I am not apt to cant of sensibility.

Instead of tiring yourself with *my* concerns, I should be glad to hear *your* plans of retirement. I suppose you would not like to be wholly shut out of society? Now I know a large village, or small town, about twelve miles off, where your family would have the advantage of very genteel society, without the hazard of being annoyed by mercantile affluence; where *you* would meet with men of information and independence; and where I have friends to whom I should be proud to introduce you. There are, besides, a coffee-room, assemblies, etc., etc., which bring people together. My mother had a house there some years, and I am well acquainted with the economy of Southwell, the name of this little commonwealth. Lastly, you will not be very remote from me; and though I am the very worst companion for young people in the world, this objection would not apply to *you*, whom I could see frequently. Your expenses, too, would be such as best suit your inclinations, more or less, as you thought proper; but very little would be requisite to enable you to enter into all the gaieties of a country life. You could be as quiet or bustling as you liked, and certainly as well situated as on the lakes of Cumberland, unless you have a particular wish to be *picturesque.*

Pray, is your Ionian friend in town? You have promised me an introduction. You mention having consulted some friends on the MSS. Is not this contrary to our usual way? Instruct Mr. Murray not to allow his shopman to call the work *Child of Harrow's Pilgrimage*!!!! as he has done to some of my astonished friends, who wrote to inquire after my *sanity* on the occasion, as well they might. I have heard nothing of Murray, whom I scolded heartily. Must I write more notes? Are there not enough? Cawthorn must be kept back with the *Hints.* I hope he is getting on with Hobhouse's quarto. Good evening.

Yours ever,

BYRON.

34. TO FRANCIS HODGSON

Newstead Abbey, Oct. 13, 1811.

You will begin to deem me a most liberal correspondent; but as my letters are free, you will overlook their frequency. I have sent you answers in prose and verse to all your late communications; and though I am invading your ease again, I don't know why, or what to put down that you are not acquainted with already. I am growing *nervous* (how you will laugh!)—but it is true,—really, wretchedly, ridiculously, fine-ladically *nervous*. Your climate kills me; I can neither read, write, or amuse myself, or any one else. My days are listless, and my nights restless; I have very seldom any society, and when I have, I run out of it. At 'this present writing', there are in the next room three *ladies*, and I have stolen away to write this grumbling letter.—I don't know that I sha'n't end with insanity, for I find a want of method in arranging my thoughts that perplexes me strangely; but this looks more like silliness than madness, as Scrope Davies would facetiously remark in his consoling manner. I must try the hartshorn of your company; and a session of Parliament would suit me well,—any thing to cure me of conjugating the accursed verb '*ennuyer*'.

When shall you be at Cambridge? You have hinted, I think, that your friend Bland is returned from Holland. I have always had a great respect for his talents, and for all that I have heard of his character; but of me, I believe he knows nothing, except that he heard my sixth form repetitions ten months together at the average of two lines a morning, and those never perfect. I remembered him and his *Slaves* as I passed between Capes Matapan, St. Angelo, and his Isle of Cerigo, and I always bewailed the absence of the *Anthology*. I suppose he will now translate Vondel,[1] the Dutch Shakespeare, and *Gysbert van Amstel* will easily be accommodated to our stage in its present state; and I presume he saw the Dutch poem, where the love of Pyramus and Thisbe is compared to the *passion* of *Christ*; also the love of *Lucifer* for Eve, and other varieties of Low Country literature. No doubt you will think me crazed to talk of such things, but they are all in black and white and good repute on the banks of every canal from Amsterdam to Alkmaar.

Yours ever,

B.

My poesy is in the hands of its various publishers; but the *Hints from Horace* (to which I have subjoined some savage lines on Methodism,[2] and ferocious notes on the vanity of the

---

[1] Joost Van Vondel (1587–1679), author of thirty-two tragedies, mostly on classical or religious themes.
[2] Lines 371–82.

triple Editory of the *Edinb. Annual Register* [1]), my *Hints*, I say, stand still, and why?—I have not a friend in the world (but you and Drury) who can construe Horace's Latin or my English well enough to adjust them for the press, or to correct the proofs in a grammatical way. So that, unless you have bowels when you return to town (I am too far off to do it for myself), this ineffable work will be lost to the world for—I don't know how many *weeks*.

Childe Harold's Pilgrimage must wait till *Murray's* is finished. He is making a tour in Middlesex, and is to return soon, when high matter may be expected. He wants to have it in quarto, which is a cursed unsaleable size; but it is pestilent long, and one must obey one's bookseller. I trust Murray will pass the Paddington Canal without being seduced by Payne and Mackinlay's example,—I say Payne and Mackinlay, supposing that the partnership held good.[2] Drury, the villain, has not written to me; 'I am never (as Mrs. Lumpkin [3] says to Tony) to be gratified with the monster's dear wild notes'.

So you are going (going indeed!) into orders. You must make your peace with the Eclectic Reviewers—they accuse you of impiety, I fear, with injustice. Demetrius, the 'Sieger of Cities', is here, with 'Gilpin Horner'.[4] The painter [5] is not necessary, as the portraits he already painted are (by anticipation) very like the new animals.—Write, and send me your 'Love Song'—but I want *paulo majora* from you. Make a dash before you are a deacon, and try a *dry* publisher.

Yours always,
B.

35. TO THOMAS MOORE

Cambridge, October 27, 1811.

SIR,

Your letter [6] followed me from Notts to this place, which will account for the delay of my reply. Your former letter I never

---

[1] ' . . . By-the-by, it is a good deal beneath Scott and Campbell, and not much above Southey, to allow the booby Ballantyne to entitle them, in the Edinburgh Annual Register (of which, by-the-by, Southey is editor), the grand poetical triumvirate of the day. . . .'

[2] Payne, a publisher, drowned himself in the Paddington Canal.

[3] An error for Mrs. Hardcastle, in Goldsmith's *She Stoops to Conquer*.

[4] Demetrius Zograffo, nicknamed after Demetrius Poliorcetes; and his other Greek servant, who seems to have resembled the Goblin Page in Scott's *Lay of the Last Minstrel* (see especially Canto II, stanza 32).

[5] J. T. Barber, who was painting his wolf and bear.

[6] An apparently insulting reference, in *English Bards, and Scotch Reviewers*, to Moore's abortive duel with Francis Jeffrey in 1806, had led Moore to demand an explanation.

had the honour to receive;—be assured, in whatever part of the world it had found me, I should have deemed it my duty to return and answer it in person.

The advertisement you mention, I know nothing of.—At the time of your meeting with Mr. Jeffrey, I had recently entered College, and remember to have heard and read a number of squibs on the occasion; and from the recollection of these I derived all my knowledge on the subject, without the slightest idea of 'giving the lie' to an address which I never beheld. When I put my name to the production, which has occasioned this correspondence, I became responsible to all whom it might concern,—to explain where it requires explanation, and, where insufficiently or too sufficiently explicit, at all events to satisfy. My situation leaves me no choice; it rests with the injured and the angry to obtain reparation in their own way.

With regard to the passage in question, *you* were certainly *not* the person towards whom I felt personally hostile. On the contrary, my whole thoughts were engrossed by one, whom I had reason to consider as my worst literary enemy, nor could I foresee that his former antagonist was about to become his champion. You do not specify what you would wish to have done: I can neither retract nor apologise for a charge of falsehood which I never advanced.

In the beginning of the week, I shall be at No. 8, St. James's Street.—Neither the letter or the friend to whom you stated your intention ever made their appearance.

Your friend, Mr. Rogers,[1] or any other gentleman delegated by you, will find me most ready to adopt any conciliatory proposition which shall not compromise my own honour,—or, failing in that, to make the atonement you deem it necessary to require.

I have the honour to be, Sir,
Your most obedient, humble servant,
BYRON.

36. TO WILLIAM HARNESS

8, St. James's Street, Dec. 8, 1811.

Behold a most formidable sheet, without gilt or black edging, and consequently very vulgar and indecorous, particularly to one of your precision; but this being Sunday, I can procure no

[1] Samuel Rogers (1763–1855), the poet, at whose table a friendly meeting between Moore and Byron was afterwards arranged.

better, and will atone for its length by not filling it. Bland I
have not seen since my last letter; but on Tuesday he dines
with me, and will meet Moore, the epitome of all that is exquisite in poetical or personal accomplishments. How Bland has
settled with Miller,[1] I know not. I have very little interest
with either, and they must arrange their concerns according to
their own gusto. I have done my endeavours, *at your request*,
to bring them together, and hope they may agree to their
mutual advantage.

Coleridge has been lecturing against Campbell.[2] Rogers was
present, and from him I derive the information. We are going
to make a party to hear this Manichean of poesy.[3]—Pole [4]
is to marry Miss Long, and will be a very miserable dog for all
that. The present ministers are to continue, and his Majesty
does continue in the same state;[5] so there's folly and madness
for you, both in a breath.

I never heard but of one man truly fortunate, and he was
Beaumarchais, the author of *Figaro*, who buried two wives and
gained three lawsuits before he was thirty.[6]

And now, child, what art thou doing? *Reading, I trust.*
I want to see you take a degree. Remember, this is the most
important period of your life; and don't disappoint your papa
and your aunt, and all your kin—besides myself. Don't you
know that all male children are begotten for the express purpose
of being graduates? and that even I am an A.M., though how
I became so the Public Orator only can resolve. Besides, you
are to be a priest; and to confute Sir William Drummond's late
book about the Bible [7] (printed, but not published), and all other
infidels whatever. Now leave Master H.'s gig, and Master S.'s
Sapphics, and become as immortal as Cambridge can make you.

You see, *Mio Carissimo*, what a pestilent correspondent I
am likely to become; but then you shall be as quiet at Newstead
as you please, and I won't disturb your studies as I do now.
When do you fix the day, that I may take you up according to

[1] William Miller, the publisher.
[2] In his lectures on Shakespeare and Milton, Coleridge had referred
slightingly to Thomas Campbell's poetry.
[3]   'the Manichean God,
       Adored through fear, strong only to destroy.'
                        COWPER, *The Task*, v, 444–5.
[4] William Wellesley Pole Wellesley, nephew of the Duke of Wellington.
[5] George III's mind had failed in the previous August.
[6] This is not strictly true.
[7] *Œdipus Judaicus*, in which many passages of the Old Testament were
explained as astronomical allegories.

contract? Hodgson talks of making a third in our journey; but we can't stow him, inside at least. Positively you shall go with me as was agreed, and don't let me have any of your *politesse* to H. on the occasion. I shall manage to arrange for both with a little contrivance. I wish H. was not quite so fat, and we should pack better. Has he left off vinous liquors? He is an excellent soul; but I don't think water would improve him, at least *in*ternally. You will want to know what I am doing—chewing tobacco.

You see nothing of my allies, Scrope Davies and Matthews [1]— they don't suit you; and how does it happen that I—who am a pipkin of the same pottery—continue in your good graces? Good night,—I will go on in the morning.

Dec. 9th.—In a morning I 'm always sullen, and to-day is as sombre as myself. Rain and mist are worse than a sirocco, particularly in a beef-eating and beer-drinking country. My bookseller, Cawthorne, has just left me, and tells me, with a most important face, that he is in treaty for a novel of Madame D'Arblay's,[2] for which 1000 guineas are asked! He wants me to read the MS. (if he obtains it), which I shall do with pleasure; but I should be very cautious in venturing an opinion on her whose *Cecilia* Dr. Johnson superintended.[3] If he lends it to me, I shall put it into the hands of Rogers and Moore, who are truly men of taste. I have filled the sheet, and beg your pardon; I will not do it again. I shall, perhaps, write again; but if not, believe, silent or scribbling, that I am,

My dearest William, ever, etc.

37. TO THOMAS MOORE

December 11, 1811.

MY DEAR MOORE,

If you please, we will drop our formal monosyllables, and adhere to the appellations sanctioned by our godfathers and godmothers. If you make it a point, I will withdraw your name;[4] at the same time there is no occasion, as I have this day postponed your election *sine die*, till it shall suit your wishes to be amongst us. I do not say this from any awkwardness the erasure of your proposal would occasion to *me*, but simply such is the state of the case; and, indeed, the longer your name is up,

[1] Henry Matthews, younger brother of C. S. Matthews.
[2] *The Wanderer, or Female Difficulties*, published in 1814.
[3] Dr. Johnson did not, however, see it till it was in print.
[4] From the list of candidates for election to the Alfred Club.

the stronger will become the probability of success, and your voters more numerous. Of course you will decide—your wish shall be my law. If my zeal has already outrun discretion, pardon me, and attribute my officiousness to an excusable motive.

I wish you would go down with me to Newstead. Hodgson will be there, and a young friend, named Harness, the earliest and dearest I ever had from the third form at Harrow to this hour. I can promise you good wine, and, if you like shooting, a manor of 4000 acres, fires, books, your own free will, and my own very indifferent company. *Balnea, vina, Venus . . .*[1]

Hodgson will plague you, I fear, with verse;—for my own part, I will conclude, with Martial, *nil recitabo tibi*;[2] and surely the last inducement is not the least. Ponder on my proposition, and believe me, my dear Moore,

Yours ever,
BYRON.

38. TO FRANCIS HODGSON

8, St. James's Street, February 16, 1812.

DEAR HODGSON,

I send you a proof. Last week I was very ill and confined to bed with stone in the kidney, but I am now quite recovered. If the stone had got into my heart instead of my kidneys, it would have been all the better. The women are gone to their relatives, after many attempts to explain what was already too clear. However, I have quite recovered *that* also, and only wonder at my folly in excepting my own strumpets from the general corruption,—albeit a two months' weakness is better than ten years. I have one request to make, which is, never mention a woman again in any letter to me, or even allude to the existence of the sex. I won't even read a word of the feminine gender;—it must all be *propria quæ maribus.*

In the spring of 1813 I shall leave England for ever. Every thing in my affairs tends to this, and my inclinations and health do not discourage it. Neither my habits nor constitution are improved by your customs or your climate. I shall find employment in making myself a good Oriental scholar. I shall retain a mansion in one of the fairest islands, and retrace, at intervals, the most interesting portions of the East In the mean time, I am adjusting my concerns, which will (when arranged) leave me with wealth sufficient even for home, but enough for a

---

[1] Sc. *corrumpunt corpora nostra.*   [2] *Epigrams*, XI, lii, 16.

principality in Turkey. At present they are involved, but I hope, by taking some necessary but unpleasant steps, to clear every thing. Hobhouse is expected daily in London: we shall be very glad to see him; and, perhaps, you will come up and 'drink deep ere he depart', if not, 'Mahomet must go to the mountain';—but Cambridge will bring sad recollections to him, and worse to me, though for very different reasons. I believe the only human being that ever loved me in truth and entirely, was of, or belonging to, Cambridge, and, in that, no change can now take place. There is one consolation in death—where he sets his seal, the impression can neither be melted or broken, but endureth for ever.

Yours always,

B.

P.S.—I almost rejoice when one I love dies young, for I could never bear to see them old or altered.

39. TO FRANCIS HODGSON

8, St. James's Street, March 5, 1812.

MY DEAR HODGSON,

We are not answerable for reports of speeches in the papers;[1] they are always given incorrectly, and on this occasion more so than usual, from the debate in the Commons on the same night. The *Morning Post* should have said *eighteen years*. However, you will find the speech, as spoken, in the Parliamentary Register, when it comes out. Lords Holland and Grenville, particularly the latter, paid me some high compliments in the course of their speeches, as you may have seen in the papers, and Lords Eldon and Harrowby answered me. I have had many marvellous eulogies repeated to me since, in person and by proxy, from divers persons ministerial—yea, ministerial! —as well as oppositionists; of them I shall only mention Sir F. Burdett. *He* says it is the best speech by a *lord* since the '*Lord* knows when', probably from a fellow-feeling in the sentiments. Lord H. tells me I shall beat them all if I persevere; and Lord G. remarked that the construction of some of my periods are very like *Burke's*!! And so much for vanity. I spoke very violent sentences with a sort of modest impudence, abused every thing and every body, and put the Lord Chancellor very much out of humour: and if I may believe what I hear,

[1] On 27 February Byron had made his first speech in the House of Lords against a bill for the severer punishment of frame-breakers.

have not lost any character by the experiment. As to my delivery, loud and fluent enough, perhaps a little theatrical. I could not recognize myself or any one else in the newspapers.

I hire myself unto Griffiths,[1] and my poesy comes out on Saturday.[2] Hobhouse is here; I shall tell him to write. My stone is gone for the present, but I fear is part of my habit. We *all* talk of a visit to Cambridge.

Yours ever,

B.

40. TO LORD HOLLAND [3]

St. James's Street, March 5, 1812.

MY LORD,

May I request your Lordship to accept a copy of the thing which accompanies this note?[4] You have already so fully proved the truth of the first line of Pope's couplet,[5]

'Forgiveness to the injured doth belong',

that I long for an opportunity to give the lie to the verse that follows. If I were not perfectly convinced that any thing I may have formerly uttered in the boyish rashness of my misplaced resentment had made as little impression as it deserved to make, I should hardly have the confidence—perhaps your Lordship may give it a stronger and more appropriate appellation—to send you a quarto of the same scribbler. But your Lordship, I am sorry to observe to-day, is troubled with the gout; if my book can produce a *laugh* against itself or the author, it will be of some service. If it can set you to *sleep*, the benefit will be yet greater; and as some facetious personage observed half a century ago, that 'poetry is a mere drug', I offer you mine as a humble assistant to the *eau médicinale*. I trust you will forgive this and all my other buffooneries, and believe me to be, with great respect,

Your Lordship's obliged and sincere servant,

BYRON.

[1] George Edward Griffiths, editor of the *Monthly Review*, for which Byron wrote some articles.
[2] The publication of *Childe Harold*, Cantos I and II, brought him instant fame.
[3] Henry Fox, third Lord Holland, the Whig statesman, whom Byron, through a misapprehension, had attacked in *English Bards*.
[4] A copy of his poem.
[5] Rather, Dryden's, in *The Conquest of Granada*, Part II, I, ii:

'Forgiveness to the injured does belong,
But they ne'er pardon, who have done the wrong.'

41. TO LADY CAROLINE LAMB [1]

May 1st, 1812.

My DEAR LADY CAROLINE,

I have read over the few poems of Miss Milbank [2] with attention. They display fancy, feeling, and a little practice would very soon induce facility of expression. Though I have an abhorrence of Blank Verse, I like the lines on Dermody [3] so much that I wish they were in rhyme. The lines in the Cave at Seaham [4] have a turn of thought which I cannot sufficiently commend, and here I am at least candid as my own opinions differ upon such subjects. The first stanza is very good indeed, and the others, with a few slight alterations, might be rendered equally excellent. The last are smooth and pretty. But these are all, has she no others? She certainly is a very extraordinary girl; who would imagine so much strength and variety of thought under that placid Countenance? It is not necessary for Miss M. to be an authoress, indeed I do not think publishing at all creditable either to men or women, and (though you will not believe me) very often feel ashamed of it myself; but I have no hesitation in saying that she has talents which, were it proper or requisite to indulge, would have led to distinction.

A friend of mine (fifty years old, and an author, but not *Rogers*) has just been here. As there is no name to the MSS. I shewed them to him, and he was much more enthusiastic in his praises than I have been. He thinks them beautiful; I shall content myself with observing that they are better, much better, than anything of Miss M.'s protegee [*sic*] Blacket. [5] You will say as much of this to Miss M. as you think proper. I say all this very sincerely. I have no desire to be better acquainted with Miss Milbank; she is too good for a fallen spirit to know, and I should like her more if she were less perfect.

Believe me, yours ever most truly,

B.

---

[1] Lady Caroline Lamb, born in 1785, was the daughter of Frederick Ponsonby, Earl of Bessborough, and wife of William Lamb, afterwards Lord Melbourne. Since meeting him at Melbourne House on 25 March, she had become infatuated with Byron.

[2] Anne Isabella ('Annabella') Milbanke, only child of Sir Ralph Milbanke, Bart., born in 1792. Byron had met her at Melbourne House, and she eventually became his wife.

[3] Thomas Dermody (1775–1802), an Irish poet, whose collected verses, called *The Harp of Erin*, appeared in 1807.

[4] Where her father had a villa.

[5] See p. 46. He had been befriended in his last years by Miss Milbanke.

42. TO WALTER SCOTT

St. James's Street, July 6, 1812.

SIR,

I have just been honoured with your letter.—I feel sorry that you should have thought it worth while to notice the 'evil works of my nonage',[1] as the thing is suppressed *voluntarily*, and your explanation is too kind not to give me pain. The Satire was written when I was very young and very angry, and fully bent on displaying my wrath and my wit, and now I am haunted by the ghosts of my wholesale assertions. I cannot sufficiently thank you for your praise; and now, waving myself, let me talk to you of the Prince Regent. He ordered me to be presented to him at a ball; and after some sayings peculiarly pleasing from royal lips, as to my own attempts, he talked to me of you and your immortalities: he preferred you to every bard past and present, and asked which of your works pleased me most. It was a difficult question. I answered, I thought the *Lay*. He said his own opinion was nearly similar. In speaking of the others, I told him that I thought you more particularly the poet of *Princes*, as *they* never appeared more fascinating than in *Marmion* and the *Lady of the Lake*. He was pleased to coincide, and to dwell on the description of your Jameses as no less royal than poetical. He spoke alternately of Homer and yourself, and seemed well acquainted with both; so that (with the exception of the Turks [2] and your humble servant) you were in very good company. I defy Murray to have exaggerated his Royal Highness's opinion of your powers, nor can I pretend to enumerate all he said on the subject; but it may give you pleasure to hear that it was conveyed in language which would only suffer by my attempting to transcribe it, and with a tone and taste which gave me a very high idea of his abilities and accomplishments, which I had hitherto considered as confined to *manners*, certainly superior to those of any living *gentleman*.

This interview was accidental. I never went to the levee; for having seen the courts of Mussulman and Catholic sovereigns, my curiosity was sufficiently allayed; and my politics being as perverse as my rhymes, I had, in fact, 'no business there'. To be thus praised by your Sovereign must be gratifying to you; and if that gratification is not alloyed by the communication

[1] *English Bards, and Scotch Reviewers*, in which Scott had been assailed for his supposed mercenary view of literature. Scott's letter, the result of an attempt at reconciliation by Murray, contained an explanation of his attitude.

[2] The Turkish ambassador and his retinue were present.

being made through me, the bearer of it will consider himself very fortunately and sincerely,

Your obliged and obedient servant,

BYRON.

P.S.—Excuse this scrawl, scratched in a great hurry, and just after a journey.

43. TO LADY CAROLINE LAMB [1]

[August, 1812?]

MY DEAREST CAROLINE,

If tears which you saw and know I am not apt to shed,—if the agitation in which I parted from you,—agitation which you must have perceived through the *whole* of this most *nervous* affair, did not commence until the moment of leaving you approached, —if all I have said and done, and am still but too ready to say and do, have not sufficiently proved what my real feelings are, and must ever be towards you, my love, I have no other proof to offer. God knows, I wish you happy, and when I quit you, or rather you, from a sense of duty to your husband and mother, quit me, you shall acknowledge the truth of what I again promise and vow, that no other in word or deed, shall ever hold the place in my affections, which is, and shall be, most sacred to you, till I am nothing. I never knew till *that moment* the *madness* of my dearest and most beloved friend; I cannot express myself; this is no time for words, but I shall have a pride, a melancholy pleasure, in suffering what you yourself can scarcely conceive, for you do not know me. I am about to go out with a heavy heart, because my appearing this evening will stop any absurd story which the event of the day might give rise to. Do you think *now* I am *cold* and *stern* and *artful*? Will even *others* think so? Will your *mother* ever—that mother to whom we must indeed sacrifice much, more, much more on my part than she shall ever know or can imagine? 'Promise not to love you!' ah, Caroline, it is past promising. But I shall attribute all concessions to the proper motive, and never cease to feel all that you have already witnessed, and more than can ever be known but to my own heart,—perhaps to yours. May God protect, forgive, and bless you. Ever, and even more than ever,

Your most attached,

BYRON.

[1] Lady Caroline's affair with Byron had become so notorious that her relatives wished her to leave England.

P.S.—These taunts which have driven you to this, my dearest Caroline, were it not for your mother and the kindness of your connections, is there anything on earth or heaven that would have made me so happy as to have made you mine long ago? and not less *now* than *then*, but *more* than ever at this time. You know I would with pleasure give up all here and all beyond the grave for you, and in refraining from this, must my motives be misunderstood? I care not who knows this, what use is made of it,—it is to *you* and to *you* only that they are *yourself* [*sic*]. I was and am yours freely and most entirely, to obey, to honour, love,—and fly with you when, where, and how you yourself *might* and *may* determine.

44. TO LADY MELBOURNE [1]

Cheltenham, September 10th, 1812.

DEAR LADY MELBOURNE,

I presume you have heard and will not be sorry to hear *again*, that *they* [2] are safely deposited in Ireland, and that the sea rolls between you and *one* of your torments; the other you see is still at your elbow. Now (if you are as sincere as I sometimes almost dream) you will not regret to hear, that I wish this to end, and it certainly shall not be renewed on my part. It is not that I love another, but loving at all is quite out of my way; I am tired of being a fool, and when I look back on the waste of time, and the destruction of all my plans last winter by this last romance, I am—what I ought to have been long ago. It is true from early habit, one must make love mechanically, as one swims. I was once very fond of both, but now as I never swim, unless I tumble into the water, I don't make love till almost obliged, though I fear *that* is not the shortest way out of the troubled waves with which in such accidents we must struggle.

But I will say no more on this topic, as I am not sure of my ground, and you can easily outwit me, as you always hitherto have done.

To-day I have had a letter from Lord Holland, wishing me to write for the opening theatre, but as all Grub Street seems engaged in the contest, I have no ambition to enter the lists, and have thrown my few ideas into the fire. I never risk

[1] Elizabeth, Lady Melbourne, 'the best, the kindest, and ablest woman I have ever known, old or young', was the mother of William Lamb, and aunt to Annabella Milbanke.

[2] Lady Caroline Lamb and her mother, Lady Bessborough.

rivalry in anything, you see the very *lowest*, as in this case, discourages me, from a sort of mixed feeling, I don't know if it be *pride*, but *you* will say it certainly is not *modesty*. I suppose your friend Twiss [1] will be *one*. I hear there are five hundred, and I wish him success. I really think he would do it well, but few men who have any character to lose, would risk it in an anonymous scramble, for the sake of their own feelings.

I have written to Lord H. to thank him and decline the chance.[2]

Betty is performing here, I fear very ill. His figure is that of a hippopotamus, his face like the bull and mouth on the panels of a heavy coach, his arms like fins fattened out of shape, his voice the gargling of an alderman with the quinsy, and his acting altogether ought to be natural, for it certainly is like nothing that *Art* has ever yet exhibited on the stage.

Will you honour me with a line at your leisure? On the most *indifferent* subjects you please, and believe me ever,

Yours very affectionately,

B.

45. TO LADY MELBOURNE

[Eywood, Presteign[3]], December 23rd, 1812.

MY DEAR LADY M.,

Your last anecdote [4] seems to show that our friend is actually possessed by 'the foul fiend Flibbertigibbet, who presides over mopping and mowing',[5] and if the provincial literati don't insert it in the *St. Albans Mercury*, the collectors of extraordinaries ought to be dismissed for malversation and omission. Seriously, though, all this forms *my* best justification. I very much fear it will not forward your interests at the next election, except amongst yᵉ ballad-makers. What will the Lady B[essborough] say? I fear it will go nigh to the recall of Sir W. Farquhar, and the ancient disorder.[6]

Was the 'odious book' (which has just attained the *summit* of *fame* by giving a name to a *very slow racehorse*) added to the conflagration? and what might be the pretty piece of eloquence

---

[1] Horace Twiss, a wit and politician.
[2] Later, at the request of the Committee, when none of the addresses submitted was found to be suitable, he furnished the lines that were spoken.
[3] The Herefordshire home of Jane Elizabeth, Countess of Oxford, with whom Byron had formed an intimacy.
[4] At Brocket Hall, Hertfordshire, Lady Caroline had burned Byron in effigy, with 'his book, ring, and chain', to the accompaniment of a chant written by herself.
[5] *King Lear*, III, iv, 120, and IV, i, 64.
[6] i.e. the temporary loss of Lady Caroline's reason.

delivered by her right trusty henchman! My letters would have added very appropriately to ye combustibles, and I regret ye omission of such exquisite ingredients.

I wrote to you yesterday (franked and directed to M[elbourne] H[ouse], not having then received ye mandate to ye contrary), and do not know that I can add anything to my details in that sheet. We are completely out of the world in this place, and have not even a *difference* to diversify the scene or amuse our correspondents and you know perhaps that the recapitulation or display of *all good* things is very insipid to auditors or beholders.

I wait the news of the reception of that same ineffable letter now in your hands, though (as I tell her) I have no great hopes of its doing the least good. It is written a little gravely but very much, nevertheless, in the usual tone, which L^dy B[essborough] is pleased to say is not 'soothing'. I am really become very indifferent as to her next proceedings, for what can she do more than she has already done?

I am much amused with ye tale of L^dy Cowper's [1] little girl; her mamma has always had a great share of my *most respectful* admiration. But I don't desire to be remembered to any of you, as I suppose the best wish you have is to forget me as soon as possible; besides which, under ye impression of C.'s correspondence, L^dy C. must conceive me to be a sucking Catiline, only less respectable. Bankes is going abroad,[2] and, as I said in my last, it is not very unlikely that I may recommence voyaging amongst the Mussulmen. If so, I claim you as a correspondent, since you *won't* give me up to the reasonable request of the moderate C., and in truth I don't wish you should. You know I have obeyed you in everything—in my suit to ye Princess of Parallelograms,[3] my breach with little *Mania*, and my subsequent acknowledgments of the *sovereignty* of *Armida*.[4] You have been my director, and are still, for I do not know anything you could not make me do, or undo; and *m'amie* (but this you *won't believe*) has not yet learned the art of *managing* me, nor superseded your authority. You would have laughed a little time ago, when I inadvertently said, talking of you, that there was nothing you could not make me do, or give up (if you

---

[1] Emily Mary, Lady Melbourne's daughter, who was married to the fifth Earl Cowper in 1805.

[2] William John Bankes was about to begin his travels in Asia Minor.

[3] Annabella Milbanke, who was a student of mathematics, had received and rejected a proposal of marriage from Byron in the previous October.

[4] Lady Oxford. Armida is a beautiful sorceress in Tasso's *Gerusalemme Liberata*.

thought it worth while)—a sentiment which did not meet with the entire approbation of my audience, but which I maintained like a Muscovite enamoured of *despotism*.

I hear little from London but the lies of the *Gazette*, and will back Buonaparte against the field still.

Pray write and tell me how your *taming* goes on. I am all acquiescence to you, and as much yours as ever, d^r L^dy M.

B.

46. TO FRANCIS HODGSON

February 3, 1813.

MY DEAR HODGSON,

I will join you in any bond for the money you require,[1] be it that or a larger sum. With regard to security, as Newstead is in a sort of abeyance between sale and purchase, and my Lancashire property very unsettled, I do not know how far I can give more than personal security, but what I can I will. At any rate you can try, and as the sum is not very considerable, the chances are favourable. I hear nothing of my own concerns, but expect a letter daily. Let me hear from you where you are and will be this month. I am a great admirer of the R[ejected] A[ddresses],[2] though I have had so great a share in the cause of their publication, and I like the C[hilde] H[arold] imitation [3] one of the best. Lady Oxford has heard me talk much of you as a relative of the Cokes, etc., and desires me to say she would be happy to have the pleasure of your acquaintance. You must come and see me at K[insham]. I am sure you would like *all* here if you knew them.

The 'Agnus'[4] is furious. You can have no idea of the horrible and absurd things she has said and done since (really from the best motives) I withdrew my homage. 'Great pleasure' is, certes, my object, but '*why bitch*, Mr. Wild?'[5] I cannot answer for the future, but the past is pretty secure; and in it I can number the last two months as worthy of the gods in *Lucretius*. I cannot review in the '*Monthly*'; in fact I can just now do nothing, at least with a pen; and I really think the days of Authorship are over with me altogether. I hear and rejoice in

---

[1] Hodgson needed £1,000 to enable him to marry.

[2] *Rejected Addresses, or the New Theatrum Poetarum*, by James and Horace Smith, a set of parodies on leading poets in the form of addresses for the opening of the Drury Lane Theatre. It appeared on 10 October 1812.

[3] *Cui Bono?*   [4] Lady Caroline Lamb.

[5] Fielding, *Jonathan Wild*, Book III, ch. viii.

Bland's and Merivale's intentions.[1] Murray has grown great, and has got him new premises in the fashionable part of the town.[2] We live here so shut out of the *monde* that I have nothing of general import to communicate, and fill this up with a 'happy new year', and drink to you and Drury.

Ever yours, dear H.,

B.

I have no intention of continuing '*Childe Harold*'. There are a few additions in the 'body of the book' of description, which will merely add to the number of pages in the next edition. I have taken Kinsham Court. The business of last summer[3] I broke off, and now the amusement of the gentle fair is writing letters literally threatening my life, and much in the style of 'Miss Mathews' in '*Amelia*', or 'Lucy' in the '*Beggar's Opera*'. Such is the reward of restoring a woman to her family, who are treating her with the greatest kindness, and with whom I am on good terms. I am still in *palatia Circes*,[4] and, being no Ulysses, cannot tell into what animal I may be converted; as you are aware of the turn of both parties, your conjectures will be very correct, I daresay, and, seriously, I am very much *attached*. She has had her share of the denunciations of the brilliant Phryne, and regards them as much as I do. I hope you will visit me at K. which will not be ready before spring, and I am very sure you would like my neighbours if you knew them. If you come down now to Kington,[5] pray come and see me.

47. TO THE HON. AUGUSTA LEIGH

4, Bennet Street, St. James's, March 26th, 1813.

MY DEAREST AUGUSTA,

I did not answer your letter, because I could not answer as I wished, but expected that every week would bring me some tidings that might enable me to reply better than by apologies. But Claughton[6] has not, will not, and, I think, cannot pay his money, and though, luckily, it was stipulated that he should never have possession till the whole was paid, the estate is still on my hands, and your brother consequently not less embarrassed than ever. This is the truth, and is all the excuse I can offer for inability, but not unwillingness, to serve you.

I am going abroad again in June, but should wish to see you

[1] The reprinting of their selections from the Greek Anthology.
[2] 50 Albemarle Street. [3] With Lady Caroline.
[4] i.e. Lady Oxford. [5] The home of the Cokes, Hodgson's relatives.
[6] The purchaser of Newstead Abbey.

before my departure. You have perhaps heard that I have been fooling away my time with different '*regnantes*'; but what better can be expected from me? I have but one *relative*, and her I never see. I have no connections to domesticate with, and for marriage I have neither the talent nor the inclination. I cannot fortune-hunt, nor afford to marry without a fortune. My parliamentary schemes are not much to my taste—I spoke twice last Session, and was told it was well enough; but I hate the thing altogether, and have no intention to 'strut another hour'[1] on that stage. I am thus wasting the best part of life, daily repenting and never amending.

On Sunday, I set off for a fortnight for Eywood, near Presteign, in Herefordshire—with the *Oxfords*. I see you put on a *demure* look at the name, which is very becoming and matronly in you; but you won't be sorry to hear that I am quite out of a more serious scrape with another singular personage[2] which threatened me last year, and trouble enough I had to steer clear of it I assure you. I hope all my nieces are well, and increasing in growth and number; but I wish you were not always buried in that bleak common near Newmarket.

I am very well in health, but not happy, nor even comfortable; but I will not bore you with complaints. I am a fool, and deserve all the ills I have met, or may meet with, but nevertheless very *sensibly*, dearest Augusta,

Your most affectionate brother,

BYRON.

48. TO WILLIAM GIFFORD

June 18, 1813.

MY DEAR SIR,

I feel greatly at a loss how to write to you at all—still more to thank you as I ought. If you knew the veneration with which I have ever regarded you, long before I had the most distant prospect of becoming your acquaintance, literary or personal, my embarrassment would not surprise you.

Any suggestion of yours, even were it conveyed in the less tender shape of the text of the *Baviad*,[3] or a Monk Mason note in Massinger,[4] would have been obeyed; I should have endeavoured to improve myself by your censure: judge then if I shall be less willing to profit by your kindness. It is not for

---

[1] See *Macbeth* v, v, 25
[2] Lady Caroline Lamb.   [3] See page 48.
[4] Gifford's edition of Massinger, 1805, which superseded that of Monck Mason and Davies, 1765.

me to bandy compliments with my elders and my betters: I receive your approbation with gratitude, and will not return my brass for your Gold by expressing more fully those sentiments of admiration, which, however sincere, would, I know, be unwelcome.

To your advice on Religious topics, I shall equally attend. Perhaps the best way will be by avoiding them altogether. The already published objectionable passages have been much commented upon, but certainly have been rather *strongly* interpreted. I am no Bigot to Infidelity, and did not expect that, because I doubted the immortality of Man, I should be charged with denying the existence of a God. It was the comparative insignificance of ourselves and *our world*, when placed in competition with the mighty whole, of which it is an atom, that first led me to imagine that our pretensions to eternity might be over-rated.

This, and being early disgusted with a Calvinistic Scotch school,[1] where I was cudgelled to Church for the first ten years of my life, afflicted me with this malady; for, after all, it is, I believe, a disease of the mind as much as other kinds of hypochondria.

I regret to hear you talk of ill-health. May you long exist! not only to enjoy your own fame, but outlive that of fifty such ephemeral adventurers as myself.

As I do not sail quite so soon as Murray may have led you to expect (not till July) I trust I have some chance of taking you by the hand before my departure, and repeating in person how sincerely and affectionately I am

Your obliged servant,

BYRON.

49. TO THOMAS MOORE

4, Benedictine Street, St. James's, July 8, 1813.

I presume by your silence that I have blundered into something noxious in my reply to your letter, for the which I beg leave to send beforehand a sweeping apology which you may apply to any, or all, parts of that unfortunate epistle. If I err in my conjecture, I expect the like from you in putting our correspondence so long in quarantine. God he knows what I have said; but he also knows (if he is not as indifferent to mortals as the *nonchalant* deities of Lucretius), that you are the last person I want to offend. So, if I have,—why the devil don't you say it at once, and expectorate your spleen?

[1] The Aberdeen Grammar School.

Rogers is out of town with Madame de Staël,[1] who hath published an Essay against Suicide, which, I presume, will make somebody shoot himself;—as a sermon by Blenkinsop, in *proof* of Christianity, sent a hitherto most orthodox acquaintance of mine out of a chapel of ease a perfect atheist. Have you found or founded a residence yet? and have you begun or finished a poem? If you won't tell me what *I* have done, pray say what you have done, or left undone, yourself. I am still in equipment for voyaging, and anxious to hear from, or of, you *before* I go, which anxiety you should remove more readily, as you think I sha'n't cogitate about you afterwards. I shall give the lie to that calumny by fifty foreign letters, particularly from any place where the plague is rife,—without a drop of vinegar or a whiff of sulphur to save you from infection. Pray write: I am sorry to say that . . .

The Oxfords have sailed almost a fortnight,[2] and my sister is in town,[3] which is a great comfort,—for, never having been much together, we are naturally more attached to each other. I presume the illuminations have conflagrated to Derby (or wherever you are) by this time.[4] We are just recovering from tumult and train oil, and transparent fripperies, and all the noise and nonsense of victory. Drury Lane had a large *M.W.*, which some thought was Marshal Wellington; others, that it might be translated into Manager Whitbread; while the ladies of the vicinity and the saloon conceived the last letter to be complimentary to themselves. I leave this to the commentators to illuminate. If you don't answer this, I sha'n't say what *you* deserve, but I think *I* deserve a reply. Do you conceive there is no Post-Bag but the Twopenny?[5] Sunburn me, if you are not too bad.

50. TO THOMAS MOORE

July 13, 1813.

. . . . .

Your letter set me at ease; for I really thought (as I hear of your susceptibility) that I had said—I know not what—but

[1] Madame de Staël (Baronne de Staël Holstein) (1766–1817), the novelist and miscellaneous writer, who had been exiled by Napoleon, had taken refuge in England in 1810.
[2] Lord and Lady Oxford left for the Continent on 28 June.
[3] Augusta had come to live in London, in rooms at St. James's Palace.
[4] The illuminations on 7 July in celebration of the battle of Vittoria had caused a fire. Moore, who had married Elizabeth Dyke, an actress, in 1811, was now settled at Mayfield Cottage, near Ashbourne, Derbyshire.
[5] Moore's *Intercepted Letters, or the Twopenny Post-bag* appeared in 1813.

something I should have been very sorry for, had it, or I, offended you;—though I don't see how a man with a beautiful wife—*his own* children,—quiet—fame—competency and friends, (I will vouch for a thousand, which is more than I will for a unit in my own behalf,) can be offended with any thing.

Do you know, Moore, I am amazingly inclined—remember I say but *inclined*—to be seriously enamoured with Lady A[delaide] F[orbes] [1]—but this * * has ruined all my prospects. However, you know her; is she *clever*, or sensible, or good-tempered? either *would* do—I scratch out the *will*. I don't ask as to her beauty—that I see; but my circumstances are mending, and were not my other prospects blackening, I would take a wife, and that should be the woman, had I a chance. I do not yet know her much, but better than I did. . . .

I want to get away, but find difficulty in compassing a passage in a ship of war. They had better let me go; if I cannot, patriotism is the word—'nay, an' they'll mouth, I'll rant as well as they'.[2] Now, what are you doing?—writing, we all hope, for our own sakes. Remember you must edit my posthumous works, with a Life of the Author, for which I will send you Confessions, dated 'Lazaretto', Smyrna, Malta, or Palermo—one can die any where.

There is to be a thing on Tuesday ycleped a national fête. The Regent and * * * are to be there, and every body else, who has shillings enough for what was once a guinea. Vauxhall is the scene—there are six tickets issued for the modest women, and it is supposed there will be three to spare. The passports for the lax are beyond my arithmetic.

P.S.—The Staël last night attacked me most furiously—said that I had 'no right to make love—that I had used * * barbarously—that I had no feeling, and was totally *in*sensible to *la belle passion*, and *had* been all my life'. I am very glad to hear it, but did not know it before. Let me hear from you anon.

51. TO THOMAS MOORE

Bennet Street, August 22, 1813.

.   .   .   .   .

As our late—I might say, deceased—correspondence had too much of the town-life leaven in it, we will now, *paulo majora*,

---

[1] Daughter of George, Earl of Granard. She never married.
[2] *Hamlet*, v, i, 306–7.

prattle a little of literature in all its branches; and first of the first—criticism. The Prince is at Brighton, and Jackson, the boxer,[1] gone to Margate, having, I believe, decoyed Yarmouth [2] to see a milling in that polite neighbourhood. Mad^e. de Staël Holstein has lost one of her young barons,[3] who has been carbonadoed by a vile Teutonic adjutant,—kilt and killed in a coffee-house at Scrawsenhawsen. Corinne is, of course, what all mothers must be,—but will, I venture to prophesy, do what few mothers could—write an Essay upon it. She cannot exist without a grievance—and somebody to see, or read, how much grief becomes her. I have not seen her since the event; but merely judge (not very charitably) from prior observation.

In a 'mail-coach copy' of the *Edinburgh*,[4] I perceive *The Giaour* [5] is second article. The numbers are still in the Leith smack—*pray which way is the wind ?* The said article is so very mild and sentimental, that it must be written by Jeffrey [6] *in love*;—you know he is gone to America to marry some fair one, of whom he has been, for several *quarters, éperdument amoureux*. Seriously — as Winifred Jenkins [7] says of Lismahago — Mr. Jeffrey (or his deputy) 'has done the handsome thing by me', and I say *nothing*. But this I will say, if you and I had knocked one another on the head in his quarrel,[8] how he would have laughed, and what a mighty bad figure we should have cut in our posthumous works. By the by, I was call'd *in* the other day to mediate between two gentlemen bent upon carnage,[9] and—after a long struggle between the natural desire of destroying one's fellow-creatures, and the dislike of seeing men play the fool for nothing,—I got one to make an apology, and the other to take it, and left them to live happy ever after. One was a peer, the other a friend untitled, and both fond of high play;— and one, I can swear for, though very mild, 'not fearful',[10] and so dead a shot, that, though the other is the thinnest of men, he would have split him like a cane. They both conducted

---

[1] John ('Gentleman') Jackson, 'my old friend and corporeal pastor and master'.
[2] Francis Conway, Earl of Yarmouth, an intimate friend of the Regent.
[3] Albert de Staël.
[4] The *Edinburgh Review*. Special copies of Edinburgh publications were sent to London by coach, the rest by sea.
[5] Published in May.
[6] Francis Jeffrey, the editor, whom Byron had believed to be the author of the review of *Hours of Idleness* in 1807.
[7] Maid to Miss Tabitha Bramble, in Smollett's *Humphrey Clinker*; she marries Captain Lismahago.
[8] See page 59.
[9] Lord Foley and Scrope Davies.   [10] *The Tempest*, I, ii, 468.

themselves very well, and I put them out of *pain* as soon as I could. . . .

There is an American *Life* of G. F. Cooke, *Scurra*, deceased, lately published.[1] Such a book!—I believe, since *Drunken Barnaby's Journal*,[2] nothing like it has drenched the press. All green-room and tap-room—drams and the drama—brandy, whisky-punch, and, *latterly*, toddy, overflow every page. Two things are rather marvellous,—first, that a man should live so long drunk, and, next, that he should have found a sober biographer. There are some very laughable things in it, nevertheless;—but the pints he swallowed, and the parts he performed, are too regularly registered.

All this time you wonder I am not gone; so do I; but the accounts of the plague are very perplexing—not so much for the thing itself as the quarantine established in all ports, and from all places, even from England. It is true, the forty or sixty days would, in all probability, be as foolishly spent on shore as in the ship; but one likes to have one's choice, nevertheless. Town is awfully empty; but not the worse for that. I am really puzzled with my perfect ignorance of what I mean to do;—not stay, if I can help it, but where to go? Sligo[3] is for the North; —a pleasant place, Petersburgh, in September, with one's ears and nose in a muff, or else tumbling into one's neckcloth or pocket-handkerchief! If the winter treated Buonaparte with so little ceremony, what would it inflict upon your solitary traveller?—Give me a *sun*, I care not how hot, and sherbet, I care not how cool, and *my* Heaven is as easily made as your Persian's.[4] *The Giaour* is now a thousand and odd lines. 'Lord Fanny spins a thousand such a day',[5] eh, Moore?—thou wilt needs be a wag, but I forgive it.

Yours ever,
BYRON.

P.S.—I perceive I have written a flippant and rather cold-hearted letter! let it go, however. I have said nothing, either, of the brilliant sex; but the fact is, I am at this moment in a

---

[1] *Memoirs of George Frederick Cooke, late of the Theatre Royal, Covent Garden*, by W. Dunlap. Cooke died in New York in 1812 through intemperance. By 'Scurra' Byron means 'buffoon'.

[2] *Drunken Barnaby's Journeys*, first published in 1638 under the title of *Barnabæ Itinerarium, or Barnabee's Journal*. Its author was probably Richard Braithwaite. [3] Lord Sligo. See page 33.

[4]   'A Persian's Heav'n is easily made,
             'Tis but black eyes and lemonade.'
                         Moore's *Twopenny Post-bag*, Letter VI.

[5] Pope, *Imitations of Horace*, I, 6.

far more serious, and entirely new, scrape than any of the last twelvemonth's,—and that is saying a good deal. . . . It is unlucky we can neither live with nor without these women.

I am now thinking and regretting that, just as I have left Newstead, you reside near it. Did you ever see it? *do*—but don't tell me that you like it. If I had known of such intellectual neighbourhood, I don't think I should have quitted it. You could have come over so often, as a bachelor,—for it was a thorough bachelor's mansion—plenty of wine and such sordid sensualities—with books enough, room enough, and an air of antiquity about all (except the lasses) that would have suited you, when pensive, and served you to laugh at when in glee. I had built myself a bath and a *vault*—and now I sha'n't even be buried in it. It is odd that we can't even be certain of a *grave*, at least a particular one. I remember, when about fifteen, reading your poems there, which I can repeat almost now,—and asking all kinds of questions about the author, when I heard that he was not dead according to the preface; wondering if I should ever see him—and though, at that time, without the smallest poetical propensity myself, very much taken, as you may imagine, with that volume. Adieu—I commit you to the care of the gods—Hindoo, Scandinavian, and Hellenic!

P.S. 2d.—There is an excellent review of Grimm's *Correspondence* and Made. de Staël [1] in this No. of the *E[dinburgh] R[eview]*. . . . Jeffrey, himself, was my critic last year; but this is, I believe, by another hand. I hope you are going on with your *grand coup*—pray do—or that damned Lucien Buonaparte will beat us all. I have seen much of his poem [2] in MS., and he really surpasses every thing beneath Tasso. Hodgson is translating him *against* another bard. You (and I believe Rogers), Scott, Gifford, and myself, are to be referred to as judges between the twain,—that is, if you accept the office. Conceive our different opinions! I think we, most of us (I am talking very impudently, you will think—*us*, indeed!) have a way of our own,—at least, you and Scott certainly have.

52. TO THOMAS MOORE

August—September, I mean—1, 1813.

I send you, begging your acceptance, Castellan,[3] and three vols. on Turkish literature,[4] not yet looked into. The *last* I

---

[1] Her *Germany*.   [2] *Charlemagne*.
[3] Castellan's *Mœurs, usages, costumes des Othomans*, 1812.
[4] Probably Toderini's *Della Letteratura Turchesca*, 1787.

will thank you to read, extract what you want, and return in a week, as they are lent to me by that brightest of Northern constellations, Mackintosh,[1]—amongst many other kind things into which India has warmed him; for I am sure your *home* Scotsman is of a less genial description.

Your Peri,[2] my dear M., is sacred and inviolable; I have no idea of touching the hem of her petticoat. Your affectation of a dislike to encounter me is so flattering, that I begin to think myself a very fine fellow. But you are laughing at me—'Stap my vitals, Tam! thou art a very impudent person';[3] and, if you are not laughing at me, you deserve to be laughed at. Seriously, what on earth can you, or have you, to dread from any poetical flesh breathing? It really puts me out of humour to hear you talk thus. . . .

The Giaour I have added to a good deal; but still in foolish fragments. It contains about 1200 lines, or rather more—now printing. You will allow me to send you a copy. You delight me much by telling me that I am in your good graces, and more particularly as to temper; for, unluckily, I have the reputation of a very bad one. But they say the devil is amusing when pleased, and I must have been more venomous than the old serpent, to have hissed or stung in your company. It may be, and would appear to a third person, an incredible thing, but I know *you* will believe me when I say, that I am as anxious for your success as one human being can be for another's,—as much as if I had never scribbled a line. Surely the field of fame is wide enough for all; and if it were not, I would not willingly rob my neighbour of a rood of it. Now you have a pretty property of some thousand acres there, and when you have passed your present Inclosure Bill, your income will be doubled, (there's a metaphor, worthy of a Templar, namely, pert and low,) while my wild common is too remote to incommode you, and quite incapable of such fertility. I send you (which return per post, as the printer would say) a curious letter from a friend of mine,[4] which will let you into the origin of *The Giaour*. Write soon.

Ever, dear Moore, yours most entirely, etc.

P.S.—This letter was written to me on account of a *different*

---

[1] Sir James Mackintosh, the philosopher and *Edinburgh* reviewer.
[2] 'A story, grafted on the amours of a Peri and a mortal', which Byron had suggested to Moore. Moore, as it happened, was already engaged on the idea.
[3] Cf. Sheridan's *Trip to Scarborough*, v, ii.
[4] A letter from Lord Sligo, giving at Byron's request the story he had heard at Athens of the girl whom Byron saved from death.

story circulated by some gentlewomen of our acquaintance, a
little too close to the text. The part erased contained merely
some Turkish names, and circumstantial evidence of the girl's
detection, not very important or decorous.

53. TO ANNE ISABELLA MILBANKE

Sep^tr 6th, 1813.

.   .   .   .   .

I look upon myself as a very facetious personage and may
appeal to most of my acquaintance (L^y M[elbourne] for instance)
in proof of my assertion. Nobody laughs more, and though
your friend Joanna Baillie [1] says somewhere that 'Laughter is
the child of misery', I do not believe her (unless indeed in a
hysteric), tho' I think it is sometimes the parent. Nothing
could do me more honor than the acquaintance of that Lady,
who does not possess a more enthusiastic admirer than myself.
She is our only dramatist since Otway [2] and Southerne; [3] I
don't except Home. [4] With all my presumed prejudice against
your sex, or rather the perversion of manners and principle in
many, which you admit in some circles, I think the worst woman
that ever existed would have made a man of very passable reputation. They are all better than us, and their faults, such as they
are, must originate with ourselves. Your sweeping sentence
'on the circles where we have met' amuses me much when I
recollect some of those who constituted that society. After all,
bad as it is, it has its *agrémens*. The great object of life is sensation—to feel that we exist, even though in pain. It is this
'craving void' which drives us to gaming—to battle—to travel
—to intemperate, but keenly felt pursuits of any description,
whose principal attraction is the agitation inseparable from their
accomplishment. I am but an awkward dissembler; as my
friend you will bear with my faults. I shall have the less con-
straint in what I say to you—firstly because I may derive some
benefit from your observations—and next because I am very
sure you can never be perverted by any paradoxes of mine.
You have said a good deal and very well too on the subject
of Benevolence systematically exerted; two lines of Pope will
explain mine (if I have any) and that of half mankind—

'Perhaps prosperity becalmed his breast;
Perhaps the Wind just shifted from the East'. [5]

---

[1] Joanna Baillie (1762–1851), the Scottish dramatist and poetess.
[2] Thomas Otway (1652–85).   [3] Thomas Southerne (1660–1746).
[4] John Home (1722–1808).   [5] *Moral Essays*, I, 111–12.

By the bye you are a *bard* also—have you q...
pursuit? Is your friend Pratt one of your c...
one of your systematic benevolents? You w...
poor Blackett which he requited by falling i...
sumptuously to be sure—like Metastasio wit...
Maria Theresa. When you can spare an inst...
course be delighted to hear from you—but do not l... ...roach
a moment on better avocations—Adieu.

Ever yours,

B.

54. TO THOMAS MOORE

September 27, 1813.

THOMAS MOORE,

(Thou wilt never be called '*true* Thomas', like He of Ercil-
doune,[1]) why don't you write to me?—as you won't, I must.
I was near you at Aston[2] the other day, and hope I soon shall
be again. If so, you must and shall meet me, and go to Matlock
and elsewhere, and take what, in *flash* dialect, is poetically
termed 'a lark', with Rogers and me for accomplices. Yesterday, at Holland House, I was introduced to Southey—the
best-looking bard I have seen for some time.[3] To have that
poet's head and shoulders, I would almost have written his
Sapphics. He is certainly a prepossessing person to look on,
and a man of talent, and all that, and—*there* is his eulogy.

* * read me *part* of a letter from you. By the foot of Pharaoh,[4]
I believe there was abuse, for he stopped short, so he did, after
a fine saying about our correspondence, and *looked*—I wish I
could revenge myself by attacking you, or by telling you that
I have *had* to defend you—an agreeable way which one's friends
have of recommending themselves by saying—'Ay, ay, *I* gave
it Mr. Such-a-one for what he said about your being a plagiary,
and a rake, and so on'. But do you know that you are one of
the very few whom I never have the satisfaction of hearing
abused, but the reverse;—and do you suppose I will forgive *that*?

I have been in the country, and ran away from the Doncaster
races. It is odd,—I was a visitor in the same house which came
to my sire as a residence with Lady Carmarthen (with whom he
adulterated before his majority—by the by, remember *she* was
not my mamma),[5]—and they thrust me into an old room, with

---

[1] Thomas the Rhymer (fl.?1220–?1297), seer and poet.
[2] Aston Hall, Rotherham, tenanted by Byron's friend, James Wedderburn Webster.
[3] 'His appearance is *Epic*', wrote Byron in his Journal on 22 November.
[4] See *Every Man in His Humour*, I, iv, 80; v, 110.
[5] She became Captain Byron's wife and the mother of Augusta.

ous picture over the chimney, which I should suppose
apa regarded with due respect, and which, inheriting the
ily taste, I looked upon with great satisfaction. I stayed a
week with the family, and behaved very well—though the lady
of the house is young, and religious, and pretty, and the master
is my particular friend. I felt no wish for any thing but a poodle
dog, which they kindly gave me. Now, for a man of my courses
not even to have *coveted*, is a sign of great amendment. Pray
pardon all this nonsense, and don't 'snub me when I 'm in
spirits'.[1]

Ever yours,
Bn.

Here 's an impromptu for you by a 'person of quality', written
last week, on being reproached for low spirits—

> When from the heart where Sorrow sits,
>   Her dusky shadow mounts too high,
> And o'er the changing aspect flits,
>   And clouds the brow, or fills the eye:
> Heed not that gloom, which soon shall sink;
>   My Thoughts their dungeon know too well—
> Back to my breast the wanderers shrink,
>   And bleed within their silent cell.

55. TO ANNE ISABELLA MILBANKE [2]

29th Novr. 1813.

No one can assume or presume less than you do, tho' very few
with whom I am acquainted possess half your claims to that
'superiority' which you are so fearful of affecting. Nor can I
recollect any expression since the commencement of our correspondence, which has in any respect diminished my opinion of
your talents,—my respect for your virtues. You wrong your-

---

[1] Goldsmith, *She Stoops to Conquer*, II.

[2] 'Yesterday, a very pretty letter from Annabella, which I answered.
What an odd situation and friendship is ours!—without one spark of love on
either side, and produced by circumstances which in general lead to coldness on one side, and aversion on the other. She is a very superior woman,
and very little spoiled, which is strange in an heiress—a girl of twenty—
a peeress that is to be, in her own right—an only child, and a *savante*,
who has always had her own way. She is a poetess—a mathematician—
a metaphysician, and yet, withal, very kind, generous, and gentle, with
very little pretension. Any other head would be turned with half her
acquisitions, and a tenth of her advantages.' (Byron, in his Journal,
30 November.)

self very much in supposing that 'the charm' has been broken by our nearer acquaintance. On the contrary, that very intercourse convinces me of the value of what I have lost, or rather never found. But I will not deny that circumstances have occurred to render it more supportable.

You will think me very capricious and apt at sudden fancies. It is true I could not exist without some object of attachment, but I have shown that I am not quite a slave to impulse. . . . But however weak (or it may merit a harsher term) I may be in my disposition to attach myself (and as society is now much the same in this as in all other European countries it were difficult to avoid it), in my search for the 'ideal',—the being to whom I would commit the whole happiness of my future life, —I have never yet seen but two approaching to the likeness. The first [1] I was too young to have a prospect of obtaining, and subsequent events have proved that my expectations might not have been fulfilled, had I ever proposed to and received my idol. *The second* [2]—the only woman to whom I ever seriously pretended as a wife—had disposed of her heart already, and I think it too late to look for a third. I shall take the world as I find it, and have seen it much the same in most climates. (More fiery in the East—a mixture of languid habits and stormy passions.) But I have no confidence, and look for no constancy, in affections founded on caprice, and lucky conformity of disposition without any fixed principles. How far this may be my case at present, I know not, and have not had time to ascertain.

I have been scribbling another poem,[3] as it is called—Turkish as before—for I can't empty my head of the East—and horrible enough, tho' not so sombre quite as the *Giaour* (that unpronounceable name), and for the sake of intelligibility it is not a fragment. The scene is in the Hellespont—a favourite *séjour* of mine, and, if you will accept it, I will send you a copy; there are some Mussulman words in it which I inflict upon you in revenge for your 'Mathematical and other superiority'.

When shall we meet in town? by the bye you won't take fright when we meet, will you? and imagine I am about to add to your thousand and one pretendants? I have taken exquisite care to prevent the possibility of that, tho' less likely than ever to become a Benedick. Indeed I have not seen (with one exception)

---

[1] Mary Duff, his cousin in Aberdeen.
[2] Mary Chaworth, his cousin, of Annesley, near Newstead. In 1805 she married John Musters.
[3] *The Bride of Abydos*.

for many years a Beatrice, and she will not be troubled to assume the part. I think we understand each other perfectly and may talk to each other occasionally without exciting speculation. The worst that can be said is that I *would* and you *won't*, and in this respect you can hardly be the sufferer and I am very sure I *shan't*. If I find my heart less philosophic on the subject than I at present believe it, I shall keep out of the way; but I now think it is well shielded—at least it has got a new suit of armour—and certainly it stood in need of it.

I have heard a rumour of another added to your list of unacceptables, and I am sorry for him, as I know that he has talent, and his pedigree assures him wit and good humour. You make sad havoc among 'us youth'. It is lucky that Mad. de Staël has published her anti-suicide at so killing a time— November too! I have not read it for fear the love of contradiction might lead me to a practical confutation. Do you know her? I don't ask if you have heard her?—her tongue is the perpetual motion.

56. TO LEIGH HUNT [1]

4, Bennet St., Dec. 2, 1813.

MY DEAR SIR,

Few things could be more welcome than your note, and on Saturday morning I will avail myself of your permission to thank you for it in person. My time has not been passed, since we met, either profitably or agreeably. A very short period after my last visit, an incident [2] occurred with which, I fear, you are not unacquainted, as report, in many mouths and more than one paper, was busy with the topic. That, naturally, gave me much uneasiness. Then I nearly incurred a lawsuit on the sale of an estate; but that is now arranged: next—but why should I go on with a series of selfish and silly details? I merely wish to assure you that it was not the frivolous forgetfulness of a mind, occupied by what is called pleasure (*not* in the true sense of Epicurus), that kept me away; but a perception of my, then, unfitness to share the society of those whom I value and wish

---

[1] James Henry Leigh Hunt (1784–1859), essayist and poet, was now serving a sentence, for libel on the Regent, in Surrey Jail. Here Byron had visited him in the previous May. With the letter Byron sent 'a copy of the two Turkish tales'. (See his Journal, 1 December.)

[2] At a ball on 6 July, Lady Caroline Lamb, after seeing Byron, had wounded herself with a knife, perhaps accidentally.

not to displease. I hate being *larmoyant*, and making a serious face among those who are cheerful.

It is my wish that our acquaintance, or, if you please to accept it, friendship, may be permanent. I have been lucky enough to preserve some friends from a very early period, and I hope, as I do not (at least now) select them lightly, I shall not lose them capriciously. I have a thorough esteem for that independence of spirit which you have maintained with sterling talent, and at the expense of some suffering. You have not, I trust, abandoned the poem you were composing, when Moore and I partook of your hospitality in the summer. I hope a time will come when he and I may be able to repay you in kind for the *latter*—for the rhyme, at least in *quantity*, you are in arrear to both.

> Believe me, very truly and affectionately yours,
> BYRON.

57. TO THOMAS MOORE

December 8, 1813.

Your letter, like all the best, and even kindest, things in this world, is both painful and pleasing. But, first, to what sits nearest. Do you know I was actually about to dedicate to you,—not in a formal inscription, as to one's *elders*,—but through a short prefatory letter, in which I boasted myself your intimate, and held forth the prospect of *your* poem; when, lo! the recollection of your strict injunctions of secrecy as to the said poem, more than *once* repeated by word and letter, flashed upon me, and marred my intents. I could have no motive for repressing my own desire of alluding to you (and not a day passes that I do not think and talk of you), but an idea that you might, yourself, dislike it. You cannot doubt my sincere admiration, waving personal friendship for the present, which, by the by, is not less sincere and deep-rooted. I have you by rote and by heart; of which *ecce signum*! When I was at Aston, on my first visit, I have a habit, in passing my time a good deal alone, of—I won't call it singing, for that I never attempt except to myself—but of uttering, to what I think tunes, your 'Oh breathe not', 'When the last glimpse', and 'When he who adores thee', with others of the same minstrel;— they are my matins and vespers. I assuredly did not intend them to be overheard, but, one morning, in comes, not *La Donna*,[1] but *Il Marito*, with a very grave face, saying, 'Byron,

---

[1] Lady Frances Wedderburn Webster.

I must request you won't sing any more, at least of *those* songs'. I stared, and said, 'Certainly, but why?'—'To tell you the truth', quoth he, 'they make my wife *cry*, and so melancholy, that I wish her to hear no more of them'.

Now, my dear M., the effect must have been from your words, and certainly not my music. I merely mention this foolish story to show you how much I am indebted to you for even your pastimes. A man may praise and praise, but no one recollects but that which pleases—at least, in composition. Though I think no one equal to you in that department, or in satire,— and surely no one was ever so popular in both,—I certainly am of opinion that you have not yet done all *you* can do, though more than enough for any one else. I want, and the world expects, a longer work from you; and I see in you what I never saw in poet before, a strange diffidence of your own powers, which I cannot account for, and which must be unaccountable, when a *Cossac* like me can appal a *cuirassier*. Your story I did not, could not, know,—I thought only of a Peri. I wish you had confided in me, not for your sake, but mine, and to prevent the world from losing a much better poem than my own, but which, I yet hope, this *clashing* will not even now deprive them of.[1] Mine is the work of a week, written, *why* I have partly told you, and partly I cannot tell you by letter—some day I will. . . .

Go on—I shall really be very unhappy if I at all interfere with you. The success of mine is yet problematical; though the public will probably purchase a certain quantity, on the presumption of their own propensity for *The Giaour* and such 'horrid mysteries'. The only advantage I have is being on the spot; and that merely amounts to saving me the trouble of turning over books which I had better read again. If *your chamber* was furnished in the same way, you have no need to *go there* to describe—I mean only as to *accuracy*—because I drew it from recollection. . . .

This last thing of mine *may* have the same fate, and I assure you I have great doubts about it. But, even if not, its little day will be over before you are ready and willing. Come out—'screw your courage to the sticking-place'.[2] Except the *Post Bag* (and surely you cannot complain of a want of success there), you have not been *regularly* out for some years. No

---

[1] On the appearance of *The Bride of Abydos*, Moore had found that it closely resembled a story which he had begun for *Lalla Rookh*.
[2] *Macbeth*, I, vii, 60.

man stands higher,—whatever you may think on a rainy day, in your provincial retreat. 'Aucun homme, dans aucune langue, n'a été, peut-être, plus complètement le poëte du cœur et le poëte des femmes. Les critiques lui reprochent de n'avoir représenté le monde ni tel qu'il est, ni tel qu'il doît être; *mais les femmes répondent qu'il l'a représenté tel qu'elles le désirent.*'— I should have thought Sismondi [1] had written this for you instead of Metastasio.

Write to me, and tell me of *yourself.* Do you remember what Rousseau said to some one—'Have we quarrelled? you have talked to me often, and never once mentioned yourself'.

P.S.—The last sentence is an indirect apology for my own egotism,—but I believe in letters it is allowed. I wish it was *mutual.* I have met with an odd reflection in Grimm; [2] it shall not—at least the bad part—be applied to you or me, though *one* of us has certainly an indifferent name—but this it is:— 'Many people have the reputation of being wicked, with whom we should be too happy to pass our lives'. I need not add it is a woman's saying—a Mademoiselle de Sommery's.

58. TO LADY MELBOURNE [3]

January 16th, 1814.

MY DEAR LADY M[E],

Lewis [4] is just returned from Oatlands, where he has been quarrelling with Staël about everything and everybody. She has not even let poor quiet *me* alone, but has discovered, first, that I am affected; and 2ndly, that I '*shut* my *eyes* during dinner!' What this last can mean I don't know, unless *she* is opposite. If I then do, she is very much obliged to me; and if at the same time I could contrive to shut my ears, she would be still more so. . . . If I really have so ludicrous a habit, will *you* tell me so—and I will try and break myself of it. In the meantime, I think the charge will amuse you. I have worse faults to find with *her* than '*shutting* her eyes'—one of which is opening her mouth too frequently.

Do not you think people are very naughty? What do you think I have this very day heard said of poor M.? [5] It provoked

[1] *De la Littérature du Midi de l'Europe.*
[2] *Correspondance Littéraire.*
[3] The substance of this letter was also entered in Byron's Journal for the day.
[4] Matthew Gregory ('Monk') Lewis (1775–1818), novelist and dramatist.
[5] Mary (Chaworth) Musters.

me beyond anything, as *he* was named as authority—why the abominable stories they circulate about Lady *W.*, of which I can say no more. All this is owing to 'dear friend'; and yet, as far as it regards 'dear friend', I must say I have very sufficing suspicions for believing them utterly false; at least, she must have altered strangely within this nine years—but this is the age of revolutions.

Her ascendancy always appeared to me that of a cunning mind over a weak one. But—but—why the woman is a fright, which, after all, is the best reason for not believing it.

I still mean to set off to-morrow,[1] unless this snow adds so much to the impracticability of the roads as to render it useless. I don't mind anything but delay; and I might as well be in London as at a sordid inn, waiting for a thaw, or the subsiding of a flood and the clearing of snow.

I wonder what *your* answer will be on *Ph.'s* [2] *letter*. I am growing rather partial to her younger sister;[3] who is very pretty, but fearfully young—and I think a *fool*. A wife, you say, would be my salvation. Now I could have but one motive for marrying into that family—and even *that* might possibly only produce a scene, and spoil everything; but at all events it would in some degree be a *revenge*, and in the very face of your compliment (*ironical*, I believe) on the want of *selfishness*, I must say that I never can quite get over the '*not*' of last summer [4]—no—though it were to become 'yea' to-morrow.

I do believe that to marry would be my wisest step—but whom? I might manage this easily with '*le père*', but I don't admire the connection—and I have not committed myself by any attentions hitherto. But all wives would be much the same. I have no heart to spare and expect none in return; but, as Moore says, 'A pretty wife is something for the fastidious vanity of a *roué* to *retire* upon'. And mine might do as she pleased, so that she had a fair temper, and a quiet way of conducting herself, leaving me the same liberty of conscience.

What I want is a companion—a friend rather than a sentimentalist. I have seen enough of love matches—and of all matches—to make up my mind to the common lot of happy couples. The only misery would be if I fell in love afterwards—which is not unlikely, for habit has a strange power over my affections. In that case I should be jealous, and then you do

---

[1] For Newstead, accompanied by Augusta.
[2] Lady Frances Wedderburn Webster.
[3] Lady Catherine Annesley.   [4] His rejection by Annabella Milbanke.

not know what a devil any bad passion makes me. I should very likely *do* all that C[aroline] *threatens* in her paroxysms; and I have more reasons than you are aware of, for mistrusting myself on this point.

Heigh-ho! Good night.

Ever y^rs most truly,

B.

P.S.—The enclosed was written last night, and I am just setting off. You shall hear from Newstead—if one ever gets there in a coach really as large as the cabin of a '74', and, I believe, meant for the Atlantic instead of the Continent.

1,000 thanks for yours of this morn; 'never loved so before'.[1] Well, then, I hope never to be loved *so* again—for what is it to the *purpose?* You wonder how I answered it? To tell you the *truth* (which I could not tell *her*), I have not answered it at all— nor shall. I feel so much inclined to believe her sincere, that I cannot sit down and coolly repay her truth with fifty falsehoods. I do not believe her for the same *reason* you *believe*, not because by writing she commits herself—and that is seldom done unless in earnest.

I shall be delighted to hear your *defence* against my insinuations, but you will make nothing of it—and he *is* very much to be envied. But you mistake me, for I do not mean in *general*; on the contrary, I coincide with him in taste but upon *one* instance.

C. was right about the poem. I have scribbled a longer one than either of the last,[2] and it is in the press, but you know I never hold forth to you on such topics—why should I? Now you will think this a piece of conceit, but, really, it is a relief to the fever of my mind to *write*; and as at present I am what they call 'popular' as an author—it enables me to serve one or two people without embarrassing anything but my brains— for I never have, nor shall avail myself of the *lucre*. And yet it would be folly merely to make presents to a bookseller, whose accounts *to* me last year are just 1,500 guineas, *without* including C[hild]e H[arold].[3] Now the odd part is, that if I were a regular stipendiary, and wanted it, probably I should not be offered *one half*. But such are mankind—always offering or denying in the wrong place. But I have written more than

---

[1] Referring to the letter from Lady Frances Webster.
[2] *The Corsair*, published in January.
[3] The copyright of *Childe Harold* and *The Corsair* Byron presented to R. C. Dallas.

enough already; and this is my last experiment on public patience—and just at present I won't try *yours* any further.

Ever, my dear L^{dy} M^e, &c.,

B.

59. TO JOHN MURRAY

Newstead Abbey, February 4, 1814.

DEAR SIR,

I need not say that your obliging letter [1] was very welcome, and not the less so for being unexpected. At the same time I received a very kind one from Mr. D'Israeli,[2] which I shall acknowledge and thank him for to-morrow.

It doubtless gratifies me much that our *Finale* has pleased, and that the Curtain drops gracefully.[3] *You* deserve it should, for your promptitude and good nature in arranging immediately with Mr. D[alla]s; and I can assure you that I esteem your entering so warmly into the subject, and writing to me so soon upon it, as a personal obligation. We shall now part, I hope, satisfied with each other. I *was* and *am* quite in earnest in my prefatory promise not to intrude any more; and this not from any affectation, but a thorough conviction that it is the best policy, and is at least respectful to my readers, as it shows that I would not willingly run the risk of forfeiting their favour in future. Besides, I have other views and objects, and think that I shall keep *this* resolution; for, since I left London, though shut up, *snow*-bound, *thaw*-bound, and tempted with all kinds of paper, the dirtiest of ink, and the bluntest of pens, I have not even been haunted by a wish to put them to their combined uses, except in letters of business—my rhyming propensity is quite gone, and I feel much as I did at Patras on recovering from my fever—weak, but in health, and only afraid of a relapse. I do most fervently hope I never shall.

I see by the *Morning Chronicle* there hath been discussion in the *Courier*;[4] and I read in the *Morning Post* a wrathful letter about Mr. Moore,[5] in which some Protestant Reader has made a sad confusion about *India* and Ireland.

[1] Informing him of the triumphant success of *The Corsair*.

[2] Isaac D'Israeli, author of the *Curiosities of Literature*.

[3] Byron had dedicated the poem to Moore 'as the last production with which I shall trespass on public patience, and your indulgence, for some years'.

[4] About the lines beginning, 'Weep, daughter of a royal line', which now first appeared with his name. In 1812 Princess Charlotte was rumoured to have wept on hearing that a new ministry would not be formed when the Prince of Wales became Regent.

[5] In reference to Byron's remarks about Moore in his epistle dedicatory.

You are to do as you please about the smaller poems; but I think removing them *now* from *The Corsair* looks like *fear*; [1] and if so, you must allow me not to be pleased. I should also suppose that, after the *fuss* of these Newspaper Esquires, they would materially assist the circulation of *The Corsair*; an object I should imagine at *present* of more importance to *yourself* than *Childe Harold's* 7th appearance. Do as you like; but don't allow the withdrawing that *poem* to draw any imputation of *dismay* upon me. I care about as much for the *Courier* as I do for the Prince, or all princes whatsoever, except Kozlovsky.[2]

Pray make my respects to Mr. Ward, whose praise I value most highly, as you well know; it is in the approbation of such men that fame becomes worth having. To Mr. G[ifford] I am always grateful, and surely not less so now than ever. And so Good Night to my Authorship.

I have been sauntering and dozing here very quietly, and not unhappily. You will be happy to hear that I have completely established my title-deeds as *marketable*, and that the Purchaser has succumbed to the terms, and fulfils them, or is to fulfil them forthwith—he is now here, and we go on very amicably together, —one in each *wing* of the Abbey. We set off on Sunday—I for town, he for Cheshire.

Mrs. Leigh is with me—much pleased with the place, and less so with me for parting with it, to which not even the price can reconcile her. Your parcel has not yet arrived—at least the *Mags*. etc.; but I have received *Childe Harold* and *The Corsair*.

I believe both are very correctly printed, which is a great satisfaction.

I thank you for wishing me in town; but I think one's success is most felt at a distance, and I enjoy my solitary self-importance in an agreeable sulky way of my own—upon the strength of your letter for which I once more thank you, and am,

Very truly yours,

B.

P.S.—Don't you think Buonaparte's next *publication* will be rather expensive to the Allies? Perry's [3] Paris letter of yesterday looks very reviving. What a Hydra and Briareus it is! I wish they would pacify: there is no end to this campaigning.

---

[1] Murray proposed to transfer them to the new edition of *Childe Harold*.
[2] Russian Minister at Turin.
[3] James Perry, editor of the *Morning Chronicle*.

60. TO LADY MELBOURNE

February 11th, 1814.

My dear Lady M.,

On my arrival in town on Wednesday, I found myself in what the learned call a dilemma, and the vulgar a scrape. Such a clash of paragraphs, and a conflict of newspapers, lampoons of all description, some good, and all hearty, the Regent (as reported) wroth; Ld Carlisle in a fury; the *Morning Post* in hysterics; and the *Courier* in convulsions of criticism and contention. To complete the farce, the Morning Papers this day announce the intention of some zealous Rosencrantz or Guildenstern to 'play upon his pipe'[1] in our house of hereditaries. This last seems a little too ludicrous to be true, but, even if so—and nothing is too ridiculous for some of them to attempt—all the motions, censures, sayings, doings and ordinances of that august body, shall never make me even endeavour to explain, or soften a syllable of the twenty words which have excited, *what* I really do not yet exactly know, as the accounts are contradictory, but be it what it may, 'as the wine is tapped it shall be drunk to the lees'. You tell me not to be 'violent', and not to 'answer'. I *have not* and shall *not* answer, and although the consequences may be, for aught I know to the contrary, exclusion from society, and all sorts of disagreeables, the '*Demon* whom I still have served, has not yet cowed my better part of man';[2] and whatever I may, and have, or shall feel, I have that within me, that bounds against opposition. I have *quick feelings*, and not very *good nerves*; but somehow they have more than once served me pretty well, when I most wanted them, and may again. At any rate I shall try.

Did you ever know anything like this? At a time when peace and war, and Emperors and Napoleons, and the destinies of the things they have made of mankind, are trembling in the balance, the Government Gazettes can devote half their attention and columns, day after day, to 8 *lines*, written two years ago, and now *republished only* (by an individual), and suggest them for the consideration of Parliament, probably about the same period with the treaty for peace.

I really begin to think myself a most important personage; what would poor Pope have given to have brought down this upon his 'epistle to Augustus'?

I think you must allow, considering all things, public and

---

[1] See *Hamlet*, III, ii, 373.　　　　[2] See *Macbeth*, v, viii, 14-18.

private, that mine has been an odd destiny. But I prate, and will spare you.

Pray when are you most visible? or will any of your 'predilections' interfere between you and me?

How is C[aroline]? It is a considerable compensation for all other disturbances, that she has left us in peace, and I do not think you will ever be further troubled with her anniversary scenes.

I am glad you like the Corsair, and was afraid he might be too larmoyant a gentleman for your favour. But all these externals are nothing to *that within*, on a subject to which I have not alluded.

Ever y^{rs} most affec^{ly},

B.

P.S.—Murray took fright and shuffled in my absence, as you say, but I made him instantly replace the lines as before. It was not time to shrink now, and if it were otherwise, they should never be expunged and never shall. All the edicts on earth could not suppress their circulation, after the foolish fuss of these journalists who merely extend the demands of curiosity by the importance they attach to two 'doggerel stanzas', as they repeatedly call them.

61. TO THOMAS MOORE

2, Albany, April 9, 1814.

Viscount Althorpe is about to be married, and I have gotten his spacious bachelor apartments in Albany, to which you will, I hope, address a speedy answer to this mine epistle.

I am but just returned to town, from which you may infer that I have been out of it; and I have been boxing, for exercise, with Jackson for this last month daily. I have also been drinking, and, on one occasion, with three other friends at the Cocoa Tree, from six till four, yea, unto five in the matin. We clareted and champagned till two—then supped, and finished with a kind of regency punch composed of madeira, brandy, and *green* tea, no *real* water being admitted therein. There was a night for you! without once quitting the table, except to ambulate home, which I did alone, and in utter contempt of a hackney-coach and my own *vis*, both of which were deemed necessary for our conveyance. And so,—I am very well, and they say it will hurt my constitution.

I have also, more or less, been breaking a few of the favourite commandments; but I mean to pull up and marry, if any one will have me. In the mean time, the other day I nearly killed myself with a collar of brawn, which I swallowed for supper, and *in*digested for I don't know how long; but that is by the by. All this gourmandise was in honour of Lent; for I am forbidden meat all the rest of the year, but it is strictly enjoined me during your solemn fast. I have been, and am, in very tolerable love; but of that hereafter as it may be.

My dear Moore, say what you will in your preface; and quiz any thing or any body,—me if you like it. Oons! dost thou think me of the *old*, or rather *elderly* school? If one can't jest with one's friends, with whom can we be facetious? You have nothing to fear from * *, whom I have not seen, being out of town when he called. He will be very correct, smooth, and all that, but I doubt whether there will be any 'grace beyond the reach of art'; [1]—and, whether there is or not, how long will you be so damned modest? As for Jeffrey, it is a very handsome thing of him to speak well of an old antagonist,—and what a mean mind dared not do. Any one will revoke praise; but—were it not partly my own case—I should say that very few have strength of mind to unsay their censure, or follow it up with praise of other things.

What think you of the review of *Levis*? [2] It beats the *Bag* and my hand-grenade hollow, as an invective, and hath thrown the Court into hysterics, as I hear from very good authority. Have you heard from * * * * * *

No more rhyme for—or rather, *from*—me. I have taken my leave of that stage, and henceforth will mountebank it no longer. I have had my day, and there's an end. The utmost I expect, or even wish, is to have it said in the *Biographia Britannica*, that I might perhaps have been a poet, had I gone on and amended. My great comfort is, that the temporary celebrity I have wrung from the world has been in the very teeth of all opinions and prejudices. I have flattered no ruling powers; I have never concealed a single thought that tempted me. They can't say I have truckled to the times, nor to popular topics, (as Johnson, or somebody, said of Cleveland,) and whatever I have gained has been at the expenditure of as much *personal* favour as possible; for I do believe never was a bard more unpopular, *quoad homo*, than myself. And now I have

---

[1] Pope, *Essay on Criticism*, i, 153.
[2] *Souvenirs et Portraits*, by M. de Levis, reviewed in the *Edinburgh*.

done;—*ludite nunc alios.* Every body may be damned, as they seem fond of it, and resolve to stickle lustily for endless brimstone.

Oh—by the by, I had nearly forgot. There is a long poem, an *Anti-Byron*, coming out, to prove that I have formed a conspiracy to overthrow, by *rhyme*, all religion and government, and have already made great progress! It is not very scurrilous, but serious and ethereal. I never felt myself important, till I saw and heard of my being such a little Voltaire as to induce such a production. Murray would not publish it, for which he was a fool, and so I told him; but some one else will, doubtless. 'Something too much of this.' [1]

Your French scheme is good, but let it be *Italian*; all the Angles will be at Paris. Let it be Rome, Milan, Naples, Florence, Turin, Venice, or Switzerland, and 'egad!' (as Bayes [2] saith,) I will connubiate and join you; and we will write a new *Inferno* in our Paradise. Pray think of this—and I will really buy a wife and a ring, and say the ceremony, and settle near you in a summer-house upon the Arno, or the Po, or the Adriatic.

Ah! my poor little pagod, Napoleon, has walked off his pedestal. He has abdicated, they say. This would draw molten brass from the eyes of Zatanai.[3] What! 'kiss the ground before young Malcolm's feet, and then be baited by the rabble's curse!' [4] I cannot bear such a crouching catastrophe. I must stick to Sylla, for my modern favourites don't do,—their resignations are of a different kind. All health and prosperity, my dear Moore. Excuse this lengthy letter.

Ever, etc.

P.S.—The *Quarterly* quotes you frequently in an article on America; and every body I know asks perpetually after you and yours. When will you answer them in person?

62. TO THOMAS MOORE

Hastings, August 3, 1814.

By the time this reaches your dwelling, I shall (God wot) be in town again probably. I have been here renewing my acquaintance with my old friend Ocean; and I find his bosom as pleasant a pillow for an hour in the morning as his daughters of Paphos could be in the twilight. I have been swimming and eating turbot, and smuggling neat brandies and silk handkerchiefs,—and listening to my friend Hodgson's raptures about a

---

[1] *Hamlet*, III, ii, 79.   [2] In Buckingham's *Rehearsal*.
[3] Satan.   [4] *Macbeth*, v, viii, 29.

pretty wife-elect of his,—and walking on cliffs, and tumbling down hills, and making the most of the *dolce far-niente* for the last fortnight. I met a son of Lord Erskine's, who says he has been married a year, and is the 'happiest of men'; and I have met the aforesaid H., who is also the 'happiest of men'; so, it is worth while being here, if only to witness the superlative felicity of these foxes, who have cut off their tails, and would persuade the rest to part with their brushes to keep them in countenance.

It rejoiceth me that you like *Lara*.[1] Jeffrey is out with his 45th Number, which I suppose you have got. He is only too kind to me, in my share of it, and I begin to fancy myself a golden pheasant, upon the strength of the plumage wherewith he hath bedecked me. But then, '*surgit amari*', etc.—the gentlemen of the *Champion*, and Perry, have got hold (I know not how) of the condolatory address to Lady Jersey on the picture-abduction by our Regent,[2] and have published them—with my name, too, smack—without even asking leave, or inquiring whether or no! Damn their impudence, and damn every thing. It has put me out of patience, and so, I shall say no more about it.

You shall have *Lara* and *Jacqueline*[3] (both with some additions) when out; but I am still demurring and delaying, and in a fuss, and so is Rogers in his way.

Newstead is to be mine again. Claughton forfeits twenty-five thousand pounds; but that don't prevent me from being very prettily ruined. I mean to bury myself there—and let my beard grow—and hate you all.

Oh! I have had the most amusing letter from Hogg, the Ettrick minstrel and shepherd.[4] He wants me to recommend him to Murray; and, speaking of his present bookseller, whose 'bills' are never 'lifted', he adds, *totidem verbis*, 'God damn him and them both'. I laughed, and so would you too, at the way in which this execration is introduced. The said Hogg is a strange being, but of great, though uncouth, powers. I think very highly of him, as a poet; but he, and half of these Scotch and Lake troubadours, are spoilt by living in little circles and petty societies. London and the world is the only place to take

[1] Of which a proof had been sent to Moore in July. He was 'enraptured'.

[2] The Regent, offended with Lady Jersey, had dismissed her portrait from his collection of the chief beauties. Byron's lines were printed in the *Champion* on 31 July, and in the *Morning Chronicle* on 1 August.

[3] *Jacqueline*, by Rogers, was to be published in the one volume with *Lara*.

[4] James Hogg (1770-1835), who was living in Edinburgh, planned a volume of verse by the foremost living poets.

the conceit out of a man—in the milling phrase. Scott, he says, is gone to the Orkneys in a gale of wind;—during which wind, he affirms, the said Scott, 'he is sure, is not at his ease,—to say the best of it'. Lord, Lord, if these home-keeping minstrels had crossed your Atlantic or my Mediterranean, and tasted a little open boating in a white squall—or a gale in 'the Gut' —or the 'Bay of Biscay', with no gale at all—how it would enliven and introduce them to a few of the sensations!—to say nothing of an illicit amour or two upon shore, in the way of essay upon the Passions, beginning with simple adultery, and compounding it as they went along.

I have forwarded your letter to Murray,—by the way, you had addressed it to *Miller*.[1] Pray write to me, and say what art thou doing? 'Not finished!'—Oons! how is this?—these 'flaws and starts' must be 'authorised by your grandam',[2] and are unbecoming of any other author. I was sorry to hear of your discrepancy with the * *s, or rather your abjuration of agreement. I don't want to be impertinent, or buffoon on a serious subject, and am therefore at a loss what to say.

I hope nothing will induce you to abate from the proper price of your poem, as long as there is a prospect of getting it. For my own part, I have *seriously* and *not whiningly* (for that is not my way—at least, it used not to be) neither hopes, nor prospects, and scarcely even wishes. I am, in some respects, happy, but not in a manner that can or ought to last,—but enough of that. The worst of it is, I feel quite enervated and indifferent. I really do not know, if Jupiter were to offer me my choice of the contents of his benevolent cask,[3] what I would pick out of it. If I was born, as the nurses say, with a 'silver spoon in my mouth', it has stuck in my throat, and spoiled my palate, so that nothing put into it is swallowed with much relish,—unless it be cayenne. However, I have grievances enough to occupy me that way too;—but for fear of adding to yours by this pestilent long diatribe, I postpone the reading of them, *sine die*.

Ever, dear M., yours, etc.

P.S.—Don't forget my godson.[4] You could not have fixed on a fitter porter for his sins than me, being used to carry double without inconvenience. * * *

[1] Murray's predecessor at 50 Albemarle Street.
[2] *Macbeth*, III, iv, 63, 66.
[3] See the *Iliad*, XXIV, 527-33.
[4] On 18 August a daughter was born to Moore, and christened Olivia Byron.

63. TO THOMAS MOORE

Newstead Abbey, Sept. 20, 1814.

> Here 's to her who long
>   Hath waked the poet's sigh!
> The girl who gave to song
>   What gold could never buy.[1]

MY DEAR MOORE,

I am going to be married—that is, I am accepted,[2] and one usually hopes the rest will follow. My mother of the Gracchi (that *are* to be), *you* think too strait-laced for me, although the paragon of only children, and invested with 'golden opinions of all sorts of men',[3] and full of 'most blest conditions'[4] as Desdemona herself. Miss Milbanke is the lady, and I have her father's invitation to proceed there in my elect capacity,—which, however, I cannot do till I have settled some business in London, and got a blue coat.

She is said to be an heiress, but of that I really know nothing certainly, and shall not enquire. But I do know, that she has talents and excellent qualities; and you will not deny her judgment, after having refused six suitors and taken me.

Now, if you have any thing to say against this, pray do; my mind 's made up, positively fixed, determined, and therefore I will listen to reason, because now it can do no harm. Things may occur to break it off, but I will hope not. In the mean time, I tell you (a *secret*, by the by,—at least, till I know she wishes it to be public) that I have proposed and am accepted. You need not be in a hurry to wish me joy, for one mayn't be married for months. I am going to town to-morrow: but expect to be here, on my way there, within a fortnight.

If this had not happened, I should have gone to Italy. In my way down, perhaps, you will meet me at Nottingham, and come over with me here. I need not say that nothing will give me greater pleasure. I must, of course, reform thoroughly; and, seriously, if I can contribute to her happiness, I shall secure my own. She is so good a person, that—that—in short, I wish I was a better.

Ever, etc.

---

[1] Moore, *Irish Melodies*, 'Drink to her'.
[2] He had made a second proposal to Annabella Milbanke on 15 September, and received her consent on 18 September.
[3] *Macbeth*, I, vii, 33.   [4] *Othello*, II, i, 249.

64. TO THE COUNTESS OF ——

Albany, October 5, 1814.

DEAR LADY * *,

Your recollection and invitation do me great honour; but I am going to be 'married, and can't come'.[1] My intended is two hundred miles off, and the moment my business here is arranged, I must set out in a great hurry to be happy. Miss Milbanke is the good-natured person who has undertaken me, and, of course, I am very much in love, and as silly as all single gentlemen must be in that sentimental situation. I have been accepted these three weeks; but when the event will take place, I don't exactly know. It depends partly upon lawyers, who are never in a hurry. One can be sure of nothing; but, at present, there appears no other interruption to this intention, which seems as mutual as possible, and now no secret, though I did not tell first,—and all our relatives are congratulating away to right and left in the most fatiguing manner.

You perhaps know the lady. She is niece to Lady Melbourne, and cousin to Lady Cowper and others of your acquaintance, and has no fault, except being a great deal too good for me, and that I must pardon, if nobody else should. It might have been *two* years ago, and, if it had, would have saved me a world of trouble. She has employed the interval in refusing about half a dozen of my particular friends, (as she did me once, by the way,) and has taken me at last, for which I am very much obliged to her. I wish it was well over, for I do hate bustle, and there is no marrying without some;—and then, I must not marry in a black coat, they tell me, and I can't bear a blue one.

Pray forgive me for scribbling all this nonsense. You know I must be serious all the rest of my life, and this is a parting piece of buffoonery, which I write with tears in my eyes, expecting to be agitated. Believe me, most seriously and sincerely your obliged servant,

BYRON.

P.S.—My best rems. to Lord * * on his return.

65. TO ANNE ISABELLA MILBANKE

. . . . .

Oc$\underline{\text{tr}}$ 7th 1814.

It gives me much pleasure to hear that Augusta has written to you. She is the least selfish and gentlest creature in being

[1] St. Luke xiv, 20.

—and more attached to me than any one in existence can be.
She was particularly desirous that I should marry and only
regretted, what I must regret a little too, that she had not
earlier the pleasure of your acquaintance. She was very anxious
for the fate and favourable reception of her letter to you. . . .

66. TO ANNE ISABELLA MILBANKE

14 Octr 1814.

.   .   .   .   .   .

I have not seen the paragraph you mention; but it cannot
speak more humbly of me in the comparison than I think.
This is one of the lesser evils to which notoriety and a carelessness of fame,—in the only good sense of the word,—has rendered
me liable,—a carelessness which I do not now feel since I have
obtained something worth caring for. The truth is that could
I have foreseen that your life was to be linked to mine,—had I
even possessed a distinct hope however distant,—I would have
been a different and better being. As it is, I have sometimes
doubts, even if I should not disappoint the future nor act hereafter unworthily of you, whether the past ought not to make
you still regret me—even that portion of it with which you are
not unacquainted.
I did not believe such a woman existed—at least for me,—
and I sometimes fear I ought to wish that she had not. I must
turn from the subject.

My love, do forgive me if I have written in a spirit that
renders you uncomfortable. I cannot embody my feelings in
words. I have nothing to desire—nothing I would see altered
in *you*—but so much in myself. I can conceive no misery equal
to mine, if I failed in making you happy,—and yet how can I
hope to do justice to those merits from whose praise there is
not a dissentient voice? . . .

67. TO THOMAS MOORE

October 15, 1814.

An there were any thing in marriage that would make a
difference between my friends and me, particularly in your
case, I would 'none on't'. My agent sets off for Durham next
week, and I shall follow him, taking Newstead and you in my
way. I certainly did not address Miss Milbanke with these

views, but it is likely she may prove a considerable *parti*. All her father can give, or leave her, he will; and from her childless uncle, Lord Wentworth, whose barony, it is supposed, will devolve on Ly. Milbanke (*his* sister), she has expectations. But these will depend upon his own disposition, which seems very partial towards her. She is an only child, and Sir R.'s estates, though dipped by electioneering, are considerable. Part of them are settled on her; but whether *that* will be *dowered* now, I do not know,—though, from what has been intimated to me, it probably will. The lawyers are to settle this among them, and I am getting my property into matrimonial array, and myself ready for the journey to Seaham, which I must make in a week or ten days.

I certainly did not dream that she was attached to me, which it seems she has been for some time. I also thought her of a very cold disposition, in which I was also mistaken—it is a long story, and I won't trouble you with it. As to her virtues, etc., etc., you will hear enough of them (for she is a kind of *pattern* in the north), without my running into a display on the subject. It is well that *one* of us is of such fame, since there is sad deficit in the *morale* of that article upon my part,—all owing to my 'bitch of a star', as Captain Tranchemont says of his planet.

Don't think you have not said enough of me in your article on T[hurlow][1]; what more could or need be said?

* * Your long-delayed and expected work—I suppose you will take fright at *The Lord of the Isles* [2] and Scott now. You must do as you like,—I have said my say. You ought to fear comparison with none, and any one would stare, who heard you were so tremulous,—though, after all, I believe it is the surest sign of talent. Good morning. I hope we shall meet soon, but I will write again, and perhaps you will meet me at Nottingham. Pray say so.

P.S.—If this union is productive, you shall name the first fruits.

68. TO LADY MELBOURNE

[Seaham], November 13th, 1814.

My dear Lady M[E],

I delivered your letters, but have only mentioned y[e] receipt of your last to myself.

---

[1] In the *Edinburgh Review*.
[2] Recently advertised, it was published in January 1815.

Do you know I have grave doubts if this will be a marriage now? Her disposition is the very reverse of our imaginings. She is overrun with fine feelings, scruples about herself and her disposition (I suppose, in fact, she means mine), and to crown all, is taken ill once every three days with I know not what. But the day before, and the day after, she seems well; looks and eats well, and is cheerful and confiding, and in short like any other person in good health and spirits. A few days ago she made one *scene*, not altogether out of C.'s style; it was too long and too trifling, in fact, for me to transcribe, but it did me no good. In the article of conversation, however, she has improved with a vengeance, but I don't much admire these same agitations upon slight occasions. I don't know, but I think it by no means improbable, you will see me in town soon. I can only interpret these things one way, and merely wait to be certain, to make my obeisance and 'exit singly'. I hear of nothing but 'feeling' from morning till night, except from Sir Ralph, with whom I go on to admiration. Lʸ M[ilbanke] too, is pretty well; but I am never sure of A. for a moment. The least word, and you know I rattle on through thick and thin (always, however, avoiding anything I think can offend her favourite notions), if only to prevent me from yawning—the least word, or alteration of tone, has some inference drawn from it. Sometimes we are too much alike, and then again too unlike. This comes of system, and squaring her notions to the devil knows what. For my part, I have lately had recourse to the eloquence of *action* (which Demosthenes calls the first part of oratory), and find it succeeds very well, and makes her very quiet; which gives me some hopes of the efficacy of the 'calming process', so renowned in 'our philosophy'. In fact, and *entre nous*, it is really amusing; she is like a child in that respect, and quite caressable into kindness, and good humour; though I don't think her temper *bad* at any time, but very *self* tormenting and anxious, and romantic.

In short, it is impossible to foresee how this will end *now*, any more than two years ago; if there is a break, it shall be her doing not mine.

Ever yʳˢ most truly,

B.

69. TO THOMAS MOORE

Halnaby, Darlington, January 10, 1815.

I was married this day week. The parson has pronounced it—Perry has announced it[1]—and the *Morning Post*, also, under the head of 'Lord Byron's Marriage'—as if it were a fabrication, or the puff-direct of a new stay-maker.

Now for thine affairs. I have redde thee upon the Fathers,[2] and it is excellent well. Positively, you must not leave off reviewing. You shine in it—you kill in it: and this article has been taken for Sydney Smith's (as I heard in town), which proves not only your proficiency in parsonology, but that you have all the airs of a veteran critic at your first onset. So, prithee, go on and prosper.

Scott's *Lord of the Isles* is out—'the mail-coach copy' I have, by special licence of Murray. * * *

Now is *your* time;—you will come upon them newly and freshly. It is impossible to read what you have lately done (verse or prose) without seeing that you have trained on tenfold. * * has floundered; * * has foundered. *I* have tried the rascals (i.e. the public) with my Harrys and Larrys, Pilgrims and Pirates. Nobody but S[outhe]y has done any thing worth a slice of bookseller's pudding, and *he* has not luck enough to be found out in doing a good thing. Now, Tom, is thy time— Oh, joyful day!—I would not take a knighthood for thy fortune'.[3] Let me hear from you soon, and

Believe me ever, etc.

P.S.—Lady Byron is vastly well. How are Mrs. Moore and Joe Atkinson's [4] 'Graces'? We must present our women to one another.

70. TO LADY MELBOURNE

Seaham, January 22nd, 1815.

MINE AUNT,

This day completes my 27th year of existence, and (save a day) my 'three weeks after marriage'. I am four years and three months older than Bell, who will be twenty-three on May 27th. I suppose this is a fair disproportion.

Yesterday I came here somewhat anent [5] my imperial will. But never mind, you know I am a very good-natured fellow, and

---

[1] In the *Morning Chronicle* on 6 January.
[2] An article in the *Edinburgh Review* on Boyd's *Select Passages from the Writings of St. Chrysostom*.
[3] *Henry IV*, Part II, v, iii, 132–3.   [4] A Dublin friend of Moore's.
[5] i.e., against: perhaps a dialectal use.

the more easily governed because I am not ashamed of being
so; and so Bell has her own way and no doubt means to keep
it; for which reason I prodigiously applaud your having written
two letters to her, and only three to me, and one of them full of
Lady Blarney [1] (by way of emetic), etc., etc., which I presume
you meant me to show. By the way, I cannot sufficiently
admire your cautious style since I became chickenpecked, but
I love thee, *ma tante*, and therefore forgive your doubts (*implied*
but not expressed), which will last till the next scrape I get into,
and then we shall wax confidential again, and I shall have good
advice. I look upon you as my good genius. I am scribbling
in my dressing-room, and Bell is in bed, so you ought to think
the length of this epistle a huge effort of complaisance.

I sent C. an answer,[2] which produced no rejoinder; thus all
is right, at least I hope so. We are all well, and Sir R[alph]
is going on Tuesday to a county meeting, to oppose continuance
of taxes. I shall stay at home quietly with Mrs. Quotem.[3]

Love and health to all my new cousins, and particularly to
Uncle M.

Ever yours most truly,

B.

71. TO THOMAS MOORE

Seaham, Stockton-on-Tees, February 2, 1815.

I have heard from London that you have left Chatsworth,
and all the women full of 'entusymusy' [4] about you, personally
and poetically; and, in particular, that 'When first I met thee' [5]
has been quite overwhelming in its effect. I told you it was one
of the best things you ever wrote, though that dog Power [6]
wanted you to omit part of it. They are all regretting your
absence at Chatsworth, according to my informant—'all the
ladies quite', etc., etc., etc. Stap my vitals!

Well, now you have got home again—which I dare say is as

---

[1] i.e. Lady Bessborough.

[2] Lady Caroline Lamb had not ceased to importune Byron in letters.

[3] Alluding to Caleb Quotem's song in *The Review, or The Wags of Windsor*,
by George Colman the Younger:

> '. . . At night by the fire, like a good, jolly cock,
>   When my day's work is done and all over,
> I tipple, I smoke, and I wind up the clock,
>   With my sweet Mrs. Quotem in clover'.

[4] i.e. enthusiasm: a mispronunciation of John Braham, the famous
Jewish tenor, who with Isaac Nathan arranged the music for Byron's
Hebrew Melodies.

[5] A song by Moore.   [6] Moore's publisher.

agreeable as a 'draught of cool small beer to the scorched palate of a waking sot'—now you have got home again, I say, probably I shall hear from you. Since I wrote last, I have been transferred to my father-in-law's, with my lady and my lady's maid, etc., etc., etc., and the treacle-moon is over, and I am awake, and find myself married. My spouse and I agree to—and in—admiration. Swift says 'no *wise* man ever married'[1]; but, for a fool, I think it the most ambrosial of all possible future states. I still think one ought to marry upon *lease*; but am very sure I should renew mine at the expiration, though next term were for ninety and nine years.

I wish you would respond, for I am here *oblitusque meorum obliviscendus et illis*.[2] Pray tell me what is going on in the way of intriguery, and how the w——s and rogues of the upper Beggar's Opera go on—or rather go off—in or after marriage; or who are going to break any particular commandment. Upon this dreary coast, we have nothing but county meetings and shipwrecks: and I have this day dined upon fish, which probably dined upon the crews of several colliers lost in the late gales. But I saw the sea once more in all the glories of surf and foam,—almost equal to the Bay of Biscay, and the interesting white squalls and short seas of Archipelago memory.

My papa, Sir Ralpho,[3] hath recently made a speech at a Durham tax-meeting; and not only at Durham, but here, several times since, after dinner. He is now, I believe, speaking it to himself (I left him in the middle) over various decanters, which can neither interrupt him nor fall asleep,—as might possibly have been the case with some of his audience.

Ever thine,

B.

I must go to tea—damn tea. I wish it was Kinnaird's[4] brandy, and with you to lecture me about it.

72. TO THOMAS MOORE

MY DEAR THOM,   March 2, 1815.

Jeffrey has sent me the most friendly of all possible letters, and has accepted H[obhouse]'s article.[5] He says he has long

---

[1] A reminiscence of *Thoughts on Various Subjects*.

[2] Horace, *Epistles*, i, xi, 9.

[3] Ralpho is the name of the trusty squire in Butler's *Hudibras*—'infallible. . . . As three- or four-legg'd Oracle' (see Part I, Canto i, 449 et seq.).

[4] Douglas James William Kinnaird, a London banker and friend of Hobhouse.

[5] A critique of Leake's *Researches in Greece*. It appeared in the *Edinburgh Review* in February.

liked not only, etc., etc., but my 'character.' This must be *your* doing, you dog—ar'n't you ashamed of yourself, knowing me so well? This is what one gets for having you for a father confessor.

I feel merry enough to send you a sad song.[1] You once asked me for some words which you would set. Now you may set or not, as you like,—but there they are in a legible hand;[2] and not in mine, but of my own scribbling; so you may say of them what you please. Why don't you write to me? I shall make you 'a speech' if you don't respond quickly.

I am in such a state of sameness and stagnation, and so totally occupied in consuming the fruits—and sauntering—and playing dull games at cards—and yawning—and trying to read old *Annual Registers* and the daily papers—and gathering shells on the shore—and watching the growth of stunted gooseberry bushes in the garden—that I have neither time nor sense to say more than

Yours ever,

B.

P.S.—I open my letter again to put a question to you. What would Lady Cork[3], or any other fashionable Pidcock[4], give to collect you and Jeffrey and me to *one* party? I have been answering his letter, which suggested this dainty query. I can't help laughing at the thoughts of your face and mine; and our anxiety to keep the Aristarch in good humour during the *early* part of a compotation, till we got drunk enough to make him 'a speech'. I think the critic would have much the best of us—of one, at least—for I don't think diffidence (I mean social) is a disease of yours.

73. TO THOMAS MOORE

March 8, 1815.

An event — the death of poor Dorset[5] — and the recollection of what I once felt, and ought to have felt now, but could not — set me pondering, and finally into the train of thought which you have in your hands. I am very glad you like them, for I flatter myself they will pass as an imitation of your style. If I could imitate it well, I

[1] 'There's not a joy the world can give like those it takes away.'
[2] Lady Byron's.
[3] Mary, Countess of Cork.
[4] Keeper of the lions at Exeter 'Change.
[5] George John Frederick Sackville, Duke of Dorset, a schoolfellow who was killed while hunting on 14th February.

should have no great ambition of originality—I wish I could make you exclaim with Dennis,[1] 'That's my thunder, by G—d!' I wrote them with a view to your setting them, and as a present to Power, if he would accept the words, and *you* did not think yourself degraded, for once in a way, by marrying them to music.

Sun-burn Nathan![2]—why do you always twit me with his vile Ebrew nasalities? Have I not told you it was all Kinnaird's doing,[3] and my own exquisite facility of temper? But thou wilt be a wag, Thomas; and see what you get for it. Now for my revenge.

Depend—and perpend—upon it that your opinion of Scott's poem will travel through one or other of the quintuple correspondents,[4] till it reaches the ear, and the liver of the author. Your adventure, however, is truly laughable—but how could you be such a potatoe? You 'a brother' (of the quill) too, 'near the throne', to confide to a man's *own publisher* (who has 'bought', or rather sold, 'golden opinions' about him) such a damnatory parenthesis! 'Between you and me', quotha—it reminds me of a passage in the *Heir at Law* [5]—'Tête-à-tête with Lady Duberly, I suppose.'—'No—tête-à-tête with *five hundred people*'; and your confidential communication will doubtless be in circulation to that amount, in a short time, with several additions, and in several letters, all signed L. H. R. O. B., etc., etc., etc.

We leave this place to-morrow, and shall stop on our way to town (in the interval of taking a house there) at Col. Leigh's, near Newmarket, where any epistle of yours will find its welcome way.

I have been very comfortable here,—listening to that damned monologue, which elderly gentlemen call conversation, and in which my pious father-in-law repeats himself every evening—save one, when he played upon the fiddle. However, they have been very kind and hospitable, and I like them and the place vastly, and I hope they will live many happy months. Bell is in health, and unvaried good-humour and behaviour. But we are all in the agonies of packing and parting; and, I suppose, by this time to-morrow I shall be stuck in the chariot with my

---

[1] John Dennis (1657–1734) introduced a new method of making stage thunder in his play, *Appius and Virginia*. The use of the thunder after the failure of this play infuriated him.

[2] Isaac Nathan, the composer and historian of music. See page 106.

[3] The *Hebrew Melodies* were written at Kinnaird's suggestion.

[4] In a letter to Longman, of Messrs. Longman, Hurst, Orme, Rees, Brown, and Co., publishers of Scott's *Lord of the Isles*, Moore had said: 'Between *you* and *me*, I don't much like Scott's poem'.

[5] By George Colman the Younger.

chin upon a band-box. I have prepared, however, another
carriage for the abigail, and all the trumpery which our wives
drag along with them.

Ever thine, most affectionately,

B.

74. TO SAMUEL TAYLOR COLERIDGE

Piccadilly, March 31, 1815.

DEAR SIR,

It will give me great pleasure to comply with your request,[1]
though I hope there is still taste enough left amongst us to
render it almost unnecessary, sordid and interested as, it must be
admitted, many of 'the trade' are, where circumstances give
them an advantage. I trust you do not permit yourself to
be depressed by the temporary partiality of what is called
'the public' for the favourites of the moment; all experience is
against the permanency of such impressions. You must have
lived to see many of these pass away, and will survive many
more—I mean personally, for *poetically*, I would not insult you
by a comparison.

If I may be permitted, I would suggest that there never was
such an opening for tragedy. In Kean, there is an actor worthy
of expressing the thoughts of the characters which you have
every power of embodying; and I cannot but regret that the
part of Ordonio was disposed of before his appearance at Drury
Lane.[2] We have had nothing to be mentioned in the same
breath with *Remorse* [3] for very many years; and I should think
that the reception of that play was sufficient to encourage
the highest hopes of author and audience. It is to be hoped
that you are proceeding in a career which could not but be
successful. With my best respects to Mr. Bowles,[4] I have the
honour to be,

Your obliged and very obedient servant,

BYRON.

P.S.—You mention my 'Satire',[5] lampoon, or whatever you
or others please to call it. I can only say that it was written

[1] That Byron should arrange for the publication of two volumes of
Coleridge's collected poetry. Murray in 1816 published a volume containing *Christabel, Kubla Khan*, and other poems.

[2] Byron was a member of the Sub-Committee of Management.

[3] By Coleridge, produced through Byron's influence in 1813.

[4] The Rev. William Lisle Bowles, Vicar of Bremhill, near Calne, where
Coleridge was staying.

[5] *English Bards, and Scotch Reviewers.*

when I was very young and very angry, and has been a thorn in my side ever since; more particularly as almost all the persons animadverted upon became subsequently my acquaintances, and some of them my friends, which is 'heaping fire upon an enemy's head', and forgiving me too readily to permit me to forgive myself. The part applied to you [1] is pert, and petulant, and shallow enough; but, although I have long done every thing in my power to suppress the circulation of the whole thing, I shall always regret the wantonness or generality of many of its attempted attacks.

75. TO LEIGH HUNT [2]

13, Piccadilly Terrace, May–June 1, 1815.

MY DEAR HUNT,

I am as glad to hear from, as I shall be to see you. We came to town, what is called late in the season; and since that time, the death of Lady Byron's uncle [3] (in the first place), and her own delicate state of health, have prevented either of us from going out much; however, she is now better, and in a fair way of going creditably through the whole process of beginning a family.

I have the alternate weeks of a private box at Drury-lane Theatre; this is my week, and I send you an admission to it for Kean's nights, Friday and Saturday next, in case you should like to see him quietly: it is close to the stage—the entrance by the private-box door—and you can go without the bore of crowding, jostling, or dressing. I also enclose you a parcel of recent letters from Paris; perhaps you may find some extracts that may amuse yourself or your readers. I have only to beg you will prevent your copyist, or printer, from mixing up any of the *English* names, or *private* matter contained therein, which might lead to a discovery of the writer; and, as the *Examiner* [4] is sure to travel back to Paris, might get him into a scrape, to say nothing of his correspondent at home. At any rate, I hope and think the perusal will amuse you. Whenever you come this way, I shall be happy to make you acquainted with Lady Byron, whom you will find any thing but a fine lady—a species of animal which you probably do not affect more than myself.

[1] Lines 255–64 and 918.
[2] Who had been released from prison on 2nd or 3rd February.
[3] Thomas, Viscount Wentworth, the bulk of whose property was entailed on his sister, Lady Milbanke, and Lady Byron.
[4] A weekly journal, of which Hunt was editor and part proprietor.

Thanks for the *Mask*[1]; there is not only poetry and thought in the body, but much research and good old reading in your prefatory matter. I hope you have not given up your narrative poem, of which I heard you speak as in progress. It rejoices me to hear of the well-doing and regeneration of the *Feast*, setting aside my own selfish reasons for wishing it success.[2] I fear you stand almost single in your liking of *Lara*; it is natural that *I* should, as being my last and most unpopular effervescence; passing by its other sins, it is too little narrative, and too metaphysical to please the greater number of readers. I have, however, much consolation in the exception with which you furnish me. From Moore I have not heard very lately: I fear he is a little humorous, because I am a lazy correspondent; but that shall be mended.

Ever your obliged and very sincere friend,

BYRON.

P.S.—'Politics!' The barking of the war-dogs for their carrion has sickened me of them for the present.

76. TO SAMUEL TAYLOR COLERIDGE

Oct. 27th, 1815.

DEAR SIR,

I have the *Christabelle* safe, and am glad to see it in such progress; surely a little effort would complete the poem. On your question with W. Scott,[3] I know not how to speak; he is a friend of mine, and, though I cannot contradict your statement, I must look to the most favourable part of it. All I have ever seen of him has been frank, fair, and warm in regard towards you, and when he repeated this very production it was with such mention as it deserves, and *that* could not be faint praise.

But I am partly in the same scrape myself, as you will see by the enclosed extract from an unpublished poem,[4] which I assure you was written before (not seeing your *Christabelle*, for that you know I never did till this day), but before I heard Mr. S[toddart] repeat it, which he did in June last, and this thing was

[1] *The Descent of Liberty, a Masque*, published in 1815.
[2] The second edition of Hunt's *Feast of the Poets* contained a long passage on Byron.
[3] Scott had heard *Christabel* recited in 1802, fourteen years before its publication, and it had influenced his *Lay of the Last Minstrel* and subsequent narrative poems.
[4] *The Siege of Corinth*, which appeared at the beginning of 1816.

begun in January and more than half written before the Summer. The coincidence is only in this particular passage,[1] and, if you will allow me, in publishing it (which I shall perhaps do *quietly* in Murray's collected Edition of my rhymes—though not *separately*), I will give the extract from you, and state that the original thought and expression have been many years in the *Christabelle*. The stories, scenes, etc., are in general quite different; mine is the siege of Corinth in 1715, when the Turks retook the Morea from the Venetians. The ground is quite familiar to me, for I have passed the Isthmus *six*, I think—*eight*, times in my way to and fro. The hero is a renegade, and, the night before the storm of the City, he is supposed to have an apparition, or wraith of his mistress, to warn him of his destiny, as he sits among the ruins of an old temple.

I write to you in the greatest hurry. I know not what you may think of this. If you like, I will cut out the passage, and do as well as I can without,—or what you please.

Ever yours,
BYRON.

P.S.—Pray write soon; I will answer the other points of your letter immediately.

77. TO LEIGH HUNT

13, Terrace, Piccadilly, September–October 30, 1815.

MY DEAR HUNT,

Many thanks for your books, of which you already know my opinion. Their external splendour should not disturb you as inappropriate—they have still more within than without. I take leave to differ with you on Wordsworth,[2] as freely as I once agreed with you; at that time I gave him credit for a promise, which is unfulfilled. I still think his capacity warrants all you say of *it* only, but that his performances since *Lyrical Ballads* are miserably inadequate to the ability which lurks within him: there is undoubtedly much natural talent spilt over the *Excursion*; but it is rain upon rocks—where it stands and stagnates, or rain upon sands—where it falls without fertilizing. Who can understand him? Let those who do, make him intelligible. Jacob Behmen, Swedenborg, and Joanna Southcote,[3] are mere types of this arch-apostle of mystery and mysticism. But I

---

[1] Stanza 19.   [2] In *The Feast of the Poets*.
[3] Joanna Southcott (1750–1814), the Methodist prophetess.

have done,—no, I have not done, for I have two petty, and perhaps unworthy objections in small matters to make to him, which, with his pretensions to accurate observation, and fury against Pope's false translation of 'the Moonlight scene in Homer'[1], I wonder he should have fallen into;—these be they: —He says of Greece in the body of his book[2]—that it is a land of

> Rivers, *fertile plains*, and *sounding* shores,
> Under a cope of *variegated* sky.

The rivers are dry half the year, the plains are barren, and the shores *still* and *tideless* as the Mediterranean can make them; the sky is any thing but variegated, being for months and months but 'darkly, deeply, beautifully blue'[3].—The next is in his notes, where he talks of our 'Monuments crowded together in the busy, etc., of a large town', as compared with the 'still seclusion of a Turkish cemetery in some *remote* place'. This is pure stuff; for *one* monument in our churchyards there are *ten* in the Turkish, and so crowded, that you cannot walk between them; that is, divided merely by a path or road; and as to '*remote* places',· men never take the trouble in a barbarous country, to carry their dead very far; they must have lived near to where they were buried. There are no cemeteries in 'remote places', except such as have the cypress and the tombstone still left, where the olive and the habitation of the living have perished. . . .

These things I was struck with, as coming peculiarly in my own way; and in both of these he is wrong; yet I should have noticed neither, but for his attack on Pope for a like blunder, and a peevish affectation about him of despising a popularity which he will never obtain. I write in great haste, and, I doubt, *not* much to the purpose; but you have it hot and hot, just as it comes, and so let it go. By-the-way, both he and you go too far against Pope's 'So when the moon', etc.; it is no translation, I know; but it is not such false description as asserted. I have read it on the spot; there is a burst, and a lightness, and a glow about the night in the Troad, which makes the 'planets vivid', and the 'pole glowing'. The moon is—at least the sky is, clearness itself; and I know no more appropriate expression for the expansion of such a heaven—o'er the scene—the plain—the sky —Ida—the Hellespont—Simois—Scamander—and the Isles—

[1] *Iliad*, VIII, 555 *et seq.*; Pope, 687-98. See Wordsworth's 'Essay Supplementary to the Preface' of *Poems*, 1815.
[2] *Excursion*, IV, 718-20.
[3] Southey, *Madoc in Wales*, V.

than that of a 'flood of glory'. I am getting horribly lengthy, and must stop: to the whole of your letter 'I say ditto to Mr. Burke', as the Bristol candidate [1] cried by way of electioneering harangue. You need not speak of morbid feelings and vexations to me; I have plenty; but I must blame partly the times, and chiefly myself: but let us forget them. *I* shall be very apt to do so when I see you next. Will you come to the theatre and see our new management? You shall cut it up to your heart's content, root and branch, afterwards, if you like; but come and see it! If not, I must come and see you.

Ever yours, very truly and affectionately,

BYRON.

78. TO THOMAS MOORE

Terrace, Piccadilly, October 31, 1815.

I have not been able to ascertain precisely the time of duration of the stock market; but I believe it is a good time for selling out, and I hope so. First, because I shall see you; and, next, because I shall receive certain monies on behalf of Lady B., the which will materially conduce to my comfort,—I wanting (as the duns say) 'to make up a sum'.

Yesterday, I dined out with a large-ish party, where were Sheridan and Colman, Harry Harris of C[ovent] G[arden], and his brother, Sir Gilbert Heathcote, Douglas Kinnaird, and others, of note and notoriety. Like other parties of the kind, it was first silent, then talky, then argumentative, then disputatious, then unintelligible, then altogethery, then inarticulate, and then drunk. When we had reached the last step of this glorious ladder, it was difficult to get down again without stumbling; and, to crown all, Kinnaird and I had to conduct Sheridan down a damned corkscrew staircase, which had certainly been constructed before the discovery of fermented liquors, and to which no legs, however crooked, could possibly accommodate themselves. We deposited him safe at home, where his man, evidently used to the business, waited to receive him in the hall.

Both he and Colman were, as usual, very good; but I carried away much wine, and the wine had previously carried away my memory; so that all was hiccup and happiness for the last hour or so, and I am not impregnated with any of the conversation. Perhaps you heard of a late answer of Sheridan to the

[1] Henry Cruger, who was returned for Bristol with Edmund Burke in 1774.

* E 93[1]

watchman who found him bereft of that 'divine particle of air', called reason, * * *. He, the watchman, found Sherry in the street, fuddled and bewildered, and almost insensible. 'Who are *you*, sir?'—no answer. 'What's your name?'—a hiccup. 'What's your name?'—Answer, in a slow, deliberate, and impassive tone—'Wilberforce!!!' Is not that Sherry all over? —and, to my mind, excellent. Poor fellow, *his* very dregs are better than the 'first sprightly runnings'[1] of others.

My paper is full, and I have a grievous headache.

P.S.—Lady B. is in full progress. Next month will bring to light (with the aid of 'Juno Lucina, *fer opem*', or rather *opes*, for the last are most wanted,) the tenth wonder of the world— Gil Blas being the eighth, and he (my son's father) the ninth.

79. TO THOMAS MOORE

January 5, 1816.

I hope Mrs. M. is quite re-established. The little girl was born on the 10th of December last; her name is Augusta *Ada* (the second a very antique family name,—I believe not used since the reign of King John). She was, and is, very flourishing and fat, and reckoned very large for her days—squalls and sucks incessantly. Are you answered? Her mother is doing very well, and up again.

I have now been married a year on the second of this month —heigh-ho! I have seen nobody lately much worth noting, except Sebastiani[2] and another general of the Gauls[3] once or twice at dinners out of doors. Sebastiani is a fine, foreign, villainous-looking, intelligent, and very agreeable man; his compatriot is more of the *petit-maître* and younger, but I should think not at all of the same intellectual calibre with the Corsican —which Sebastiani, you know, is, and a cousin of Napoleon's.

Are you never to be expected in town again? To be sure, there is no one here of the fifteen hundred fillers of hot rooms, called the fashionable world. My approaching papa-ship detained us for advice, etc., etc., though I would as soon be here as any where else on this side of the Straits of Gibraltar.

I would gladly—or, rather, sorrowfully—comply with your request of a dirge for the poor girl you mention. But how can I write on one I have never seen or known? Besides, you will

---

[1] Dryden, *Aureng-zebe*, IV, i.
[2] François Horace Bastien de la Porta, Comte Sebastiani.
[3] Auguste Charles Joseph, Comte de Flahault.

do it much better yourself. I could not write upon any thing, without some personal experience and foundation: far less on a theme so peculiar. Now, you have both in this case; and, if you had neither, you have more imagination, and would never fail.[1]

This is but a dull scrawl, and I am but a dull fellow. Just at present, I am absorbed in 500 contradictory contemplations, though with but one object in view—which will probably end in nothing, as most things we wish do. But never mind,—as somebody says, 'for the blue sky bends over all'[2]. I only could be glad, if it bent over me where it is a little bluer; like the 'skyish top of blue Olympus'[3], which, by the way, looked very white when I last saw it.

Ever, etc.

80. TO JOHN MURRAY
February 20, 1816.

Dear Sir,

To return to *our* business—your epistles are vastly agreeable. With regard to the observations on carelessness, etc.,[4] I think, with all humility, that the gentle reader has considered a rather uncommon, and designedly irregular versification for haste and negligence. The measure is not that of any of the other poems, which (I believe) were allowed to be tolerably correct, according to Bysshe[5] and the fingers—or ears—by which bards write, and readers reckon. Great part of *The Siege* is in (I think) what the learned call Anapests, (though I am not sure, being heinously forgetful of my metres and my *Gradus*), and many of the lines intentionally longer or shorter than its rhyming companion; and the rhyme also occurring at greater or less intervals of caprice or convenience.

I mean not to say that this is right or good, but merely that I could have been smoother, had it appeared to me of advantage; and that I was not otherwise without being aware of the deviation, though I now feel sorry for it, as I would undoubtedly rather please than not. My wish has been to try at something different from my former efforts; as I endeavoured to make them differ from each other. The versification of *The Corsair* is not that of *Lara*; nor *The Giaour* that of *The Bride*; *Childe*

---

[1] See Moore's lines, 'Weep not for those' (*Sacred Songs*).
[2] Coleridge, *Christabel*, Part I, 331.
[3] *Hamlet*, v, i, 275.
[4] In the reviews of *The Siege of Corinth* and *Parisina*.
[5] Edward Bysshe's *Art of English Poetry*, 1702.

Harold is again varied from these; and I strove to vary the last somewhat from *all* of the others.

Excuse all this damned nonsense and egotism. The fact is, that I am rather trying to think on the subject of this note, than really thinking on it. I did not know you had called; you are always admitted and welcome when you choose.

Yours, etc., etc.,

BN.

P.S.—You need not be in any apprehension or grief on my account: [1] were I to be beaten down by the world and its inheritors, I should have succumbed to many things—years ago. You must not mistake my *not* bullying for dejection; nor imagine that because I feel, I am to faint:—but enough for the present.

I am sorry for Sotheby's [2] row. What the devil is it about? I thought it all settled; and if I can do any thing about him or *Ivan* still, I am ready and willing. I do not think it proper for me just now to be much behind the scenes, but I will see the committee and Moore upon it, if S. likes.

If you see Mr. Sotheby, will you tell him that I wrote to Mr. Coleridge, on getting Mr. Sotheby's note, and have, I hope, done what Mr. S. wished on that subject?

81. TO LEIGH HUNT

DEAR HUNT,   Feb. 26, 1816.

Your letter would have been answered before, had I not thought it probable that, as you were in town for a day or so, I should have seen you. I don't mean this as a hint at reproach for not calling, but merely that of course I should have been very glad if you had called in your way home or abroad, as I always would have been, and always shall be. With regard to the circumstances to which you allude, there is no reason why you should not speak openly to me on a subject already sufficiently rife in the mouths and minds of what is called 'the world'. Of the 'fifty reports', it follows that forty-nine must have more or less error and exaggeration; but I am sorry to say, that on the main and essential point of an intended, and, it may be, an inevitable separation, I can contradict none.

[1] At Byron's request Lady Byron had left with Ada for Kirkby Mallory, her parents' home, on 15 January. She then signified her wish for a separation. Rumours of the cause, unfavourable to Byron, were already abroad.

[2] William Sotheby, author and man of fortune. 'Ivan' was one of *Five Tragedies* published in 1814.

At present I shall say no more—but this is not from want of confidence: in the mean time, I shall merely request a suspension of opinion. Your prefatory letter to *Rimini*,[1] I accepted as it was meant—as a public compliment and a private kindness. I am only sorry that it may, perhaps, operate against you as an inducement, and, with some, a pretext for attack, on the part of the political and personal enemies of both;—not that this can be of much consequence, for in the end the work must be judged by its merits, and, in that respect, you are well armed. Murray tells me it is going on well, and, you may depend upon it, there is a substratum of poetry, which is a foundation for solid and durable fame. The objections (*if* there be objections, for this is a *pre*sumption, and not an *as*sumption) will be merely as to the mechanical part, and such, as I stated before, the usual consequences of either novelty or revival. I desired Murray to forward to you a pamphlet with two things of mine in it, the most part of both of them, and of one in particular, *written* before *others* of my composing, which have preceded them in *publication*; they are neither of them of much pretension, nor intended for it. You will, perhaps, wonder at my dwelling so much and so frequently on former subjects and scenes; but the fact is, that I found them fading fast from my memory; and I was, at the same time, so partial to their *place* (and events connected with it), that I have stamped them, while I could, in such colours as I could trust to *now*, but might have confused and misapplied *hereafter*, had I longer delayed the attempted delineation.

82. TO THOMAS MOORE

February 29, 1816.

I have not answered your letter [2] for a time; and, at present, the reply to part of it might extend to such a length, that I shall delay it till it can be made in person, and then I will shorten it as much as I can.

In the mean time, I am at war 'with all the world and his wife'; or rather, 'all the world and *my* wife' are at war with me, and have not yet crushed me,—whatever they *may* do. I don't know that in the course of a hair-breadth existence I was ever, at home or abroad, in a situation so completely uprooting

---

[1] The dedication to Byron.
[2] A tactful inquiry as to the truth of the rumours concerning the separation.

of present pleasure, or rational hope for the future, as this same. I say this, because I think so, and feel it. But I shall not sink under it the more for that mode of considering the question—I have made up my mind.

By the way, however, you must not believe all you hear on the subject; and don't attempt to defend me. If you succeeded in that, it would be a mortal, or an immortal, offence—who can bear refutation? I have but a very short answer for those whom it concerns; and all the activity of myself and some vigorous friends have not yet fixed on any tangible ground or personage, on which or with whom I can discuss matters, in a summary way, with a fair pretext;—though I nearly had *nailed one* yesterday, but he evaded by—what was judged by others —a satisfactory explanation. I speak of *circulators*—against whom I have no enmity, though I must act according to the common code of usage, when I hit upon those of the serious order.

Now for other matters—poesy, for instance. Leigh Hunt's poem is a devilish good one—quaint, here and there, but with the substratum of originality, and with poetry about it, that will stand the test. I do not say this because he has inscribed it to me, which I am sorry for, as I should otherwise have begged you to review it in the *Edinburgh*. It is really deserving of much praise, and a favourable critique in the *E. R.* would but do it justice, and set it up before the public eye, where it ought to be.

How are you? and where? I have not the most distant idea what I am going to do myself—or with myself—or where—or what. I had, a few weeks ago, some things to say that would have made you laugh; but they tell me now that I must not laugh, and so I have been very serious—and am.

I have not been very well—with a *liver* complaint—but am much better within the last fortnight, though still under Iatrical advice. I have latterly seen a little of * *.

* * I must go and dress to dine. My little girl is in the country, and, they tell me, is a very fine child, and now nearly three months old. Lady Noel [1] (my mother-in-law, or, rather, *at* law) is at present overlooking it. Her daughter (Miss Milbanke that was) is, I believe, in London with her father. A Mrs. C. [2] (now a kind of housekeeper and spy of Lady N.'s), who, in her better days, was a washerwoman, is supposed to

---

[1] The Milbankes had changed their name to Noel, in compliance with Lord Wentworth's will.

[2] Mrs. Clermont, successively lady's maid to Lady Milbanke and governess to Annabella. Byron's suspicions found vent on 29 March in the vituperative lines, *A Sketch*.

be—by the learned—very much the occult cause of our late domestic discrepancies.

In all this business, I am the sorriest for Sir Ralph. He and I are equally punished, though *magis pares quam similes* in our affliction. Yet it is hard for both to suffer for that fault of one, and so it is—I shall be separated from my wife; he will retain his.

Ever, etc.

83. TO THOMAS MOORE

March 8, 1816.

I rejoice in your promotion as Chairman and Charitable Steward, etc., etc. These be dignities which await only the virtuous. But then, recollect you are *six* and *thirty*, (I speak this enviously—not of your age, but the 'honour—love—obedience—troops of friends'[1], which accompany it), and I have eight years good to run before I arrive at such hoary perfection; by which time,—if I *am* at all,—it will probably be in a state of grace or progressing merits.

I must set you right in one point, however. The fault was *not*—no, nor even the misfortune—in my 'choice' (unless in *choosing at all*)—for I do not believe—and I must say it, in the very dregs of all this bitter business—that there ever was a better, or even a brighter, a kinder, or a more amiable and agreeable being than Lady B. I never had, nor can have, any reproach to make her, while with me. Where there is blame, it belongs to myself, and, if I cannot redeem, I must bear it.

Her nearest relatives are a * * * *—my circumstances have been and are in a state of great confusion—my health has been a good deal disordered, and my mind ill at ease for a considerable period. Such are the causes (I do not name them as excuses) which have frequently driven me into excess, and disqualified my temper for comfort. Something also may be attributed to the strange and desultory habits which, becoming my own master at an early age, and scrambling about, over and through the world, may have induced. I still, however, think that, if I had had a fair chance, by being placed in even a tolerable situation, I might have gone on fairly. But that seems hopeless, —and there is nothing more to be said. At present—except my health, which is better (it is odd, but agitation or contest of any kind gives a rebound to my spirits and sets me up for the time)—I have to battle with all kinds of unpleasantnesses, including private and pecuniary difficulties, etc., etc.

[1] *Macbeth*, v, iii, 22.

I believe I may have said this before to you, but I risk repeating it. It is nothing to bear the *privations* of adversity, or, more properly, ill fortune; but my pride recoils from its *indignities*. However, I have no quarrel with that same pride, which will, I think, buckler me through every thing. If my heart could have been broken, it would have been so years ago, and by events more afflicting than these.

I agree with you (to turn from this topic to our shop), that I have written too much. The last things were, however, published very reluctantly by me, and for reasons I will explain when we meet. I know not why I have dwelt so much on the same scenes, except that I find them fading, or *confusing* (if such a word may be) in my memory, in the midst of present turbulence and pressure, and I felt anxious to stamp before the die was worn out. I now break it. With those countries, and events connected with them, all my really poetical feelings begin and end. Were I to try, I could make nothing of any other subject, and that I have apparently exhausted. 'Woe to him', says Voltaire, 'who says all he could say on any subject.' There are some on which, perhaps, I could have said still more: but I leave them all, and not too soon.

Do you remember the lines I sent you early last year, which you still have? I don't wish (like Mr. Fitzgerald, in the *Morning Post*) [1] to claim the character of 'Vates' in all its translations, but were they not a little prophetic? I mean those beginning, 'There's not a joy the world can,' etc. etc., on which I rather pique myself as being the truest, though the most melancholy, I ever wrote.

What a scrawl have I sent you! You say nothing of yourself, except that you are a Lancasterian churchwarden, [2] and an encourager of mendicants. When are you out? and how is your family? My child is very well and flourishing, I hear; but I must see also. I feel no disposition to resign it to the contagion of its grandmother's society, though I am unwilling to take it from the mother. It is weaned, however, and something about it must be decided.

Ever, etc.

[1] William Thomas Fitzgerald, in his poem, *The White Cockade*, published in the *Morning Post* on 13 January 1814, recalled that he had prophesied the fall of Napoleon.

[2] Moore had presided at a meeting of the Lancasterian Society, which was connected with the educational system of Joseph Lancaster.

84. TO LADY BYRON

Mivart's Hotel [Easter] Sunday April [14] 1816.

'More last words'—not many—and such as you will attend
to—answer I do not expect—nor does it import—but you will
hear me.——I have just parted from Augusta—almost the last
being you had left me to part with—and the only unshattered
tie of my existence—wherever I may go—and I am going far [1]
—you and I can never meet again in this world—nor in the
next—Let this content or atone.—If any accident occurs to
me—be kind to *her,*—if she is then nothing—to her children;—
Some time ago—I informed you that with the knowledge
that any child of ours was already provided for by other and
better means—I had made my will in favor of her and her
children—as prior to my marriage:—this was not done in
prejudice to you for we had not then differed—and even this is
useless during your life by the settlements—I say therefore—
be kind to her and hers—for never has she acted or spoken
otherwise towards you—she has ever been your friend—this
may seem valueless to one who has now so many:——be kind
to her—however—and recollect that though it may be advantage to you to have lost your husband—it is sorrow to her to
have the waters now—or the earth hereafter—between her and
her brother.—

She is gone—I need hardly add that of this request she knows
nothing—your late compliances have not been so extensive—
as to render this an encroachment:—I repeat it—(for deep
resentments have but *half* recollections) that you once did
promise me thus much—do not forget it—nor deem it cancelled
it was not a vow.———

Mr. Wharton has sent me a letter with one question and two
pieces of intelligence—to the question I answer that the carriage
is yours—and as it has only carried us to Halnaby—and London
—and you to Kirkby—I hope it will take you many a more
propitious journey.—

The receipts can remain—unless troublesome, if so—they
can be sent to Augusta—and through her I would also hear of
my little daughter—my address will be left for Mrs. Leigh.—
The ring is of no lapidary value—but it contains the hair of a
king and an ancestor—which I should wish to preserve to Miss
Byron.—

[1] Public indignation against Byron was so great that he decided to leave
England.

To a subsequent letter of Mr. Wharton's I have to reply that it is the 'law's delay'[1] not mine,—and that when he and Mr. H. have adjusted the tenor of the bond [2]—I am ready to sign.

Y^{rs} Ever

very truly

BYRON.

85. TO ISAAC NATHAN

MY DEAR NATHAN,   Piccadilly, Tuesday evening.

I have to acknowledge the receipt of your very seasonable bequest,[3] which I duly appreciate; the unleavened bread shall certainly accompany me in my pilgrimage; and, with a full reliance on their efficacy, the *Motsas* shall be to me a charm against the destroying Angel wherever I may sojourn; his serene highness, however, will, I hope, be polite enough to keep at a desirable distance from my person, without the necessity of besmearing my *door posts* or *upper lintels* with the blood of any animal. With many thanks for your kind attention, believe me, my dear Nathan,

Yours very truly,

BYRON.

86. TO THE HON. AUGUSTA LEIGH

MY HEART,   Bruxelles, [Wednesday,] May 1st, 1816.

We [4] are detained here for some petty carriage repairs, having come out of our way to the Rhine on purpose, after passing through Ghent, Antwerp, and Mechlin. I have written to you twice,—once from Ostend, and again from Ghent. I hope most truly that you will receive my letters, not as important in themselves, but because you wish it, and so do I. It would be difficult for me to write anything amusing; this country has been so frequently described, and has so little for description, though a good deal for observation, that I know not what to say of it, and one don't like talking only of oneself. We saw at

---

[1] *Hamlet*, III, i, 72.

[2] The deed of separation, which was signed on 21 April. On the 25th Byron sailed for Ostend.

[3] Some Passover Cakes, which Nathan, after parting from Byron, had sent with this wish: 'As a certain angel at a certain hour, by his presence, ensured the safety of a whole nation, may the same guardian spirit pass with your Lordship to that land where the fates may have decreed you to sojourn for a while!'

[4] He was accompanied by a doctor, John William Polidori; William Fletcher and Robert Rushton; and Berger, a Swiss servant.

Antwerp the famous basons of Bonaparte for his navy, which are very superb—as all his undertakings were, and as for churches, and pictures, I have stared at them till my brains are like a guide-book;—the last (though it is heresy to say so) don't please me at all. I think Rubens a very great dauber, and prefer Vandyke a hundred times over (but then I know nothing about the matter). Rubens' women have all red gowns and red shoulders—to say nothing of necks, of which they are more liberal than charming; it may all be very fine, and I suppose it may be Art, for 'tis not Nature.

As the low Countries did not make part of my plan (except as a route), I feel a little anxious to get out of them. Level roads don't suit me, as thou knowest; it must be up hill or down, and then I am more *au fait*. Imagine to yourself a succession of avenues with a Dutch Spire at the end of each, and you see the road;—an accompaniment of highly cultivated farms on each side, intersected with small canals or ditches, and sprinkled with very neat and clean cottages, a village every two miles,—and you see the country; not a rise from Ostend to Antwerp—a molehill would make the inhabitants think that the Alps had come here on a visit; it is a perpetuity of plain and an eternity of *pavement* (on the *road*), but it is a country of great apparent comfort, and of singular though *tame* beauty, and, were it not out of my way, I should like to survey it less cursorily. The towns are wonderfully fine. The approach to Brussels is beautiful, and there is a fine palace to the right in coming. . . .

87. TO JOHN CAM HOBHOUSE

MY DEAR H^E. Bruxelles, May 1st, 1816.

You will be surprised that we are not more 'en avant', and so am I, but Mr. Baxter's wheel and springs have not done their duty, for which I beg that you will abuse him like a pickpocket (that is—*He*—the said Baxter being the *pickpocket*) and say that I expect a deduction, having been obliged to come out of the way to this place, which was not in my route, for repairs, which however I hope to have accomplished, so as to put us in motion in a day or two.

We passed through Ghent, Antwerp, and Mechlin, and thence diverged here, having seen all the sights, pictures, docks, basons, and having climbed up steeples, etc., etc., and so forth. The first thing, after the flatness and fertility of the country, which struck me, was the beauty of the towns, Bruges first, where, you may tell Douglas Kinnaird, on entering at sunset, I over-took a crew of beggarly looking gentlemen, not unlike Oxberry, headed by a monarch with a staff, the very fac-simile of King Clause in the said D. K.'s revived drama.[1]

We lost our way in the dark, or rather twilight, not far from Ghent, by the stupidity of the postilion (*one* only, by the way, to four horses), which produced an alarm of intended robbery amongst the uninitiated, whom I could not convince that four or five well-armed people were not immediately to be plundered and anatomized by a single person, fortified with a horsewhip to be sure, but, nevertheless, a little encumbered with large jack boots, and a tight jacket that did not fit him.

The way was found again without loss of life or limb. I thought the learned Fletcher at least would have known better after our Turkish expeditions, and defiles and banditti, and guards, etc., etc., than to have been so valorously alert, without at least a better pretext for his superfluous courage.

I don't mean to say that they were frightened, but were vastly suspicious, without any cause.

At Ghent we stared at pictures; and climbed up a steeple, 450 steps in altitude, from which I had a good view and notion of these *paesi bassi*.

Next day we broke down, by a damned wheel (on which Baxter should be broken) pertinaciously refusing its stipulated rotation. This becalmed us at Lo-Kristy (2 leagues from Ghent) and obliged us to return for repairs; at Lo-Kristy I came to anchor in the house of a Flemish blacksmith (who was ill of a fever for which Dr. Dori[2] physicked him—I daresay he is dead by now), and saw somewhat of Lo-Kristy; Low-country low-life, which regaled me much; besides, it being a Sunday, all the world were on their way to mass, and I had the pleasure of seeing a number of very ordinary women in extraordinary garments:—we found the 'Contadini', however, very good-natured and obliging, though not at all useful.

At Antwerp we pictured—churched—and steepled again, but the principal street and *bason* pleased me most—poor dear Buonaparte!!! and the foundries, etc., etc. As for Rubens, I was glad to see his tomb on account of that ridiculous description (in Smollett's *P. Pickle*) of Pallet's absurdity at his monument —but as for his works, and his superb 'tableaux', he seems to me (who by the way know nothing of the matter) the most glaring—flaring—staring—harlotry impostor that ever passed

---

[1] *The Merchant of Bruges.*　　　　[2] Dr. Polidori.

a trick upon the senses of mankind,—it is not nature—it is not art—with the exception of some linen (which hangs over the cross in one of his pictures) which, to do it justice, looked like a very handsome table-cloth—I never saw such an assemblage of florid nightmares as his canvas contains; his portraits seem clothed in pulpit cushions.

On the way to Mechlin, a wheel, and a *spring* too gave way; that is, the one went, and the other would not go; so we came off here to get into dock. I hope we shall sail shortly. On to Geneva.

Will you have the goodness to get at my account with Hoares? I believe there must be a balance in my favour, as I did not draw a great deal previously to going:—whatever there may be, over the two thousand five hundred, they can send by you, to me in a further credit, when you come out.

I wish you to enquire (for fear any tricks might be played with my drafts)—*my* banker's books, left with you, will shew you exactly what I have drawn; and you can let them have the book, to make out the remainder of the account.

All I have to urge to Hanson, or to our friend Douglas K., is to *sell* [1] if possible.

All kind things to Scrope and the rest.

Ever yrs. most truly and obligedly,
B.

P.S.—If you hear of my child let me know any good of her health and well-doing.

88. TO JOHN MURRAY

Ouchy, near Lausanne, June 27, 1816.

DEAR SIR,

I am thus far (kept by stress of weather) on my way back to Diodati [2] (near Geneva) from a voyage in my boat round the Lake; and I enclose you a sprig of *Gibbon's Acacia* and some rose-leaves from his garden, which, with part of his house, I have just seen. You will find honourable mention, in his *Life*, made of this 'Acacia', when he walked out on the night of concluding his history.[3] The garden and *summer-house*, where he composed, are neglected, and the last utterly decayed; but they still show it as his 'Cabinet', and seem perfectly aware of his memory.

---

[1] To sell Newstead.
[2] The Villa Diodati, which Byron had taken on 10 June. At Geneva he first met Shelley.
[3] *The Decline and Fall of the Roman Empire.*

My route through Flanders, and by the Rhine, to Switzerland, was all I expected, and more.

I have traversed all Rousseau's ground, with the *Héloise* [1] before me; and am struck, to a degree, with the force and accuracy of his descriptions and the beauty of their reality. Meillerie, Clarens, and Vevay, and the Château de Chillon, are places of which I shall say little, because all I could say must fall short of the impressions they stamp.

Three days ago, we [2] were most nearly wrecked in a Squall off Meillerie, and driven to shore. I ran no risk, being so near the rocks, and a good swimmer; but our party were wet, and incommoded a good deal, the wind was strong enough to blow down some trees, as we found at landing, however, all is righted and right, and we are thus far on return.

Dr. Polidori is not here, but at Diodati, left behind in hospital with a sprained ancle, acquired in tumbling from a wall—he can't jump.

I shall be glad to hear you are well, and have received for me certain helms and swords, sent from Waterloo, which I rode over with pain and pleasure.

I have finished a third canto of *Childe Harold* (consisting of one hundred and seventeen stanzas), longer than either of the two former, and in some parts, it may be, better; but of course on that *I* cannot determine. I shall send it by the first safe-looking opportunity.

Ever very truly yours,

B.

89. TO JOHN MURRAY

Diodati, near Geneva, July 22d, 1816.

DEAR SIR,

I wrote to you a few weeks ago, and Dr. P[olidori] received your letter; but the packet has not made its appearance, nor the epistle, of which you gave notice therein. I enclose you an advertisement, which was copied by Dr. P[olidori], and which appears to be about the most impudent imposition that ever issued from Grub Street. [3] I need hardly say that I know nothing of all this trash, nor whence it may spring,—'Odes to St. Helena',—'Farewells to England', etc., etc.; and if it can

---

[1] *Julie, ou La Nouvelle Héloïse*, 1760.   [2] Byron and Shelley.
[3] James Johnston, a London publisher, was attempting to pass off as Byron's some poems, namely: *Lord Byron's Farewell to England, Ode to St. Helena, To my Daughter on the Morn of her Birth*, and *To the Lily of France*.

be disavowed, or is worth disavowing, you have full authority
to do so. I never wrote, nor conceived, a line on any thing of
the kind, any more than of two other things with which I was
saddled—something about 'Gaul', and another about 'Mrs.
La Valette'; and as to the 'Lily of *France*', I should as soon
think of celebrating a turnip. On the 'Morning of my
Daughter's Birth', I had other things to think of than verses;
and should never have dreamed of such an invention, till Mr.
Johnston and his pamphlet's advertisement broke in upon me
with a new light on the Crafts and subtilties of the Demon of
printing,—or rather publishing.

I did hope that some succeeding lie would have superseded
the thousand and one which were accumulated during last
winter. I can forgive whatever may be said *of* or against me,—
but not what they make me say or sing for myself. It is enough
to answer for what I have written; but it were too much for
Job himself to bear what one has not. I suspect that when the
Arab Patriarch wished that his 'Enemy had written a book',[1]
he did not anticipate his own name on the title-page. I feel
quite as much bored with this foolery as it deserves, and more
than I should be, if I had not a headache.

Of *Glenarvon*,[2] Madame de Staël told me (ten days ago, at
Copet) marvellous and grievous things; but I have seen nothing
of it but the Motto, which promises amiably 'for us and for our
tragedy'.[3] If such be the posy, what should the ring be? 'a
name to all succeeding',[4] etc. The generous moment selected
for the publication is probably its kindest accompaniment, and
—truth to say—the time was well chosen. I have not even a
guess at the contents, except from the very vague accounts I
have heard, and I know but one thing which a woman can say
to the purpose on such occasions, and that she might as well
for her own sake keep to herself, which by the way they very
rarely can—the old reproach against their admirers of '*Kiss* and
tell', bad as it is, is surely somewhat less than —— and publish.

I ought to be ashamed of the Egotism of this letter. It is
not my fault altogether, and I shall be but too happy to drop
the subject when others will allow me.

[1] Job xxxi, 35.
[2] An autobiographical novel, just published, by Lady Caroline Lamb.
Lord Glenarvon is Byron.
[3] *Hamlet*, iii, ii, 159.
[4] The motto of the second edition was taken from *The Corsair*:
    'He left a name to all succeeding times,
     Link'd with one virtue and a thousand crimes'.

I am in tolerable plight, and in my last letter told you what I had done in the way of all rhyme. I trust that you prosper, and that your authors are in good condition. I should suppose your Stud has received some increase, by what I hear. *Bertram* [1] must be a good horse; does he run next meeting? and does the *Quarterly* cover still at so much the mare and the groom? I hope you will beat the Row.

Yours alway, very truly,
B.

90. TO THE HON. AUGUSTA LEIGH

Diodati—Geneva, Sept. 8th, 1816.

MY DEAREST AUGUSTA,

By two opportunities of private conveyance I have sent answers to your letter delivered by Mr. H.[2] S——[3] is on his return to England and may probably arrive before this. He is charged with a few packets of seals—necklaces—balls, etc. and—I know not what—formed of Chrystals, Agates, and other stones, *all of* them *from Mont Blanc* bought and brought by me on and from the spot—expressly for you to divide among yourself and the children, including also your niece Ada, for whom I selected a ball (of Granite—a *soft* substance by the way—but the only one there) wherewithall to roll and play when she is old enough, and mischievous enough, and moreover a Chrystal necklace; and anything else you may like to add for her—the love!

The rest are for you and the nursery, but particularly Georgiana,[4] who has sent me a very nice letter. I hope Scrope will carry them all safely, as he promised. There are seals and all kinds of fooleries, pray like them, for they come from a very curious place (nothing like it *hardly* in all I ever saw) to say nothing of the giver.

And so—Lady B. has been 'kind to you' you tell me—'very kind'—umph—it is as well she should be kind to some of us, and I am glad she has the heart and the discernment to be still *your* friend; you was ever so to her. I heard the other day that she was very unwell.[5] I was shocked enough—and sorry

---

[1] *Bertram, or the Castle of Aldobrand*, a tragedy by the Rev. Charles Robert Maturin, which was extremely successful on the stage. Murray published it.

[2] Hobhouse and Scrope Davies had arrived, at the end of August.

[3] Scrope.

[4] Mrs. Leigh's eldest daughter.

[5] See his 'Lines on hearing that Lady Byron was Ill'.

enough, God knows, but never mind; H. tells me however that she is *not* ill; that she *had* been indisposed, but is better and well to do—This is a relief. As for me I am in good health, and fair, though very unequal spirits; but for all that—she—or rather the Separation—has broken my heart. I feel as if an Elephant had trodden on it. I am convinced I shall never get over it —but I try. I had enough before I knew her and more than enough, but time and agitation had done something for me; but this last wreck has affected me very differently. If it were *acutely* it would not signify; but it is not that—I breathe lead. While the storm lasted and you were all pitying and comforting me with condemnation in Piccadilly, it was bad enough and violent enough, but it's worse now; I have neither strength nor spirits nor inclination to carry me through anything which will clear my brain or lighten my heart. I mean to cross the Alps at the end of this month, and go—God knows where—by Dalmatia up to the Arnauts again, if nothing better can be done; I have still a world before me—this—or the next. H—— has told me all the strange stories in circulation of me and mine—*not* true. I have been in some danger on the lake (near Meillerie) but nothing to speak of; and as to all these 'mistresses' —Lord help me—I have had but one.[1] Now don't scold—but what could I do? A foolish girl, in spite of all I could say or do, would come after me, or rather went before for I found her here, and I have had all the plague possible to persuade her to go back again, but at last she went.[2] Now dearest, I do most truly tell thee that I could not help this, that I did all I could to prevent it, and have at last put an end to it. I was not in love nor have any love left for any, but I could not exactly play the Stoic with a woman who had scrambled eight hundred miles to unphilosophize me, besides I had been regaled of late with so many 'two courses and a *desert*' [3] (Alas!) of aversion, that I was fain to take a little love (if pressed particularly) by way of novelty. And now you know all that I know of that matter, and it's over. Pray write, I have heard nothing since your last, at least a month or five weeks ago. I go out very little, except into the *air*, and on journeys, and on the water, and to Coppet, where Me de Staël has been particularly kind and friendly towards me, and, (I hear) fought battles without number in my very indifferent cause. It has (they say) made quite as

[1] Clara Mary Jane ('Claire') Clairmont, a stepdaughter of William Godwin. She had accompanied Shelley and Mary Godwin to Geneva.
[2] The Shelley party left for England on 29 August.
[3] See *She Stoops to Conquer*, II, ii.

much noise on this as the other side of 'La Manche'—Heaven knows why, but I seem destined to set people by the ears.

Don't hate me, but believe me ever

Yrs. most affec^{ly}

B.

91. TO THE HON. AUGUSTA LEIGH

My dearest Augusta,   Ouchy. Sep^t 17. 1816.

I am thus far [1] on my way to the Bernese Alps and the Grindenwald, and the *Yung frau* (that is the 'Wild woman' being interpreted—as it is so perverse a mountain that no other sex would suit it), which journey may occupy me about eight days or so, and then it is my intention to return to Geneva, preparatory to passing the Simplon—

Continue you to direct as usual to Geneva. I have lately written to you several letters (3 or 4 by post and two by hand) and I have received all yours very safely. I rejoice to have heard that you are well. You have been in London too lately, and H. tells me that at your levée he generally found Ld F. Bentinck—pray why is that fool so often a visitor? is he in love with you? I have recently broken through my resolution of not speaking to you of Lady B— but do not on that account name her to me. It is a relief—a partial relief to me to talk of her sometimes to you—but it would be none to hear of her. *Of* her you are to judge for yourself but do not altogether forget that she has destroyed your brother. Whatever my faults might or may have been——*She*—was not the person marked out by providence to be their avenger. One day or another her conduct will recoil on her own head; *not* through *me,* for my feelings towards her are not those of Vengeance, but—mark—if she does not end miserably *tôt ou tard*. She may think—talk—or act as she will, and by any process of cold reasoning and a jargon of 'duty and acting for the best', etc. etc., impose upon her own feelings and those of others for a time—but woe unto her—the wretchedness she has brought upon the man to whom she has been everything evil [except in one respect] [2] will flow back into its fountain. I may thank the strength of my constitution that has enabled me to bear all this, but those who bear the longest and the most do not suffer the least. I do not think a human being could endure more mental torture than that woman has directly and indirectly inflicted upon me— within the present year.

[1] On a tour with Hobhouse.   [2] Erased.

She has (for a time at least) separated me from my child—and from you—but I turn from the subject for the present.

To-morrow I repass Clarens and Vevey; if in the new and more extended tour I am making, anything that I think may please you occurs, I will detail it.

Scrope has by this time arrived with my little presents for you and yours and Ada. I still hope to be able to see you next Spring, perhaps you and one or two of the children could be spared some time next year for a little tour *here* or in France with me of a month or two. I think I could make it pleasing to you, and it should be no expense to L[eigh] or to yourself. Pray think of this hint. You have no idea how very beautiful great part of this country is—and *women* and *children* traverse it with ease and expedition. I would return from any distance at any time to see you, and come to England for you; and when you consider the chances against our—but I won't relapse into the dismals and anticipate long absences—

The great obstacle would be that you are so admirably yoked —and necessary as a housekeeper—and a letter writer—and a place-hunter to that very helpless gentleman your Cousin, that I suppose the usual self-love of an elderly person would interfere between you and any scheme of recreation or relaxation, for however short a period.

What a fool was I to marry—and *you* not very wise—my dear—we might have lived so single and so happy—as old maids and bachelors; I shall never find any one like you—nor you (vain as it may seem) like me. We are just formed to pass our lives together, and therefore—we—at least—I—am by a crowd of circumstances removed from the only being who could ever have loved me, or whom I can unmixedly feel attached to.

Had you been a Nun—and I a Monk—that we might have talked through a grate instead of across the sea—no matter—my voice and my heart are

ever thine—
B.

92. TO JOHN MURRAY

Diodati, Sept. 29th, 1816.

MY DEAR SIR,

I am very much flattered by Mr. Gifford's good opinion of the MSS.,[1] and shall be still more so if it answers your expectations and justifies his kindness. I liked it myself, but that must

---

[1] *The Prisoner of Chillon* and other poems.

go for nothing. The feelings with which much of it was written need not be envied me. With regard to the price, I fixed *none*, but left it to Mr. Kinnaird, and Mr. Shelley, and yourself, to arrange. Of course, they would do their best; and as to yourself, I knew you would make no difficulties. But I agree with Mr. K. perfectly, that the concluding *five hundred* should be only *conditional*; and for my own sake, I wish it to be added, only in case of your selling a certain number, *that number* to be fixed by *yourself*. I hope this is fair. In every thing of this kind there must be risk; and till that be past, in one way or the other, I would not willingly add to it, particularly in times like the present. And pray always recollect that nothing could mortify me more—no failure on my own part—than having made you lose by any purchase from me.

The Monody [1] was written by request of Mr. K. for the theatre. I did as well as I could; but where I have not my choice I pretend to answer for nothing. Mr. Hobhouse and myself are just returned from a journey of lakes and mountains. We have been to the Grindenwald, and the Jung-frau, and stood on the summit of the Wengeren Alp, and seen torrents of nine hundred feet in fall, and Glaciers of all dimensions: we have heard Shepherds' pipes, and Avalanches, and looked on the clouds foaming up from the valleys below us, like the spray of the ocean of hell. Chamouni, and that which it inherits, we saw a month ago: but (though Mont Blanc is higher), it is not equal in wildness to the Jung-frau, the Eighers, the Shreckhorn, and the Rose Glaciers.

We set off for Italy next week. The road is within this month infested with Bandits, but we must take our chance and such precautions as are requisite.

Ever yours very truly,
Byron.

P.S.—My best remembrances to Mr. G[ifford]. Pray say all that can be said from me to him.

I am sorry that Mr. M. did not like Phillips's picture. I thought it was reckoned a good one. If he had made the speech on the original, perhaps he would have been more readily forgiven by the proprietor and the painter of the portrait. Do not forget to consult Mrs. Leigh on the lines to her; [2] they must not be published without her full consent and approbation.

---

[1] *A Monody on the Death of R. B. Sheridan*, which was spoken at Drury Lane on 7 September.

[2] The *Epistle to Augusta*, which was not published till 1830.

93. TO THOMAS MOORE

Verona, November 6, 1816.

My dear Moore,

Your letter, written before my departure from England, and addressed to me in London, only reached me recently. Since that period, I have been over a portion of that part of Europe which I had not already seen. About a month since, I crossed the Alps from Switzerland to Milan, which I left a few days ago, and am thus far on my way to Venice, where I shall probably winter. Yesterday I was on the shores of the Benacus,[1] with his *fluctibus et fremitu*. Catullus's Sirmium [2] has still its name and site, and is remembered for his sake: but the very heavy autumnal rains and mists prevented our quitting our route, (that is, Hobhouse and myself, who are at present voyaging together,) as it was better not to see it at all than to a great disadvantage.

I found on the Benacus the same tradition of a city still visible in calm weather below the waters, which you have preserved of Lough Neagh, 'When the clear, cold eve's declining'.[3] I do not know that it is authorised by records; but they tell you such a story, and say that the city was swallowed up by an earthquake. We moved to-day over the frontier to Verona, by a road suspected of thieves,—'the wise *convey* it call',[4]—but without molestation. I shall remain here a day or two to gape at the usual marvels,—amphitheatre, paintings, and all that time-tax of travel,—though Catullus, Claudian,[5] and Shakspeare have done more for Verona than it ever did for itself. They still pretend to show, I believe, the 'tomb of all the Capulets' [6]—we shall see.

Among many things at Milan, one pleased me particularly, viz. the correspondence (in the prettiest love-letters in the world) of Lucretia Borgia with Cardinal Bembo, (who, *you say*, made a very good cardinal,) and a lock of her hair, and some Spanish verses of hers,—the lock very fair and beautiful. I took one single hair of it as a relic, and wished sorely to get a copy of one or two of the letters; but it is prohibited: *that* I don't mind; but it was impracticable; and so I only got some of them by heart. They are kept in the Ambrosian Library, which I often visited to look them over—to the scandal of the librarian,

---

[1] The Lago di Garda. [2] Catullus, *Carmina*, xxxi.
[3] *Irish Melodies*, 'Let Erin remember the days of old'.
[4] *Merry Wives of Windsor*, I, iii, 32. [5] *Epigrams*, II.
[6] Juliet's tomb in a Franciscan monastery.

who wanted to enlighten me with sundry valuable MSS., classical, philosophical, and pious. But I stick to the Pope's daughter, and wish myself a cardinal.

I have seen the finest parts of Switzerland, the Rhine, the Rhone, and the Swiss and Italian lakes; for the beauties of which I refer you to the Guide-book. The north of Italy is tolerably free from the English; but the south swarms with them, I am told. Madame de Staël I saw frequently at Copet, which she renders remarkably pleasant. She has been particularly kind to me. I was for some months her neighbour, in a country-house called Diodati, which I had on the Lake of Geneva. My plans are very uncertain; but it is probable that you will see me in England in the spring. I have some business there. If you write to me, will you address to the care of Mons. Hentsch, *Banquier*, Geneva, who receives and forwards my letters. Remember me to Rogers, who wrote to me lately, with a short account of your poem,[1] which, I trust, is near the light. He speaks of it most highly.

My health is very endurable, except that I am subject to casual giddiness and faintnesses, which is so like a fine lady, that I am rather ashamed of the disorder. When I sailed, I had a physician [2] with me, whom, after some months of patience, I found it expedient to part with, before I left Geneva some time. On arriving at Milan, I found this gentleman in very good society, where he prospered for some weeks; but, at length, at the theatre, he quarrelled with an Austrian officer, and was sent out by the government in twenty-four hours. I was not present at his squabble; but, on hearing that he was put under arrest, I went and got him out of his confinement, but could not prevent his being sent off, which, indeed, he partly deserved, being quite in the wrong, and having begun a row for row's sake. I had preceded the Austrian government some weeks myself, in giving him his congé from Geneva. He is not a bad fellow, but very young and hot-headed, and more likely to incur diseases than to cure them. Hobhouse and myself found it useless to intercede for him. This happened some time before we left Milan. He is gone to Florence.

At Milan I saw, and was visited by, Monti, the most celebrated of the living Italian poets. He seems near sixty; in face he is like the late Cooke the actor. His frequent changes in politics have made him very unpopular as a man. I saw many more of their literati; but none whose names are well known in

---

[1] *Lalla Rookh.*   [2] Polidori.

England, except Acerbi.[1] I lived much with the Italians, particularly with the Marquis of Breme's family, who are very able and intelligent men, especially the Abbate. There was a famous improvisatore [2] who held forth while I was there. His fluency astonished me; but, although I understand Italian, and speak it (with more readiness than accuracy), I could only carry off a few very common-place mythological images, and one line about Artemisia, and another about Algiers, with sixty words of an entire tragedy about Eteocles and Polynices.[3] Some of the Italians liked him—others called his performance '*seccatura*'[4] (a devilish good word, by the way) and all Milan was in controversy about him.

The state of morals in these parts is in some sort lax. A mother and son were pointed out at the theatre, as being pronounced by the Milanese world to be of the Theban dynasty [5]— but this was all. The narrator (one of the first men in Milan) seemed to be not sufficiently scandalised by the taste or the tie. All society in Milan is carried on at the opera: they have private boxes, where they play at cards, or talk, or any thing else; but (except at the Cassino) there are no open houses, or balls, etc., etc. * * * * *

The peasant girls have all very fine dark eyes, and many of them are beautiful. There are also two dead bodies in fine preservation—one Saint Carlo Boromeo,[6] at Milan; the other not a saint, but a chief, named Visconti,[7] at Monza—both of which appeared very agreeable. In one of the Boromean isles (the Isola bella), there is a large laurel—the largest known—on which Buonaparte, staying there just before the battle of Marengo, carved with his knife the word 'Battaglia'. I saw the letters, now half worn out and partly erased.

Excuse this tedious letter. To be tiresome is the privilege of old age and absence; I avail myself of the latter, and the former I have anticipated. If I do not speak to you of my own affairs, it is not from want of confidence, but to spare you and myself. My day is over—what then?—I have had it. To be sure, I have shortened it; and if I had done as much by this letter, it would have been as well. But you will forgive that, if not the other faults of

Yours ever and most affectionately, B.

---

[1] Giuseppe Acerbi (1773–1846), who had lived and published in England.
[2] Probably Sgricchi (see Medwin's *Conversations*, pages 165–6).
[3] The twin sons of Œdipus and Jocasta.   [4] i.e. tedious stuff.
[5] Œdipus and Jocasta.
[6] Who died in 1584.   [7] Ettore Visconti, killed in 1413.

P.S.—November 7, 1816.

I have been over Verona. The amphitheatre is wonderful—beats even Greece. Of the truth of Juliet's story they seem tenacious to a degree, insisting on the fact—giving a date (1303), and showing a tomb. It is a plain, open, and partly decayed sarcophagus, with withered leaves in it, in a wild and desolate conventual garden, once a cemetery, now ruined to the very graves. The situation struck me as very appropriate to the legend, being blighted as their love. I have brought away a few pieces of the granite, to give to my daughter and my nieces. Of the other marvels of this city, paintings, antiquities, etc., excepting the tombs of the Scaliger princes, I have no pretensions to judge. The Gothic monuments of the Scaligers pleased me, but 'a poor virtuoso am I',[1] and ever yours.

94. TO JOHN MURRAY

Venice, November 25, 1816.

DEAR SIR,

It is some months since I have heard from or of you—I think, not since I left Diodati. From Milan I wrote once or twice; but have been here some little time, and intend to pass the winter without removing. I was much pleased with the Lago di Garda, and with Verona, particularly the amphitheatre, and a sarcophagus in a Convent garden, which they show as Juliet's: they insist on the *truth* of her history. Since my arrival at Venice, the lady of the Austrian governor [2] told me that between Verona and Vicenza there are still ruins of the castle of the *Montecchi*, and a chapel once appertaining to the Capulets. Romeo seems to have been of *Vicenza* by the tradition; but I was a good deal surprised to find so firm a faith in Bandello's novel, which seems really to have been founded on a fact.

Venice pleases me as much as I expected, and I expected much. It is one of those places which I know before I see them, and has always haunted me the most after the East. I like the gloomy gaiety of their gondolas, and the silence of their canals. I do not even dislike the evident decay of the city, though I regret the singularity of its vanished costume; however, there is much left still; the Carnival, too, is coming.

[1]
> '. . . I swear I can't love for antiquity's sake,
> Such a poor virtuoso am I.'
>
> Moore, *Little's Poems*, 'To Mrs. ——.

[2] Countess Goetz.

St. Mark's, and indeed Venice, is most alive at night. The theatres are not open till *nine*, and the society is proportionably late. All this is to my taste; but most of your countrymen miss and regret the rattle of hackney coaches, without which they can't sleep.

I have got remarkably good apartments in a private house:[1] I see something of the inhabitants (having had a good many letters to some of them); I have got my gondola; I read a little, and luckily could speak Italian (more fluently though than accurately) long ago. I am studying, out of curiosity, the *Venetian* dialect, which is very naïve, and soft, and peculiar, though not at all classical; I go out frequently, and am in very good contentment.

The *Helen* of Canova (a bust which is in the house of Madame the Countess d'Albrizzi,[2] whom I know) is, without exception, to my mind, the most perfectly beautiful of human conceptions, and far beyond my ideas of human execution.

> In this beloved marble view
>   Above the works and thoughts of Man,
> What Nature *could*, but *would not*, do,
>   And Beauty and Canova *can*!
> Beyond Imagination's power,
>   Beyond the Bard's defeated art,
> With Immortality her dower,
>   Behold the *Helen* of the *heart*!

Talking of the 'heart' reminds me that I have fallen in love, which, except falling into the Canal (and that would be useless as I can swim), is the best (or worst) thing I could do. I am therefore in love—fathomless love; but lest you should make some splendid mistake, and envy me the possession of some of those princesses or countesses with whose affections your English voyagers are apt to invest themselves, I beg leave to tell you, that my goddess is only the wife of a 'Merchant of Venice';[3] but then she is pretty as an Antelope, is but two-and-twenty years old, has the large, black, Oriental eyes, with the Italian countenance, and dark glossy hair, of the curl and colour of Lady Jersey's. Then she has the voice of a lute, and the song of a Seraph (though not quite so sacred), besides a long postscript of graces, virtues, and accomplishments, enough to furnish

---

[1] That of Segati, a draper, in the Frezzeria.
[2] Isabella Teotochi, Countess Albrizzi, at whose assemblies the most distinguished men of the day met.
[3] Marianna Segati.

out a new chapter for Solomon's Song. But her great merit is finding out mine—there is nothing so amiable as discernment. Our little arrangement is completed; the usual oaths having been taken, and every thing fulfilled according to the 'understood relations' [1] of such liaisons.

The general race of women appear to be handsome; but in Italy, as on almost all the Continent, the highest orders are by no means a well-looking generation, and indeed reckoned by their countrymen very much otherwise. Some are exceptions, but most of them as ugly as Virtue herself.

If you write, address to me here, *poste restante,* as I shall probably stay the winter over. I never see a newspaper, and know nothing of England, except in a letter now and then from my Sister. Of the MS. sent you I know nothing, except that you have received it, and are to publish it, etc., etc.: but when, where, and how, you leave me to guess. But it don't much matter.

I suppose you have a world of works passing through your process for next year? When does Moore's poem appear? I sent a letter for him, addressed to your care, the other day.

So Mr. Frere [2] is married; and you tell me in a former letter that he had 'nearly forgotten that he was so'. He is fortunate.

Yours ever, and very truly,

B.

95. TO THE HON. AUGUSTA LEIGH

My dearest Augusta,   Venice. Dec[r] 18th, 1816.

I have received one letter dated 19th Nov[r] I think (or rather earlier by a week or two perhaps), since my arrival in Venice, where it is my intention to remain probably till the Spring. The place pleases me. I have found some pleasing society—and the *romance* of the situation—and it's extraordinary appearance—together with all the associations we are accustomed to connect with Venice, have always had a charm for me, even before I arrived here; and I have not been disappointed in what I have seen.

I go every morning to the Armenian Convent [3] (of *friars not Nuns*—my child) to study the language, I mean the *Armenian* language, (for as you perhaps know—I am versed in the Italian which I speak with fluency rather than accuracy,) and if you ask me my reason for studying this out of the way language—

---

[1] *Macbeth,* III; iv, 124.
[2] John Hookham Frere, the diplomatist and author, married, on 12 September, Elizabeth Jemima, Dowager Countess of Erroll.
[3] The Armenian Mekhitarist Convent, on the island of St. Lazzaro.

I can only answer that it is Oriental and difficult, and employs me—which are—as you know my Eastern and difficult way of thinking—reasons sufficient. Then I have fallen in love with a very pretty Venetian of two and twenty, with great black eyes. She is married—and so am I—which is very much to the purpose. We have formed and sworn an eternal attachment, which has already lasted a lunar month, and I am more in love than ever, and so is the lady—at least she says so. She does not plague me (which is a wonder) and I verily believe we are one of the happiest—unlawful couples on this side of the Alps. She is very handsome, very Italian or rather Venetian, with something more of the Oriental cast of countenance; accomplished and musical after the manner of her nation. Her spouse is a very good kind of man who occupies himself elsewhere, and thus the world goes on here as elsewhere. This adventure came very opportunely to console me, for I was beginning to be 'like Sam Jennings very *unappy*' but at present —at least for a month past—I have been very tranquil, very loving, and have not so much embarrassed myself with the tortures of the last two years and that virtuous monster Miss Milbanke, who had nearly driven me out of my senses.— [curse her.] [1]

Hobhouse is gone to Rome with his brother and sister—but returns here in February: you will easily suppose that I was not disposed to stir from my present position.

I have not heard recently from England and wonder if Murray has published the po's sent to him; and I want to know if you don't think them very fine and all that—Goosey my love—don't they make you 'put finger in eye?'

You can have no idea of my thorough wretchedness from the day of my parting from you till nearly a month ago though I struggled against it with some strength. At present I am better—thank Heaven above—and woman beneath—and I will be a very good boy. Pray remember me to the babes, and tell me of little *Da*—who by the way—is a year old and a few days over.

My love to you all and to Aunt *Sophy*: [2] pray tell *her* in particular that I have consoled myself; and tell Hodgson that his prophecy is accomplished. He said—you remember—I should be in love with an Italian—so I am.—

ever dearest yrs.
B.

---

[1] Erased, probably by Mrs. Leigh.   [2] Sophia Byron (see page 3).

P.S.—I forgot to tell you—that the *Demoiselle* [1]—who returned to England from Geneva—went there to produce a new baby B., who is now about to make his appearance. [2] You wanted to hear some adventures—there are enough I think for one epistle.—Pray address direct to Venice—Poste Restante.

96. TO THE HON. AUGUSTA LEIGH

MY DEAREST AUGUSTA,   Venice, Decr 19th 1816.

I wrote to you a few days ago. Your letter of the 1st is arrived, and you have 'a *hope*' [3] for me, it seems: what '*hope*', child? my dearest Sis. I remember a methodist preacher who, on perceiving a profane grin on the faces of part of his congregation, exclaimed 'no *hopes* for them as *laughs*'. And thus it is with us: we laugh too much for hopes, and so even let them go. I am sick of sorrow, and must even content myself as well as I can: so here goes—I won't be woeful again if I can help it.

My letter to my moral Clytemnestra [4] required no answer, and I would rather have none. I was wretched enough when I wrote it, and had been so for many a long day and month: at present I am less so, for reasons explained in my late letter (a few days ago); and as I never pretend to be what I am not, you may tell her if you please that I am recovering, and the reason also if you like it.

I do not agree with you about Ada: [5] there was *equivocation* in the answer, and it shall be settled one way or the other. I wrote to Hanson to take proper steps to prevent such a removal of my daughter, and even the probability of it.

I have heard of Murray's squabble with one of his brethren, who is an impudent impostor, and should be trounced.

You do not say whether the *true po's* are out: I hope you like them.

You are right in saying that I like Venice: it is very much what you would imagine it, but I have no time just now for description. The Carnival is to begin in a week, and with it the mummery of masking.

I have not been out a great deal, but quite as much as I like. I am going out this evening in my *cloak* and *Gondola*—there are

[1] Claire Clairmont.
[2] A girl was born on 12 January, 1817, and named Allegra.
[3] Probably that religious feeling would influence him.
[4] Lady Byron.
[5] Hearing that it was intended to take the child abroad, he had written to forbid it.

two nice Mrs. Radcliffe [1] words for you. And then there is the place of St. Mark, and conversaziones, and various fooleries, besides many *nau*: indeed, every body is *nau*, so much so, that a lady with only *one lover* is not reckoned to have overstepped the modesty of marriage—that being a regular thing. Some have two, three, and so on to twenty, beyond which they don't account; but they generally begin by one. The husbands of course belong to any body's wives—but their own. . . .

The music here is famous, and there will be a whole tribe of singers and dancers during the Carnival, besides the usual theatres.

The Society here is something like our own, except that the women sit in a semicircle at one end of the room, and the men stand at the other.

I pass my mornings at the Armenian convent studying Armenian,—my evenings here and there. To-night I am going to the Countess Albrizzi's, one of the *noblesse*. I have also been at the Governor's, who is an Austrian, and whose wife, the Countess Goetz, appears to me in the little I have seen of her a very amiable and pleasing woman, with remarkably good manners, as many of the German women have.

There are no English here, except birds of passage, who stay a day and then go on to Florence or Rome.

I mean to remain here till Spring. When you write address *directly* here, as in your present letter.

Ever, dearest, yours,

B.

97. TO THOMAS MOORE

Venice, December 24, 1816.

I have taken a fit of writing to you, which portends postage— once from Verona—once from Venice, and again from Venice— *thrice* that is. For this you may thank yourself; for I heard that you complained of my silence—so, here goes for garrulity.

I trust that you received my other twain of letters. My 'way of life' [2] (or 'May of life', which is it, according to the commentators?)—my 'way of life' is fallen into great regularity. In the morning I go over in my gondola to babble Armenian with the friars of the convent of St. Lazarus, and to help one of them in correcting the English of an English and Armenian

---

[1] Ann Radcliffe (1764–1823), authoress of *The Mysteries of Udolpho*.
[2] *Macbeth*, v, iii, 22.

grammar which he is publishing. In the evenings I do one of many nothings—either at the theatres, or some of the conversaziones, which are like our routs, or rather worse, for the women sit in a semicircle by the lady of the mansion, and the men stand about the room. To be sure, there is one improvement upon ours—instead of lemonade with their ices, they hand about stiff *rum-punch—punch*, by my palate; and this they think *English*. I would not disabuse them of so agreeable an error,—'no, not for Venice'. [1]

Last night I was at the Count Governor's, which, of course, comprises the best society, and is very much like other gregarious meetings in every country,—as in ours,—except that, instead of the Bishop of Winchester, you have the Patriarch of Venice, and a motley crew of Austrians, Germans, noble Venetians, foreigners, and, if you see a quiz, you may be sure he is a Consul. Oh, by the way, I forgot, when I wrote from Verona, to tell you that at Milan I met with a countryman of yours—a Colonel [Fitzgerald], a very excellent, good-natured fellow, who knows and shows all about Milan, and is, as it were, a native there. He is particularly civil to strangers, and this is his history,—at least, an episode of it.

Six-and-twenty years ago, Col. [Fitzgerald], then an ensign, being in Italy, fell in love with the Marchesa [Castiglione], and she with him. The lady must be, at least, twenty years his senior. The war broke out; he returned to England, to serve —not his country, for that 's Ireland—but England, which is a different thing; and *she*—heaven knows what she did. In the year 1814, the first annunciation of the definitive treaty of peace (and tyranny) was developed to the astonished Milanese by the arrival of Col. [Fitzgerald], who, flinging himself full length at the feet of Madame [Castiglione], murmured forth, in half-forgotten Irish Italian, eternal vows of indelible constancy. The lady screamed, and exclaimed, 'Who are you?' The Colonel cried, 'What! don't you know me? I am so and so', etc. etc., etc.; till, at length, the Marchesa, mounting from reminiscence to reminiscence, through the lovers of the intermediate twenty-five years, arrived at last at the recollection of her *povero* sub-lieutenant. She then said, 'Was there ever such virtue?' (that was her very word) and, being now a widow, gave him apartments in her palace, reinstated him in all the rights of wrong, and held him up to the admiring world as a miracle of incontinent fidelity, and the unshaken Abdiel of absence.

[1] *Merchant of Venice*, IV, i, 230.

Methinks this is as pretty a moral tale as any of Marmontel's.[1] Here is another. The same lady, several years ago, made an escapade with a Swede, Count Fersen (the same whom the Stockholm mob quartered and lapidated not very long since), and they arrived at an Osteria on the road to Rome or thereabouts. It was a summer evening, and, while they were at supper, they were suddenly regaled by a symphony of fiddles in an adjacent apartment, so prettily played, that, wishing to hear them more distinctly, the Count rose, and going into the musical society, said, 'Gentlemen, I am sure that, as a company of gallant cavaliers, you will be delighted to show your skill to a lady, who feels anxious', etc., etc. The men of harmony were all acquiescence—every instrument was tuned and toned, and, striking up one of their most ambrosial airs, the whole band followed the Count to the lady's apartment. At their head was the first fiddler, who, bowing and fiddling at the same moment, headed his troop and advanced up the room. Death and discord!—it was the Marquis himself, who was on a serenading party in the country, while his spouse had run away from town. The rest may be imagined—but, first of all, the lady tried to persuade him that she was there on purpose to meet him, and had chosen this method for an harmonic surprise. So much for this gossip, which amused me when I heard it, and I send it to you in the hope it may have the like effect. Now we'll return to Venice.

The day after to-morrow (to-morrow being Christmas-day) the Carnival begins. I dine with the Countess Albrizzi and a party, and go to the opera. On that day the Phenix, (not the Insurance Office, but the theatre of that name) opens: I have got me a box there for the season, for two reasons, one of which is, that the music is remarkably good. The Contessa Albrizzi, of whom I have made mention, is the De Staël of Venice; not young, but a very learned, unaffected, good-natured woman; very polite to strangers, and, I believe, not at all dissolute, as most of the women are. She has written very well on the works of Canova, and also a volume of Characters,[2] besides other printed matter. She is of Corfu, but married a dead Venetian —that is, dead since he married.

My flame (my *Donna* whom I spoke of in my former epistle, my Marianna) is still my Marianna, and I her—what she pleases. She is by far the prettiest woman I have seen here, and the most lovable I have met with any where—as well as one of the

---

[1] Jean François Marmontel (1723–99), author of the *Contes Moraux*.
[2] *Opere di scultura e di plastica di A. Canova*, 1809; *Ritratti*, 1807.

most singular. I believe I told you the rise and progress of our *liaison* in my former letter. Lest that should not have reached you, I will merely repeat, that she is a Venetian, two-and-twenty years old, married to a merchant well to do in the world, and that she has great black oriental eyes, and all the qualities which her eyes promise. Whether being in love with her has steeled me or not, I do not know; but I have not seen many other women who seem pretty. The nobility, in particular, are a sad-looking race—the gentry rather better. And now, what art *thou* doing?

> What are you doing now,
>   Oh Thomas Moore?
> What are you doing now,
>   Oh Thomas Moore?
> Sighing or suing now,
> Rhyming or wooing now,
> Billing or cooing now,
>   Which, Thomas Moore?

Are you not near the Luddites?[1] By the Lord! if there's a row, but I'll be among ye! How go on the weavers—the breakers of frames—the Lutherans of politics—the reformers?

> As the Liberty lads o'er the sea
> Bought their freedom, and cheaply, with blood,
>   So we, boys, we
>   Will *die* fighting, or *live* free,
> And down with all kings but King Ludd!

> When the web that we weave is complete,
> And the shuttle exchanged for the sword,
>   We will fling the winding-sheet
>   O'er the despot at our feet,
> And dye it deep in the gore he has pour'd.

> Though black as his heart its hue,
> Since his veins are corrupted to mud,
>   Yet this is the dew
>   Which the tree shall renew
> Of Liberty, planted by Ludd!

There's an amiable *chanson* for you—all impromptu. I have

---

[1] Named after Ned Lud, a village boy who began the practice of smashing machinery.

written it principally to shock your neighbour * *[1] who is all clergy and loyalty—mirth and innocence—milk and water.

> But the Carnival 's coming,
> Oh Thomas Moore,
> The Carnival 's coming,
> Oh Thomas Moore;
> Masking and mumming,
> Fifing and drumming,
> Guitarring and strumming,
> Oh Thomas Moore.

The other night I saw a new play,—and the author. The subject was the sacrifice of Isaac. The play succeeded, and they called for the author—according to continental custom—and he presented himself, a noble Venetian, Mali—or Malapiero, by name. Mala was his name, and *pessima* his production,—at least, I thought so; and I ought to know, having read more or less of five hundred Drury Lane offerings, during my coadjutor-ship with the sub-and-super Committee.

When does your Poem of Poems come out? I hear that the E[dinburgh] R[eview] has cut up Coleridge's *Christabel*, and declared against me for praising it.[2] I praised it, firstly, because I thought well of it; secondly, because Coleridge was in great distress, and after doing what little I could for him in essentials, I thought that the public avowal of my good opinion might help him further, at least with the booksellers. I am very sorry that J[effrey] has attacked him, because, poor fellow, it will hurt him in mind and pocket. As for me, he 's welcome—I shall never think less of J[effrey] for any thing he may say against me or mine in future.

I suppose Murray has sent you, or will send (for I do not know whether they are out or no) the poem, or poesies, of mine, of last summer. By the mass! they 're sublime—*Ganion Coheriza* [3]—gainsay who dares! Pray, let me hear from you, and of you, and, at least, let me know that you have received these three letters. Direct right *here, poste restante*.

Ever and ever, etc.

P.S.—I heard the other day of a pretty trick of a bookseller,[4]

---

[1] Perhaps Francis Hodgson, who on 18 July had been appointed to the living of Bakewell, Derbyshire.

[2] He had called it 'a wild and singularly original and beautiful poem'.

[3] *Dhandeon co heirogha*, the motto of the Macdonalds of Clanranald.

[4] James Johnston. See page 128.

who has published some damned nonsense, swearing the bastards
to me, and saying he gave me five hundred guineas for them.
He lies—I never wrote such stuff, never saw the poems, nor the
publisher of them, in my life, nor had any communication,
directly or indirectly, with the fellow.   Pray say as much for
me, if need be. I have written to Murray, to make him contradict
the impostor.

98. TO JOHN MURRAY

Venice, Dec. 27, 1816.

DEAR SIR,

As the Demon of silence seems to have possessed you, I am
determined to have my revenge in postage. This is my sixth
or seventh letter since summer and Switzerland.   My last was
an injunction to contradict and consign to confusion that
Cheapside impostor,[1] who (I heard by a letter from your Island)
had thought proper to append my name to his spurious poesy,
of which I know nothing, nor of his pretended purchase or
copyright. I hope you have, at least, received *that* letter.

As the news of Venice must be very interesting to you, I will
regale you with it.

Yesterday being the feast of St. Stephen, every mouth was
put in motion.   There was nothing but fiddling and playing on
the virginals, and all kinds of conceits and divertisements, on
every canal of this aquatic city.   I dined with the Countess
Albrizzi and a Paduan and Venetian party, and afterwards went
to the opera, at the Fenice theatre (which opens for the Carnival
on that day)—the finest, by the way, I have ever seen; it beats
our theatres hollow in beauty and scenery, and those of Milan
and Brescia bow before it.   The opera and its Syrens were much
like all other operas and women, but the subject of the said
opera was something edifying; it turned—the plot and conduct
thereof—upon a fact narrated by Livy [2] of a hundred and fifty
married ladies having *poisoned* a hundred and fifty husbands in
the good old times.   The bachelors of Rome believed this
extraordinary mortality to be merely the common effect of
matrimony or a pestilence; but the surviving Benedicts, being
all seized with the cholic, examined into the matter, and found
that 'their possets had been drugged';[3] the consequence of

---

[1] An injunction restraining Johnston from publishing the spurious
poems was granted on 28 November.
[2] Book VIII, c. 18.   [3] *Macbeth*, II, ii, 7.

which was much scandal and several suits at law. This is really and truly the subject of the Musical piece at the Fenice; and you can't conceive what pretty things are sung and recitativoed about the *horrenda strage*. The conclusion was a lady's head about to be chopped off by a Lictor, but (I am sorry to say) he left it on, and she got up and sung a trio with the two Consuls, the Senate in the background being chorus. The ballet was distinguished by nothing remarkable, except that the principal she-dancer went into convulsions because she was not applauded on her first appearance; and the manager came forward to ask if there was 'ever a physician in the theatre'. There was a Greek one in my box, whom I wished very much to volunteer his services, being sure that in this case these would have been the last convulsions which would have troubled the *Ballerina*; but he would not. The crowd was enormous; and in coming out, having a lady under my arm, I was obliged, in making way, almost to 'beat a Venetian and traduce the state',[1] being compelled to regale a person with an English punch in the guts, which sent him as far back as the squeeze and the passage would admit. He did not ask for another; but, with great signs of disapprobation and dismay, appealed to his compatriots, who laughed at him.

I am going on with my Armenian studies in a morning, and assisting and stimulating in the English portion of an English and Armenian grammar, now publishing at the convent of St. Lazarus.

The Superior of the Friars is a bishop, and a fine old fellow, with the beard of a meteor. My spiritual preceptor, pastor and master, Father Paschal, is also a learned and pious soul: he was two years in England.

I am still dreadfully in love with the Adriatic lady[2] whom I spoke of in a former letter (and *not* in *this*—I add, for fear of mistakes; for the only one mentioned in the first part of this epistle is elderly and bookish, two things which I have ceased to admire), and love in this part of the world is no sinecure. This is also the season when every body make up their intrigues for the ensuing year, and cut for partners for the next deal.

And now, if you don't write, I don't know what I won't say or do, nor what I will: send me some news—good news.

Yours very truly, etc., etc., etc.

B.

---

[1] *Othello*, v, ii, 353.　　　　[2] Marianna Segati.

P.S.—Remember me to Mr. G[ifford], with all duty.

I hear that the E[dinburgh] R[eview] has cut up Coleridge's *Christabel*, and me for praising it, which omen, I think, bodes no great good to your forthcome or coming Canto [1] and Castle (of Chillon): my run of luck within the last year seems to have taken a turn every way; but never mind, I will bring myself through in the end—if not, I can but be where I began: in the mean time, I am not displeased to be where I am—I mean, at Venice. My Adriatic nymph is this moment here, and I must therefore repose from this letter, 'rocked by the beating of her heart'.[2]

99. TO JOHN MURRAY

Venice, Jan. 2, 1817.

DEAR SIR,

Your letter has arrived. Pray, in publishing the 3d canto, have you *omitted* any passage or passages? I hope *not*; and indeed wrote to you on my way over the Alps to prevent such an accident—say in your next whether or not the *whole* of the canto (as sent to you) has been published. I wrote to you again the other day, (*twice*, I think), and shall be glad to hear of the reception of those letters.

To-day is the 2d of January. On this day *3* years ago *The Corsair's* publication is dated, I think, in my letter to Moore. On this day *two* years I married—'Whom the Lord loveth he chasteneth—blessed be the name of the Lord.'—I shan't forget the day in a hurry, and will take care to keep the Anniversary before the Evening is over. It is odd enough that I this day received a letter from you announcing the publication of *Cd. Hd.*, etc., etc., on the day of the date of *The Corsair*; and that I also received one from my Sister, written on the 10th of Decr., my daughter's birth-day (and relative chiefly to my daughter), and arriving on the day of the date of my marriage, this present 2d of January, the month of my birth,—and various other Astrologous matters, which I have no time to enumerate.

By the way, you might as well write to Hentsch, my Genevese banker, and enquire whether the *two packets* consigned to his care were or were not delivered to Mr. St. Aubyn, or if they are still in his keeping. One contains papers, letters, and all the

---

[1] Canto III of *Childe Harold*, published in November.
[2] From the translation of the twelfth Love Epistle of Aristænetus, attributed by Moore to Sheridan, l. 42; see also *Venus and Adonis*, 1185-6.

original MS. of your 3ᵈ canto, as first conceived; and the other, some bones from the field of Morat.¹ Many thanks for your news, and the good spirits in which your letter is written.

Venice and I agree very well; but I do not know that I have any thing new to say, except of the last new opera, which I sent in my late letter. The Carnival is commencing, and there is a good deal of fun here and there—besides business; for all the world are making up their intrigues for the season—changing, or going on upon a renewed lease. I am very well off with Marianna, who is not at all a person to tire me; firstly, because I do not tire of a woman *personally*, but because they are generally bores in their disposition; and, secondly, because she is amiable, and has a tact which is not always the portion of the fair creation; and, thirdly, she is very pretty; and, fourthly— but there is no occasion for further specification. I have passed a great deal of my time with her since my arrival at Venice, * * . . . * * * * * So far we have gone on very well; as to the future, I never anticipate—'*Carpe diem*'—the past at least is one's own, which is one reason for making sure of the present. So much for my proper liaison.

The general state of morals here is much the same as in the Doges' time; a woman is virtuous (according to the code) who limits herself to her husband and one lover; those who have two, three, or more, are a little *wild*; but it is only those who are indiscriminately diffuse, and form a low connection, such as the Princess of Wales with her courier,² (who, by the way, is made a knight of Malta,) who are considered as overstepping the modesty of marriage. In Venice, the Nobility have a trick of marrying with dancers or singers: and, truth to say, the women of their own order are by no means handsome; but the general race- the women of the 2ᵈ and other orders, the wives of the Advocates, merchants, and proprietors, and untitled gentry, are mostly *bel' sangue*, and it is with these that the more amatory connections are usually formed: there are also instances of stupendous constancy. I know a woman of fifty who never had but one lover, who dying early, she became devout, renouncing all but her husband: she piques herself, as may be presumed, upon this miraculous fidelity, talking of it occasionally with a species of misplaced morality, which is rather amusing. There is no convincing woman here, that she is in

¹ Where the Swiss defeated Charles the Bold, Duke of Burgundy, in 1476.
² Caroline, who had left England in 1814, was in 1820 accused of adultery with Bartolommeo Bergami, her courier.

the smallest degree deviating from the rule of right or the fitness of things, in having an *Amoroso*: the great sin seems to lie in concealing it, or in having more than one; that is, unless such an extension of the prerogative is understood and approved of by the prior claimant.

In my case, I do not know that I had any predecessor, and am pretty sure that there is no participator; and am inclined to think, from the youth of the party, and from the frank undisguised way in which every body avows everything in this part of the world, when there is anything to avow, as well as from some other circumstances, such as the marriage being recent, etc., etc., etc., that this is the *premier pas*: it does not much signify.

In another sheet, I send you some sheets of a grammar, English and Armenian, for the use of the Armenians, of which I promoted, and indeed induced, the publication: (it cost me but a thousand francs—French livres.) I still pursue my lessons in the language, without any rapid progress, but advancing a little daily. Padre Paschal, with some little help from me, as translator of his Italian into English, is also proceeding in an MS. Grammar for the *English* acquisition of Armenian, which will be printed also, when finished.

We want to know if there are any *Armenian types* or letter-press in England—at Oxford, Cambridge, or elsewhere? You know, I suppose, that, many years ago, the two Whistons published in England an original text of a history of Armenia, with their own Latin translation? Do those types still exist? and where? Pray enquire among your learned acquaintance.

When this grammar (I mean the one now printing) is done, will you have any objection to take 40 or fifty copies, which will not cost in all above five or ten guineas, and try the curiosity of the learned with a sale of them? Say yes or no, as you like. I can assure you that they have some very curious books and MS., chiefly translations from Greek originals now lost. They are, besides, a much respected and learned community, and the study of their language was taken up with great ardour by some literary Frenchmen in Buonaparte's time.

I have not done a stitch of poetry since I left Switzerland, and have not, at present, the *estro* upon me: the truth is, that you are *afraid* of having a *4th* canto *before* September, and of another copyright; but I have at present no thoughts of resuming that poem nor of beginning any other. If I write, I think of trying prose; but I dread introducing living people, or applications which might be made to living people: perhaps one day or other, I may attempt some work of fancy in prose, descriptive of Italian manners and of human passions; but at present I am preoccupied. As for poesy, mine is the *dream* of my sleeping Passions; when they are awake, I cannot speak their language, only in their Somnambulism, and just now they are not dormant.

If Mr. G[ifford] wants *carte blanche* as to *The Siege of Corinth*, he has it, and may do as he likes with it.

I sent you a letter contradictory of the Cheapside man (who invented the story you speak of) the other day. My best respects to Mr. Gifford, and such of my friends as you may see at your house. I wish you all prosperity and new year's gratulation, and am

Yours, ever and truly,

B.

100. TO THOMAS MOORE

Venice, January 28, 1817.

Your letter of the 8th is before me. The remedy for your plethora is simple—abstinence. I was obliged to have recourse to the like some years ago, I mean in point of *diet*, and, with the exception of some convivial weeks and days, (it might be months, now and then), have kept to Pythagoras ever since. For all this, let me hear that you are better. You must not *indulge* in 'filthy beer', nor in porter, nor eat *suppers*—the last are the devil to those who swallow dinner. * * * *

I am truly sorry to hear of your father's misfortune [1]—cruel at any time, but doubly cruel in advanced life. However, you will, at least, have the satisfaction of doing your part by him, and, depend upon it, it will not be in vain. Fortune, to be sure, is a female, but not such a b * * as the rest (always excepting your wife and my sister from such sweeping terms); for she generally has some justice in the long run. I have no spite against her, though between her and Nemesis I have had some sore gauntlets to run—but then I have done my best to deserve no better. But to *you*, she is a good deal in arrear, and she will come round—mind if she don't: you have the vigour of life, of independence, of talent, spirit, and character all with you. What you can do for yourself, you have done and will do; and surely there are some others in the world who would not be sorry to be of use, if you would allow them to be useful, or at least attempt it.

[1] John Moore had lost his post of barrack-master in Dublin.

I think of being in England in the spring. If there is a row, by the sceptre of King Ludd, but I 'll be one; and if there is none, and only a continuance of 'this meek, piping time of peace',[1] I will take a cottage a hundred yards to the south of your abode, and become your neighbour; and we will compose such canticles, and hold such dialogues, as shall be the terror of the *Times* (including the newspaper of that name), and the wonder, and honour, and praise, of the *Morning Chronicle* and posterity.

I rejoice to hear of your forthcoming in February—though I tremble for the 'magnificence' which you attribute to the new *Childe Harold*. I am glad you like it; it is a fine indistinct piece of poetical desolation, and my favourite. I was half mad during the time of its composition, between metaphysics, mountains, lakes, love unextinguishable, thoughts unutterable, and the nightmare of my own delinquencies. I should, many a good day, have blown my brains out, but for the recollection that it would have given pleasure to my mother-in-law; and, even *then*, if I could have been certain to haunt her —— but I won't dwell upon these trifling family matters.

Venice is in the *estro* of her carnival, and I have been up these last two nights at the ridotto [2] and the opera, and all that kind of thing. Now for an adventure. A few days ago a gondolier brought me a billet without a subscription, intimating a wish on the part of the writer to meet me either in gondola or at the island of San Lazaro, or at a third rendezvous, indicated in the note. 'I know the country's disposition well; — in Venice they do let Heaven see those tricks they dare not show',[3] etc., etc.; so, for all response, I said that neither of the three places suited me; but that I would either be at home at ten at night *alone*, or be at the ridotto at midnight, where the writer might meet me masked. At ten o'clock I was at home and alone (Marianna was gone with her husband to a conversazione), when the door of my apartment opened, and in walked a well-looking and (for an Italian) *bionda* girl of about nineteen, who informed me that she was married to the brother of my *amorosa*, and wished to have some conversation with me. I made a decent reply, and we had some talk in Italian and Romaic (her mother being a Greek of Corfu), when lo! in a very few minutes in marches, to my very great astonishment, Marianna Segati, *in propriâ personâ*, and after making a most polite curtsy

---

[1] *Richard III*, I, i, 24.   [2] Masked ball.
[3] *Othello*, III, iii, 201-3.

to her sister-in-law and to me, without a single word seizes her said sister-in-law by the hair, and bestows upon her some sixteen slaps, which would have made your ear ache only to hear their echo. I need not describe the screaming which ensued. The luckless visitor took flight. I seized Marianna, who, after several vain efforts to get away in pursuit of the enemy, fairly went into fits in my arms; and, in spite of reasoning, eau de Cologne, vinegar, half a pint of water, and God knows what other waters beside, continued so till past midnight.

After damning my servants for letting people in without apprizing me, I found that Marianna in the morning had seen her sister-in-law's gondolier on the stairs, and, suspecting that his apparition boded her no good, had either returned of her own accord, or been followed by her maids or some other spy of her people to the conversazione, from whence she returned to perpetrate this piece of pugilism. I had seen fits before, and also some small scenery of the same genus in and out of our island: but this was not all. After about an hour, in comes— who? why, Signor Segati, her lord and husband, and finds me with his wife fainting upon a sofa, and all the apparatus of confusion, dishevelled hair, hats, handkerchiefs, salts, smelling-bottles—and the lady as pale as ashes, without sense or motion. His first question was, 'What is all this?' The lady could not reply—so I did. I told him the explanation was the easiest thing in the world; but in the mean time it would be as well to recover his wife—at least, her senses. This came about in due time of suspiration and respiration.

You need not be alarmed—jealousy is not the order of the day in Venice, and daggers are out of fashion; while duels, on love matters, are unknown—at least, with the husbands. But, for all this, it was an awkward affair; and though he must have known that I made love to Marianna, yet I believe he was not, till that evening, aware of the extent to which it had gone. It is very well known that almost all the married women have a lover; but it is usual to keep up the forms, as in other nations. I did not, therefore, know what the devil to say. I could not out with the truth, out of regard to her, and I did not choose to lie for my sake;—besides, the thing told itself. I thought the best way would be to let her explain it as she chose (a woman being never at a loss—the devil always sticks by them)—only determining to protect and carry her off, in case of any ferocity on the part of the Signor. I saw that he was quite calm. She went to bed, and next day—how they settled it, I know not, but settle it they did.   Well—then I had to explain to Marianna about   this   never-to-be-sufficiently-confounded   sister-in-law; which I did by swearing innocence, eternal constancy, etc., etc. * * * But the sister-in-law, very much discomposed with being treated in such wise, has (not having her own shame before her eyes) told the affair to half Venice, and the servants (who were summoned by the fight and the fainting) to the other half. But, here, nobody minds such trifles, except to be amused by them.   I don't know whether you will be so, but I have scrawled a long letter out of these follies.

Believe me ever, etc.

101. TO THE HON. AUGUSTA LEIGH

Venice, February 25th, 1817.

DEAREST AUGUSTA,

I believe you have received all my letters, for I sent you no description of Venice, beyond a slight sketch in a letter which I perceive has arrived, because you mention the 'Canal, etc.', that was the longest letter I have written to you from this city of the seventy islands.

Instead of a description of the lady [1] whom Aunt Sophy wants to have described, I will show you her picture, which is just finished for me, some of these days or other.   The Carnival is over, but I am not in a descriptive mood, and will reserve all my wonders for word of mouth, when I see you again.   I have nothing which would make you laugh much, except a battle some weeks ago in my apartment, between two of the fair 'sect' (sisters in law) which ended in the flight of one and the fits of the other, and a great deal of confusion and eau de Cologne, and asterisks, and all that.   The cause was—one paying me an evening visit.   The other was gone out to a Conversazione, as was supposed for the evening, but lo and behold, in about half an hour she returned and entering my room, without a word, administered (before I could prevent her) about sixteen such slaps to her relation, as would have made your ear ache only to hear them.   The assaulted lady screamed and ran away, the assailant attempted pursuit, but being prevented by me, fairly went into asterisks, which cost a world of water of all sorts, besides fine speeches to appease, and even then she declared herself a very ill used person, although victorious over a much

[1] Marianna Segati.

taller woman than herself. Besides she wronged my innocence, for nothing could be more innocent than my colloquy with the other. You may tell this to Sophy if she wants amusement. I repeat (as in my former letter) that I really and truly know nothing of P. P.[1]

I have published nothing but what you know already.

I am glad to hear of Ada's progress in her mother tongue, I hope you will see her again soon. What you 'hope' may be, I do not know, if you mean a reunion between Lady B. and me, it is too late. It is now a year, and I have repeatedly offered to make it up, with what success you know. At present if she would rejoin me to-morrow, *I* would not accept the proposition. I have no spirit of hatred against her, however, I am too sensitive not to feel injuries, but far too proud to be vindictive. She's a fool, and when you have said that, it is the most that can be said for her.

ever very truly yrs.,

B.

102. TO THOMAS MOORE

Venice, February 28, 1817.

You will, perhaps, complain as much of the frequency of my letters now, as you were wont to do of their rarity. I think this is the fourth within as many moons. I feel anxious to hear from you, even more than usual, because your last indicated that you were unwell. At present, I am on the invalid regimen myself. The Carnival—that is, the latter part of it, and sitting up late o' nights, had knocked me up a little. But it is over— and it is now Lent, with all its abstinence and sacred music.

The mumming closed with a masked ball at the Fenice, where I went, as also to most of the ridottos, etc., etc.; and, though I did not dissipate much upon the whole, yet I find 'the sword wearing out the scabbard',[2] though I have but just turned the corner of twenty-nine.

So we'll go no more a roving
So late into the night,
Though the heart be still as loving,
And the moon be still as bright.

[1] *The Tales of my Landlord*, which began to appear in December 1816, were assigned to 'Peter, or Patrick, Pattieson', whom Mrs. Leigh believed to be Byron.

[2] 'La lame use le fourreau.'

> For the sword outwears its sheath,
>   And the soul wears out the breast,
> And the heart must pause to breathe,
>   And Love itself have rest.
>
> Though the night was made for loving,
>   And the day returns too soon,
> Yet we 'll go no more a roving
>   By the light of the moon.

I have lately had some news of litter*atoor*, as I heard the editor of the *Monthly* [1] pronounce it once upon a time. I hear that W. W. [2] has been publishing and responding to the attacks of the *Quarterly*, in the learned Perry's *Chronicle*. I read his poesies [3] last autumn, and amongst them found an epitaph on his bull-dog, and another on *myself*. But I beg leave to assure him (like the astrologer Partridge [4]) that I am not only alive now, but was alive also at the time he wrote it. * * Hobhouse has (I hear, also) expectorated a letter against the *Quarterly*, addressed to me. I feel awkwardly situated between him and Gifford, both being my friends.

And this is your month of going to press—by the body of Diana! (a Venetian oath,) I feel as anxious—but not fearful for you—as if it were myself coming out in a work of humour, which would, you know, be the antipodes of all my previous publications. I don't think you have any thing to dread but your own reputation. You must keep up to that. As you never showed me a line of your work, I do not even know your measure; but you must send me a copy by Murray forthwith, and then you shall hear what I think. I dare say you are in a pucker. Of all authors, you are the only really *modest* one I ever met with,—which would sound oddly enough to those who recollect your morals when you were young—that is, when you were *extremely* young—I don't mean to stigmatize you either with years or morality.

I believe I told you that the *E[dinburgh]* *R[eview]* had attacked me, in an article on Coleridge (I have not seen it)—'*Et tu*, Jeffrey?'—'there is nothing but roguery in villanous man'.[5] But I absolve him of all attacks, present and future; for I think he had already pushed his clemency in my behoof to the

---

[1] G. E. Griffiths.   [2] Wedderburn Webster.

[3] *Waterloo and other Poems*, 1816, in which were some 'Lines on Lord B——n's Portrait'.

[4] John Partridge, the victim of Swift's elaborate practical joke in 1708.

[5] *Henry IV*, Part I, ii, iv, 137.

utmost, and I shall always think well of him. I only wonder he did not begin before, as my domestic destruction was a fine opening for all the world, of which all who could did well to avail themselves.

If I live ten years longer, you will see, however, that it is not over with me—I don't mean in literature, for that is nothing; and it may seem odd enough to say, I do not think it my vocation. But you will see that I shall do something or other—the times and fortune permitting—that, 'like the cosmogony, or creation of the world, will puzzle the philosophers of all ages'.[1] But I doubt whether my constitution will hold out. I have, at intervals, exorcised it most devilishly.

I have not yet fixed a time of return, but I think of the spring. I shall have been away a year in April next. You never mention Rogers, nor Hodgson, your clerical neighbour, who has lately got a living near you. Has he also got a child yet?—his desideratum, when I saw him last. * * *

Pray let me hear from you, at your time and leisure, believing me ever and truly and affectionately, etc.

103. TO LADY BYRON

Venice, March 5th 1817.

A letter from Mr. Hanson apprizes me of the result of his correspondence with Sir Ralph Noel (of which he has transmitted a copy), and of his interviews with Dr. Lushington[2] on the subject of our daughter. I am also informed of a bill in Chancery[3] filed against me last Spring by Sir Ralph Noel, of which this is the first intimation, and of the subject of which I am ignorant.

Whatever may be the result of these discussions and the measures, which have led to them, and to which they may lead, remember, that I have not been the first to begin; but, being begun, neither shall I be the first to recede. I feel at length convinced that the feeling which I had cherished through all and in spite of all, namely—the hope of a reconciliation and reunion, however remote,—is indubitably useless; and although, all things considered, it could not be very sanguine, still it was sincere, and I cherished it as a sickly infatuation: and now I part with it with a regret, perhaps bitterer of [than] that which I felt in parting with yourself.

[1] *The Vicar of Wakefield*, chap. xiv.
[2] Dr. Stephen Lushington, the lawyer who advised the separation.
[3] The purpose of which was to make Ada a ward in Chancery.

It was generally understood, if not expressed, that all legal proceedings were to terminate in the act of our separation: to what then I am to attribute the bill, of which I am apprized, I am at a loss to conjecture. The object, however, is evident: it is to deprive me of my paternal right over my child, which I have the less merited, as I neither abused nor intended to abuse it. You and yours might have been satisfied with the outrages I have already suffered, if not by your design, at least by your means. I know your defence and your apology—duty and Justice; but *Qui n'est que juste, est dur*: or if the French aphorism should seem light in the balance, I could refer you to an older language and a higher authority for the condemnation of conduct, which you may yet live to condemn in your own heart.

Throughout the whole of this unhappy business, I have done my best to avoid the bitterness, which, however, is yet amongst us; and it would be as well if even you at times recollected, that the man who has been sacrificed in fame, in feelings, in every thing, to the convenience of your family, was he whom you once loved, and who—whatever you may imagine to the contrary—loved you. If you conceive that I could be actuated by revenge against you, you are mistaken: I am not humble enough to be vindictive. Irritated I may have been, and may be—is it a wonder? but upon such irritation, beyond its momentary expression, I have not acted, from the hour that you quitted me to that in which I am made aware that our daughter is to be the entail of our disunion, the inheritor of our bitterness. If you think to reconcile yourself to yourself by accumulating harshness against me, you are again mistaken: you are not happy, nor even tranquil, nor will you ever be so, even to the very moderate degree which is permitted to general humanity. For myself, I have a confidence in my Fortune, which will yet bear me through. *Ταὐτόματον ἡμῶν κάλλιον βουλεύεται.*[1] The reverses, which have occurred, were what I should have expected; and, in considering you and yours merely as the instruments of my more recent adversity, it would be difficult for me to blame you, did not every thing appear to intimate a deliberate intention of as wilful malice on your part as could well be digested into a system. However, time and Nemesis will do that, which I would not, even were it in my power remote or immediate. You will smile at this piece of prophecy—do

[1] 'Chance arranges things better than we do.'—Menander, *Monostichoi*, 726.

so, but recollect it: it is justified by all human experience. No one was ever even the involuntary cause of great evils to others, without a requital: I have paid and am paying for mine—so will you.

104. TO THOMAS MOORE

Venice, March 10, 1817.

I wrote again to you lately, but I hope you won't be sorry to have another epistle. I have been unwell this last month, with a kind of slow and low fever, which fixes upon me at night, and goes off in the morning; but, however, I am now better. In spring it is probable we may meet; at least I intend for England, where I have business, and hope to meet you in *your* restored health and additional laurels.

Murray has sent me the *Quarterly* and the *Edinburgh*.[1] When I tell you that Walter Scott is the author of the article in the former, you will agree with me that such an article is still more honourable to him than to myself. I am perfectly pleased with Jeffrey's also, which I wish you to tell him, with my remembrances—not that I suppose it is of any consequence to him, or ever could have been, whether I am pleased or not,—but simply in my private relation to him, as his well-wisher, and it may be one day as his acquaintance. I wish you would also add, what you know, that I was not, and, indeed, am not even *now*, the misanthropical and gloomy gentleman he takes me for, but a facetious companion, well to do with those with whom I am intimate, and as loquacious and laughing as if I were a much cleverer fellow.

I suppose now I shall never be able to shake off my sables in public imagination, more particularly since my moral * * [Clytemnestra?] clove down my fame. However, nor that, nor more than that, has yet extinguished my spirit, which always rises with the rebound.

At Venice we are in Lent, and I have not lately moved out of doors, my feverishness requiring quiet, and—by way of being more quiet—here is the Signora Marianna just come in and seated at my elbow.

Have you seen * * *'s book of poesy? and, if you have seen it, are you not delighted with it? And have you—I really cannot go on. There is a pair of great black eyes looking over my shoulder, like the angel leaning over St. Matthew's, in the

---

[1] Containing reviews of the Third Canto of *Childe Harold*.

old frontispieces to the Evangelists,—so that I must turn and answer them instead of you.

Ever, etc.

105. TO THOMAS MOORE

Venice, March 25, 1817.

I have at last learned, in default of your own writing (or *not* writing—which should it be? for I am not very clear as to the application of the word *default*), from Murray two particulars of (or belonging to) you; one, that you are removing to Hornsey, which is, I presume, to be nearer London; and the other, that your poem is announced by the name of *Lalla Rookh*. I am glad of it,—first that we are to have it at last, and next, I like a tough title myself—witness *The Giaour* and *Childe Harold*, which choked half the Blues [1] at starting. Besides, it is the tail of Alcibiades's dog,[2]—not that I suppose you want either dog or tail. Talking of tail, I wish you had not called it a '*Persian Tale*'.[3] Say a 'Poem', or 'Romance', but not 'Tale'. I am very sorry that I called some of my own things 'Tales', because I think that they are something better. Besides, we have had Arabian, and Hindoo, and Turkish, and Assyrian Tales. But, after all, this is frivolous in me; you won't, however, mind my nonsense.

Really and truly, I want you to make a great hit, if only out of self-love, because we happen to be old cronies; and I have no doubt you will—I am sure you *can*. But you are, I'll be sworn, in a devil of a pucker; and *I* am *not* at your elbow, and Rogers *is*. I envy him; which is not fair, because he does not envy any body. Mind you send to me—that is, make Murray send—the moment you are forth.

I have been very ill with a slow fever, which at last took to flying, and became as quick as need be. But, at length, after a week of half-delirium, burning skin, thirst, hot headache, horrible pulsation, and no sleep, by the blessing of barley water, and refusing to see any physician, I recovered. It is an epidemic of the place, which is annual, and visits strangers. Here follow some versicles, which I made one sleepless night.

I read the 'Christabel',[4]
Very well:

[1] i.e. bluestockings. Assemblies of literary ladies first became popular in England in 1750.
[2] i.e. the chief beauty. (See North's *Plutarch*.)
[3] An 'Oriental Romance' was Moore's actual title.
[4] By Coleridge. See page 110.

I read the 'Missionary'; [1]
  Pretty—very:
I tried at 'Ilderim'; [2]
  Ahem!
I read a sheet of 'Marg'ret of *Anjou*'; [3]
  Can you?
I turn'd a page of Webster's 'Waterloo'; [4]
  Pooh! pooh!
I look'd at Wordsworth's milk-white 'Rylstone Doe': [5]
  Hillo!
I read 'Glenarvon', too, by Caro. Lamb [6]—
  God damn!

I have not the least idea where I am going, nor what I am to do. I wished to have gone to Rome; but at present it is pestilent with English—a parcel of staring boobies, who go about gaping and wishing to be at once cheap and magnificent. A man is a fool who travels now in France or Italy, till this tribe of wretches is swept home again. In two or three years the first rush will be over, and the Continent will be roomy and agreeable.

I stayed at Venice chiefly because it is not one of their 'dens of thieves'; and here they but pause and pass. In Switzerland it was really noxious. Luckily, I was early, and had got the prettiest place on all the Lake before they were quickened into motion with the rest of the reptiles. But they crossed me every where. I met a family of children and old women half-way up the Wengen Alp (by the Jungfrau) upon mules, some of them too old and others too young to be the least aware of what they saw.

By the way, I think the Jungfrau, and all that region of Alps, which I traversed in September—going to the very top of the Wengen, which is not the highest (the Jungfrau itself is inaccessible) but the best point of view—much finer than Mont-Blanc and Chamouni, or the Simplon. I kept a journal of the whole for my sister Augusta, part of which she copied and let Murray see.

---

[1] *The Missionary of the Andes, a Poem*, by W. L. Bowles, 1815.
[2] *Ilderim, a Syrian Tale*, by H. Gally Knight, 1816.
[3] *Margaret of Anjou, a Poem*, by Margaret Holford, 1816.
[4] See page 158.
[5] *The White Doe of Rylstone, or the Fate of the Nortons, a Poem*, by W. Wordsworth, 1815.
[6] See page 129.

I wrote a sort of mad Drama,[1] for the sake of introducing the Alpine scenery in description: and this I sent lately to Murray. Almost all the *dram. pers.* are spirits, ghosts, or magicians, and the scene is in the Alps and the other world, so you may suppose what a Bedlam tragedy it must be: make him show it you. I sent him all three acts piecemeal, by the post, and suppose they have arrived.

I have now written to you at least six letters, or letter*ets*, and all I have received in return is a note about the length you used to write from Bury Street to St. James's Street, when we used to dine with Rogers, and talk laxly, and go to parties, and hear poor Sheridan now and then. Do you remember one night he was so tipsy, that I was forced to put his cocked hat on for him,—for he could not,—and I let him down at Brookes's, much as he must since have been let down into his grave. Heigh ho! I wish I was drunk—but I have nothing but this damned barley-water before me.

I am still in love,—which is a dreadful drawback in quitting a place, and I can't stay at Venice much longer. What I shall do on this point I don't know. The girl means to go with me, but I do not like this for her own sake. I have had so many conflicts in my own mind on this subject, that I am not at all sure they did not help me to the fever I mentioned above. I am certainly very much attached to her, and I have cause to be so, if you knew all. But she has a child; and though, like all the 'children of the sun'[2], she consults nothing but passion, it is necessary I should think for both; and it is only the virtuous, like * * * *, who can afford to give up husband and child, and live happy ever after.

The Italian ethics are the most singular ever met with. The perversion, not only of action, but of reasoning, is singular in the women. It is not that they do not consider the thing itself as wrong, and very wrong, but *love* (the *sentiment* of love) is not merely an excuse for it, but makes it an *actual virtue*, provided it is disinterested, and not a *caprice*, and is confined to one object. They have awful notions of constancy; for I have seen some ancient figures of eighty pointed out as *Amorosi* of forty, fifty, and sixty years' standing. I can't say I have ever seen a husband and wife so coupled.

Ever, etc.

P.S.—Marianna, to whom I have just translated what I

---

[1] *Manfred*, which was published in June 1817.
[2] Young, *The Revenge*, v, ii.

have written on our subject to you, says—'If you loved me thoroughly, you would not make so many fine reflections, which are only good *forbirsi i scarpi*',—that is, 'to clean shoes withal',—— a Venetian proverb of appreciation, which is applicable to reasoning of all kinds.

106. TO JOHN MURRAY

Venice, April 9, 1817.

DEAR SIR,

Your letters of the 18th and 20th are arrived. In my own I have given you the rise, progress, decline, and fall of my recent malady. It is *gone* to the Devil: I won't pay him so bad a compliment as to say it *came* from him;—*he* is too much of a Gentleman. It was nothing but a slow fever, which quickened its pace towards the end of its journey. I had been bored with it some weeks—with nocturnal burnings and morning perspirations; but I am quite well again, which I attribute to having had neither medicine nor Doctor thereof.

In a few days I set off for Rome: such is my purpose. I shall change it very often before Monday next, but do you continue to direct and address to *Venice*, as heretofore. If I go, letters will be forwarded: I say '*if*', because I never know what I shall do till it is done; and as I mean most firmly to set out for Rome, it is not unlikely I may find myself at St. Petersburg.

You tell me to 'take care of myself';—faith, and I will. I won't be posthumous yet, if I can help it. Notwithstanding, only think what a 'Life and Adventures', while I am in full scandal, would be worth, together with the *membra* of my writing-desk, the sixteen beginnings of poems never to be finished! Do you think I would not have shot myself last year, had I not luckily recollected that Mrs. Clermont,[1] and Lady Noel, and all the old women in England would have been delighted;—besides the agreeable 'Lunacy', of the 'Crowner's Quest', and the regrets of two or three or half a dozen? Be assured that I *would live* for two reasons, or more;—there are one or two people whom I have to put out of the world, and as many into it, before I can 'depart in peace'; if I do so before, I have not fulfilled my mission. Besides, when I turn thirty, I will turn devout; I feel a great vocation that way in Catholic churches, and when I hear the organ.

[1] See page 120.

So Webster is writing again![1] Is there no Bedlam in Scotland? nor thumb-screw? nor gag? nor handcuff? I went upon my knees to him almost, some years ago, to prevent him from publishing a political pamphlet, which would have given him a livelier idea of 'Habeas Corpus' than the world will derive from his present production upon that suspended subject, which will doubtless be followed by the suspension of other (his Majesty's) subjects.

I condole with Drury Lane, and rejoice with Sotheby,—that is, in a modest way,—on the tragical end of the new tragedy.[2]

You and Leigh Hunt have quarrelled then, it seems? I introduce him and his poem [3] to you, in the hope that (malgré politics) the union would be beneficial to both, and the end is eternal enmity; and yet I did this with the best intentions: I introduce Coleridge and Christabel, and Coleridge runs away with your money; my friend Hobhouse quarrels, too, with the Quarterly: and (except the last) I am the innocent Istmhus (damn the word! I can't spell it, though I have crossed that of Corinth a dozen times) of these enmities.

I will tell you something about Chillon.—A Mr. De Luc, ninety years old, a Swiss, had it read to him, and is pleased with it,—so my sister writes. He said that he was with Rousseau at Chillon, and that the description is perfectly correct. But this is not all: I recollected something of the name, and find the following passage in The Confessions, vol. 3, page 247, liv. 8th:—

'De tous ces amusemens celui qui me plût davantage fut une promenade autour du Lac, que je fis en bateau avec De Luc père, sa bru, ses deux fils, et ma Thérèse. Nous mîmes sept jours à cette tournée par le plus beau temps du monde. J'en gardai le vif souvenir des sites qui m'avoient frappé à l'autre extrémité du Lac, et dont je fis la description, quelques années après, dans la Nouvelle Héloïse.'

This nonagenarian, De Luc, must be one of the deux fils. He is in England—infirm, but still in faculty. It is odd that he should have lived so long, and not wanting in oddness that he should have made this voyage with Jean Jacques, and afterwards, at such an interval, read a poem by an Englishman (who

---

[1] A pamphlet on the recent suspensions of the Habeas Corpus Act.
[2] Maturin's second tragedy, Manuel, produced at Drury Lane on 8 March, ran only five nights.
[3] The Story of Rimini.

had made precisely the same circumnavigation) upon the same scenery.

As for *Manfred*, it is of no use sending *proofs*; nothing of that kind comes. I sent the whole at different times. The 2 first acts are the best; the third so so: but I was blown with the first and second heats. You must call it 'a poem', for it is *no drama*, and I do not choose to have it called by so Sotheby-ish a name—a 'poem in dialogue', or—Pantomime, if you will; any thing but a green-room Synonime; and this is your motto—

> There are more things in heaven and earth, Horatio,
> Than are dreamt of in your philosophy.

Yours ever,
B.

My love and thanks to Mr. G[ifford].

Don't forget my tooth powder; its of no use to send it by the damned and double damned conveyances, but by some private hand—by Mr. Kinnaird,—or Mr. Davies if they come out,—or any body. Let it be left at my bankers here, Siri and Wilhalm. I mean to be in Venice again in July.

Nothing yet whatever from the foreign office. Why do you send anything to such a 'den of thieves' as that?

107. TO THE HON. AUGUSTA LEIGH

Florence, May 27th, 1817.

MY DEAREST AUGUSTA,

I am thus far on my return from Rome to Venice. From Rome I wrote to you at some length. Hobhouse [1] is gone to Naples for a short time.

I received a letter or two from you during my stay—one old, and one new. My health is reestablished, and has continued so through some very warm weather, and a good deal of horse and mountain exercise and scrambling; for I lived out of doors ever since my arrival.

I shall be glad to hear from or of you, and of your children and mine. By the way, it seems that I have got another— a *daughter* [2] by that same lady, whom you will recognize by what I said of her in former letters—I mean *her* who returned to England to become a Mamma incog., and whom I pray the Gods to keep there. I am a little puzzled how to dispose of

---

[1] Hobhouse had spent five months in Rome studying the antiquities.
[2] Allegra. See page 142.

this new production (which is two or three months old, though I did not receive the accounts till at Rome), but shall probably send for and place it in a Venetian convent, to become a good Catholic, and (it may be) a *Nun*, being a character somewhat wanted in our family.

They tell me it is very pretty, with blue eyes and *dark* hair; and, although I never was attached nor pretended attachment to the mother, still in case of the eternal war and alienation which I foresee about my legitimate daughter, Ada, it may be as well to have something to repose a hope upon. I must love something in my old age, and probably circumstances will render this poor little creature a great and, perhaps, my only comfort. . . .

108. TO JOHN MURRAY

Venice, May 30, 1817.

DEAR SIR,

I returned from Rome two days ago, and have received your letter; but no sign nor tidings of the parcel sent through Sir —— Stuart, which you mention. After an interval of months, a packet of *Tales*, etc., found me at Rome; but this is all, and may be all that ever will find me. The post seems to be the only sane conveyance; and *that only for letters*. From Florence I sent you a poem on Tasso, and from Rome the new third act of *Manfred*, and by Dr. Polidori two pictures for my sister. I left Rome, and made a rapid journey home. You will continue to direct here as usual. Mr. Hobhouse is gone to Naples: I should have run down there too for a week, but for the quantity of English whom I heard of there. I prefer hating them at a distance; unless an earthquake, or a good real eruption of Vesuvius, were insured to reconcile me to their vicinity.

I know no other situation except Hell which I should feel inclined to participate with them—as a race, always excepting several individuals. There were few of them in Rome, and I believe none whom you know, except that old Blue-*bore* Sotheby, who will give a fine account of Italy, in which he will be greatly assisted by his total ignorance of Italian, and yet this is the translator of Tasso.

The day before I left Rome I saw three robbers guillotined. The ceremony—including the *masqued* priests; the half-naked executioners; the bandaged criminals; the black Christ and his banner; the scaffold; the soldiery; the slow procession, and the quick rattle and heavy fall of the axe; the splash of the blood, and the ghastliness of the exposed heads—is altogether more impressive than the vulgar and ungentlemanly dirty 'new drop', and dog-like agony of infliction upon the sufferers of the English sentence. Two of these men behaved calmly enough, but the first of the three died with great terror and reluctance, which was very horrible. He would not lie down; then his neck was too large for the aperture, and the priest was obliged to drown his exclamations by still louder exhortations. The head was off before the eye could trace the blow; but from an attempt to draw back the head, notwithstanding it was held forward by the hair, the first head was cut off close to the ears: the other two were taken off more cleanly. It is better than the oriental way, and (I should think) than the axe of our ancestors. The pain seems little; and yet the effect to the spectator, and the preparation to the criminal, are very striking and chilling. The first turned me quite hot and thirsty, and made me shake so that I could hardly hold the opera-glass (I was close, but determined to see, as one should see every thing, once, with attention); the second and third (which shows how dreadfully soon things grow indifferent), I am ashamed to say, had no effect on me as a horror, though I would have saved them if I could.

It is some time since I heard from you—the *12th April* I believe.

> Yours ever truly,
> B.

109. TO THE HON. AUGUSTA LEIGH

Venice. June 3ᵈ, 1817.

DEAREST AUGUSTA,

I returned home a few days ago from Rome but wrote to you on the road; at Florence I believe, or Bologna. The last city you know—or do not know—is celebrated for the production of Popes—Cardinals—painters—and sausages—besides a female professor of anatomy, who has left there many models of the art in waxwork, some of them not the most decent.—I have received all your letters, I believe, which are full of woes, as usual, megrims and mysteries; but my sympathies remain in suspense, for, for the life of me I can't make out whether your disorder is a broken heart or the earache—or whether it is *you* that have been ill or the children—or what your melancholy and mysterious apprehensions tend to, or refer to, whether to Caroline Lamb's novels — Mrs. Clermont's evidence — Lady

Byron's magnanimity—or any other piece of imposture; I know nothing of what you are in the doldrums about at present. I should think all that could affect *you* must have been over long ago; and as for me—leave me to take care of myself. I may be ill or well—in high or low spirits—in quick or obtuse state of feelings—like any body else, but I can battle my way through; better than your exquisite piece of helplessness G[eorge] L[eigh] or that other poor creature George Byron, who will be finely helped up in a year or two with his new state of life— I should like to know what they would do in my situation, or in any situation. I wish well to your George, who is the best of the two a devilish deal—but as for the other I shan't forget him in a hurry, and if I ever forgive or allow an opportunity to escape of evincing my sense of his conduct (and of more than his) on a certain occasion—write me down—what you will, but do not suppose me asleep. 'Let them look to their bond' —sooner or later time and Nemesis will give me the ascendant— and then 'let them look to their bond'. I do not of course allude only to that poor wretch, but to all—to the 3^d and 4th generation of these accursed Amalekites and the woman who has been the stumbling block of my ——

June 4th 1817.

I left off yesterday at the stumbling block of my Midianite marriage—but having received your letter of the 20th May I will be in good humour for the rest of this letter. I had hoped you would likc the miniatures, at least one of them, which is in pretty good health; the other is thin enough to be sure—and so was I—and in the ebb of a fever when I sate for it. By the 'man of fashion' I suppose you mean that poor piece of affectation and imitation Wilmot—another disgrace to me and mine —that fellow. I regret not having shot him, which the persuasions of others—and circumstances which at that time would have rendered combats presumptions against my cause—prevented. I wish you well of your indispositions which I hope are slight, or I should lose my senses.

Yours ever

very and truly,

B.

110. TO JOHN MURRAY

DEAR SIR,　　　　　　　　La Mira, near Venice, June 17, 1817.

It gives me great pleasure to hear of Moore's success—and the more so that I never doubted that it would be complete.

Whatever good you can tell me of him and his poem will be most acceptable: I feel very anxious indeed to receive it. I hope that he is as happy in his fame and reward as I wish him to be; for I know no one who deserves both more—if any, so much.

Now to business [of] our own. For the drama [1] I required three hundred guineas, and desire no more, and for the other [2]—three hundred guineas, and will take no less. When you say that the Drama is of the same length, and will form the same-sized publication as most of the preceding, it is probable that you will charge the same price to the purchaser, and in that case (unless the publication fails altogether) will probably be not less a gainer than upon the former. At least it seems that you can hardly be a loser—when the author's demand has not been a *third* of what you have already paid for productions of the like calibre. Do you mean to say that it is dearer or shorter than Mr. R.'s *Jaqueline*? or than my *Lara*? or than *The Giaour*? or the *Bride*? Or do you mean to say that it is inferior to these as Poetry? or that its dramatic form renders it less susceptible of profit? I will tell you that to you, from its being the first poem of mine in that form, it must to a certain degree be more advantageous, as far as an object of curiosity, and although it is not a drama properly—but a dialogue, still it contains poetry and passion—although I by no means look on it as the best— or conceive that it will be the most fortunate of compositions by the same writer.

When therefore you talk to me as of its being a dear purchase, I answer you in so many words, that if I had not named the prior price (with which by the way I was satisfied and had no wish to enlarge) *you* would yourself have offered me a greater, and, if you would not, I could find those who would.

As to the other poem I look upon that as good of its kind, and the price not at all out of proportion to what writers require and obtain.

You are to print in what form you please—that is your concern; as far as your connection with myself has gone, you are the best judge, how far you have lost or gained—probably sometimes one and sometimes the other, but when you come to me with your '*can*' and talk to me about the copy of *Manfred* as if the 'force of purchase would no further go—to *make* a book he separates the *two*',[3] I say unto you, verily, it is not so; or, as the Foreigner said to the Waiter, after asking him to bring

---

[1] *Manfred*. [2] *The Lament of Tasso*.
[3] Parodying Dryden's famous lines, *Under Milton's Picture*.

a glass of water, to which the man answered 'I will, sir,'—'You *will*!—God damn,—I say, you *mush*!' And I will submit this to the decision of any person or persons to be appointed by both, on a fair examination of the circumstances of this as compared with the preceding publications. So there's for you. There is always some row or other previously to all our publications: it should seem that, on approximating, we can never quite get over the natural antipathy of author and bookseller, and that more particularly the ferine nature of the latter must break forth.

You are out about the third [*sic*] Canto: I have not done, nor designed, a line of continuation to that poem. I was too short a time at Rome for it, and have no thoughts of recommencing. But if I ever do, I will put it to market to the best bidder and will desert at once to the '*Row*', if you come over me with your pitiful-hearted speeches about 'can' and 'not', of which if you are not ashamed, you deserve to be the publisher of *Saul* [1] on your Sole account—(paying the author five pounds copyright) with all expenses for ever, now, and to posterity.

I cannot well explain to you by letter what I conceive to be the origin of Mrs. Leigh's notion about *Tales of My Landlord*; but it is some points of the characters of Sir E. Manley and Burley, as well as one or two of the jocular portions, on which it is founded, probably.

If you have received Dr. Polidori, as well as a parcel of books, and you can be of use to him, be so. I never was much more disgusted with any human production than with the eternal nonsense, and *tracasseries*, and emptiness, and ill humour, and vanity of that young person; but he has some talent, and is a man of honour, and has dispositions of amendment, in which he has been aided by a little subsequent experience, and may turn out well. Therefore, use your government interest for him, for he is improved and improvable.

Yours ever truly,
B^N.

111. TO THOMAS MOORE

La Mira, Venice, July 10, 1817.

Murray, the Mokanna [2] of booksellers, has contrived to send me extracts from *Lalla Rookh* by the post. They are taken from some magazine, and contain a short outline and quotations from the two first Poems. I am very much delighted with what

---

[1] A poem by William Sotheby.
[2] Perhaps in reference to the Veiled Mokanna of Moore's *Lalla Rookh*.

is before me, and very thirsty for the rest. You have caught the colours as if you had been in the rainbow, and the tone of the East is perfectly preserved; so that * * * and its author must be somewhat in the background, and learn that it requires something more than to have been upon the hunch of a drome-dary to compose a good oriental story. I am glad you have changed the title from 'Persian Tale'. * * * *

I suspect you have written a devilish fine composition, and I rejoice in it from my heart; because 'the Douglas and the Percy both together are confident against a world in arms.'[1] I hope you won't be affronted at my looking on us as 'birds of a feather'; though, on whatever subject you had written, I should have been very happy in your success.

There is a simile of an orange-tree's 'flowers and fruits',[2] which I should have liked better if I did not believe it to be a reflection on * * *.

Do you remember Thurlow's poem to Sam—'*When* Rogers';[3] and that damned supper at Rancliffe's that ought to have been a *dinner*? 'Ah, Master Shallow, we have heard the chimes at midnight'.[4] But,

> My boat is on the shore,
>   And my bark is on the sea;
> But, before I go, Tom Moore,
>   Here 's a double health to thee!
>
> Here 's a sigh to those who love me,
>   And a smile to those who hate;
> And whatever sky 's above me,
>   Here 's a heart for every fate.
>
> Though the ocean roar around me,
>   Yet it still shall bear me on;
> Though a desert should surround me,
>   It hath springs that may be won.

[1] *Henry IV*, Part I, v, i, 117.
[2]
> 'Just then, beneath some orange-trees,
>   Whose fruit and blossoms in the breeze
>   Were wantoning together, free,
>   Like Age at play with Infancy . . .'
>   *Lalla Rookh*, 'Paradise and the Peri', 212–15.

[3] Lord Thurlow's *Poems on Several Occasions*, 1813. At the time Byron thought the lines so ridiculous that in a letter to Moore he parodied them.
[4] *Henry IV*, Part II, iii, ii, 228.

> Were 't the last drop in the well,
>   As I gasp'd upon the brink,
> Ere my fainting spirit fell,
>   'Tis to thee that I would drink.
>
> With that water, as this wine,
>   The libation I would pour
> Should be—peace with thine and mine,
>   And a health to thee, Tom Moore.

This should have been written fifteen moons ago—the first stanza was. I am just come out from an hour's swim in the Adriatic; and I write to you with a black-eyed Venetian girl before me, reading Boccaccio.

Last week I had a row on the road (I came up to Venice from my casino, a few miles on the Paduan road, this blessed day, to bathe) with a fellow in a carriage, who was impudent to my horse. I gave him a swingeing box on the ear, which sent him to the police, who dismissed his complaint. Witnesses had seen the transaction. He first shouted, in an unseemly way, to frighten my palfry. I wheeled round, rode up to the window, and asked him what he meant. He grinned, and said some foolery, which produced him an immediate slap in the face, to his utter discomfiture. Much blasphemy ensued, and some menace, which I stopped by dismounting and opening the carriage door, and intimating an intention of mending the road with his immediate remains, if he did not hold his tongue. He held it.

Monk Lewis is here—'how pleasant!' He is a very good fellow, and very much yours. So is Sam—so is every body—and amongst the number,

Yours ever,

P.S.—What think you of *Manfred*?   B.

112. TO JOHN MURRAY

DEAR SIR,   September 15, 1817.

I enclose a sheet for correction, if ever you get to another edition.[1] You will observe that the blunder in printing makes it appear as if the Château was *over* St. Gingo, instead of being on the opposite shore of the Lake, over Clarens. So, separate the paragraphs, otherwise my *to*pography will seem as inaccurate as your *ty*pography on this occasion.

[1] Of *The Prisoner of Chillon*.

The other day I wrote to convey my proposition with regard to the 4th and concluding canto. I have gone over and extended it to one hundred and fifty stanzas, which is almost as long as the two first were originally, and longer by itself than any of the smaller poems except *The Corsair*. Mr. Hobhouse has made some very valuable and accurate notes of considerable length, and you may be sure I will do for the text all that I can to finish with decency. I look upon *Childe Harold* as my best; and as I begun, I think of concluding with it. But I make no resolutions on that head, as I broke my former intention with regard to *The Corsair*. However, I fear that I shall never do better; and yet, not being thirty years of age, for some moons to come, one ought to be progressive as far as Intellect goes for many a good year. But I have had a devilish deal of wear and tear of mind and body in my time, besides having published too often and much already. God grant me some judgement! to do what may be most fitting in that and every thing else, for I doubt my own exceedingly.

I have read *Lalla Rookh*, but not with sufficient attention yet, for I ride about, and lounge, and ponder, and—two or three other things; so that my reading is very desultory, and not so attentive as it used to be. I am very glad to hear of its popularity, for Moore is a very noble fellow in all respects, and will enjoy it without any of the bad feeling which success—good or evil—sometimes engenders in the men of rhyme. Of the poem itself, I will tell you my opinion when I have mastered it: I say of the *poem*, for I don't like the *prose* at all—at all; and in the mean time, the 'Fire worshippers' is the best, and the 'Veiled Prophet' the worst, of the volume.

With regard to poetry in general, I am convinced, the more I think of it, that he and *all* of us—Scott, Southey, Wordsworth, Moore, Campbell, I,—are all in the wrong, one as much as another; that we are upon a wrong revolutionary poetical system, or systems, not worth a damn in itself, and from which none but Rogers and Crabbe are free; and that the present and next generations will finally be of this opinion. I am the more confirmed in this by having lately gone over some of our classics, particularly *Pope*, whom I tried in this way,—I took Moore's poems and my own and some others, and went over them side by side with Pope's, and I was really astonished (I ought not to have been so) and mortified at the ineffable distance in point of sense, harmony, effect, and even *Imagination*, passion, and *Invention*, between the little Queen Anne's man, and us of

the Lower Empire.   Depend upon it, it is all Horace then, and
Claudian now, among us; and if I had to begin again, I would
model myself accordingly.   Crabbe's the man, but he has got
a coarse and impracticable subject, and Rogers, the Grandfather
of living poetry, is retired upon half-pay, (I don't mean as
a Banker),[1]—

> Since pretty Miss Jaqueline,
> With her nose aquiline,[2]

and has done enough, unless he were to do as he did formerly.

113. TO JOHN MURRAY

Venice, January 8, 1818.

1

My dear Mr. Murray,
You 're in a damned hurry
    To set up this ultimate Canto;
But (if they don't rob us)
You 'll see Mr. Hobhouse
    Will bring it safe in his portmanteau.

2

For the Journal [3] you hint of,
As ready to print off,
    No doubt you do right to commend it;
But as yet I have writ off,
The devil a bit of
    Our *Beppo*; [4] when copied, I 'll send it.

[1] Rogers was formerly a banker.
[2] Recalling a rhyme which Byron scribbled in his copy of *English Bards,
and Scotch Reviewers*, on or before 14 July 1816:

> Pretty Miss Jaqueline
> Had a nose aquiline;
> And would assert rude
> Things of Miss Gertrude:
> While Mr. Marmion
> Led a great army on,
> Making Kehama look
> Like a fierce Mamaluke.

[3] *The Edinburgh Monthly Magazine*, in which Murray had purchased a
share, began to appear in April 1817.
[4] Published in February 1818.

3

In the mean time you 've 'Galley' [1]
Whose verses all tally,
   Perhaps you may say he 's a Ninny,
But if you abashed are
Because of *Alashtar*,
    He 'll drivel another *Phrosine*.

4

Then you 've Sotheby's tour,[2]
No great things, to be sure,—
   You could hardly begin with a less work;
For the pompous rascallion,
Who don't speak Italian
   Nor French, must have scribbled by guess-work.

5

No doubt he 's a rare man
Without knowing German
   Translating his way up Parnassus,
And now still absurder
He meditates Murder
   As you 'll see in the trash he calls *Tasso's*.

6

But you 've others his betters,
The real men of letters,
   Your Orators—Critics—and—Wits,—
And I 'll bet that your Journal
(Pray is it diurnal?)
   Will pay with your luckiest hits.

7

You can make any loss up
With 'Spence' [3] and his Gossip,
   A work which must surely succeed;
Then Queen Mary's Epistle-craft,[4]

[1] Henry Gally Knight, whose *Phrosyne, a Grecian Tale*, and *Alashtar, an Arabian Tale*, were published in 1817. To Byron they were 'worse than trash, the sublime of mediocrity'.
[2] *Farewell to Italy, and Occasional Poems*, 1818.
[3] *Observations, Anecdotes, and Characters of Books and Men*, by the Rev. Joseph Spence. It appeared in 1820.
[4] *The Life of Mary Queen of Scots*, by George Chalmers, 1819.

With the new 'Fytte' of 'Whistlecraft',[1]
Must make people purchase and read.

8

Then you 've General Gordon,[2]
Who girded his sword on,
    To serve with a Muscovite Master,
And help him to polish
A nation so owlish,
    They thought shaving their beards a disaster.

9

For the man, '*poor and shrewd*', *
With whom you 'd conclude
    A compact without more delay,
Perhaps some such pen is
Still extant in Venice;
    But please, sir, to mention *your pay*.

10

Now tell me some news
Of your friends and the Muse
    Of the Bar, or the Gown, or the House,
From Canning, the tall wit,
To Wilmot the small wit,
    Ward's creeping Companion and *Louse*,

11

Who 's so damnably bit
With fashion and Wit,
    That he crawls on the surface like Vermin,
But an Insect in both,—
By his Intellect's growth
    Of what size you may quickly determine.[3]

---

[1] John Hookham Frere's *Prospectus and Specimen of an Intended National Work, by William and Robert Whistlecraft. . . . Intended to comprise the most interesting particulars relating to King Arthur and his Round Table,* 1817–18.

[2] Thomas Gordon, who had served in the Russian Army from 1813 to 1815.

* '*Vide* your letter'.

[3] The remaining three stanzas are unpublishable.

114. TO THOMAS MOORE

Venice, February 2, 1818.

Your letter of December 8th arrived but this day, by some delay, common but inexplicable. Your domestic calamity [1] is very grievous, and I feel with you as much as I *dare* feel at all. Throughout life, your loss must be my loss, and your gain my gain; and, though my heart may ebb, there will always be a drop for you among the dregs.

I know how to feel with you, because (selfishness being always the substratum of our damnable clay) I am quite wrapt up in my own children. Besides my little legitimate, I have made unto myself an *il*-legitimate since (to say nothing of one before), and I look forward to one of these as the pillar of my old age, supposing that I ever reach—which I hope I never shall—that desolating period. I have a great love for my little Ada, though perhaps she may torture me like * * * * *

Your offered address will be as acceptable as you can wish. I don't much care what the wretches of the world think of me —all *that's* past. But I care a good deal what *you* think of me, and, so say what you like. You *know* that I am not sullen; and, as to being *savage*, such things depend on circumstances. However, as to being in good humour in *your* society, there is no great merit in that, because it would be an effort, or an insanity, to be otherwise.

I don't know what Murray may have been saying or quoting.[2] I called Crabbe and Sam the fathers of present Poesy; and said, that I thought—except them—*all* of '*us youth*' were on a wrong tack. But I never said that we did not sail well. Our fame will be hurt by *admiration* and *imitation*. When I say *our*, I mean *all* (Lakers included), except the postscript of the Augustans. The next generation (from the quantity and facility of imitation) will tumble and break their necks off our Pegasus, who runs away with us; but we keep the *saddle*, because we broke the rascal and can ride. But though easy to mount, he is the devil to guide; and the next fellows must go back to the riding-school and the manège, and learn to ride the 'great horse'.

Talking of horses, by the way, I have transported my own, four in number, to the Lido (*beach* in English), a strip of some ten miles along the Adriatic, a mile or two from the city; so that I not only get a row in my gondola, but a spanking gallop of

---

[1] Moore's daughter Barbara died on 18 September, 1817.
[2] See page 175.

some miles daily along a firm and solitary beach, from the fortress to Malamocco, the which contributes considerably to my health and spirits.

I have hardly had a wink of sleep this week past. We are in the agonies of the Carnival's last days, and I must be up all night again, as well as to-morrow. I have had some curious masking adventures this Carnival; but, as they are not yet over, I shall not say on. I will work the mine of my youth to the last veins of the ore, and then—good night. I have lived, and am content.

Hobhouse went away before the Carnival began, so that he had little or no fun. Besides, it requires some time to be thoroughgoing with the Venetians; but of all this anon, in some other letter. * * * * *

I must dress for the evening. There is an opera and ridotto, and I know not what, besides balls; and so, ever and ever yours,

B.

P.S.—I send this without revision, so excuse errors. I delight in the fame and fortune of *Lalla*, and again congratulate you on your well-merited success.

115. TO JOHN MURRAY

Venice, Feb. 20, 1818.

Dear Sir,

I have to thank Mr. Croker for the arrival, and you for the Continents, of the parcel which came last week, much quicker than any before, owing to Mr. C.'s kind attention, and the official exterior of the bags; and all safe, except much fraction amongst the magnesia, of which only two bottles came entire; but it is all very well, and I am exceedingly obliged to you.

The books I have read, or rather am reading. Pray, who may be the Sexagenarian,[1] whose gossip is very amusing? Many of his sketches I recognize, particularly Gifford, Mackintosh, Drummond, Dutens, H. Walpole, Mrs. Inchbald, Opie, etc., with the Scotts, Loughborough, and most of the divines and lawyers, besides a few shorter hints of authors, and a few lines about a certain '*Noble Author*', characterised as Malignant and Sceptical, according to the good old story, 'as it was in the beginning, is now, but *not* always shall be': do you know such

[1] *The Sexagenarian, or Recollections of a Literary Life*, by the Rev. William Beloe, 1817.

a person, Master Murray? eh?—And pray, of the Booksellers, which be *you*? the dry, the dirty, the honest, the opulent, the finical, the splendid, or the Coxcomb Bookseller? 'Stap my vitals', but the author grows scurrilous in his grand Climacteric!

I remember to have seen Porson [1] at Cambridge, in the Hall of our College, and in private parties, but not frequently: and I never can recollect him except as drunk or brutal, and generally both: I mean in an evening, for in the hall he dined at the Dean's table, and I at the Vice-master's, so that I was not near him; and he then and there appeared sober in his demeanour, nor did I ever hear of excess or outrage on his part in public,— Commons, college, or Chapel; but I have seen him in a private party of undergraduates, many of them freshmen and strangers —take up a poker to one of them, and heard him use language as blackguard as his action. I have seen Sheridan drunk, too, with all the world; but his intoxication was that of Bacchus, and Porson's that of Silenus. Of all the disgusting brutes, sulky, abusive, and intolerable, Porson was the most bestial, as far as the few times that I saw him went, which were only at William Bankes's (the Nubian Discoverer's) rooms. I saw him once go away in a rage, because nobody knew the name of the 'Cobbler of Messina',[2] insulting their ignorance with the most vulgar terms of reprobation. He was tolerated in this state amongst the young men for his talents—as the Turks think a Madman inspired, and bear with him. He used to recite, or rather vomit, pages of all languages, and could hiccup Greek like a Helot; and certainly Sparta never shocked her children with a grosser exhibition than this man's intoxication.

I perceive, in the book you sent me, a long account of him; of Gilbert Wakefield's account of him, which is very savage, I cannot judge, as I never saw him sober, except in *Hall* or Combination-room; and then I was never near enough to hear, and hardly to see him. Of his drunken deportment I can be sure, because I saw it.

With the Reviews I have been much entertained. It requires to be as far from England as I am to relish a periodical paper properly: it is like Soda-water in an Italian Summer. But what cruel work you make with Lady Morgan![3]—You should recollect that she is a woman; though, to be sure, they are now

---

[1] Richard Porson (1759–1808), Professor of Greek, to whom a large part of Beloe's book is devoted.
[2] Possibly Vatinius of Beneventum.
[3] Lady Morgan's *France* was noticed in the *Quarterly Review*.

and then very provoking: still, as authoresses, they can do no great harm; and I think it a pity so much good invective should have been laid out upon her, when there is such a fine field of us Jacobin gentlemen for you to work upon. It is perhaps as bitter a Critique as ever was written, and enough to make sad work for Dr. Morgan, both as a husband and an Apothecary, unless she should say as Pope did, of some attack upon him, 'that it is as good for *her* as a dose of *Hartshorn*'.[1]

I heard from Moore lately, and was very sorry to be made aware of his domestic loss. Thus it is—*medio de fonte leporum* [2] —in the acmé of his fame and of his happiness comes a drawback as usual.

His letter, somehow or other, was more than two months on the road, so that I could only answer it the other day. What you tell me of Rogers in your last letter is like him; but he had best let *us*, that is one of us, if not both, alone. He cannot say that I have not been a sincere and a warm friend to him, till the black drop of his liver oozed through, too palpably to be overlooked. Now, if I once catch him at any of his jugglery with me or mine, let him look to it, for, if I spare him then, write me down a good-natured gentleman; and the more that I have been deceived,—the more that I once relied upon him,— I don't mean his petty friendship (what is that to me?), but his *good* will, which I really tried to obtain, thinking him at first a good fellow,—the more will I pay off the balance; and so, if he values his quiet, let him look to it; in three months I could restore him to the Catacombs.

Mr. Hoppner,[3] whom I saw this morning, has been made the father of a very fine boy.—Mother and child doing very well indeed. By this time Hobhouse should be with you, and also certain packets, letters, etc., of mine, sent since his departure.— I am not at all well in health within this last eight days. My remembrances to Gifford and all friends.

Yours,

B.

P.S.—In the course of a month or two, Hanson will have probably to send off a clerk with conveyances to sign (Newstead being sold [4] in November last for ninety-four thousand and five hundred pounds), in which case I supplicate supplies of articles

---

[1] Letter to Warburton, 12 January, 1743-4.
[2] Lucretius, *De Rerum Natura*, iv, 1133.
[3] Richard Belgrave Hoppner, English Consul at Venice.
[4] To Major Thomas Wildman, an old schoolfellow of Byron's.

as usual, for which desire Mr. Kinnaird to settle from funds in their bank, and deduct from my account with him.

P.S.—To-morrow night I am going to see *Otello*, an opera from our *Othello*, and one of Rossini's best, it is said. It will be curious to see in Venice the Venetian story itself represented, besides to discover what they will make of Shakespeare in Music.

116. TO SAMUEL ROGERS

Venice, March 3ᵈ, 1818.

DEAR ROGERS,

I have not, as you say, 'taken to wife the Adriatic'; but if the Adriatic will take my wife, I shall be very glad to marry her instead. In the mean time, I have had wife enough; as the Grammar has it, *tædet vitæ, pertæsum est conjugii*. However, the last part of this exquisite quotation only is applicable to my case; I like life very well in my own way.

I heard of Moore's loss from himself in a letter which was delayed upon the road three months. I was sincerely sorry for it, but in such cases what are words? The villa you speak of is one at Este, which Mr. Hoppner (Consul-general here) has transferred to me. I have taken it for two years as a place of villeggiatura. The situation is very beautiful, indeed, among the Euganean hills, and the house very fair. The vines are luxuriant to a great degree, and all the fruits of the earth abundant. It is close to the old castle of the Estes, or Guelphs, and within a few miles of Arqua, which I have visited twice, and hope to visit often.

Last summer (except an excursion to Rome) I passed upon the Brenta. In Venice I winter, transporting my horses to the Lido, bordering the Adriatic (where the fort is), so that I get a gallop of some miles daily along the strip of beach which reaches the Malamocco, when in health; but within these few weeks I have been unwell. At present I am getting better. The Carnival was short, but a good one. I don't go out much, except during the time of masques; but there are one or two *conversazioni*, where I go regularly, just to keep up the system, as I had letters to their givers, and they are particular on such points; and now and then, though very rarely, to the Governor's.

It is a very good place for women. * * * I like the dialect and their manner very much. There is a *naïveté* about them which is very winning, and the romance of the place is a mighty adjunct; the *bel sangue* is not, however, now amongst the *dame* or higher orders; but all under *i fazzioli*, or kerchiefs (a white kind of veil which the lower orders wear upon their heads);—the *vesta zendale*, or old national female costume, is no more. The city, however, is decaying daily, and does not gain in population. However, I prefer it to any other in Italy; and here have I pitched my staff, and here do I purpose to reside for the remainder of my life, unless events, connected with business not to be transacted out of England, compel me to return for that purpose; otherwise I have few regrets, and no desires to visit it again for its own sake. I shall probably be obliged to do so, to sign papers for my affairs, and a proxy for the Whigs, and to see Mr. Waite, for I can't find a good dentist here, and every two or three years one ought to consult one. About seeing my children, I must take my chance. One I shall have sent here; and I shall be very happy to see the legitimate one, when God pleases, which he perhaps will some day or other. As for my mathematical Medea, I am as well without her.

Your account of your visit to F[onthill] is very striking. could you beg of *him*[1] for *me* a copy in MS. of the remaining *Tales*?[2] I think I deserve them, as a strenuous and public admirer of the first one. I will return it when read, and make no ill use of the copy, if granted. Murray would send me out anything safely. If ever I return to England, I should like very much to see the author, with his permission. In the mean time, you could not oblige me more than by obtaining me the perusal I request, in French or English,—all's one for that, though I prefer Italian to either. I have a French copy of *Vathek* which I bought at Lausanne. I can read French with great pleasure and facility, though I neither speak nor write it. Now Italian I *can* speak with some fluency, and write sufficiently for my purposes, but I don't like their *modern* prose at all; it is very heavy, and so different from Machiavelli.

They say Francis is Junius;[3] I think it looks like it. I remember meeting him at Earl Grey's at dinner. Has not he lately married a young woman? and was not he Madame Talleyrand's *Cavalier servente* in India years ago?

I read my death in the papers, which was not true. I see they are marrying the remaining singleness of the royal family.[4]

---

[1] William Beckford.
[2] Unpublished episodes to *Vathek*.
[3] Sir Philip Francis was asserted to be the author of the *Letters of Junius*.
[4] The Dukes of Clarence and Cambridge.

They have brought out *Fazio* [1] with great and deserved success at Covent Garden: that's a good sign. I tried, during the directory, to have it done at Drury Lane, but was overruled; as also in an effort I made in favour of Sotheby's trash, which I did to oblige the mountebank, who has since played me a trick, or two (I suspect), which perhaps he may remember as well as his airs of patronage, which he affects with young writers, and affected both *to* me and *of* me many a long year. He sent me (unless the *handwriting* be a most extraordinary coincidental mistake) an anonymous note at Rome about the 'Poeshie' of 'Chillon etc.' I can swear also to his phrases, particularly the word 'effulgence'. Well—I say nothing.

If you think of coming into this country, you will let me know perhaps beforehand. I suppose Moore won't move. Rose [2] is here, and has made a *relazione* with a Venetian lady, rather in years, but not ugly—at least by candlelight. I saw them the other night at Madame Albrizzi's: he talks of returning in May. My love to the Hollands.

Ever yours very truly and affect^ly,

BYRON.

P.S.—They have been crucifying *Othello* into an opera (*Otello*, by Rossini): the music good, but lugubrious; but as for the words, all the real scenes with Iago cut out, and the greatest nonsense inserted; the handkerchief turned into a *billet-doux*, and the first singer would not *black* his face, for some exquisite reasons assigned in the preface. Scenery, dresses, and music very good.

117. TO THOMAS MOORE

Palazzo Mocenigo, Canal Grande, Venice, June 1, 1818.

Your letter is almost the only news, as yet, of Canto fourth, and it has by no means settled its fate—at least, does not tell me how the 'Poeshie' has been received by the public. But, I suspect, no great things,—firstly, from Murray's 'horrid stillness'; secondly, from what you say about the stanzas running into each other, which I take *not* to be *yours*, but a notion you have been dinned with among the Blues. The fact is, that the *terza rima* of the Italians, which always *runs* on and in, may have led me into experiments, and carelessness into conceit—

---

[1] By Henry Hart Milman.　　[2] William Stewart Rose, poet.

or conceit into carelessness—in either of which events failure
will be probable, and my fair woman, *superne*, end in a fish;[1]
so that *Childe Harold* will be like the mermaid, my family crest,
with the fourth Canto for a tail thereunto. I won't quarrel
with the public, however, for the 'Bulgars' are generally right;
and if I miss now, I may hit another time:—and so, the 'gods
give us joy'.[2]

You like *Beppo*, that's right. * * * I have not had the
Fudges[3] yet, but live in hopes. I need not say that your
successes are mine. By the way, Lydia White[4] is here, and has
just borrowed my copy of *Lalla Rookh*. * *

Hunt's letter is probably the exact piece of vulgar coxcombry
you might expect from his situation. He is a good man, with
some poetical elements in his chaos; but spoilt by the Christ-
Church Hospital and a Sunday newspaper,—to say nothing of
the Surrey gaol, which conceited him into a martyr. But he
is a good man. When I saw *Rimini* in MS., I told him that I
deemed it good poetry at bottom, disfigured only by a strange
style. His answer was, that his style was a system, or *upon
system*, or some such cant; and, when a man talks of system, his
case is hopeless: so I said no more to him, and very little to
any one else.

He believes his trash of vulgar phrases tortured into compound
barbarisms to be *old* English; and we may say of it as Aimwell[5]
says of Captain Gibbet's regiment, when the Captain calls it
an 'old corps',—'the *oldest* in Europe, if I may judge by your
uniform'. He sent out his *Foliage*[6] by Percy Shelley * * *,
and, of all the ineffable Centaurs that were ever begotten by
Self-love upon a Night-mare, I think 'this monstrous Sagittary'[7]
the most prodigious. *He* (Leigh H.) is an honest charlatan,
who has persuaded himself into a belief of his own impostures,
and talks Punch in pure simplicity of heart, taking himself (as
poor Fitzgerald said of *him*self in the *Morning Post*)[8] for *Vates*
in both senses, or nonsenses, of the word. Did you look at the
translations of his own which he prefers to Pope and Cowper,
and says so?[9]—Did you read his skimble-skamble about

---

[1] 'Desinat in piscem mulier formosa superne'.—Horace, *Ars Poetica*, 4.
[2] *As You Like It*, III, iii, 47.
[3] Moore's *Fudge Family in Paris*, published in 1818.
[4] A fashionable bluestocking, whom Byron had known in London.
[5] In Farquhar's *Beaux' Stratagem*.
[6] *Foliage, or Poems Original and Translated*, 1818.
[7] *Troilus and Cressida*, V, v, 14.
[8] See page 122.
[9] In the Preface.

Wordsworth being at the head of his own *profession*, in the *eyes* of *those* who followed it? I thought that poetry was an *art*, or an *attribute*, and not a *profession*;—but be it one, is that * * * * * * at the head of *your* profession in *your* eyes? I 'll be curst if he is of *mine*, or ever shall be. He is the only one of us (but of us he is not) whose coronation I would oppose. Let them take Scott, Campbell, Crabbe, or you, or me, or any of the living, and throne him;—but not this new Jacob Behmen, this * * * * * * whose pride might have kept him true, even had his principles turned as perverted as his *soi-disant* poetry.

But Leigh Hunt is a good man, and a good father—see his Odes to all the Masters Hunt;—a good husband—see his Sonnet to Mrs. Hunt;—a good friend—see his Epistles to different people;—and a great coxcomb and a very vulgar person in every thing about him. But that 's not his fault, but of circumstances.

.   .   .

.   .   .

I do not know any good model for a life of Sheridan [1] but that of *Savage*. Recollect, however, that the life of such a man may be made far more amusing than if he had been a Wilber-force; [2]—and this without offending the living, or insulting the dead. The Whigs abuse him; however, he never left them, and such blunderers deserve neither credit nor compassion.—As for his creditors,—remember, Sheridan *never had* a shilling, and was thrown, with great powers and passions, into the thick of the world, and placed upon the pinnacle of success, with no other external means to support him in his elevation. Did Fox * * * *pay his* debts?—or did Sheridan take a subscription? Was the Duke of Norfolk's drunkenness more excusable than his? Were his intrigues more notorious than those of all his contemporaries? and is his memory to be blasted, and theirs respected? Don't let yourself be led away by clamour, but compare him with the coalitioner Fox, and the pensioner Burke, as a man of principle, and with ten hundred thousand in personal views, and with none in talent, for he beat them all *out* and *out*. Without means, without connexion, without character, (which might be false at first, and make him mad afterwards from desperation,) he beat them all, in all he ever attempted. But alas, poor human nature! Good night—or rather, morning. It is four, and the dawn gleams over the Grand Canal, and unshadows the Rialto.

---

[1] Moore's *Life of Sheridan* came out in 1825.   [2] See page 116.

I must to bed; up all night—but, as George Philpot [1] says, 'it's life, though, damme, it's life!'

Ever yours,

B.

Excuse errors—no time for revision. The post goes out at noon, and I shan't be up then. I will write again soon about your *plan* for a publication.

118. TO JOHN CAM HOBHOUSE [2]

Venice, June, 1818.

SIR,

With great grief I inform you of the death of my late dear Master, my Lord, who died this morning at ten of the Clock of a rapid decline and slow fever, caused by anxiety, sea-bathing, women, and riding in the Sun against my advice.

He is a dreadful loss to every body, mostly to me, who have lost a master and a place—also, I hope you, Sir, will give me a charakter.

I saved in his service as you know several hundred pounds. God knows how, for I don't, nor my late master neither; and if my wage was not always paid to the day, still it was or is to be paid sometime and somehow. You, Sir, who are his executioner won't see a poor Servant wronged of his little all.

My dear Master had several phisicians and a Priest: he died a Papish, but is to be buried among the Jews in the Jewish burying ground; for my part I don't see why—he could not abide them when living nor any other people, hating whores who asked him for money.

He suffered his illness with great patience, except that when in extremity he twice damned his friends and said they were selfish rascals—you, Sir, particularly and Mr. Kinnaird, who had never answered his letters nor complied with his repeated requests. He also said he hoped that your new tragedy would be damned—God forgive him—I hope that my master won't be damned like the tragedy.

His nine whores are already provided for, and the other servants; but what is to become of me? I have got his Cloathes and Carriages, and Cash, and everything; but the Consul quite against law has clapt his seal and taken an inventary and swears that *he* must account to my Lord's heirs—who they are

<hr>

[1] In Murphy's play, *The Citizen*.
[2] A letter feigned to be written by William Fletcher, Byron's valet.

I don't know—but they ought to consider poor Servants and above all his Vally de Sham.

My Lord never grudged me perquisites—my wage was the least I got by him; and if I did keep the Countess (she is, or ought to be, a Countess, although she is upon the town) Marietta Monetta Piretta, after passing my word to you and my Lord that I would not never no more—still he was an indulgent master, and only said I was a damned fool, and swore and forgot it again. What could I do? she said as how she should die, or kill herself if I did not go with her, and so I did—and kept her out of my Lord's washing and ironing—and nobody can deny that, although the charge was high, the linen was well got up.

Hope you are well, Sir—am, with tears in my eyes,

Yours faithfoolly to command,
W.^M FLETCHER.

P.S.—If you know any Gentleman in want of a Wally— hope for a charakter. I saw your late Swiss Servant in the Galleys at Leghorn for robbing an Inn—he produced your recommendation at his trial.

119. TO THE HON. AUGUSTA LEIGH

Venice, August 3^d 1818.

DEAREST AUGUSTA,

I am not uncomfortable, but have been obliged to scold Hobhouse, etc., for not doing a thing or two for me in England in the way of business. At present they are done, and I am graciously appeased.

My little girl, Allegra (the child I spoke to you of), has been with me these three months:[1] she is very pretty, remarkably intelligent, and a great favourite with every body; but, what is remarkable, much more like Lady Byron than her mother— so much so as to stupefy the learned Fletcher and astonish me. Is it not odd? I suppose she must also resemble her sister, Ada: she has very blue eyes, and that singular forehead, fair curly hair, and a devil of a Spirit—but that is Papa's.

I am in health, and yours,

B.

[1] She had been brought from England to Milan by Claire Clairmont and the Shelleys.

120. TO THOMAS MOORE

Venice, September 19, 1818.

An English newspaper here would be a prodigy, and an opposition one a monster; and except some extracts *from* extracts in the vile, garbled Paris gazettes, nothing of the kind reaches the Veneto-Lombard public, who are, perhaps the most oppressed in Europe. My correspondences with England are mostly on business, and chiefly with my attorney, who has no very exalted notion, or extensive conception, of an author's attributes; for he once took up an *Edinburgh Review*, and, looking at it a minute, said to me, 'So, I see you have got into the magazine',—which is the only sentence I ever heard him utter upon literary matters, or the men thereof.

My first news of your Irish Apotheosis [1] has, consequently, been from yourself. But, as it will not be forgotten in a hurry, either by your friends or your enemies, I hope to have it more in detail from some of the former, and, in the mean time, I wish you joy with all my heart. Such a moment must have been a good deal better than Westminster Abbey,—besides being an assurance of *that* one day (many years hence, I trust), into the bargain.

I am sorry to perceive, however, by the close of your letter, that even *you* have not escaped the *surgit amari*, etc., and that your damned deputy has been gathering such 'dew from the still *vext* Bermoothes' [2] — or rather *vexatious*. Pray, give me some items of the affair, as you say it is a serious one; and, if it grows more so, you should make a trip over here for a few months, to see how things turn out. I suppose you are a violent admirer of England by your staying so long in it. For my own part, I have passed, between the age of one-and-twenty and thirty, half the intervenient years out of it without regretting any thing, except that I ever returned to it at all, and the gloomy prospect before me of business and parentage obliging me, one day, to return to it again,—at least, for the transaction of affairs, the signing of papers, and inspecting of children.

I have here my natural daughter, by name Allegra,—a pretty little girl enough, and reckoned like papa. Her mamma is

---

[1] The enthusiastic welcome Moore had received in Dublin in the previous June.

[2] *The Tempest*, I, ii, 228–9. Since 1803 Moore had been Registrar to the Admiralty in Bermuda, discharging his duties by deputy. By the defalcation of the deputy he became liable for £6,000.

English,—but it is a long story, and — there's an end. She is about twenty months old. * * *

I have finished the first canto (a long one, of about 180 octaves) of a poem in the style and manner of *Beppo*, encouraged by the good success of the same. It is called *Don Juan*, and is meant to be a little quietly facetious upon every thing. But I doubt whether it is not—at least, as far as it has yet gone—too free for these very modest days. However, I shall try the experiment, anonymously; and if it don't take, it will be discontinued. It is dedicated to Southey in good, simple, savage verse, upon the Laureat's politics, and the way he got them. But the bore of copying it out is intolerable; and if I had an amanuensis he would be of no use, as my writing is so difficult to decipher.

> My poem's Epic, and is meant to be
> Divided in twelve books, each book containing,
> With love and war, a heavy gale at sea—
> A list of ships, and captains, and kings reigning—
> New characters, etc., etc.

The above are two stanzas, which I send you as a brick of my Babel, and by which you can judge of the texture of the structure.

In writing the *Life* of Sheridan, never mind the angry lies of the humbug Whigs. Recollect that he was an Irishman and a clever fellow, and that *we* have had some very pleasant days with him. Don't forget that he was at school at Harrow, where, in my time, we used to show his name—R. B. Sheridan, 1765,— as an honour to the walls. Remember * * * * * * *. Depend upon it that there were worse folks going, of that gang, than ever Sheridan was.

What did Parr [1] mean by 'haughtiness and coldness?' I listened to him with admiring ignorance, and respectful silence. What more could a talker for fame have?—they don't like to be answered. It was at Payne Knight's I met him, where he gave me more Greek than I could carry away. But I certainly meant to (and *did*) treat him with the most respectful deference.

I wish you a good night, with a Venetian benediction, '*Benedetto te, e la terra che ti fara!*'—'May you be blessed, and the *earth* which you will *make!*'—is it not pretty? You would think it still prettier if you had heard it, as I did two hours

---

[1] Dr. Samuel Parr, a former assistant master at Harrow, to whom Moore had applied for information about Sheridan.

ago, from the lips of a Venetian girl, with large black eyes, a face like Faustina's, and the figure of a Juno—tall and energetic as a Pythoness, with eyes flashing, and her dark hair streaming in the moonlight—one of those women who may be made any thing. I am sure if I put a poniard into the hand of this one, she would plunge it where I told her,—and into *me*, if I offended her. I like this kind of animal, and am sure that I should have preferred Medea to any woman that ever breathed. You may, perhaps, wonder that I don't in that case * * *[1] I could have forgiven the dagger or the bowl,—any thing, but the deliberate desolation piled upon me, when I stood alone upon my hearth, with my household gods shivered around me. * * Do you suppose I have forgotten or forgiven it? It has comparatively swallowed up in me every other feeling, and I am only a spectator upon earth, till a tenfold opportunity offers. It may come yet. There are others more to be blamed than * * * *, and it is on these that my eyes are fixed unceasingly.

121. TO THE HON. AUGUSTA LEIGH

Venice, Sep^{tr} 21st, 1818.

DEAREST AUGUSTA,

I particularly beg that you will contrive to get the enclosed letter safely delivered to Lady Frances,[2] and if there is an answer to let me have it. You can write to her first and state that you have such a letter—at my request—for there is no occasion for any concealment at least with *her*—and pray oblige me so far, for many reasons.

If the Queen dies [3] you are no more a Maid of Honour—is it not so? Allegra is well, but her mother (whom the Devil confound) came prancing the other day over the Appennines—to see her *shild*; which threw my Venetian loves (who are none of the quietest) into great combustion; and I was in a pucker till I got her to the Euganean hills,[4] where she and the child now are, for the present. I declined seeing her for fear that the consequence might be an addition to the family; she is to have the child a month with her, and then to return herself to Lucca, or Naples, where she was with her relatives (she is English you

---

[1] The suppressed passages must refer to Lady Byron, whom on p. 184 he styles his 'mathematical Medea.'
[2] Lady Frances Wedderburn Webster.
[3] Queen Charlotte died on 17 November, 1818.
[4] To his villa at Este.

know), and to send Allegra to Venice again. I lent her my house at Este for her maternal holidays. As troubles don't come single, here is another confusion. The chaste wife of a baker [1]—having quarrelled with her tyrannical husband—has run away *to* me (God knows without being invited), and resists all the tears and penitence and beg-pardons of her disconsolate Lord, and the threats of the police, and the priest of the parish besides; and swears she won't give up her unlawful love (myself), for any body, or any thing. I assure you I have begged her in all possible ways too to go back to her husband, promising her all kinds of eternal fidelity into the bargain, but she only flies into a fury; and as she is a very tall and formidable Girl of three and twenty, with the large black eyes and handsome face of a pretty fiend, a correspondent figure and a carriage as haughty as a Princess—with the violent passions and capacities for mischief of an Italian when they are roused—I am a little embarrassed with my unexpected acquisition. However she keeps my household in rare order, and has already frightened the learned Fletcher out of his remnants of wits more than once; we have turned her into a housekeeper. As the morals of this place are very lax, all the women commend her and say she has done right—especially her own relations. You need not be alarmed—I know how to manage her—and can deal with anything but a cold blooded animal such as Miss Milbanke. The worst is that she won't let a woman come into the house, unless she is as old and frightful as possible; and has sent so many to the right about that my former female acquaintances are equally frightened and angry. She is extremely fond of the child, and is very cheerful and goodnatured, when not jealous; but Othello himself was a fool to her in that respect. Her soubriquet in her family was *la Mora* from her colour, as she is very dark (though clear of complexion), which literally means *the Moor* so that I have 'the Moor of Venice' in propria persona as part of my household. She has been here this month. I had known her (and fifty others) more than a year, but did not anticipate this escapade, which was the fault of her booby husband's treatment —who now runs about repenting and roaring like a bull calf. I told him to take her in the devil's name, but she would not stir; and made him a long speech in the Venetian dialect which was more entertaining to anybody than to him to whom it was addressed. You see Goose—that there is no quiet in this world. —so be a good woman—and repent of y[r] sins.——

[1] Margarita Cogni, whose full story is told in the letter on page 217.

122. TO LADY BYRON

Venice, Nov! 18ᵗʰ 1818.

Sir Samuel Romilly [1] has cut his throat for the loss of his wife. It is now nearly three years since he became, in the face of his compact (by a retainer—previous, and, I believe, general), the advocate of the measures and the Approver of the proceedings, which deprived me of mine. I would not exactly, like Mr. Thwackum, when Philosopher Square bit his own tongue—'saddle him with a Judgement'; [2] but

> This even-handed Justice
> Commends the ingredients of our poisoned Chalice
> To our own lips. [3]

This Man little thought, when he was lacerating my heart according to law, while he was poisoning my life at it's sources, aiding and abetting in the blighting, branding, and exile that was to be the result of his counsels in their indirect effects, that in less than thirty-six moons—in the pride of his triumph as the highest candidate for the representation of the Sister-City of the mightiest of Capitals—in the fullness of his professional career—in the greenness of a healthy old age—in the radiance of fame, and the complacency of self-earned riches—that a domestic affliction would lay him in the earth, with the meanest of malefactors, in a cross-road with the stake in his body, if the verdict of insanity did not redeem his ashes from the sentence of the laws he had lived upon by interpreting or misinterpreting, and died in violating.

This man had eight children, lately deprived of their mother: could he not live? Perhaps, previous to his annihilation, he felt a portion of what he contributed his legal mite to make me feel; but I have lived—lived to see him a Sexagenary Suicide.

It was not in vain that I invoked Nemesis in the midnight of Rome from the awfullest of her ruins. [4]

Fare you well.

B.

123. TO JOHN MURRAY

Venice, November 24th, 1818.

DEAR SIR,

Mr. Hanson has been here a week and went five days ago; he brought nothing but his papers, some corn-rubbers, and a

---

[1] A former Solicitor-General, and Lady Byron's legal adviser. His wife died on 29 October, and he committed suicide four days later.
[2] Fielding, *Tom Jones*, Book v, chap. ii.   [3] *Macbeth*, i, vii, 10-12.
[4] See *Childe Harold*, Canto iv, stanzas cxxx–cxxxviii.

kaleidoscope. 'For what we have received, the L
thankful!'—for without his aid I shall not be so.

He—Hanson—left everything else in Chancery I
except your copy-paper for the last canto, etc.,
a degree of parchment, he brought with him.

You may imagine his reception; he swore the books were a
'waggon-load'. If they were, he should have come in a waggon
—he would in that case have come quicker than he did.

Lord Lauderdale set off from hence twelve days ago, accompanied by a cargo of poesy [1] directed to Mr. Hobhouse—all spick and span, and in MS. You will see what it is like. I have given it to Master Southey, [2] and he shall have more before I have done with him. I understand the scoundrel said, on his return from Switzerland two years ago, that 'Shelley and I were in a league of Incest, etc., etc.' He is a burning liar! [3] for the women to whom he alludes are not sisters—one being Godwin's daughter, by Mary Wollstonecraft, and the other daughter of the *present* (second) Mrs. G^n, by a *former* husband; and in the next place, if they had even been so, there was no *promiscuous intercourse* whatever.

You may make what I say here as public as you please—more particularly to Southey, whom I look upon, and will say as publicly, to be a dirty, lying rascal; and will prove it in ink—or in his blood, if I did not believe him to be too much of a poet to risk it. If he had forty reviews at his back—as he has the *Quarterly*—I would have at him in his scribbling capacity, now that he has begun with me; but I will do nothing underhand. Tell him what I say from *me*, and everyone else you please.

You will see what I have said if the parcel arrives safe. I understand *Coleridge* went about repeating Southey's lie with pleasure. I can believe it, for I had done him what is called a favour. [4] I can understand Coleridge's abusing me, but how or why *Southey*—whom I had never obliged in any sort of way, or done him the remotest service—should go about fibbing and calumniating is more than I readily comprehend.

Does he think to put me down with his *canting*—not being able to do so with his poetry? We will try the question. I have read his review of Hunt, [5] where he has attacked Shelley in an oblique and shabby manner. Does he know what that

---

[1] *Don Juan*, Canto 1, *Mazeppa*, and the *Ode on Venice*.
[2] In the Dedication to *Don Juan*.   [3] Cf. *Othello*, v, ii, 129.
[4] See page 110.   Byron also sent him £100.
[5] Hunt's *Foliage*, in the *Quarterly*.

..ew has done? I will tell you. It has *sold* an edition of ..e *Revolt of Islam*, which, otherwise, nobody would have thought of reading, and few who read can understand—I for one.

Southey would have attacked me, too, there, if he durst further than by hints about Hunt's friends in general; and some outcry about an 'Epicurean system', carried on by men of the most opposite habits, tastes, and opinions in life and poetry (I believe), that ever had their names in the same volume— Moore, Byron, Shelley, Hazlitt, Haydon,[1] Leigh Hunt, Lamb [2] —what resemblance do ye find among all or any of these men? and how could any sort of system or plan be carried on, or attempted amongst them? However, let Mr. Southey look to himself—since the wine is tapped, let him drink it.

I got some books a few weeks ago—many thanks; amongst them is *Israeli's* new edition.[3] It was not fair in you to show him my copy of his former one, with all the marginal notes and nonsense made in Greece when I was not two-and-twenty, and which certainly were not meant for his perusal, nor for that of his readers. I have a great respect for *Israeli* and his talents, and have read his works over and over and over repeatedly, and have been amused by them greatly, and in structed often. Besides, I hate giving pain unless provoked and he is an author, and must feel like his brethren: and although his liberality repaid my marginal flippancies with a compliment —the highest compliment—that don't reconcile me to myself nor to *you*—it was a breach of confidence to do this without my leave. I don't know a living man's books I take up so often or lay down more reluctantly, as *Israeli's*; and I never will forgive you—that is, for many weeks. If he had got out of humour I should have been less sorry, but even then, I should have been sorry; but, really, he has heaped his 'coals of fire' so handsomely upon my head, that they burn unquenchably.

You ask me of the two reviews—I will tell you. Scott's is the review of one poet on another—his friend; and Wilson' the review of a poet, too, on another—his *idol*; for he likes me better than he chooses to avow to the public, with all his eulogy I speak, judging only from the article, for I don't know him personally.

So Sir Samuel Romilly has cut his throat for the loss of his wife. Three years ago (nearly), when, after a long and general

---

[1] Benjamin Robert Haydon, the painter, and friend of Keats.
[2] The Hon. George Lamb, third son of the first Viscount Melbourne.
[3] Isaac D'Israeli's *Literary Character*, first published in 1795.

retainer, he deserted to Miss Milbanke, and did his best, or his worst, to destroy me, or make me destroy myself, did he dream that in less than thirty-six months a domestic deprivation would level him in a cross-road, but for a lying verdict of lunacy?

There would have been some excuse for such a fit at twenty-seven—but at sixty-four! Could not the dotard wait till his drivelling did it? You see that Nemesis is not yet extinct, for I had not forgot Sir S. in my imprecation, which involved many. I never will dissemble—it may be very fine to forgive—but I would not have forgiven him living, and I will not affect to pity him dead. There are others of that set (of course I except the women, who were mere instruments—all but one) who have throats; but whether they will be cut by their own hands, or no, is yet to be shown. There is much to be done; and you may yet see that what ought to be done upon those my enemies will be.

Here is a long letter—can you read it?

Yours ever,
BYRON.

124. TO JOHN MURRAY

Venice, January 25, 1819.

DEAR SIR,

You will do me the favour to print privately (for private distribution) fifty copies of *Don Juan*.[1] The list of the men to whom I wish it to be presented, I will send hereafter. The other two poems had best be added to the collective edition: I do not approve of *their* being published separately. *Print Don Juan entire*, omitting, of course, the lines on Castlereagh, as I am not on the spot to meet him. I have a second Canto ready, which will be sent by and bye. By this post, I have written to Mr. Hobhouse, addressed to your care.

Yours ever truly,
B.

P.S.—I have acquiesced in the request and representation; and having done so, it is idle to detail my arguments in favour of my own Self-love and 'Poeshie'; but I *protest*. If the poem has poetry, it would stand; if not, fall: the rest is 'leather and prunella',[2] and has never yet affected any human production

[1] Byron's friends, Hobhouse, Kinnaird, Scrope Davies, Moore, and Frere, had advised strongly against its publication. Cantos I and II appeared on 15 July, 1819, without name of author or publisher.
[2] Pope, *Essay on Man*, IV, 204.

'pro or con'. Dullness is the only annihilator in such cases. As to the Cant of the day, I despise it, as I have ever done all its other finical fashions, which become you as paint became the Antient Britons. If you admit this prudery, you must omit half Ariosto, La Fontaine, Shakespeare, Beaumont, Fletcher, Massinger, Ford, all the Charles Second writers; in short, *something* of most who have written before Pope and are worth reading, and much of Pope himself. *Read him*—most of you *don't*—but *do*—and I will forgive you; though the inevitable consequence would be that you would burn all I have ever written, and all your other wretched Claudians of the day (except Scott and Crabbe) into the bargain. I wrong Claudian, who *was* a *poet*, by naming him with such fellows; but he was the *ultimus Romanorum*, the tail of the Comet, and these persons are the tail of an old Gown cut into a waistcoat for Jackey; but being both *tails*, I have compared one with the other, though very unlike, like all Similies. I write in a passion and a Sirocco, and I was up till six this morning at the Carnival; but I *protest* as I did in my former letter.

125. TO THE HON. DOUGLAS KINNAIRD

MY DEAR DOUGLAS,   Venice, January 27th, 1819.

I have received a very clever letter from Hobhouse against the publication of *Don Juan*, in which I understand you have acquiesced (you be damned). I acquiesce too, but reluctantly.

This acquiescence is some thousands of pounds out of my pocket, the very thought of which brings tears into my eyes. I have imbibed such a love for money, that I keep some sequins in a drawer, to count and cry over them once a week; and if it was not for a turn for women (which I hope will be soon worn out), I think I should be able, not only to clear off, but to accumulate.

God only knows how it rends my heart to part with the idea of the sum I should have received from a fair bargain of my recent 'poeshie'. The sequins are the great consideration—as for the applauses of posterity, I would willingly sell the reversion at a discount—even to Mr. Southey, who seems fond of it; as if people's grandchildren were to be wiser than their forefathers—although, no doubt, the simple chances of change are in favour of the deuce-ace turning up last—just as in the overturn of a coach, the odds are that your backside will be the first out of the window.

I say, that as for fame and all that, it is for such persons as Fortune chooses—and so is money. And so on account of this damned prudery, and the reviews, and an outcry, and posterity, a gentleman who has 'a proper regard for his fee' is to be curtailed of his '*darics*' (I am reading about Greece and Persia). This comes of consulting friends. I will see you all damned before I consult you again. What do you mean now by giving advice when you are asked for it? Don't you know that it is like asking a man how he does, and that the answer in both cases should always be '*Very well*, I thank you'?

Yours ever,

B.

P.S.—Give my love to Frere, and tell him he is right, but I never will forgive him, or any of you.

126. TO JOHN MURRAY

Dear Sir,   Venice, April 6, 1819.

The Second Canto of *Don Juan* was sent, on Saturday last, by post, in 4 packets, two of 4, and two of three sheets each, containing in all two hundred and seventeen stanzas, octave measure. But I will permit no curtailments, except those mentioned about Castlereagh and the two *Bobs* in the Introduction. You sha'n't make *Canticles* of my Cantos. The poem will please, if it is lively; if it is stupid, it will fail; but I will have none of your damned cutting and slashing. If you please, you may publish *anonymously*; it will perhaps be better; but I will battle my way against them all, like a Porcupine.

So you and Mr. Foscolo,[1] etc., want me to undertake what you call a 'great work'? an Epic poem, I suppose, or some such pyramid. I'll try no such thing; I hate tasks. And then 'seven or eight years!' God send us all well this day three months, let alone years. If one's years can't be better employed than in sweating poesy, a man had better be a ditcher. And works, too!—is *Childe Harold* nothing? You have so many '*divine*' poems, is it nothing to have written a *Human* one? without any of your worn-out machinery. Why, man, I could have spun the thoughts of the four cantos of that poem into twenty, had I wanted to book-make, and its passion into as

[1] Ugo Foscolo (1778–1827), the Italian poet, dramatist, and critic, had settled in England in 1816.

many modern tragedies. Since you want *length*, you shal
have enough of *Juan*, for I 'll make 50 cantos.

And Foscolo, too! Why does *he* not do something more than
the *Letters of Ortis*, and a tragedy, and pamphlets?[1] He has
good fifteen years more at his command than I have: what has
he done all that time?—proved his Genius, doubtless, but no
fixed its fame, nor done his utmost.

Besides, I mean to write my best work in *Italian*, and it wil
take me nine years more thoroughly to master the language
and then if my fancy exist, and I exist too, I will try what
can do *really*. As to the Estimation of the English which you
talk of, let them calculate what it is worth, before they insul
me with their insolent condescension.

I have not written for their pleasure. If they are pleased
it is that they chose to be so; I have never flattered their
opinions, nor their pride; nor will I. Neither will I mak
'Ladies books' *al dilettar le femine e la plebe*. I have written
from the fullness of my mind, from passion, from impulse, from
many motives, but not for their 'sweet voices'. [2]

I know the precise worth of popular applause, for few
Scribblers have had more of it; and if I chose to swerve int
their paths, I could retain it, or resume it, or increase it. But
neither love ye, nor fear ye; and though I buy with ye and sel
with ye, and talk with ye, I will neither eat with ye, drink wit
ye, nor pray with ye.[3] They made me, without my search,
species of popular Idol; they, without reason or judgement
beyond the caprice of their good pleasure, threw down the Imag
from its pedestal; it was not broken with the fall, and they would
it seems, again replace it—but they shall not.

You ask about my health: about the beginning of the year
was in a state of great exhaustion, attended by such debilit
of Stomach that nothing remained upon it; and I was oblige
to reform my 'way of life', which was conducting me from th
'yellow leaf' to the Ground, with all deliberate speed. I ar
better in health and morals, and very much yours ever,

B[N]

P.S.—Tell Mrs. Leigh I have never had 'my Sashes', and
want some tooth-powder, the red, by all or any means.

---

[1] *Lettere di Jacopo Ortis*, 1798; *Tieste*, 1797; Essays on the Italian writer
He was also the author of poems, translations, and two other tragedies.
[2] *Coriolanus*, II, iii, 119.
[3] Cf. *The Merchant of Venice*, I, iii, 36.

127. TO THE HON. DOUGLAS KINNAIRD

Dear Douglas, Venice, April 24th, 1819.

Damn '*the Vampire*'.[1] What do I know of Vampires? It must be some bookselling imposture; contradict it in a solemn paragraph.

I sent off on April 3rd the 2nd canto of *Don Juan* addressed to Murray, I hope it is arrived—by the Lord it is a Capo d'Opera, so full 'of pastime and prodigality', but you sha'n't decimate nor mutilate, no—'rather than that, come critics into the list, and champion me to the uttermost'.[2]

Nor you, nor that rugged rhinoceros Murray, have ever told me, in answer to *fifty* times the question, if he ever received the additions to Canto *first*, entitled 'Julia's letter', and also some four stanzas for the beginning.

I have fallen in love, within the last month, with a Roma-gnuola Countess from Ravenna,[3] the spouse of a year of Count Guiccioli, who is sixty—the girl twenty.

She is as fair as sunrise, and warm as noon, but she is young, and was not content with what she had done, unless it was to be turned to the advantage of the public, and so she made an éclat, which rather astonished even the Venetians, and electrified the Conversazioni of the Benzona, the Albrizzi, and the Michelli, and made her husband look embarrassed.

They have been gone back to Ravenna some time, but they return in the winter. She is the queerest woman I ever met with, for in general they cost one something one way or other, whereas by an odd combination of circumstances, I have proved an expense to HER, which is not *my* custom, but an accident; however it don't matter.

She is a sort of Italian Caroline Lamb, except that she is much prettier, and not so savage. But she has the same red-hot head, the same noble disdain of public opinion, with the super-structure of all that Italy can add to such natural dispositions.

She is also of the Ravenna noblesse, educated in a convent, sacrificed to wealth, filial duty, and all that.

I am damnably in love, but they are gone, for many months —and nothing but hope keeps me alive *seriously*.

Yours ever,

B.

[1] A tale, written by Dr. Polidori, and published as Byron's by Henry Colburn in the *New Monthly Magazine*.
[2] Cf. *Macbeth*, III, i, 71-2.
[3] Teresa, daughter of Count Ruggiero Gamba.

128. TO JOHN MURRAY

Venice, May 15, 1819.

DEAR SIR,

I have received and return by this post, under another Cover, the first proof of *Don Juan*. Before the Second can arrive, it is probable that I may have left Venice, and the length of my absence is so uncertain, that you had better proceed to the publication without boring me with more proofs. I send by last post an addition—and a new copy of 'Julia's Letter', perceiving or supposing the former one in winter did not arrive.

Mr. Hobhouse is at it again about indelicacy. There is *no indelicacy*; if he wants *that*, let him read Swift, his great Idol, but his Imagination must be a dunghill, with a Viper's nest in the middle, to engender such a supposition about this poem. For my part, I think you are all crazed. * * * Request him not 'to put me in a phrenzy', as Sir Anthony Absolute says 'though he was not the indulgent father that I am'.[1]

I have got your extract, and the *Vampire*. I need not say it is *not mine*. There is a rule to go by: you are my publisher (till we quarrel), and what is not published by you is not written by me.

The story of Shelley's agitation [2] is true. I can't tell what seized him, for he don't want courage. He was once with me in a gale of Wind, in a small boat, right under the rocks between Meillerie and St. Gingo. We were five in the boat—a servant, two boatmen, and ourselves. The sail was mismanaged, and the boat was filling fast. He can't swim. I stripped off my coat—made him strip off his and take hold of an oar, telling him that I thought (being myself an expert swimmer) I could save him, if he would not struggle when I took hold of him—unless we got smashed against the rocks, which were high and sharp, with an awkward surf on them at that minute. We were then about a hundred yards from shore, and the boat in peril. He answered me with the greatest coolness, that 'he had no notion of being saved, and that I would have enough to do to save myself, and begged not to trouble me'. Luckily the boat righted, and, baling, we got round a point into St. Gingo, where the inhabitants came down and embraced the boatmen on their escape, the Wind having been high enough to

[1] *The Rivals*, I, ii; II, i.
[2] Given in the 'Extract of a Letter from Geneva', which is prefixed to *The Vampire*. It describes the effect upon Shelley of ghost stories, and the repetition of the beginning of *Christabel*, one evening at Geneva.

tear up some huge trees from the Alps above us, as we saw next day.

And yet the same Shelley, who was as cool as it was possible to be in such circumstances (of which I am no judge myself, as the chance of swimming naturally gives self possession when near shore), certainly had the fit of phantasy which Polidori describes, though *not exactly* as he describes it.

The story of the agreement to write the Ghost-books is true; but the ladies are *not* sisters. One is Godwin's daughter by Mary Wollstonecraft, and the other the *present* Mrs. Godwin's daughter by a former husband. So much for Scoundrel Southey's story of '*incest*'; neither was there *any promiscuous intercourse* whatever. Both are an invention of that execrable villain Southey, whom I will term so as publicly as he deserves. Mary Godwin (now Mrs. Shelley) wrote *Frankenstein*,[1] which you have reviewed, thinking it Shelley's. Methinks it is a wonderful work for a girl of nineteen,—*not* nineteen, indeed, at that time. I enclose you the beginning of mine, by which you will see how far it resembles Mr. Colburn's publication. If you choose to publish it in the *Edinburgh Magazine* (*Wilson's and Blackwood's*) you may, *stating why*, and with such explanatory proem as you please. I never went on with it, as you will perceive by the date. I began it in an old account-book of Miss Milbanke's, which I kept because it contains the word 'Household', written by her twice on the inside blank page of the covers, being the only two scraps I have in the world in her writing, except her name to the Deed of Separation. Her letters I sent back except those of the quarrelling correspondence, and those, being documents, are placed in possession of a third person (Mr. Hobhouse), with copies of several of my own; so that I have no kind of memorial whatever of her, but these *two* words,—and her actions. I have torn the leaves containing the part of the Tale out of the book, and enclose them with this sheet.

Next week I set out for Romagna—at least in all probability. You had better go on with the publications without waiting to hear farther, for I have other things in my head. 'Mazeppa' and 'The Ode' *Separate*—what think you? *Juan anonymously*, without the dedication, for I won't be shabby and attack Southey under Cloud of night.

What do you mean? First you seem hurt by my letter, and then, in your next, you talk of its 'power', and so forth. This is a damned blind story, Jack; but never mind, go on.'

[1] Published in 1818, and reviewed by Scott in the *Edinburgh Magazine*.

You may be sure I said nothing *on purpose* to plague you; but if you will put me 'in a phrenzy, I will never call you Jack again'.[1] I remember nothing of the epistle at present.

What do you mean by Polidori's *Diary*?[2] Why, I defy him to say any thing about me, but he is welcome. I have nothing to reproach me with on his score, and I am much mistaken if that is not his *own* opinion. But why publish the names of the two girls? and in such a manner?—what a blundering piece of exculpation! *He* asked Pictet, etc., to dinner, and of course was left to entertain them.[3] I went into Society *solely* to present *him* (as I told him), that he might return into good company if he chose; it was the best thing for his youth and circumstances for myself, I had done with Society, and, having presented him withdrew to my own 'way of life'. It is true that I returned without entering Lady Dalrymple Hamilton's, because I saw it full. It is true that Mrs. Hervey[4] (she writes novels) fainted at my entrance into Coppet, and then came back again. On her fainting, the Duchesse de Broglie exclaimed, 'This is too much—at *sixty-five* years of age!'—I never gave 'the English' an opportunity of 'avoiding' me; but I trust that, if ever I do, they will seize it.

I am, yours very truly,

B.

129. TO JOHN MURRAY

Venice, May 18, 1819.

DEAR SIR,

Yesterday I wrote to Mr. Hobhouse and returned the proof under cover to you. Tell Mr. Hobhouse that in the Ferrara Story I told him, the phrase was *Vi riveresco Signor Cognate* and *not Cognato mio* as I stated yesterday by mistake.

I wrote to you in haste and at past two in the morning having besides had an accident. In going, about an hour and a half ago, to a rendezvous with a Venetian girl (unmarried and the daughter of one of their nobles), I tumbled into the Grand Canal and, not choosing to miss my appointment by the delays of changing, I have been perched in a balcony with my wet clothes on ever since, till this minute that on my return I have slipped

---

[1] *The Rivals*, I, ii; II, i.

[2] A journal which he kept for Murray when on tour with Byron in 1816

[3] Polidori's version of the story was that 'having invited M. Pictet and Bonstetten to dinner, [Byron] went on to the lake to Chillon, leaving [Polidori] to receive them and make apologies'.

[4] Probably Elizabeth Hervey, authoress of *Amabel* and other novels.

into my dressing-gown. My foot slipped in getting into my Gondola to set out (owing to the cursed slippery steps of their palaces), and in I flounced like a Carp, and went dripping like a Triton to my Sea nymph and had to scramble up to a grated window:—

> Fenced with iron within and without
> Lest the lover get in or the Lady get out.[1]

She is a very dear friend of mine, and I have undergone some trouble on her account, for last winter the truculent tyrant her flinty-hearted father, having been informed by an infernal German, Countess Vorsperg (their next neighbour), of our meetings, they sent a priest to me, and a Commissary of police, and they locked the Girl up, and gave her prayers and bread and water, and our connection was cut off for some time; but the father hath lately been laid up, and the brother is at Milan, and the mother falls asleep, and the Servants are naturally on the wrong side of the question, and there is no Moon at Midnight just now, so that we have lately been able to recommence; the fair one is eighteen; her name, Angelina; the family name, of course, I don't tell you.

She proposed to me to divorce my mathematical wife, and I told her that in England we can't divorce except for *female* infidelity. 'And pray, (said she), how do you know what she may have been doing these last three years?' I answered that I could not tell, but that the * * * was not quite so flourishing in Great Britain as with us here. 'But,' she said, 'can't you get rid of her?' 'Not more than is done already (I answered): You would not have me *poison her*?' Would you believe it? She made me *no answer*. Is not that a true and odd national trait? It spoke more than a thousand words, and yet this is a little, pretty, sweet-tempered, quiet feminine being as ever you saw, but the Passions of a Sunny Soil are paramount to all other considerations. An unmarried Girl naturally wishes to be married: if she can marry and love at the same time it is well, but at any rate she must love. I am not sure that my pretty paramour was herself fully aware of the inference to be drawn from her dead Silence, but even the unconsciousness of the latent idea was striking to an observer of the Passions; and I never strike out a thought of another's or of my own without trying to trace it to its Source.

[1] Compare Herrick, *No Lock against Letcherie* (Poems, ed. Moorman, p. 97).

I wrote to Mr. H. pretty fully about our matters. In a
few days I leave Venice for Romagna. Excuse this scrawl, for I
write in a state of shivering from having sat in my dripping
drapery, and from some other little accessories which affect this
husk of our immortal Kernel.

Tell Augusta that I wrote to her by yesterday's post, addressed
to your Care. Let me know if you come out this Summer
that I may be in the way, and come to me; don't go to an Inn.
I do not know that I can promise you any pleasure; 'our way
of life' is so different in these parts, but I insure to myself a
great deal in seeing you, and in endeavouring (however vainly)
to prove to you that I am, very truly,

Yours ever,

B.

P.S.—I have read Parson Hodgson's *Friends*[1] in which he
seems to display his knowledge of the subject by a Covert attack
or two on some of his own. He probably wants another Living;
at least I judge so by the prominence of his piety, although he
was always pious—even when he was kept by a Washerwoman
on the New Road. I have seen him Cry over her picture, which
he generally wore under his left Armpit. But he is a good man,
and I have no doubt does his duty by his Parish. As to the
poetry of his New fangled Stanza, I wish they would write the
octave or the Spenser; we have no other legitimate measure of
that kind. He is right in defending *Pope* against the bastard
Pelicans of the poetical winter day, who add insult to their
Parricide by sucking the blood of the parent of English *real*
poetry—poetry without fault,—and then spurning the bosoms
which fed them.

130. TO RICHARD BELGRAVE HOPPNER

Padua, June 2^d, 1819.

My dear Hoppner,

When you see that learned Clerk Edgecombe,[2] will you tell
him in your most agreeable manner, that the repairs of the
Carriages, which he stated to be so complete as to warrant
him in paying a hundred francs above the agreement, are very
far from doing credit to him or the Coachmaker here? The

---

[1] *The Friends: a Poem*, published by Murray in 1818.
[2] Richard Edgecombe, one of Hoppner's clerks, whom Byron employed
as his accountant.

wheels of the Servants' carriage had not *been touched*; the wheels of my own made rather worse than before, and, so far from being *cleaned*, they had not even wiped the *Glasses*.   Will you hint to him that, if I don't find my Palazzo and Casini, in town and country, in rather better order at my *ritorno* than I found the carriages at setting out, I will remit him to be Supercargo to a Venetian fishing boat.   And now he may go home and beat Mrs. Edgecombe.

I am just setting off for Ferrara.   Mengaldo gave me a letter to the Podesta, Count Mosti, for which I am grateful which is a troublesome sensation.   I am proceeding in no very good humour, for La G[uiccioli]'s instructions are rather calculated to produce an *éclat*—and perhaps a scene—than any decent iniquity.   I had a letter from her on Monday, which merely repeated the directions she had given me before, with the addition of something about her own house.

Now to go to cuckold a Papal Count, who, like Candide, has already been 'the death of two men one of whom was a priest', in his own house is rather too much for my modesty, when there are several other places at least as good for the purpose.   She says they must go to Bologna in the middle of June, and why the devil then drag me to Ravenna?   However, I shall determine nothing till I get to Bologna, and probably take some time to decide when I am there, so that, the Gods willing, you may probably see me again soon.   The Charmer forgets that a man may be whistled anywhere *before*, but that *after*—a Journey in an Italian June is a Conscription, and therefore she should have been less liberal in Venice, or less exigent at Ravenna.

If I was not the most constant of men, I should now be swimming from the Lido, instead of smoking in the dust of Padua.

Should there be letters from England, let them wait my return. And do look at my house and (not lands but) Waters, and scold, and deal out the monies to Edgecombe with an air of reluctance, and a shake of the head, and put queer questions to him, and turn up your nose when he answers.

Make my respects to the Consuless—and to the Chevalier, and to Scotin, and to all the Counts and Countesses of our acquaintance.

And believe me, ever your disconsolate and affectionate,

B.

131. TO JOHN MURRAY

Bologna, June 7, 1819.

DEAR SIR,

Tell Mr. Hobhouse that I wrote to him a few days ago from Ferrara. It will therefore be idle in him or you to wait for any further answers or returns of proofs from Venice, as I have directed that no English letters be sent after me. The publication can be proceeded in without, and I am already sick of your remarks, to which I think not the least attention ought to be paid.

Tell Mr. Hobhouse that, since I wrote to him, I had availed myself of my Ferrara letters, and found the society much younger and better there than at Venice. I was very much pleased with the little the shortness of my stay permitted me to see of the Gonfaloniere Count Mosti, and his family and friends in general.

I have been picture-gazing this morning at the famous Domenichino and Guido, both of which are superlative. I afterwards went to the beautiful Cimetery of Bologna, beyond the walls, and found, besides the superb Burial-ground, an original of a *Custode*, who reminded me of the grave-digger in Hamlet. He has a collection of Capuchins' skulls, labelled on the forehead, and taking down one of them, said, 'This was Brother Desiderio Berro, who died at forty—one of my best friends. I begged his head of his brethren after his decease, and they gave it me. I put it in lime and then boiled it. Here it is, teeth and all, in excellent preservation. He was the merriest, cleverest fellow I ever knew. Wherever he went, he brought joy; and when any one was melancholy, the sight of him was enough to make him cheerful again. He walked so actively, you might have taken him for a dancer—he joked— he laughed—oh! he was such a Frate as I never saw before, nor ever shall again!'

He told me that he had himself planted all the Cypresses in the Cimetery; that he had the greatest attachment to them and to his dead people; that since 1801 they had buried fifty-three thousand persons. In showing some older monuments, there was that of a Roman girl of twenty, with a bust by Bernini.[1] She was a Princess Barberini, dead two centuries ago: he said that, on opening her grave, they had found her hair complete, and 'as yellow as gold'. Some of the epitaphs at Ferrara pleased

[1] Giovanni Lorenzo Bernini (1598–1680).

me more than the more splendid monuments of Bologna; for instance:—

> Martini Luigi
> Implora pace.

> Lucrezia Picini
> Implora eterna quiete.

Can any thing be more full of pathos? Those few words say all that can be said or sought: the dead had had enough of life; all they wanted was rest, and this they '*implore*'. There is all the helplessness, and humble hope, and deathlike prayer, that can arise from the grave—'*implora pace*'. I hope, whoever may survive me, and shall see me put in the foreigners' burying-ground at the Lido, within the fortress by the Adriatic, will see those two words, and no more, put over me. I trust they won't think of 'pickling, and bringing me home to Clod or Blunderbuss Hall'.[1] I am sure my bones would not rest in an English grave, or my clay mix with the earth of that country. I believe the thought would drive me mad on my deathbed, could I suppose that any of my friends would be base enough to convey my carcase back to your soil. I would not even feed your worms, if I could help it.

So, as Shakespeare says of Mowbray, the banished Duke of Norfolk, who died at Venice (see *Richard II*), that he, after fighting

> Against black pagans, Turks, and Saracens,
> And toil'd with works of war, retir'd himself
> To Italy; and there, at *Venice*, gave
> His body to that *pleasant* country's earth,
> And his pure soul unto his Captain Christ,
> Under whose colours he had fought so long.[2]

Before I left Venice, I had returned to you your late, and Mr. Hobhouse's, sheets of *Juan*. Don't wait for further answers from me, but address yours to Venice, as usual. I know nothing of my own movements; I may return there in a few days, or not for some time. All this depends on circumstances. I left Mr. Hoppner very well, as well as his son and Mrs. Hoppner. My daughter Allegra was well too, and is growing pretty; her hair is growing darker, and her eyes are blue. Her temper and her ways, Mr. Hoppner says, are like mine, as well as her features: she will make, in that case, a manageable young lady.

I never hear any thing of Ada, the little Electra of my

---

[1] *The Rivals*, v, iii.   [2] *Richard II*, iv, i, 95–100.

Mycenæ; the moral Clytemnestra is not very communicative of her tidings, but there will come a day of reckoning, even if I should not live to see it.

I have at least seen Romilly shivered who was one of the assassins. When that felon, or lunatic (take your choice he must be one and might be both), was doing his worst to uproot my whole family tree, branch, and blossoms; when, after taking my retainer, he went over to them; when he was bringing desolation on my hearth and destruction on my household Gods, did he think that, in less than three years, a natural event—a severe domestic—but an unexpected and common domestic calamity,—would lay his carcase in a cross road, or stamp his name in a verdict of Lunacy? Did he (who in his drivelling sexagenary dotage had not the courage to survive his Nurse—for what else was a wife to him at his time of life?)—reflect or consider what my feelings must have been, when wife, and child, and sister, and name, and fame, and country were to be my sacrifice on his legal altar—and this at a moment when my health was declining, my fortune embarrassed, and my mind had been shaken by many kinds of disappointment, while I was yet young and might have reformed what might be wrong in my conduct, and retrieved what was perplexing in my affairs. But the wretch is in his grave. I detested him living, and I will not affect to pity him dead; I still loathe him—as much as we can hate dust—but that is nothing.

What a long letter I have scribbled!

Yours truly,

B.

P.S.—Here, as in Greece, they strew flowers on the tombs. I saw a quantity of rose-leaves, and entire roses, scattered over the graves at Ferrara. It has the most pleasing effect you can imagine.

132. TO RICHARD BELGRAVE HOPPNER

Ravenna, June 20th, 1819.

MY DEAR HOPPNER,

I wrote to you a week ago (particularly begging a line in answer by return of post) to request you would send off Augustine with the two Grey saddle horses, and the Carriage and Carriage Horses, saddles, etc., to wait for me at the *Pellegrino*—(the Inn there) in *Bologna*. To this letter and one of the same purport to Mr. Scott, I have had no answer, which makes me uneasy as I shall probably not return to Venice for some time. I wished my English letters also to be forwarded with Augustine to Bologna. If there was any want of Money, Siri and Willhalm would equip him.

Pray write to me here (*Ravenna*) by next post; it will reach me in time, and do not let Augustine delay a moment for the non-sense of that son of a bitch Edgecombe, who may probably be the cause of his dawdling.

I wrote to you from Padua, and from Bologna, and since from Ravenna. I find my situation very agreeable, but want my horses very much, there being good riding in the environs. I can fix no time for my return to Venice—it may be soon or late—or not at all—it all depends on the *Dama*,[1] whom I found very seriously in *bed* with a cough and spitting of blood, etc., all of which has subsided, and something else has recommenced. Her miscarriage has made her a good deal thinner; and I found all the people here firmly persuaded that she would never recover;—they were mistaken, however.

My letters were useful as far as I employed them; and I like both the place and people, though I don't trouble the latter more than I can help. *She* manages very well * * * * * but if I come away with a Stiletto in my gizzard some fine afternoon, I shall not be astonished.

I can't make *him* out at all—he visits me frequently, and takes me out (like Whittington, the Lord Mayor) in a coach and *six* horses. The fact appears to be, that he is completely *governed* by her—for that matter, so am I. The people here don't know what to make of us, as he had the character of jealousy with all his wives—this is the third. He is the richest of the Ravennese, by their own account, but is not popular among them.

By the aid of a Priest, a Chambermaid, a young Negro-boy, and a female friend, we are enabled to carry on our unlawful loves, as far as they can well go, though generally with some peril, especially as the female friend and priest are at present out of town for some days, so that some of the precautions devolve upon the Maid and Negro.

Now do pray—send off Augustine—and carriage—and cattle to Bologna without fail or delay—or I shall lose my remaining Shred of senses.

Don't forget this. My coming—going—and every thing depends upon *her* entirely just as Mrs. Hoppner—(to whom I remit my reverences) said, in the true spirit of female prophecy.

[1] The Countess Guiccioli.

You are but a shabby fellow not to have written before—and
I am,

Truly yours,

B.

P.S.—Address by return of Post to me—at *Ravenna*.

133. TO JOHN MURRAY

Ravenna. June 29, 1819.

DEAR SIR,

The letters have been forwarded from Venice, but I trust that you
will not have waited for further alterations—I will make none.

You ask me to spare Romilly—ask the worms. His dust
can suffer nothing from the truth being spoken, and, if it *could*,
how did he behave to me? You may talk to the Wind, which
will carry the Sound, and to the Caves, which will echo you,
but *not* to me on the subject of a villain who wronged me,
whether dead or alive.

I have no time to return you the proofs—publish without
them. I am glad you think the poesy good; and as to 'thinking
of the effect', think *you* of the sale, and leave me to pluck the
Porcupines who may point their quills at you.

I have been here (at Ravenna) these four weeks, having left
Venice a month ago;—I came to see my *Amica*, the Countess
Guiccioli, who has been, and still continues, very unwell. * *
She is only twenty years old, but not of a strong constitution.
* * She has a perpetual cough and an intermittent fever, but
bears up most *gallantly* in every sense of the word. Her husband (this is his third wife) is the richest noble of Ravenna,
and almost of Romagna; he is also *not* the youngest, being upwards of threescore, but in good preservation. All this will
appear strange to you, who do not understand the Meridian
morality, nor our way of life in such respects, and I cannot at
present expound the difference;—but you would find it much
the same in these parts. At Faenza there is Lord Kinnaird with
an opera girl; and at the inn in the same town is a Neapolitan
Prince, who serves the wife of the Gonfaloniere of that city.
I am on duty here—so you see 'Così fan tu*tti* e tut*te*'.

I have my horses here—*saddle* as well as carriage—and ride
or drive every day in the forest, the *Pineta*, the scene of Boccaccio's novel, and Dryden's fable of Honoria,[1] etc., etc., and
I see my *Dama* every day at the proper (and improper) hours;

[1] 'Theodore and Honoria', in *Fables*, 1700.

but I feel seriously uneasy about her health, which seems very precarious. In losing her, I should lose a being who has run great risks on my account, and whom I have every reason to love—but I must not think this possible. I do not know what I *should* do if she died, but I ought to blow my brains out—and I hope that I should. Her husband is a very polite personage, but I wish he would not carry me out in his Coach and Six, like Whittington and his Cat.

You ask me if I mean to continue *D. J.*, etc. How should I know? what encouragement do you give me, all of you, with your nonsensical prudery? publish the two Cantos, and then you will see. I desired Mr. Kinnaird to speak to you on a little matter of business: either he has not spoken, or you have not answered. You are a pretty pair, but I will be even with you both. I perceive that Mr. Hobhouse has been challenged by Major Cartwright [1]—Is the Major 'so cunning of fence'? [2] why did not they fight?—they ought.

Yours ever truly,

B.

Address your answer to *Venice* as usual.

134. TO RICHARD BELGRAVE HOPPNER

Ravenna. July 2, 1819.

Thanks for your letter and for Madame's. I will answer it directly. Will you recollect whether I did not consign to you one or two receipts of Madame Mocenigo's for house-rent— (I am not sure of this, but think I did—if not, they will be in my drawers)—and will you desire Mr. Dorville [3] to have the goodness to see if Edgecombe has *receipts* to all payments *hitherto* made by him on my account, and that there are *no debts* at Venice? On your answer, I shall send order of further remittance to carry on my household expenses, as my present return to Venice is very problematical; and it may happen— but I can say nothing positive—every thing with me being indecisive and undecided, except the disgust which Venice excites when fairly compared with any other city in this part of Italy. When I say *Venice*, I mean the *Venetians*—the city itself

---

[1] The quarrel arose out of the Westminster election of March 1819, in which Hobhouse was defeated—as he thought, through Major Cartwright's influence.

[2] *Twelfth Night*, III, iv, 312. [3] Vice-Consul at Venice.

is superb as its history—but the people are what I never thought them till they taught me to think so.

The best way will be to leave Allegra with Antonio's spouse till I can decide something about her and myself—but I thought that you would have had an answer from Mrs. V[avassou]r.[1] You have had bore enough with me and mine already.

I greatly fear that the Guiccioli is going into a consumption, to which her constitution tends. Thus it is with every thing and every body for whom I feel any thing like a real attachment;—'War, death, or discord, doth lay siege to them'.[2] I never even could keep alive a dog that I liked or that liked me.[3] Her symptoms are obstinate cough of the lungs, and occasional fever, etc., etc., and there are latent causes of an eruption in the skin, which she foolishly repelled into the system two years ago: but I have made them send her case to Aglietti; and have begged him to come—if only for a day or two—to consult upon her state. * * *

If it would not bore Mr. Dorville, I wish he would keep an eye on E[dgecombe] and on my other ragamuffins. I might have more to say, but I am absorbed about La Gui. and her illness. I cannot tell you the effect it has upon me.

The horses came, etc., etc., and I have been galloping through the pine forest daily.

Believe me, etc.

P.S.—My benediction on Mrs. Hoppner, a pleasant journey among the Bernese tyrants, and safe return. You ought to bring back a Platonic Bernese for my reformation. If any thing happens to my present *Amica*, I have done with the passion for ever—it is my *last* love. As to libertinism, I have sickened myself of that, as was natural in the way I went on, and I have at least derived that advantage from vice, to *love* in the better sense of the word. *This* will be my last adventure—I can hope no more to inspire attachment, and I trust never again to feel it.

135. TO LADY BYRON [4]

Ravenna. July 20th, 1819.

I have received from Holstein (I believe) the annexed paper of the Baroness of Hohenhausen, etc. and the enclosed letter of a Mr. Jacob (or Jacobssen) and as they 'ardently wish it could

---

[1] An English widow who wished to adopt Allegra.
[2] *A Midsummer Night's Dream*, I, i, 142.
[3] See page 53.   [4] Enclosing verses of a German poet.

reach you' I transmit it. You will smile, as I have done, at the importance which they attach to such things, and the effect which they conceive capable of being produced by composition, but the Germans are still a young and a romantic people, and live in an ideal world. Perhaps it may not offend you, however it may surprise, that the good people on the frontiers of Denmark have taken an interest in your domestic Affairs, which have now, I think, nearly made the tour of Europe, and been discussed in most of its languages, to as little purpose as in our own. If you like to retain the enclosed, you can do so, an indication to my Sister that you have received the letter will be a sufficient answer. I will not close this sheet without a few words more. Fletcher has complained to me of your declining to give his wife a character, on account of your 'doubts of her veracity in some circumstances a short time before she left you'. If your doubts allude to her testimony on your case during the then discussion, you *must* or at least ought to be the best judge how far she spoke truth or not; *I* can only say that She never had directly or indirectly, through me or mine, the slightest inducement to the contrary, nor am I indeed perfectly aware of what her Evidence was, never having seen her nor communicated with her at that period or since. I presume that you will weigh well your justice before you deprive the woman of the means of obtaining her bread. No one can be more fully aware than I am of the utter inefficacy of any words of mine to you on this or on any other subject, but I have discharged my duty to Truth in stating the above, and now do yours.

The date of my letter, indeed my letter itself, may surprize you, but I left Venice in the beginning of June, and came down into Romagna; there is the famous forest of Boccaccio's Story and Dryden's fable hardby, the Adriatic not far distant, and the Sepulchre of Dante within the walls. I am just going to take a Canter (for I have resumed my Tartar habits since I left England) in the cool of the Evening, and in the shadow of the forest till the Ave Maria. I have got both my saddle and Carriage horses with me, and don't spare them, in the cooler part of the day. But I shall probably return to Venice in a short time. Ravenna itself preserves perhaps more of the old Italian manners than any City in Italy. It is out of the way of travellers and armies, and thus they have retained more of their originality. They make love a good deal, and assassinate a little. The department is governed by a Cardinal Legate (Alberoni was once Legate here) to whom I have been presented and who told me some singular anecdotes of past times—of Alfieri etc. and others. I tried to discover for Leigh Hunt some traces of Francesca, but except her father Guido's [1] tomb, and the mere notice of the fact in the Latin commentary of Benvenuto da Imola in MS. in the library, I could discover nothing for him. He (Hunt) has made a sad mistake about 'old Ravenna's *clear-shewn towers* and *bay*' the city lies so low that you must be close upon it before it is 'shewn' at all, and the Sea had retired *four miles* at least, long before Francesca was born, and as far back as the Exarchs and Emperors. They tell me that at Rimini they know as little about her now—as they do here—so I have not gone there, it lies in the way to Rome, but I was at Rome in 1817. This is odd, for at Venice I found many traditions of the old Venetians, and at Ferrara a plentiful assortment of the House of Este, with the remains of the very Mirror, whose reflection cost at least a dozen lives, including those of Parisina and Ugo. I was wrong in placing those two naughty people in a garden.[2] Parisina was a Malatesta of Rimini, and her daughter by Niccolo of Este was also put to death by some Italian Chief her husband in nearly the same manner as her mother. Her name was Ginevra. So that including the alliance of Francesca with Launcelot Malatesta of Rimini, that same Malatesta family appears to have been but indifferently fortunate in their matrimonial speculations—I have written to you thus much, because in writing to you at all I may as well write much as little. I have not heard of Ada for many months but they say 'no news is good news' she must now be three years and almost eight months old. You must let her be taught Italian as soon as she can be taught any language but her own, and pray let her be musical, that is if She has a turn that way. I presume that Italian being a language of mine, will not prevent you from recollecting my request at the proper time. I am etc.,

B.

Bologna. August 31st, 1819.

This letter was written as far back as July 20th at Ravenna, but I delayed putting it in the post till my return here which will account for the interval between the date and the arrival of the letter, *if* it arrives. Pray state to Augusta that you have received it, on account of the inclosures. I want no other answer. I should like to have a picture of Miss Byron, when she can conveniently sit to Holmes or any other painter. Addio.

[1] Guido Vecchio da Polenta (*d.* 1310).   [2] See his *Parisina*, 1816.

136. TO JOHN MURRAY

Ravenna, August 1, 1819.

[Address your answer to Venice, however.]

DEAR SIR,

Don't be alarmed. You will see me defend myself gaily—that is, if I happen to be in Spirits; and by *Spirits*, I don't mean your meaning of the word, but the spirit of a bull-dog when pinched, or a bull when pinned—it is then that they make best sport—and as my Sensations under an attack are probably a happy compound of the united energies of those amiable animals, you may perhaps see what Marrall calls 'rare sport', [1] and some good tossing and goring, in the course of the controversy. But I must be in the right cue first, and I doubt I am almost too far off to be in a sufficient fury for the purpose; and then I have effeminated and enervated myself with love and the summer in these last two months.

I wrote to Mr. Hobhouse the other day, and foretold that Juan would either fail entirely or succeed completely—there will be no medium: appearances are not favourable; but as you write the day after publication, it can hardly be decided what opinion will predominate. You seem in a fright, and doubtless with cause. Come what may, I never will flatter the million's canting in any shape: circumstances may or may not have placed me at times in a situation to lead the public opinion, but the public opinion never led, nor ever shall lead, me. I will not sit 'on a degraded throne'; so pray put Messrs. Southey, or Sotheby, or Tom Moore, or Horace Twiss upon it—they will all of them be transported with their coronation.

You have bought Harlow's [2] drawings of Margarita and me rather dear methinks; but since you desire the story of Margarita Cogni, you shall be told it, though it may be lengthy.

Her face is of the fine Venetian cast of the old Time, and her figure, though perhaps too tall, not less fine—taken altogether in the national dress.

In the summer of 1817, Hobhouse and myself were sauntering on horseback along the Brenta one evening, when, amongst a group of peasants, we remarked two girls as the prettiest we had seen for some time. About this period, there had been great distress in the country, and I had a little relieved some of the

---

[1] Massinger, *A New Way to Pay Old Debts*, v, i, 318.

[2] George Henry Harlow (1787–1819), the portrait painter, visited Italy in 1818.

people. Generosity makes a great figure at very little cost in
Venetian livres, and mine had probably been exaggerated—as
an Englishman's. Whether they remarked us looking at them
or no, I know not; but one of them called out to me in Venetian,
'Why do not you, who relieve others, think of us also?' I turned
round and answered her—'*Cara, tu sei troppo bella e giovane per
aver' bisogno del' soccorso mio*'. She answered, 'If you saw my
hut and my food, you would not say so'. All this passed half
jestingly, and I saw no more of her for some days.

A few evenings after, we met with these two girls again, and
they addressed us more seriously, assuring us of the truth of
their statement. They were cousins; Margarita married, the
other single. As I doubted still of the circumstances, I took
the business up in a different light, and made an appointment
with them for the next evening. Hobhouse had taken a fancy
to the single lady, who was much shorter in stature, but a very
pretty girl also. They came attended by a third woman, who
was cursedly in the way, and Hobhouse's charmer took fright
(I don't mean at Hobhouse, but at not being married—for here
no woman will do anything under adultery), and flew off; and
mine made some bother—at the propositions, and wished to
consider of them. I told her, 'if you really are in want, I will
relieve you without any conditions whatever, and you may
make love with me or no just as you please—*that* shall make no
difference; but if you are not in absolute necessity, this is naturally a rendezvous, and I presumed that you understood this
when you made the appointment'. She said that she had no
objection to make love with me, as she was married, and all
married women did it: but that her husband (a baker) was
somewhat ferocious, and would do her a mischief. In short,
in a few evenings we arranged our affairs, and for two years, in
the course of which I had more women than I can count or
recount, she was the only one who preserved over me an ascendancy which was often disputed, and never impaired. As she
herself used to say publicly, 'It don't matter, he may have five
hundred; but he will always come back to me'.

The reasons of this were, firstly, her person—very dark, tall,
the Venetian face, very fine black eyes—and certain other
qualities which need not be mentioned. She was two and
twenty years old, and, never having had children, had not
spoilt her figure * * * * * * * * She was, besides, a thorough
Venetian in her dialect, in her thoughts, in her countenance,
in every thing, with all their naïveté and Pantaloon humour.

Besides, she could neither read nor write, and could not plague me with letters,—except twice that she paid sixpence to a public scribe, under the piazza, to make a letter for her, upon some occasion, when I was ill and could not see her. In other respects she was somewhat fierce and *prepotente*, that is, overbearing, and used to walk in whenever it suited her, with no very great regard to time, place, nor persons; and if she found any women in her way, she knocked them down.

When I first knew her, I was in *relazione* (*liaison*) with la Signora Segati, who was silly enough one evening at Dolo, accompanied by some of her female friends, to threaten her; for the Gossips of the Villeggiatura had already found out, by the neighing of my horse one evening, that I used to 'ride late in the night' to meet the Fornarina. Margarita threw back her veil (*fazziolo*), and replied in very explicit Venetian, '*You* are *not* his *wife*: *I* am *not* his *wife*: *you* are his *Donna*, and *I* am his *Donna*: *your* husband is a cuckold, and *mine* is another. For the rest, what *right* have you to reproach me? if he prefers what is mine to what is yours, is it my fault? if you wish to secure him, tie him to your petticoat-string; but do not think to speak to me without a reply, because you happen to be richer than I am'. Having delivered this pretty piece of eloquence (which I transiate as it was related to me by a bye-stander), she went on her way, leaving a numerous audience with Madame Segati, to ponder at her leisure on the dialogue between them.

When I came to Venice for the Winter, she followed. I never had any regular *liaison* with her, but whenever she came I never allowed any other connection to interfere with her; and as she found herself out to be a favourite, she came pretty often. But she had inordinate Self-love, and was not tolerant of other women, except of the Segati, who was, as she said, my regular *Amica*, so that, I being at that time somewhat promiscuous, there was great confusion and demolition of head-dresses and handkerchiefs; and sometimes my servants, in 'redding the fray'[1] between her and other feminine persons, received more knocks than acknowledgements for their peaceful endeavours. At the *Cavalchina*, the masqued ball on the last night of the Carnival, where all the World goes, she snatched off the mask of Madame Contarini, a lady noble by birth, and decent in conduct, for no other reason, but because she happened to be leaning on my arm. You may suppose what a cursed noise this made; but this is only one of her pranks.

[1] Cf. *Old Mortality*, chap. iv.

At last she quarrelled with her husband, and one evening ran away to my house. I told her this would not do: she said she would lie in the street, but not go back to him; that he beat her (the gentle tigress), spent her money, and scandalously neglected his Oven. As it was Midnight I let her stay, and next day there was no moving her at all. Her husband came, roaring and crying, and entreating her to come back:—*not* she! He then applied to the Police, and they applied to me: I told them and her husband to *take* her; I did not want her; she had come, and I could not fling her out of the window; but they might conduct her through that or the door if they chose it. She went before the Commissary, but was obliged to return with that *becco ettico* ('consumptive cuckold'), as she called the poor man, who has a Ptisick. In a few days she ran away again. After a precious piece of work, she fixed herself in my house, really and truly without my consent, but, owing to my indolence, and not being able to keep my countenance; for if I began in a rage, she always finished by making me laugh with some Venetian pantaloonery or another; and the Gipsy knew this well enough, as well as her other powers of persuasion, and exerted them with the usual tact and success of all She-things—high and low, they are all alike for that.

Madame Benzone also took her under her protection, and then her head turned. She was always in extremes, either crying or laughing; and so fierce when angered, that she was the terror of men, women, and children—for she had the strength of an Amazon, with the temper of Medea. She was a fine animal, but quite untameable. *I* was the only person that could at all keep her in any order, and when she saw me really angry (which they tell me is rather a savage sight), she subsided. But she had a thousand fooleries: in her *fazziolo*, the dress of the lower orders, she looked beautiful; but, alas! she longed for a hat and feathers, and all I could say or do (and I said much) could not prevent this travestie. I put the first into the fire; but I got tired of burning them, before she did of buying them, so that she made herself a figure—for they did not at all become her.

Then she would have her gowns with a *tail*—like a lady, forsooth: nothing would serve her but '*l'abito colla coua*', or *cua*, (that is the Venetian for '*la Coda*', the tail or train,) and as her cursed pronunciation of the word made me laugh, there was an end of all controversy, and she dragged this diabolical tail after her every where.

In the mean time, she beat the women and stopped my letters. I found her one day pondering over one: she used to try to find out by their shape whether they were feminine or no; and she used to lament her ignorance, and actually studied her Alphabet, on purpose (as she declared) to open all letters addressed to me and read their contents.

I must not omit to do justice to her housekeeping qualities: after she came into my house as *donna di governo*, the expences were reduced to less than half, and every body did their duty better—the apartments were kept in order, and every thing and every body else, except herself.

That she had a sufficient regard for me in her wild way, I had many reasons to believe. I will mention one. In the autumn, one day, going to the Lido, with my Gondoliers, we were overtaken by a heavy squall, and the Gondola put in peril—hats blown away, boat filling, oar lost, tumbling sea, thunder, rain in torrents, night coming, and wind encreasing. On our return, after a tight struggle, I found her on the open steps of the Mocenigo palace, on the Grand Canal, with her great black eyes flashing through her tears, and the long dark hair, which was streaming drenched with rain over her brows and breast. She was perfectly exposed to the storm; and the wind blowing her hair and dress about her tall thin figure, and the lightning flashing round her, with the waves rolling at her feet, made her look like Medea alighted from her chariot, or the Sibyl of the tempest that was rolling around her, the only living thing within hail at that moment except ourselves. On seeing me safe, she did not wait to greet me, as might be expected, but calling out to me—*Ah! can' della Madonna, xe esto il tempo per andar' al' Lido?* (Ah! Dog of the Virgin, is this a time to go to Lido?) ran into the house, and solaced herself with scolding the boatmen for not foreseeing the '*temporale*'. I was told by the servants that she had only been prevented from coming in a boat to look after me, by the refusal of all the Gondoliers of the Canal to put out into the harbour in such a moment: and that then she sate down on the steps in all the thickest of the Squall, and would neither be removed nor comforted. Her joy at seeing me again was moderately mixed with ferocity, and gave me the idea of a tigress over her recovered Cubs.

But her reign drew near a close. She became quite ungovernable some months after; and a concurrence of complaints, some true, and many false—'a favourite has no friend'[1]

[1] Gray, *On the Death of a Favourite Cat.*

—determined me to part with her. I told her quietly that she must return home (she had acquired a sufficient provision for herself and mother, etc., in my service,) and She refused to quit the house. I was firm, and she went, threatening knives and revenge. I told her that I had seen knives drawn before her time, and that if she chose to begin, there was a knife, and fork also, at her service on the table, and that intimidation would not do. The next day, while I was at dinner, she walked in, (having broke open a glass door that led from the hall below to the staircase, by way of prologue,) and, advancing strait up to the table, snatched the knife from my hand, cutting me slightly in the thumb in the operation. Whether she meant to use this against herself or me, I know not—probably against neither—but Fletcher seized her by the arms, and disarmed her. I then called my boatmen, and desired them to get the Gondola ready, and conduct her to her own house again, seeing carefully that she did herself no mischief by the way. She seemed quite quiet, and walked down stairs. I resumed my dinner.

We heard a great noise: I went out, and met them on the staircase, carrying her up stairs. She had thrown herself into the Canal. That she intended to destroy herself, I do not believe; but when we consider the fear women and men who can't swim have of deep or even of shallow water, (and the Venetians in particular, though they live on the waves,) and that it was also night, and dark, and very cold, it shows that she had a devilish spirit of some sort within her. They had got her out without much difficulty or damage, excepting the salt water she had swallowed, and the wetting she had undergone.

I foresaw her intention to refix herself, and sent for a Surgeon, enquiring how many hours it would require to restore her from her agitation; and he named the time. I then said, 'I give you that time, and more if you require it; but at the expiration of the prescribed period, if *She* does not leave the house, *I* will'.

All my people were consternated—they had always been frightened at her, and were now paralyzed: they wanted me to apply to the police, to guard myself, etc., etc., like a pack of snivelling servile boobies as they were. I did nothing of the kind, thinking that I might as well end that way as another; besides, I had been used to savage women, and knew their ways.

I had her sent home quietly after her recovery, and never saw her since, except twice at the opera, at a distance amongst the audience. She made many attempts to return, but no more violent ones. And this is the story of Margarita Cogni, as far as it belongs to me.

I forgot to mention that she was very devout, and would cross herself if she heard the prayer-time strike—sometimes when that ceremony did not appear to be much in unison with what she was then about.

She was quick in reply; as, for instance—One day when she had made me very angry with beating somebody or other, I called her a *Cow* (*Cow*, in Italian, is a sad affront and tantamount to the feminine of dog in English). I called her '*Vacca*'. She turned round, curtesied, and answered, '*Vacca tua*, '*Celenza*' (i.e. *Eccelenza*). '*Your* Cow, please your Excellency'. In short, she was, as I said before, a very fine Animal, of considerable beauty and energy, with many good and several amusing qualities, but wild as a witch and fierce as a demon. She used to boast publicly of her ascendancy over me, contrasting it with that of other women, and assigning for it sundry reasons, physical and moral, which did more credit to her person than her modesty. True it was, that they all tried to get her away, and no one succeeded till her own absurdity helped them. Whenever there was a competition, and sometimes one would be shut in one room and one in another to prevent battle, she had generally the preference.

Yours very truly and affectionately,

B.

P.S.—The Countess G[uiccioli] is much better than she was. I sent you, before leaving Venice, a letter containing the real original sketch which gave rise to the *Vampire*, etc.: did you get it?

137. TO JOHN MURRAY

Ravenna, August 9, 1819.

DEAR SIR,

I wrote a long letter in answer to yours of the 16th July the other day, giving you an account of Margarita Cogni, as you wished. But I omitted to tell you her answer when I reproached her for snatching Madame Contarini's mask at the Cavalchina. I represented to her that she was a lady of high birth, '*una dama*', etc. She answered, '*Se Ella è dama, mi* (*io*) *son*' *Veneziana*'—'If she is a lady, I am a Venetian'. This would have been fine a hundred years ago—the pride of the nation rising up against the pride of Aristocracy: but, alas! Venice, and her people, and her nobles, are alike returning fast to the Ocean; and where there is no independence, there can be no real self-respect.

I believe that I mistook or misstated one of her phrases in my letter: it should have been—'*Can' della Madonna! cosa vus' tu? Esto non è tempo per andar' a Lido*'. I do not remember how I had worded it, but have a general idea of having blundered.

Talking of blunders reminds me of Ireland—Ireland of Moore. What is this I see in Galignani[1] about 'Bermuda—Agent—deputy—appeal—attachment', etc.?[2] what is the matter? is it anything in which his friends can be of use to him? Pray inform me.

Of *Don Juan* I hear nothing further from *you*—you chicken-hearted, silver-paper Stationer, you! But the papers don't seem so fierce as the letter you sent seemed to anticipate, by their extracts at least in *Galignani's Messenger*. I never saw such a set of fellows as you are: and then the pains taken to exculpate the modest publisher—he had remonstrated, forsooth! I will write a preface that *shall* exculpate *you* and Hobhouse, etc., completely, on that point; but, at the same time, I will cut you all up (and *you* in particular), like Gourds. You have no more soul than the Count de Caylus[3] (who assured his friends, on his death-bed, that he had none, and that *he* must know better than they whether he had one or no,) and no more blood than a Water-Melon! And I see there hath been asterisks, and what Perry used to call 'domned cutting and slashing'. But, never mind.

I write in haste—tomorrow I set off for Bologna—I write to you with thunder, lightning, etc., and all the winds of heaven whistling through my hair, and the racket of preparation to boot. My 'Mistress dear', who hath 'fed my heart upon smiles and wine'[4] for the last two months, set off for Bologna with her husband this morning, and it seems that I follow him at three to-morrow morning. I cannot tell how our romance will end, but it hath gone on hitherto most erotically—such perils and escapes—Juan's are a child's play in comparison. The fools think that all my *Poeshie* is always allusive to my *own* adventures: I have had at one time or another better and more

---

[1] i.e. *The Messenger*, a journal published in Paris by John Anthony Galignani.

[2] See page 190. Unable to satisfy his claimants, Moore had taken refuge in Paris.

[3] 1692–1765.   [4] Moore, *Irish Melodies*, 'The Legacy'.

extraordinary and perilous and pleasant than these, any day of the week, if I might tell them; but that must never be.

I hope Mrs. M. has accouched.

Yours ever,

B.

138. TO JOHN MURRAY

Bologna, August 12, 1819.

DEAR SIR,

I do not know how far I may be able to reply to your letter, for I am not very well to-day. Last night I went to the representation of Alfieri's *Mirra*, the last two acts of which threw me into convulsions. I do not mean by that word a lady's hysterics, but the agony of reluctant tears, and the choaking shudder, which I do not often undergo for fiction. This is but the second time for anything under reality; the first was on seeing Kean's Sir Giles Overreach.[1] The worst was, that the '*dama*', in whose box I was, went off in the same way, I really believe more from fright than any other sympathy—at least with the players: but she has been ill, and I have been ill, and we are all languid and pathetic this morning, with great expenditure of Sal Volatile. But to return to your letter of the 23d of July.

You are right, Gifford is right, Crabbe is right, Hobhouse is right—you are all right, and I am all wrong; but do, pray, let me have that pleasure. Cut me up root and branch; quarter me in the *Quarterly*; send round my *disjecti membra poetæ*, like those of the Levite's Concubine;[2] make me, if you will, a spectacle to men and angels; but don't ask me to alter, for I can't:—I am obstinate and lazy—and there's the truth.

But, nevertheless, I will answer your friend C[ohen],[3] who objects to the quick succession of fun and gravity, as if in that case the gravity did not (in intention, at least) heighten the fun. His metaphor is, that 'we are never scorched and drenched at the same time'. Blessings on his experience! Ask him these questions about 'scorching and drenching'. Did he never play at Cricket, or walk a mile in hot weather? Did he never spill a dish of tea over himself in handing the cup to his charmer, to the great shame of his nankeen breeches? Did he never swim in the sea at Noonday with the Sun in his eyes and on his head, which all the foam of Ocean could not cool? Did he never draw his foot out a tub of too hot water, damning his

---

[1] In Massinger's *New Way to Pay Old Debts*.
[2] See Judges xix, 29.   [3] Francis Cohen, a critic and historian.

eyes and his valet's? * * * * * Was he ever in a Turkish bath, that marble paradise of sherbet and Sodomy? Was he ever in a cauldron of boiling oil, like St. John? or in the sulphureous waves of hell? (where he ought to be for his 'scorching and drenching at the same time'). Did he never tumble into a river or lake, fishing, and sit in his wet cloathes in the boat, or on the bank, afterwards 'scorched and drenched', like a true sportsman? 'Oh for breath to utter!' [1]—but make him my compliments; he is a clever fellow for all that—a very clever fellow.

You ask me for the plan of Donny Johnny: I *have* no plan —I *had* no plan; but I had or have materials; though if, like Tony Lumpkin, I am 'to be snubbed so when I am in spirits', [2] the poem will be naught, and the poet turn serious again. If it don't take, I will leave it off where it is, with all due respect to the Public; but if continued, it must be in my own way. You might as well make Hamlet (or Diggory) [3] 'act mad' in a strait waistcoat as trammel my buffoonery, if I am to be a buffoon: their gestures and my thoughts would only be pitiably absurd and ludicrously constrained. Why, Man, the Soul of such writing is its licence; at least the *liberty* of that *licence*, if one likes—*not* that one should abuse it: it is like trial by Jury and Peerage and the Habeas Corpus—a very fine thing, but chiefly in the *reversion*; because no one wishes to be tried for the mere pleasure of proving his possession of the privilege.

But a truce with these reflections. You are too earnest and eager about a work never intended to be serious. Do you suppose that I could have any intention but to giggle and make giggle?—a playful satire, with as little poetry as could be helped, was what I meant: and as to the indecency, do, pray, read in Boswell what *Johnson*, the sullen moralist, says of *Prior* and Paulo Purgante. [4]

Will you get a favour done for me? *You* can, by your Government friends, Croker, Canning, or my old Schoolfellow Peel, and I can't. Here it is. Will you ask them to appoint (*without salary or emolument*) a noble Italian [5] (whom I will name afterwards) Consul or Vice-Consul for Ravenna? He is a man of very large property,—noble, too; but he wishes to

---

[1] *Henry IV*, Part I, ii, iv, 248.   [2] *She Stoops to Conquer*, ii.
[3] In Jackman's *All the World's a Stage*.
[4] *Paulo Purganti and his Wife*. Johnson when questioned said: 'There is nothing in Prior that will excite to lewdness. If Lord Hailes thinks there is, he must be more combustible than other people'.
[5] Count Guiccioli.

have a British protection, in case of changes. Ravenna is near the sea. He wants *no emolument* whatever: that his office might be useful, I know; as I lately sent off from Ravenna to Trieste a poor devil of an English Sailor, who had remained there sick, sorry, and penniless (having been set ashore in 1814), from the want of any accredited agent able or willing to help him homewards. Will you get this done? It will be the greatest favour to me. If you do, I will then send his name and condition, subject, of course, to rejection, if *not* approved when known.

I know that in the Levant you make consuls and Vice-Consuls, perpetually, of foreigners. This man is a Patrician, and has twelve thousand a year. His motive is a British protection in case of new Invasions. Don't you think Croker would do it for us? To be sure, *my interest* is rare!! but, perhaps a brother-wit in the Tory line might do a good turn at the request of so harmless and long absent a Whig, particularly as there is no *salary* nor *burthen* of any sort to be annexed to the office.

I can assure you, I should look upon it as a great obligation; but, alas! that very circumstance may, very probably, operate to the contrary—indeed, it ought. But I have, at least, been an honest and an open enemy. Amongst your many splendid Government Connections, could not you, think you, get our Bibulus [1] made a Consul? Or make me one, that I may make him my Vice. You may be assured that, in case of accidents in Italy, he would be no feeble adjunct—as you would think if you knew his property.

What is all this about Tom Moore? but why do I ask? since the state of my own affairs would not permit me to be of use to him, although they are greatly improved since 1816, and may, with some more luck and a little prudence, become quite Clear. It seems his Claimants are *American* merchants? *There* goes *Nemesis*! Moore abused America. It is always thus in the long run:—Time, the Avenger. You have seen every trampler down, in turn, from Buonaparte to the simplest individuals. You saw how some were avenged even upon my insignificance, and how in turn Romilly paid for his atrocity. It is an odd World; but the Watch has its mainspring, after all.

So the Prince has been repealing Lord Ed. Fitzgerald's forfeiture? [2] *Ecco un' Sonnetto !*

[1] Consul with Julius Caesar in 59 B.C., though his enemy.
[2] Lord Edward Fitzgerald (1763–98) had been attainted for high treason.

To be the father of the fatherless,
To stretch the hand from the throne's height, and raise
    His offspring, who expired in other days
To make thy Sire's Sway by a kingdom less,—
This is to be a Monarch, and repress
    Envy into unutterable praise.
Dismiss thy Guard, and trust thee to such traits,
For who would lift a hand, except to bless?
Were it not easy, Sir, and is 't not sweet
To make thyself beloved? and to be
Omnipotent by Mercy's means? for thus
Thy Sovereignty would grow but more complete,
A Despot thou, and yet thy people free,
And by the Heart, not Hand, enslaving us.

There, you dogs: there 's a Sonnet for you: you won't have such as that in a hurry from Mr. Fitzgerald.[1] You may publish it with my name, an ye wool. He deserves all praise, bad and good; it was a very noble piece of principality. Would you like an epigram—a translation?

> If for silver, or for gold,
>   You could melt ten thousand pimples
>   Into half a dozen dimples,
> Then your face we might behold,
>   Looking, doubtless, much more smugly,
>   Yet even then 'twould be damned ugly.

This was written on some Frenchwoman, by Rulhières,[2] I believe. And so 'good-morrow t' ye, good Master lieutenant.'[3]

Yours,

BYRON.

139. TO JOHN CAM HOBHOUSE

MY DEAR HOBHOUSE,   Bologna, August 23rd, 1819.

I have received a letter from Murray containing the *British Review's* eleventh article. Had you any conception of a man's tumbling into such a trap as Roberts has done?[4] Why it is precisely what he was wished to do.

---

[1] William Thomas Fitzgerald, See page 122.
[2] Claude Carloman de Rulhière (1735–91).
[3] *Othello*, III, i, 44.
[4] William Roberts, the editor of the *British Review*, in reviewing *Don Juan* indignantly denied that Byron had 'bribed My Grandmother's Review,—the British'. (See *Don Juan*, I, stanzas ccix–ccx.)

I have enclosed an epistle for publication with a queer signature [1] (to Murray, who should keep the anonymous still about D. Juan) in answer to Roberts, which pray approve if you can. It is written in an evening and morning in haste, with ill-health and worse nerves. I am so bilious, that I nearly lose my head, and so nervous that I cry for nothing; at least to-day I burst into tears, all alone by myself, over a cistern of gold-fishes, which are not pathetic animals.

I can assure you it is not Mr. Roberts, or any of his crew that can affect me; but I have been excited and agitated, and exhausted mentally and bodily all this summer, till I sometimes begin to think not only 'that I shall die at top first',[2] but that the moment is not very remote. I have had no particular cause of griefs, except the usual accompaniments of all unlawful passions.

I have to do with a woman rendered perfectly disinterested by her situation in life, and young and amiable and pretty; in short as good, and at least as attentive as anything of the sex can be, with all the advantages and disadvantages of being scarcely twenty years old, and only two out of her Romagnuolo convent at Faenza.

But I feel—and I feel it bitterly—that a man should not consume his life at the side and on the bosom of a woman, and a stranger; that even the recompense, and it is much, is not enough, and that this Cicisbean existence [3] is to be condemned.

But I have neither the strength of mind to break my chain, nor the insensibility which would deaden its weight. I cannot tell what will become of me—to leave, or to be left would at present drive me quite out of my senses; and yet to what have I conducted myself?

I have, luckily, or unluckily, no ambition left; it would be better if I had, it would at least awake me; whereas at present I merely start in my sleep.

I think I wrote to you last week, but really (like Lord Grizzle [4]) cannot positively tell.

Why don't you write? pray do—never mind *Don Juan*, let him tumble—and let me too—like Jack and Gill.

---

[1] *A Letter to the Editor of 'My Grandmother's Review'*, signed, 'Wortley Clutterbuck'. It was published later in the *Liberal*.
[2] Swift's remark of himself, when he saw an elm withered in the upper branches.
[3] A *cicisbeo* is the recognized gallant of a married woman.
[4] In Fielding's *Tom Thumb*.

Write, and believe me—as long as I can keep my sanity, ever yours most truly and affect^{ly},

B.

140. TO JOHN MURRAY

DEAR SIR,   Bologna, August 24, 1819.

I wrote to you by last post, enclosing a buffooning letter for publication, addressed to the buffoon Roberts, who has thought proper to tie a canister to his own tail. It was written off hand, and in the midst of circumstances not very favourable to facetiousness, so that there may, perhaps, be more bitterness than enough for that sort of small acid punch. You will tell me.

Keep the *anonymous*, in every case: it helps what fun there may be; but if the matter grows serious about *Don Juan*, and you feel *yourself* in a scrape, or *me* either, *own that I am the author*. *I* will never *shrink*; and if *you* do, I can always answer you in the question of Guatimozin to his minister—each being on his own coals.[1]

I wish that I had been in better spirits, but I am out of sorts, out of nerves; and now and then (I begin to fear) out of my senses. All this Italy has done for me, and not England: I defy all of you, and your climate to boot, to make me mad. But if ever I do really become a Bedlamite, and wear a strait waistcoat, let me be brought back among you; your people will then be proper compagny.

I assure you what I here say and feel has nothing to do with England, either in a literary or personal point of view. All my present pleasures or plagues are as Italian as the Opera. And after all, they are but trifles, for all this arises from my *dama's* being in the country for three days (at Capofiume); but as I could never live for but one human being at a time, (and, I assure you, *that one* has never been *myself*, as you may know by the consequences, for the *Selfish* are *successful* in life,) I feel alone and unhappy.

I have sent for my daughter from Venice, and I ride daily, and walk in a Garden, under a purple canopy of grapes, and sit by a fountain, and talk with the Gardener of his toils, which seem greater than Adam's, and with his wife, and with his Son's wife, who is the youngest of the party, and, I think, talks best of the three. Then I revisit the Campo Santo, and my old friend, the Sexton, has two—but *one* the prettiest daughter

[1] When the minister showed signs of giving way under torture Guatimozin is said to have asked: 'Am I now reposing on a bed of flowers?'

imaginable; and I amuse myself with contrasting her beautiful and innocent face of fifteen with the skulls with which he has peopled several cells, and particularly with that of one skull dated 1766, which was once covered (the tradition goes,) by the most lovely features of Bologna—noble and rich. When I look at these, and at this girl—when I think of what *they were*, and what *she* must be—why, then, my dear Murray, I won't shock you by saying what I think. It is little matter what becomes of us 'bearded men', but I don't like the notion of a beautiful woman's lasting less than a beautiful tree—than her own picture—her own shadow, which won't change so to the Sun as her face to the mirror. I must leave off, for my head aches consumedly: I have never been quite well since the night of the representation of Alfieri's *Mirra,* a fortnight ago.

Yours ever,

B.

141. TO THE COUNTESS GUICCIOLI [1]

My dear Teresa,

Bologna, August 25, 1819.

I have read this book in your garden;—my love, you were absent, or else I could not have read it. It is a favourite book of yours, and the writer was a friend of mine. You will not understand these English words, and *others* will not understand them—which is the reason I have not scrawled them in Italian. But you will recognize the handwriting of him who passionately loved you, and you will divine that, over a book which was yours, he could only think of love. In that word, beautiful in all languages, but most so in yours—*Amor mio*—is comprised my existence here and hereafter. I feel I exist here, and I fear that I shall exist hereafter,—to *what* purpose you will decide; my destiny rests with you, and you are a woman, eighteen years of age, and two out of a convent. I wish that you had stayed there, with all my heart,—or, at least, that I had never met you in your married state.

But all this is too late. I love you, and you love me,—at least, you *say so*, and *act* as if you *did* so, which last is a great consolation in all events. But *I* more than love you, and cannot cease to love you.

Think of me, sometimes, when the Alps and the ocean divide us,—but they never will, unless you *wish* it.

Byron.

[1] This letter was written in the last page of the Countess's copy of Madame de Staël's *Corinne*.

142. TO JOHN CAM HOBHOUSE

Venice, Oct. 3rd, 1819.

DEAR HOBHOUSE,

I wrote to Murray last week and begged him to reassure you of my health and sanity, as far as I know at present. At Bologna I was out of sorts in health and spirits. Here—I have health at least.

My South American project, of which I believe I spoke to you (as you mention it)—was this. I perceived by the inclosed paragraphs [1] that advantageous offers were—or are to be held out to settlers in the Venezuela territory. My affairs in England are nearly settled or in prospect of settlement; in Italy I have no debts, and I could leave it when I choose. The Anglo-Americans are a little too coarse for me, and their climate too cold, and I should prefer the others. I could soon grapple with the Spanish language. Ellice or others would get me letters to Bolivar and his government, and if men of little, or no property are encouraged there, surely with present income, and—if I could sell Rochdale—with some capital, I might be suffered as a landholder there, or at least a tenant, and if possible, and legal—a Citizen. I wish you would speak to *Perry* of the *M[orning] C[hronicle]*—who is their Gazetteer—about this, and ask like Jeremy Diddler [2]—not for eighteen pence—but information on the subject. I assure you that I am very *serious* in the idea, and that the notion has been about me for a long time, as you will see by the worn state of the advertisement.

I should go there with my natural daughter, Allegra—now nearly three years old, and with me here,—and pitch my tent for good and all.

I am not tired of Italy, but a man must be a Cicisbeo and a Singer in duets, and a connoisseur of Operas—or nothing—here. I have made some progress in all these accomplishments, but I can't say that I don't feel the degradation. Better be an unskilful Planter, an awkward settler,—better be a hunter, or anything, than a flatterer of fiddlers, and fan carrier of a woman. I like women—God he knows—but the more their system here developes upon me, the worse it seems, after Turkey too; here the *polygamy* is all on the female side. I have been an intriguer, a husband, a whoremonger, and now I am a Cavalier Servente —by the holy! it is a strange sensation. After having belonged

---

[1] Newspaper cuttings.   [2] In Kenney's *Raising the Wind*.

in my own and other countries to the intriguing, the married, and the keeping parts of the town,—to be sure an honest arrangement is the best, and I have had that too, and have—they expect it to be for *life*, thereby, I presume, excluding longevity. But let us be serious, if possible.

You must not talk to me of England, that is out of the question. I had a house and lands, and a wife and child, and a name there—once—but all these things are transmuted or sequestered. Of the last, and best, ten years of my life, nearly six have been passed out of it. I feel no love for the soil after the treatment I received before leaving it for the last time, but I do not hate it enough to wish to take a part in its calamities, as on either side harm must be done before good can accrue; revolutions are not to be made with rosewater. My taste for revolution is abated, with my other passions.

Yet I want a country, and a home, and—if possible—a free one. I am not yet thirty-two years of age. I might still be a decent Citizen, and found a house, and a family as good—or better—than the former. I could at all events occupy myself rationally, my hopes are not high, nor my ambition extensive, and when tens of thousands of our countrymen are colonizing (like the Greeks of old in Sicily and Italy) from so many causes, does my notion seem visionary or irrational? There is no freedom in Europe—that 's certain; it is besides a worn out portion of the globe. What I should be glad of is *information* as to the encouragement, the means required, and what is acceded, and what would be my probable reception. Perry—or Ellice or many merchants would be able to tell you this for me. I won't go there to travel, but to settle. Do not laugh at me; you will, but I assure you I am quite in earnest if the thing be practicable. I do not want to have anything to do with war projects, but to go there as a settler, and if as a citizen all the better, my own government would not, I think, refuse me permission, if they know their own interest; such fellows as I am are no desideratum for Sidmouth [1] at present, I think. Address to me at Venice. I should of course come to Liverpool, or some town on your coast, to take my passage and receive my credentials. Believe me,

Ever yours most truly,
BYRON.

---

[1] Henry Addington, Viscount Sidmouth, was Home Secretary.

143. TO JOHN MURRAY

Venice, October 29, 1819.

DEAR MURRAY,

Yours of the 15th came yesterday. I am sorry that you do not mention a large letter addressed to *your care* for Lady Byron, from me, at Bologna, two months ago. Pray tell me, was this letter received and forwarded?

You say nothing of the Vice Consulate for the Ravenna patrician, from which it is to be inferred that the thing will not be done.

I had written about a hundred stanzas of a *third* Canto to *Don Juan*, but the reception of the two first is no encouragement to you nor me to proceed.

I had also written about 600 lines of a poem, the *Vision* (or *Prophecy*) of *Dante*,[1] the subject a view of Italy in the ages down to the present—supposing Dante to speak in his own person, previous to his death, and embracing all topics in the way of prophecy, like Lycophron's *Cassandra*.[2] But this and the other are both at a standstill for the present.

I gave Moore,[3] who is gone to Rome, my *Life* in MS., in 78 folio sheets, brought down to 1816. But this I put into his hands for *his* care, as he has some other MSS. of mine—a journal kept in 1814, etc. Neither are for publication during my life; but when I am cold you may do what you please. In the mean time, if you like to read them you may, and show them to any body you like—I care not.

The *Life* is *Memoranda*, and not *Confessions*. I have left out all my *loves* (except in a general way), and many other of the most important things (because I must not compromise other people), so that it is like the play of *Hamlet*—'the part of Hamlet omitted by particular desire'. But you will find many opinions, and some fun, with a detailed account of my marriage and its consequences, as true as a party concerned can make such accounts, for I suppose we are all prejudiced.

I have never read over this life since it was written, so that I know not exactly what it may repeat or contain. Moore and I passed some merry days together; but so far from 'seducing me to England', as you suppose, the account he gave of me and mine was of any thing but a nature to make me wish to return:

---

[1] Published, with *Marino Faliero*, in April 1821.

[2] *Circa* 284 B.C.

[3] Moore, touring with Lord John Russell, had spent a few days in Venice.

it is not such opinions of the public that would weigh with me one way or the other; but I think they should weigh with others of my friends before they ask me to return to a place for which I have no great inclination.

I probably must return for business, or in my way to America. Pray, did you get a letter for Hobhouse, who will have told you the contents? I understood that the Venezuelan commissioners had orders to treat with emigrants; now I want to go there. I should not make a bad South-American planter, and I should take my natural daughter, Allegra, with me, and settle. I wrote at length to Hobhouse, to get information from Perry, who, I suppose, is the best topographer and trumpeter of the new Republicans. Pray write.

Yours ever,

B.

P.S.—Moore and I did nothing but laugh: he will tell you of 'my whereabouts',[1] and all my proceedings at this present; they are as usual. You should not let those fellows publish false *Don Juans*;[2] but do not put *my name*, because I mean to cut Roberts up like a gourd, in the preface, if I continue the poem.

144. TO RICHARD BELGRAVE HOPPNER

October 29, 1819.

My dear Hoppner,

The Ferrara Story is of a piece with all the rest of the Venetian manufacture; you may judge. I only changed horses there since I wrote to you after my visit in June last. '*Convent*'— and '*carry off*' quotha!—and '*girl*'—I should like to know *who* has been carried off—except poor dear *me*. I have been more ravished myself than any body since the Trojan war; but as to the arrest and it's causes—one is as true as the other, and I can account for the invention of neither. I suppose it is some confusion of the tale of the F[ornarina]—and of M̃ᵉ Guiccioli— and half a dozen more—but it is useless to unravel the web, when one has only to brush it away.

I shall settle with Muster Edgecombe who looks very blue at your *in-decision*, and swears that he is the best arithmetician in Europe; and so I think also, for he makes out two and two to be five.

---

[1] *Macbeth*, II, i, 58.
[2] *Don John, Canto the Third*, by W. Hone, and *Don Juan Unread*, by Dr. Maginn, 1819.

You may see me next week. I have a horse or two more (five in all) and I shall repossess myself of Lido, and I will rise earlier, and we will go and shake our livers over the beach as heretofore—if you like, and we will make the Adriatic roar again with our hatred of that now empty Oyster shell without it's pearl—the city of Venice.

Murray sent me a letter yesterday; the impostors have published *two* new *third* Cantos of *Don Juan*; the devil take the impudence of some blackguard bookseller or other there*for*.

Perhaps I did not make myself understood. He told me the sale had not been great—1200 out of 1500 quarto I believe (which is nothing after selling 13000 of *The Corsair* in one day) but that the 'best judges, etc.', had said it was very fine, and clever, and particularly good English, and poetry, and all those consolatory things which are not, however, worth a single copy to a bookseller;—and as to the author—of course I am in a damned passion at the bad taste of the times, and swear there is nothing like posterity, who of course must know more of the matter than their Grandfathers.

There has been an eleventh commandment to the women not to read it—and what is still more extraordinary they seem not to have broken it. But that can be of little import to them, poor things, for the reading or non-reading a book will never keep * * * [them from evil];—but it is of import to Murray, who will be in scandal for his aiding as publisher.

He is bold howsomedever—wanting two more cantos against the winter. I think that he had better not, for by the larkins! it will only make a new row for him.

Edgecombe is gone to Venice to-day to consign my chattels to t' other fellow.

Count G. comes to Venice next week and I am requested to consign his wife to him, which shall be done—with all her linen.

What you say of the long evenings at the Mira, or Venice, reminds me of what *Curran*[1] said to Moore—'so—I hear—you have married a pretty woman—and a very good creature too—an excellent creature — pray — um — *how do you pass your evenings?*' it is a devil of a question that, and perhaps as easy to answer with a wife as with a mistress; but surely they are longer than the nights. I am all for morality now, and shall confine myself henceforward to the strictest adultery, which you will please to recollect is all that that virtuous wife of mine has left me.

[1] John Philpot Curran, the Irish judge and orator, who died in 1817.

If you go to Milan, pray leave at least a *Vice-Consul*—the only Vice that will ever be wanting in Venice. D'Orville is a good fellow. But you should go to England in the Spring with me, and plant Mrs. Hoppner at Berne with her relations for a few months.

I wish you had been here (at Venice I mean not the Mira) when Moore was here; we were very merry and tipsy—he *hated* Venice by the way, and swore it was a sad place.

So—Madame Albrizzi's health is in danger, poor woman. * * * Moore told me that at Geneva they had made a devil of a story of the Fornaretta—'young lady seduced—subsequent abandonment—leap into the grand canal—her being in the hospital of *fous* in consequence'. I should like to know who was nearest being made '*fou*' and be damned to them. Don't you think me in the interesting character of a very ill used gentleman?

I hope your little boy is well. Allegrina is flourishing like a pome-granate blossom.

Yours ever,
BYRON.

145. TO JOHN MURRAY

Venice, November 8, 1819.

DEAR MURRAY,

Mr. Hoppner has lent me a copy of *Don Juan*, Paris Edition, which he tells me is read in Switzerland by Clergymen and ladies with considerable approbation. In the second Canto, you must alter the 49th Stanza to

'Twas twilight, and the sunless day went down
    Over the waste of waters, like a veil
Which if withdrawn would but disclose the frown
    Of one whose hate is masked but to assail:
Thus to their hopeless eyes the Night was shown,
    And grimly darkled o'er their faces pale,
And the dim desolate deep; twelve days had fear
Been their familiar, and now Death was here.

And, in Stanza 208 of the same canto, make the sixth line run

Newly a

Strong palpitation rises, 'tis her boon.

Otherwise there is a syllable too few.

On referring to the MS. I found that I had stupidly blundered all the rhymes of the 49th stanza, such as they are printed. Cast your eye over; you will perceive the necessity of the alteration.

I have been ill these eight days with a tertian fever, caught in the country on horseback in a thunderstorm: yesterday I had the fourth attack. The two last were very smart, the first day as well as the last being preceded by vomiting. It is the fever of the place and the Season. I feel weakened, but not unwell, in the intervals, except headache and lassitude.

Count G. has arrived in Venice, and has presented his Spouse (who had preceded him two months for her health and the pre-scriptions of Dr. Aglietti) with a paper of conditions, regulations of hours and conduct and morals, etc., etc., which he insists on her accepting, and she persists in refusing. I am expressly, it should seem, excluded by this treaty, as an indispensible preliminary; so that they are in high discussion, and what the result may be I know not, particularly as they are consulting friends.

To-night, as Countess G. observed me poring over *Don Juan*, she stumbled by mere chance on the 137th Stanza of the first Canto, and asked me what it meant. I told her, 'Nothing—but "your husband is coming."' [1] As I said this in Italian, with some emphasis, she started up in a fright, and said, '*Oh my God, is* he *coming?*' thinking it was *her own*, who either was or ought to have been at the theatre. You may suppose we laughed when she found out the mistake. You will be amused, as I was;—it happened not three hours ago.

I wrote to you last week, but have added nothing to the third Canto since my fever, nor to the *Prophecy of Dante*. Of the former there are about 110 octaves done; of the latter about 500 lines—perhaps more. Moore saw the third *Juan*, as far as it then went. I do not know if my fever will let me go on with either, and the tertian lasts, they say, a good while. I had it in Malta on my way home, and the Malaria fever in Greece the year before that. The Venetian is not very fierce, but I was delirious one of the nights with it, for an hour or two, and, on my senses coming back, found Fletcher sobbing on one side of the bed, and la Contessa G. weeping on the other; so that I had no want of attendance. I have not yet taken any physician, because, though I think they may relieve in Chronic disorders, such as Gout and the like, etc., etc., etc. (though they can't

[1] 'For God's sake, madam—madam—here's my master.'

cure them)—just as Surgeons are necessary to set bones and tend wounds—yet I think fevers quite out of their reach, and remediable only by diet and Nature.

I don't like the taste of bark, but I suppose that I must take it soon.

Tell Rose [1] that somebody at Milan (an Austrian, Mr. Hoppner says) is answering his book. William Bankes is in quarantine at Trieste. I have not lately heard from you. Excuse this paper: it is long paper shortened for the occasion. What folly is this of Carlile's trial? [2] why let him have the honours of a martyr? it will only advertise the books in question.

Yours ever,

B.

P.S.—As I tell you that the Guiccioli business is on the eve of exploding in one way or the other, I will just add that, without attempting to influence the decision of the Contessa, a good deal depends upon it. If she and her husband make it up, you will, perhaps, see me in England sooner than you expect: if not, I shall retire with her to France or America, change my name, and lead a quiet provincial life. All this may seem odd, but I have got the poor girl into a scrape; and as neither her birth, nor her rank, nor her connections by birth or marriage are inferior to my own, I am in honour bound to support her through: besides, she is a very pretty woman—ask Moore—and not yet one and twenty.

If she gets over this and I get over my tertian, I will, perhaps, look in at Albemarle Street, some of these days, *en passant* to Bolivar.

146. TO THE HON. AUGUSTA LEIGH

Venice. Novr 28th 1819.

MY DEAREST AUGUSTA,

Yours of the 11th came to-day—many thanks. I may be wrong, and right or wrong, have lived long enough not to defend opinions; but my doubts of the funds were Douglas Kinnaird's, who also told me that at the investment Lady B. or her agents had demurred. I know nothing of England but

---

[1] See page 185. The book may be his *Letters from the North of Italy to Henry Hallam, Esq.*, 1819.

[2] Richard Carlile, journalist and printer, was tried and sentenced for republishing Paine's *Age of Reason*, and an American work, *Principles of Nature*.

through Douglas and Hobhouse, who are alarming reformers, and the Paris papers which are full of bank perplexities. The Stake concerns you and your children who are in part my heirs, and Lady B—— and her child who have a jointure and all that to come out of it. She may do as she pleases—I merely suggest —it is all your affair as much as mine. Since I wrote to you last I have had with all my household and family a sharp tertian fever. I have got *well* but Allegra is still laid up though convalescent; and her nurse—and half my ragamuffins—Gondoliers, Nurses—cook—footmen etc. I cured myself without bark, but all the others are taking it like trees. I have also had another hot crater, in the shape of a scene with Count Guiccioli who quarrelled with his wife, who refused to go back to him, and wanted to stay with me—and elope—and be as good as married. At last they made it up—but there was a dreadful scene; if I had not loved her better than myself, I could not have resisted her wish but at thirty one years, as I have, and *such years* as they have been—you may be sure—knowing the world that I would rather sacrifice myself ten times over—than the girl, who did not know the extent of the step she was so eager to take. He behaved well enough, saying 'take your lover or retain me—but you shan't have both', the lady would have taken her lover as in duty bound—not to do—but on representing to her the destruction it would bring on her family (five unmarried sisters) and all the probable consequences— she had the reluctant good grace to acquiesce and return with him to Ravenna. But this business has rendered Italy hateful to me, and as I left England on account of my own wife, I leave Italy because of another's. You need not be frightened—there was no fighting—nobody fights here—they sometimes assassinate, but generally by proxy—and as to intrigue, it is the only employment; but elopements and separations are still more serious than even with us being so uncommon, and indeed needless; as excepting an occasionally jealous old gentleman— every body lets their spouses have a man or two—provided he be taken with decency. But the Guiccioli was romantic and had read 'Corinna'—in short she was a kind of Italian Caroline Lamb—but very pretty and gentle, at least to me; for I never knew so docile a creature as far as we lived together, except that she had a great desire to leave her husband who is sixty years old—and not pleasant. There was the deuce—for her father's family (a very noble one of Ravenna), were furious against the *husband*—(not against me) for his unreasonable

ways. You must not dislike *her*, for she was a great admirer
of *you*, and used to collect and seal up all *your letters* to me as
they came that they might not be lost or mixed with other
papers; and she was a very amiable and accomplished woman,
with however some of the drawbacks of the Italian character
now corrupted for ages.

All this—and my fever—have made me low and ill; but the
moment Allegra is better we shall set off over the Tyrolese
Alps, and find our way to England as we can, to the great
solace of Mr Fletcher, who may perhaps find his family not less
increased than his fortune during his absence. I cannot fix
any day for departure or arrival—so much depending on circumstances—but we are to be in voyage as soon as it can be undertaken with safety to the child's health. As to the Countess G.
if I had been single and could have married her by getting her
divorced, she would probably have been of the party; but this
being out of the question—though *she* was as 'all for love or
the world well lost' [1]—I, who know what 'love' and 'the world'
both are, persuaded her to keep her station in society.

Pray let Ada's picture be *portable* as I am likely to see more
of the portrait than of the original. Excuse this scrawl. Think
that within this month I have had a *fever—an Italian husband
and wife quarrelling;—*a sick family—and *the preparation for
a December journey over the mountains of the Tyrol all brewing
at once in my cauldron.*

yours

P.S.—I enclose *her* last letter to me by which you may judge
for yourself—that it was a serious business—I have felt it such,
but—it was my duty to do as I did as her husband offered to
forgive everything if she would return with him to Ravenna
and give up her liaison.——

I will talk to you of my American scheme when I see you—

147. TO LADY BYRON

Ravenna, Decr. 31st, 1819.

Anything—like or unlike—copy or original [2] will be welcome,
I can make no comparison, and find no fault, it is enough for
me to have something to remind me of what is yours and mine,
and which, whatever may be mine, will I hope be yours while

---

[1] The title of Dryden's tragedy on Antony and Cleopatra.
[2] Referring to his request for a picture of Ada. See page 216.

you breathe. It is my wish to give you as little further trouble as can be helped, the time and the mode of sending the picture you can choose; I have been taught waiting if not patience. The wretchedness of the past should be sufficient for you and me without adding wittingly to the future more bitterness than that of which time and eternity are pregnant. While we do not approximate we may be gentle, and feel at a distance what we once felt without mutual or self-reproach. This time five years (the fault is not mine but of Augusta's letter 10th Decr. which arrived to-day) I was on my way to our funeral marriage. I hardly thought then that your bridegroom as an exile would one day address you as a stranger; and that Lady and Lord Byron would become byewords of division. This time four years I suspected it as little. I speak to you from another country, and as it were from another world, for this city of Italy is out of the track of armies and travellers, and is more of the old time. That I think of you is but too obvious, for three hours have not passed, since in society where I ought not to think of you, though Italian customs and Italian, perhaps even English, passions attach more importance and duty to such liaisons than to any nuptial engagement, the principal person concerned said to me—'tu pensi di tua moglie'—it was so right a conjecture that I started and answered why do you think so? The answer was—'because you are so serious—and she is the woman whom I believe tu ami piu ed ami sempre'— If this had been said in a moment of anger or of playfulness, I should have thought it the consequence of ill humour or curiosity, but it was said without any such prologue, in a time of indifferent things and much good company, Countesses and Marchionesses and all the noble blood of the descendants of Guido di Polenta's—cotemporaries with names eloquent of the middle ages.

I was nearly on the point of setting out for England in November, but a fever the *epidemic* of the Season stopped me with other reasons; Augusta can tell you all about me and mine if you think either worth the enquiry. But the object of my writing is to come.

It is this—I saw Moore three months ago and gave to his care a long Memoir written up to the Summer of 1816, of my life which I had been writing since I left England. It will not be published till after my death, and in fact it is a 'Memoir' and not 'confessions'. I have omitted the most important and decisive events and passions of my existence not to compromise others. But it is not so with the part you occupy, which is long and minute, and I could wish you to see, read and mark any part or parts that do not appear to coincide with the truth. The truth I have always stated—but there are two ways of looking at it—and your way may not be mine. I have never revised the papers since they were written. You may read them and mark what you please. I wish you [to] know what I think and say of you and yours. You will find nothing to flatter you, nothing to lead you to the most remote supposition that we could ever have been, or be happy together. But I do not choose to give to another generation statements which we cannot arise from the dust to prove or disprove—without letting you see fairly and fully what I look upon you to have been, and what I depict you as being. If seeing this, you can detect what is false, or answer what is charged, do so—*your mark* shall not be erased.

You will perhaps say *why* write my life? Alas!—I say so too, but they who have traduced it and blasted it, and branded me, should know—that it is they, and not I—are the cause. It is no great pleasure to have lived, and less to live over again the details of existence, but the last becomes sometimes a necessity and even a duty.

If you choose to see this you may, if you do not—you have at least had the option.[1]

January 1st.   B.

148. TO THOMAS MOORE

January 2, 1820.

MY DEAR MOORE,

> To-day it is my wedding day,
> And all the folks would stare,
> If wife should dine at Edmonton,
> And I should dine at Ware.

Or *thus:*

> Here 's a happy new year! but with reason
> I beg you 'll permit me to say—
> Wish me *many* returns of the *season*,
> But as *few* as you please of the *day*.

[1] Lady Byron declined to see the Memoir, because she considered 'the publication or circulation of such a composition at any time as prejudicial to Ada's future happiness'. In the subsequent destruction of the Memoir, however, by Byron's friends and executors, she had no part.

My this present writing is to direct you that, *if she chooses*, she may see the MS. Memoir in your possession. I wish her to have fair play, in all cases, even though it will not be published till after my decease. For this purpose, it were but just that Lady B. should know what is there said of her and hers, that she may have full power to remark on or respond to any part or parts, as may seem fitting to herself. This is fair dealing, I presume, in all events.

To change the subject, are you in England? I send you an epitaph for Castlereagh:—

> [Posterity will ne'er survey
> A nobler grave than this;
> Here lie the bones of Castlereagh:
> Stop traveller, * *]

Another for Pitt:

> With death doom'd to grapple,
> Beneath this cold slab, he
> Who lied in the Chapel
> Now lies in the Abbey.

The gods seem to have made me poetical this day:[1]—

> In digging up your bones, Tom Paine,
> Will. Cobbett has done well:
> You visit him on earth again,
> He 'll visit you in hell.

Or,

> You come to him on earth again,
> He 'll go with you to hell.

Pray let not these versiculi go forth with *my* name, except among the initiated, because my friend H. has foamed into a reformer, and, I greatly fear, will subside into Newgate; since the Honourable House, according to Galignani's Reports of Parliamentary Debates, are menacing a prosecution to a pamphlet of his.[2] I shall be very sorry to hear of any thing but good for him, particularly in these miserable squabbles; but these are the natural effects of taking a part in them.

For my own part, I had a sad scene since you went. Count Gu. came for his wife, and *none* of those consequences which

---

[1] See *As You Like It*, III, iii, 16 and 24.

[2] Hobhouse was then actually in Newgate, his pamphlet, *A Trifling Mistake in Thomas Lord Erskine's recent Preface*, having been voted a breach of privilege.

Scott prophesied ensued. There was no damages, as in England, and so Scott lost his wager. But there was a great scene, for she would not, at first, go back with him—at last, she *did* go back with him; but he insisted, reasonably enough, that all communication should be broken off between her and me. So, finding Italy very dull, and having a fever tertian, I packed up my valise, and prepared to cross the Alps; but my daughter fell ill, and detained me.

After her arrival at Ravenna, the Guiccioli fell ill again too; and at last, her father (who had, all along, opposed the *liaison* most violently till now) wrote to me to say that she was in such a state that *he* begged me to come and see her,—and that her husband had acquiesced, in consequence of her relapse, and that *he* (her father) would guarantee all this, and that there would be no further scenes in consequence between them, and that I should not be compromised in any way. I set out soon after, and have been here ever since. I found her a good deal altered, but getting better:—*all* this comes of reading *Corinna*.

The Carnival is about to begin, and I saw about two or three hundred people at the Marquis Cavalli's the other evening, with as much youth, beauty, and diamonds among the women, as ever averaged in the like number. My appearance in waiting on the Guiccioli was considered as a thing of course. The Marquis is her uncle, and naturally considered me as her relation.

The paper is out, and so is the letter. Pray write. Address to Venice, whence the letters will be forwarded.

Yours, etc.,

B.

149. TO JOHN MURRAY

Ravenna, February 21, 1820.

DEAR MURRAY,

The Bulldogs will be very agreeable: I have only those of this country, who, though good, and ready to fly at any thing, yet have not the tenacity of tooth and Stoicism in endurance of my canine fellow-citizens: then pray send them by the readiest conveyance—perhaps best by Sea. Mr. Kinnaird will disburse for them, and deduct from the amount on your application or on that of Captain Fyler.

I see the good old King[1] is gone to his place: one can't help being sorry, though blindness, and age, and insanity, are

---

[1] George III died on 29 January.

supposed to be drawbacks on human felicity; but I am not at all sure that the latter, at least, might not render him happier than any of his subjects.

I have no thoughts of coming to the Coronation, though I should like to see it, and though I have a right to be a puppet in it; but my division with Lady Byron, which has drawn an equinoctial line between me and mine in all other things, will operate in this also to prevent my being in the same procession.

By Saturday's post I sent you four packets, containing Cantos third and fourth of D[on] J[uan]; recollect that these two cantos reckon only as *one* with you and me, being, in fact, the third Canto cut into two, because I found it too long. Remember this, and don't imagine that there could be any other motive. The whole is about 225 Stanzas, more or less, and a lyric of 96 lines, so that they are no longer than the first *single* cantos: but the truth is, that I made the first too long, and should have cut those down also had I thought better. Instead of saying in future for so many cantos, say so many *Stanzas* or pages: it was Jacob Tonson's [1] way, and certainly the best: it prevents mistakes. I might have sent you a dozen cantos of 40 Stanzas each,—those of *the Minstrel* (Beattie's) [2] are no longer,—and ruined you at once, if you don't suffer as it is; but recollect you are not *pinned down* to anything you say in a letter, and that, calculating even these two cantos as *one* only (which they were and are to be reckoned), you are not bound by your offer: act as may seem fair to all parties.

I have finished my translation of the first Canto of the *Morgante Maggiore* of Pulci, which I will transcribe and send: it is the parent, not only of *Whistlecraft*, but of all jocose Italian poetry. You must print it side by side with the original Italian, because I wish the reader to judge of the fidelity: it is stanza for stanza, and often line for line, if not word for word.

You ask me for a volume of manners, etc., on Italy: perhaps I am in the case to know more of them than most Englishmen, because I have lived among the natives, and in parts of the country where Englishmen never resided before (I speak of Romagna and this place particularly); but there are many reasons why I do not choose to touch in print on such a subject. I have lived in their houses and in the heart of their families, sometimes merely as '*amico di casa*', and sometimes as '*Amico*

---

[1] Jacob Tonson (?1656–1736), publisher to Dryden and the Augustan writers.
[2] James Beattie (1735–1803), whose *Minstrel* appeared in 1771 and 1774.

di cuore' of the *Dama,* and in neither case do I feel myself
authorized in making a book of them. Their moral is not your
moral; their life is not your life; you would not understand it:
it is not English, nor French, nor German, which you would all
understand. The Conventual education, the Cavalier Servi-
tude, the habits of thought and living are so entirely different,
and the difference becomes so much more striking the more you
live intimately with them, that I know not how to make you
comprehend a people, who are at once temperate and profligate,
serious in their character and buffoons in their amusements,
capable of impressions and passions, which are at once *sudden*
and *durable* (what you find in no other nation), and who actually
have *no society* (what we would call so), as you may see by their
Comedies: they have no real comedy, not even in Goldoni; and
that is because they have no Society to draw it from.

Their Conversazioni are not Society at all. They go to the
theatre to talk, and into company to hold their tongues. The
women sit in a circle, and the men gather into groupes, or they
play at dreary *Faro* or *'Lotto reale',* for small sums. Their
Academie are Concerts like our own, with better music and more
form. Their best things are the Carnival balls and masquerades,
when every body runs mad for six weeks. After their dinners
and suppers, they make extempore verses and buffoon one
another; but it is in a humour which you would not enter into,
ye of the North.

In their houses it is better. I should know something of the
matter, having had a pretty general experience among their
women, from the fisherman's wife up to the *Nobil' Donna,*
whom I serve. Their system has its rules, and its fitnesses, and
decorums, so as to be reduced to a kind of discipline or game at
hearts, which admits few deviations, unless you wish to lose it.
They are extremely tenacious, and jealous as furies; not permitting their lovers even to marry if they can help it, and
keeping them always close to them in public as in private whenever they can. In short, they transfer marriage to adultery,
and strike the *not* out of that commandment. The reason is,
that they marry for their parents, and love for themselves.
They exact fidelity from a lover as a debt of honour, while
they pay the husband as a tradesman, that is, not at all. You
hear a person's character, male or female, canvassed, not as
depending on their conduct to their husbands or wives, but to
their mistress or lover. And—and—that's all. If I wrote a
quarto, I don't know that I could do more than amplify what

I have here noted. It is to be observed that while they do all this, the greatest outward respect is to be paid to the husbands, not only by the ladies, but by their *Serventi*—particularly if the husband serves no one himself (which is not often the case, however): so that you would often suppose them relations— the *Servente* making the figure of one adopted into the family. Sometimes the ladies run a little restive and elope, or divide, or make a scene; but this is at starting, generally, when they know no better, or when they fall in love with a foreigner, or some such anomaly,—and is always reckoned unnecessary and extravagant.

You enquire after 'Dante's prophecy': I have not done more than six hundred lines, but will vaticinate at leisure.

Of the bust [1] I know nothing. No Cameos or Seals are to be cut here or elsewhere that I know of, in any good style. Hobhouse should write himself to Thorwalsen: the bust was made and paid for three years ago.

Pray tell Mrs. Leigh to request Lady Byron to urge forward the transfer from the funds, which Hanson is opposing, because he has views of investment for some Client of his own, which I can't consent to. I wrote to Lady B. on business this post, addressed to the care of Mr. D. Kinnaird.

Somebody has sent me some American abuse of *Mazeppa* and 'the Ode': in future I will compliment nothing but Canada, and desert to the English.

By the king's death Mr. H[obhouse], I hear, will stand for Westminster: I shall be glad to hear of his standing any where except in the pillory, which, from the company he must have lately kept (I alway except Burdett, and Douglas K., and the genteel part of the reformers), was perhaps to be apprehended. I was really glad to hear it was for libel instead of larceny; for, though impossible in his own person, he might have been taken up by mistake for another at a meeting. All reflections on his present case and place are so *Nugatory*,[2] that it would be useless to pursue the subject further. I am out of all patience to see my friends sacrifice themselves for a pack of blackguards, who disgust one with their Cause, although I have always been a friend to and a Voter for reform. If Hunt had addressed the language to me which he did to Mr. H. last election, I would not have descended to call out such a miscreant who won't fight;

---

[1] A bust of Byron which Hobhouse had commissioned the sculptor Thorwaldsen to execute.

[2] See pages 244 and 271.

but have passed my sword-stick through his body, like a dog's, and then thrown myself on my Peers, who would, I hope, have weighed the provocation: at any rate, it would have been as public a Service as Walworth's chastisement of Wat. Tyler. If we must have a tyrant, let him at least be a gentleman who has been bred to the business, and let us fall by the axe and not by the butcher's cleaver.

No one can be more sick of, or indifferent to, politics than I am, if they let me alone; but if the time comes when a part must be taken one way or the other, I shall pause before I lend myself to the views of such ruffians, although I cannot but approve of a Constitutional amelioration of long abuses.

Lord George Gordon, and Wilkes, and Burdett, and Horne Tooke, were all men of education and courteous deportment: so is Hobhouse; but as for these others, I am convinced that Robespierre was a Child, and Marat a Quaker in comparison of what they would be, could they throttle their way to power.

Yours ever,

B.

150. TO JOHN MURRAY

Ravenna, April 16, 1820.

. Dear Murray,

Post after post arrives without bringing any acknowledgement from you of the different packets (excepting the first) which I have sent within the last two months, all of which ought to be arrived long ere now; and as they were announced in other letters, you ought at least to say whether they are come or not. You are not expected to write frequent or long letters, as your time is much occupied; but when parcels that have cost some pains in the composition, and great trouble in the copying, are sent to you, I should at least be put out of Suspense by the immediate acknowledgement, per return of post, addressed *directly* to *Ravenna*. I am naturally—knowing what continental *posts* are—anxious to hear that they are arrived; especially as I loathe the task of copying so much, that if there was a human being that could copy my blotted MSS. he should have all they can ever bring for his trouble. All I desire is two lines, to say, such a day I received such a packet: there are now at least *six* unacknowledged. This is neither kind nor courteous.

I have, besides, another reason for desiring you to be speedy, which is, that there is THAT brewing in Italy which will speedily cut off all security of communication, and set all your Anglo-travellers flying in every direction, with their usual fortitude in foreign tumults. The Spanish and French affairs[1] have set the Italians in a ferment; and no wonder: they have been too long trampled on. This will make a sad scene for your exquisite traveller, but not for the resident, who naturally wishes a people to redress itself. I shall, if permitted by the natives, remain to see what will come of it, and perhaps to take a turn with them, like Dugald Dalgetty [2] and his horse, in case of business; for I shall think it by far the most interesting spectacle and moment in existence, to see the Italians send the Barbarians of all nations back to their own dens. I have lived long enough among them to feel more for them as a nation than for any other people in existence; but they want Union, and they want principle; and I doubt their success. However, they will try, probably; and if they do, it will be a good cause. No Italian can hate an Austrian more than I do; unless it be the English, the Austrians seem to me the most obnoxious race under the Sky.

But I doubt, if anything be done, it won't be so quietly as in Spain. To be sure, Revolutions are not to be made with Rose-water, where there are foreigners as Masters.

Write while you can; for it is but the toss up of a Paul that there will not be a row that will somewhat retard the Mail by and bye.

Address right to *Ravenna*.

Yours,

B.

151. TO JOHN MURRAY

Ravenna, April 23, 1820.

Dear Murray,

The proofs don't contain the *last* stanzas of Canto second, but end abruptly with the 105th Stanza.

I told you long ago that the new Cantos were *not* good, and I also *told you a reason*: recollect, I do not oblige you to publish them; you may suppress them, if you like, but I can alter nothing. I have erased the six stanzas about those two impostors, Southey and Wordsworth (which I suppose will give you great pleasure), but I can do no more. I can neither recast, nor replace; but I give you leave to put it all into the fire, if you like, or *not* to publish, and I think that 's sufficient.

I told you that I wrote on with no good will—that I had been, *not* frightened, but *hurt* by the outcry, and, besides that, when I wrote last November, I was ill in body, and in very great distress

---

[1] Revolutionary movements in both countries.
[2] In *A Legend of Montrose*.

of mindabout some private things of my own; but *you would*
have it: so I sent it to you, and to make it lighter, *cut* it in two—
but I can't piece it together again. I can't cobble: I must
'either make a spoon or spoil a horn',[1]—and there's an end;
for there's no remeid: but I leave you free will to suppress the
whole, if you like it.

About the *Morgante Maggiore, I won't have a line omitted*:
it may circulate, or it may not; but all the Criticism on earth
shan't touch a line, unless it be because it is *badly* translated.
Now you say, and I say, and others say, that the translation is
a good one; and so it shall go to press as it is.   Pulci must answer
for his own irreligion: I answer for the translation only.

I am glad you have got the *Dante*; and there should be by
this time a translation of his Francesca of Rimini arrived to
append to it.

I sent you a quantity of *prose* observations in answer to
Wilson,[2] but I shall not publish them *at present*: keep them by
you as *documents*.

Pray let Mr. Hobhouse look to the *Italian* next time in the
proofs: *this time*, while I am scribbling to you, they are corrected
by one who passes for the prettiest woman in Romagna, and even
the Marches, as far as Ancona—be the other who she may.

I am glad you like my answer to your enquiries about Italian
Society: it is fit you should like *something*, and be damned to you.

My love to Scott. I shall think higher of knighthood ever
after for his being dubbed.[3] By the way, he is the first poet
titled for his talent in Britain: it has happened abroad before
now; but on the continent titles are universal and worthless.
Why don't you send me *Ivanhoe* and the *Monastery*? [4] I have
never written to Sir Walter, for I know he has a thousand things,
and I a thousand nothings, to do; but I hope to see him at
Abbotsford before very long, and I will sweat his Claret for him,
though Italian abstemiousness has made my brain but a shilpit [5]
concern for a Scotch sitting *inter pocula*.   I love Scott and Moore,
and all the better brethren; but I hate and abhor that puddle of
waterworms whom you have taken into your troop in the
history line I see.   I am obliged to end abruptly.

Yours,

B.

---

[1] See *Rob Roy,* chap. xxii.
[2] i.e. a review of *Don Juan* in the *Edinburgh Magazine* for August 1819
which he attributed to John Wilson.
[3] Scott was made a baronet on 1 April.   [4] Both published in 1820.
[5] Weak, a word from Scott.

P.S.—You say that *one half*[1] is very good: you are *wrong*;
for, if it were, it would be the finest poem in existence. *Where*
is the poetry of which *one half* is good? is it the *Æneid*? is it
Milton's? is it *Dryden*'s? is it any one's except *Pope*'s and Goldsmith's, of which *all* is good? and yet these two last are the poets
your pond poets would explode. But if *one half* of the two new
Cantos be good in your opinion, what the devil would you have
more? No—no: no poetry is *generally* good—only by fits and
starts—and you are lucky to get a sparkle here and there. You
might as well want a Midnight *all stars* as rhyme all perfect.

We are on the verge of a *row* here. Last night they have
overwritten all the city walls with 'Up with the Republic!'
and 'death to the Pope!' etc., etc. This would be nothing in
London, where the walls are privileged, and where, when somebody went to Chancellor Thurlow to tell him, as an alarming
sign, that he had seen 'Death to the king' on the park wall,
old Thurlow asked him if he had ever seen '*' chalked on the
same place, to which the alarmist responding in the affirmative,
Thurlow resumed 'and so have I for these last thirty years,
and yet it never * * * *'. But here it is a different thing:
they are not used to such fierce political inscriptions, and the
police is all on the alert, and the Cardinal glares pale through
all his purple.

April, 24, 1820, 8 o'clock, P.M.

The police have been, all Noon and after, searching for the
Inscribers, but have caught none as yet. They must have been
all night about it, for the 'Live republics—death to popes and
priests', are innumerable, and plastered over all the palaces:
ours has plenty. There is 'down with the Nobility', too—they
are down enough already, for that matter. A very heavy rain
and wind having come on, I did not get on horseback to go out
and 'skirr the country'; but I shall mount to-morrow, and take
a canter among the peasantry, who are a savage, resolute race,
always riding with guns in their hands. I wonder they don't
suspect the Serenaders, for they play on the guitar all night,
here as in Spain, to their Mistresses.

Talking of politics, as Caleb Quotem[2] says, pray look at the
Conclusion of my Ode on *Waterloo*, written in the year 1815,
and, comparing it with the Duke de Berri's catastrophe in 1820:[3]

---

[1] Of *Don Juan*.
[2] The original Caleb Quotem, in Henry Lee's *Throw Physic to the Dogs*.
[3] He was murdered by a saddler on 20 February.

tell me if I have not as good a right to the character of '*Vates*', in both senses of the word, as Fitzgerald [1] and Coleridge?

'Crimson tears will follow yet'—

and have not they?

I can't pretend to foresee what will happen among you Englishers at this distance, but I vaticinate a *row* in Italy; in whilk case, I don't know that I won't have a finger in it. I dislike the Austrians, and think the Italians infamously oppressed; and if they begin, why, I will recommend 'the erection of a Sconce upon Drumsnab',[2] like Dugald Dalgetty.

152. TO JOHN MURRAY

Ravenna, May 20th, 1820.

DEAR MURRAY,

First and foremost, you must forward my letter to *Moore* dated *2d January*, which I said you might open, but desired you *to forward*. Now, you should really not forget these little things, because they do mischief among friends. You are an excellent man, a great man, and live among great men, but do pray recollect your absent friends and authors.

I return you the packets. The prose (the *Edin. Mag.* answer) looks better than I thought it would, and *you may publish it*: there will be a row, but I'll fight it out one way or another. You are wrong: I never had those '*two* ladies',[3] upon my honour! Never believe but *half* of such stories. Southey was a damned scoundrel to spread such a lie of a woman, whose mother he did his best to get and could not.

So you and Hobhouse have squabbled about my ballad: you should not have circulated it; but I am glad you are by the ears, you both deserve it—he for having been in Newgate, and *you* for not being there.

Excuse haste: if you knew what I have on hand, you would.

In the first place, *your packets*; then a letter from Kinnaird, on the most urgent business: another from Moore, about a communication to Lady B[yron] of importance; a fourth from the mother of Allegra; and, fifthly, at Ravenna, the Contessa G. is on the eve of being divorced on account of our having been taken together *quasi* in the fact, and, what is worse, that she did not *deny* it: but the Italian public are on our side, particularly the women,—and the men also, because they say that *he*

[1] See page 122.   [2] *A Legend of Montrose*, chap. x.   [3] See page 195.

had no business to take the business up now after a year of toleration. The law is against him, because he slept with his wife after her admission. All her relations (who are numerous, high in rank, and powerful) are furious *against him* for his conduct, and his not wishing to be cuckolded at *three*score, when every one else is at ONE. I am warned to be on my guard, as he is very capable of employing *Sicarii*—this is Latin as well as Italian, so you can understand it; but I have arms, and don't mind them, thinking that I can pepper his ragamuffins if they don't come unawares, and that, if they do, one may as well end that way as another; and it would besides serve *you* as an advertisement:—

> 'Man may escape from rope or gun, etc.
> But he who takes Woman, Woman, Woman,' etc.[1]

Yours,

B.

P.S.—I have looked over the press, but Heaven knows how: think what I have on hand and the post going out tomorrow. Do you remember the epitaph on Voltaire?

> 'Cy gît l'enfant gâté,' etc.

> 'Here lies the spoilt child
> Of the World which he spoil'd.'

The original is in Grimm [2] and Diderot, etc., etc., etc.

153. TO THOMAS MOORE

Ravenna, May 24, 1820.

I wrote to you a few days ago. There is also a letter of January last for you at Murray's, which will explain to you why I am here. Murray ought to have forwarded it long ago. I enclose you an epistle from a countrywoman of yours at Paris, which has moved my entrails. You will have the goodness, perhaps, to enquire into the truth of her story, and I will help her as far as I can,—though not in the useless way she proposes. Her letter is evidently unstudied, and so natural, that the orthography is also in a state of nature.

Here is a poor creature, ill and solitary, who thinks, as a last resource, of translating you or me into French! Was there ever such a notion? It seems to me the consummation of despair. Pray enquire, and let me know, and, if you could

---

[1] *The Beggar's Opera*, ii, viii.   [2] *Correspondance Littéraire.*

draw a bill on me *here* for a few hundred francs, at your banker's, I will duly honour it,—that is, if she is not an impostor. If not, let me know, that I may get something remitted by my banker Longhi, of Bologna, for I have no correspondence myself at Paris: but tell her she must not translate;—if she does, it will be the height of ingratitude.

I had a letter (not of the same kind, but in French and flattery) from a Madame Sophie Gail, of Paris, whom I take to be the spouse of a Gallo-Greek of that name.[1] Who is she? and what is she? and how came she to take an interest in my *poeshie* or its author? If you know her, tell her, with my compliments, that, as I only *read* French, I have not answered her letter; but would have done so in Italian, if I had not thought it would look like an affectation. I have just been scolding my monkey for tearing the seal of her letter, and spoiling a mock book, in which I put rose leaves. I had a civet-cat the other day, too; but it ran away, after scratching my monkey's cheek, and I am in search of it still. It was the fiercest beast I ever saw, and like * * in the face and manner.

I have a world of things to say; but, as they are not come to a *dénouement*, I don't care to begin their history till it is wound up. After you went, I had a fever, but got well again without bark. Sir Humphry Davy was here the other day, and liked Ravenna very much. He will tell you any thing you may wish to know about the place and your humble servitor.

Your apprehensions (arising from Scott's) were unfounded. There are *no damages* in this country, but there will probably be a separation between them, as her family, which is a principal one, by its connections, are very much against *him*, for the whole of his conduct;—and he is old and obstinate, and she is young and a woman, determined to sacrifice every thing to her affections. I have given her the best advice, viz. to stay with him,—pointing out the state of a separated woman, (for the priests won't let lovers live openly together, unless the husband sanctions it,) and making the most exquisite moral reflections, —but to no purpose. She says, 'I will stay with him, if he will let you remain with me. It is hard that I should be the only woman in Romagna who is not to have her *Amico*; but, if not, I will not live with him; and as for the consequences, love, etc., etc., etc.'—you know how females reason on such occasions.

He says he has let it go on till he can do so no longer. But

[1] She was the wife of Jean Baptiste Gail, Professor of Greek Literature in the Collège de France.

he wants her to stay, and dismiss me; for he does not like to pay back her dowry and to make an alimony. Her relations are rather for the separation, as they detest him,—indeed, so does every body. The populace and the women are, as usual, all for those who are in the wrong, viz. the lady and her lover. I should have retreated, but honour, and an erysipelas which has attacked her, prevent me,—to say nothing of love, for I love her most entirely, though not enough to persuade her to sacrifice every thing to a frenzy. 'I see how it will end; she will be the sixteenth Mrs. Shuffleton'.[1]

My paper is finished, and so must this letter.

Yours ever,

B.

P.S.—I regret that you have not completed the Italian Fudges.[2] Pray, how come you to be still in Paris? Murray has four or five things of mine in hand—the new *Don Juan*, which his back-shop synod don't admire;—a translation of the first canto of Pulci's *Morgante Maggiore*, excellent;—a short ditto from Dante, not so much approved: the *Prophecy of Dante*, very grand and worthy, etc., etc., etc.:—a furious prose answer to Blackwood's 'Observations on *Don Juan*', with a savage Defence of Pope—likely to make a row. The opinions above I quote from Murray and his Utican senate;—you will form your own, when you see the things.

You will have no great chance of seeing me, for I begin to think I must finish in Italy. But, if you come my way, you shall have a tureen of macaroni. Pray tell me about yourself, and your intents.

My trustees are going to lend Earl Blessington [3] sixty thousand pounds (at six per cent.) on a Dublin mortgage. Only think of my becoming an Irish absentee!

154. TO THOMAS MOORE

Ravenna, June 1, 1820.

I have received a Parisian letter from W[edderburn] W[ebster], which I prefer answering through you, if that worthy be still at Paris, and, as he says, an occasional visitor of yours. In

---

[1] *John Bull, or the Englishman's Fireside*, by George Colman the Younger, ii, ii.

[2] A proposed continuation of his *Fudge Family in Paris*.

[3] Charles John Gardiner, second Viscount Mountjoy and first Earl of Blessington.

November last he wrote to me a well-meaning letter, stating, for some reasons of his own, his belief that a reunion might be effected between Lady B. and myself. To this I answered as usual; and he sent me a second letter, repeating his notions, which letter I have never answered, having had a thousand other things to think of. He now writes as if he believed that he had offended me by touching on the topic; and I wish you to assure him that I am not at all so,—but, on the contrary, obliged by his good nature. At the same time acquaint him *the thing is impossible. You know this*, as well as I,—and there let it end.

I believe that I showed you his epistle in autumn last. He asks me if I have heard of *my* 'laureat' at Paris,—somebody who has written 'a most sanguinary *Epître*' against me; [1] but whether in French, or Dutch, or on what score, I know not, and he don't say,—except that (for my satisfaction) he says it is the best thing in the fellow's volume. If there is anything of the kind that I *ought* to know, you will doubtless tell me. I suppose it to be something of the usual sort;—he says, he don't remember the author's name.

I wrote to you some ten days ago, and expect an answer at your leisure.

The separation business still continues, and all the world are implicated, including priests and cardinals. The public opinion is furious against *him*, because he ought to have cut the matter short *at first*, and not waited twelve months to begin. He has been trying at evidence, but can get none *sufficient*; for what would make fifty divorces in England won't do here—there must be the *most decided* proofs. * * *

It is the first cause of the kind attempted in Ravenna for these two hundred years; for, though they often separate, they assign a different motive. You know that the continental incontinent are more delicate than the English, and don't like proclaiming their coronation in a court, even when nobody doubts it.

All her relations are furious against him. The father has challenged him—a superfluous valour, for he don't fight, though suspected of two assassinations—one of the famous Monzoni of Forli. Warning was given me not to take such long rides in the Pine Forest without being on my guard; so I take my stiletto and a pair of pistols in my pocket during my daily rides.

[1] Lamartine's *Premières Méditations Poétiques* contained a poem, 'L'Homme—à Lord Byron'.

I won't stir from this place till the matter is settled one way or the other. She is as femininely firm as possible; and the opinion is so much against him, that the *advocates* decline to undertake his cause, because they say that he is either a fool or a rogue—fool, if he did not discover the liaison till now; and rogue, if he did know it, and waited, for some bad end, to divulge it. In short, there has been nothing like it since the days of Guido di Polenta's family,[1] in these parts.

If the man has me taken off, like Polonius 'say, he made a good end', [2]—for a melodrame. The principal security is, that he has not the courage to spend twenty scudi—the average price of a clean-handed bravo—otherwise there is no want of opportunity, for I ride about the woods every evening, with one servant, and sometimes an acquaintance, who latterly looks a little queer in solitary bits of bushes.

Good bye.—Write to yours ever, etc.

155. TO THOMAS MOORE

Ravenna, June 9, 1820.

Galignani has just sent me the Paris edition of your works (which I wrote to order), and I am glad to see my old friends with a French face. I have been skimming and dipping, in and over them, like a swallow, and as pleased as one. It is the first time that I had seen the Melodies without music; and, I don't know how, but I can't read in a music-book—the crotchets confound the words in my head, though I recollect them perfectly when *sung*. Music assists my memory through the ear, not through the eye; I mean, that her quavers perplex me upon paper, but they are a help when heard. And thus I was glad to see the words without their borrowed robes;—to my mind they look none the worse for their nudity.

The biographer has made a botch of your life [3]—calling your father 'a *venerable old* gentleman', and prattling of 'Addison', and 'dowager countesses'. If that damned fellow was to *write my* life, I would certainly *take his*. And then, at the Dublin dinner, you have 'made a speech' (do you recollect, at Douglas K.'s, 'Sir, he made me a speech?') too complimentary to the

---

[1] See page 216.   [2] *Hamlet*, iv, v, 186.
[3] The 'Sketch of Thomas Moore' prefixed to the collected edition of his works.

'living poets', and somewhat redolent of universal praise. I am but too well off in it, but * * *

You have not sent me any poetical or personal news of yourself. Why don't you complete an Italian *Tour of the Fudges*? I have just been turning over *Little*, which I knew by heart in 1803, being then in my fifteenth summer. Heigho! I believe all the mischief I have ever done, or sung, has been owing to that confounded book of yours.

In my last I told you of a cargo of 'Poeshie', which I had sent to M. at his own impatient desire;—and, now he has got it, he don't like it, and demurs. Perhaps he is right. I have no great opinion of any of my last shipment, except a translation from Pulci, which is word for word, and verse for verse.

I am in the third act of a Tragedy;[1] but whether it will be finished or not, I know not: I have, at this present, too many passions of my own on hand to do justice to those of the dead. Besides the vexations mentioned in my last, I have incurred a quarrel with the Pope's carabiniers, or *gens d'armerie*, who have petitioned the Cardinal against my liveries, as resembling too nearly their own lousy uniform. They particularly object to the epaulettes, which all the world with us have on upon gala days. My liveries are of the colours conforming to my arms, and have been the family hue since the year 1066.

I have sent a trenchant reply, as you may suppose; and have given to understand that, if any soldados of that respectable corps insult my servants, I will do likewise by their gallant commanders; and I have directed my ragamuffins, six in number, who are tolerably savage, to defend themselves, in case of aggression; and, on holidays and gaudy days, I shall arm the whole set, including myself, in case of accidents or treachery. I used to play pretty well at the broad-sword, once upon a time, at Angelo's; but I should like the pistol, our national buccaneer weapon, better, though I am out of practice at present. However, I can 'wink and hold out mine iron'.[2] It makes me think (the whole thing does) of Romeo and Juliet—'now, Gregory, remember thy *swashing* blow'.[3]

All these feuds, however, with the Cavalier for his wife, and the troopers for my liveries, are very tiresome to a quiet man, who does his best to please all the world, and longs for fellowship and good will. Pray write.

I am yours, etc.

---

[1] *Marino Faliero.*   [2] *Henry V*, ii, i, 8.
[3] *Romeo and Juliet*, i, i, 70.

156. TO THOMAS MOORE

Ravenna, July 13, 1820.

To remove or increase your Irish anxiety about my being 'in a wisp',[1] I answer your letter forthwith; premising that, as I am a '*Will* of the wisp', I may chance to flit out of it. But, first, a word on the Memoir;—I have no objection, nay, I would rather that *one* correct copy was taken and deposited in honourable hands, in case of accidents happening to the original; for you know that I have none, and have never even *re*-read, nor, indeed, *read* at all what is there written; I only know that I wrote it with the fullest intention to be 'faithful and true'[2] in my narrative, but *not* impartial—no, by the Lord! I can't pretend to be that, while I feel. But I wish to give every body concerned the opportunity to contradict or correct me.

I have no objection to any proper person seeing what is there written,—seeing it was written, like every thing else, for the purpose of being read, however much many writings may fail in arriving at that object.

With regard to 'the wisp', the Pope has pronounced *their separation*. The decree came yesterday from Babylon,—it was *she* and *her friends* who demanded it, on the grounds of her husband's (the noble Count Cavalier's) extraordinary usage. *He* opposed it with all his might because of the alimony, which has been assigned, with all her goods, chattels, carriage, etc., to be restored by him. In Italy they can't divorce. He insisted on her giving me up, and he would forgive every thing,— even the adultery, which he swears that he can prove by 'famous witnesses'. But, in this country, the very courts hold such proofs in abhorrence, the Italians being as much more delicate in public than the English, as they are more passionate in private.

The friends and relatives, who are numerous and powerful, reply to him—'*You*, yourself, are either fool or knave,—fool, if you did not see the consequences of the approximation of these two young persons,—knave, if you connive at it. Take your choice,—but don't break out (after twelve months of the closest intimacy, under your own eyes and positive sanction) with a scandal, which can only make you ridiculous and her unhappy'.

He swore that he thought our intercourse was purely amicable, and that *I* was more partial to him than to her, till melancholy testimony proved the contrary. To this they answer, that 'Will of *this* wisp' was not an unknown person, and that

---

[1] i.e. in a scrape.   [2] Revelation, xx, 6.

'*clamosa Fama*' had not proclaimed the purity of my morals;—
that *her* brother, a year ago, wrote from Rome to warn him
that his wife would infallibly be led astray by this *ignis fatuus*,
unless he took proper measures, all of which he neglected to
take, etc., etc.

Now he says that he encouraged my return to Ravenna, to
see '*in quanti piedi di acqua siamo*', and he has found enough
to drown him in. In short,

> 'Ce ne fut pas le tout; sa femme se plaignit—
> Procès—La parenté se joint en excuse et dit
> Que du *Docteur* venoit tout le mauvais ménage;
> Que cet homme étoit fou, que sa femme étoit sage.
> On fit casser le mariage.'[1]

It is best to let the women alone, in the way of conflict, for they
are sure to win against the field. She returns to her father's
house, and I can only see her under great restrictions—such is
the custom of the country. The relations behaved very well:
—I offered any settlement, but they refused to accept it, and
swear she *shan't* live with G. (as he has tried to prove her faith-
less), but that he shall maintain her; and, in fact, a judgment
to this effect came yesterday. I am, of course, in an awkward
situation enough.

I have heard no more of the carabiniers who protested against
my liveries. They are not popular, those same soldiers, and,
in a small row, the other night, one was slain, another wounded,
and divers put to flight, by some of the Romagnuole youth,
who are dexterous, and somewhat liberal of the knife. The
perpetrators are not discovered, but I hope and believe that
none of my ragamuffins were in it, though they are somewhat
savage, and secretly armed, like most of the inhabitants. It is
their way, and saves sometimes a good deal of litigation.

There is a revolution at Naples. If so, it will probably leave
a card at Ravenna in its way to Lombardy.

Your publishers seem to have used you like mine. M. has
shuffled, and almost insinuated that my last productions are
dull. Dull, sir!—damme, dull! I believe he is right. He begs
for the completion of my tragedy of *Marino Faliero*, none of
which is yet gone to England. The fifth act is nearly completed, but it is dreadfully long—40 sheets of long paper of
4 pages each—about 150 when printed; but 'so full of pastime
and prodigality'[2] that I think it will do.

---

[1] La Fontaine, 'Le Roi Candaule et le Maître en Droit'.
[2] Farquhar, *The Recruiting Officer*, v, i.

Pray send and publish your *Pome* upon me; and don't be afraid of praising me too highly. I shall pocket my blushes.

'Not actionable!'—*Chantre d'enfer!*[1]—by * * that's 'a speech', and I won't put up with it. A pretty title to give a man for doubting if there be any such place!

So my Gail is gone—and Miss Mahony won't take money. I am very glad of it—I like to be generous, free of expense. But beg her not to translate me.

Oh, pray tell Galignani that I shall send him a screed of doctrine if he don't be more punctual. Somebody *regularly detains two*, and sometimes *four*, of his *Messengers* by the way. Do, pray, entreat him to be more precise. News are worth money in this remote kingdom of the Ostrogoths.

Pray, reply. I should like much to share some of your Champagne and La Fitte, but I am too Italian for Paris in general. Make Murray send my letter to you—it is full of *epigrams*.

Yours, etc.

157. TO JOHN MURRAY

Ravenna, August 31ˢᵗ, 1820.

Dear Murray,

I *have 'put my Soul* into the tragedy' (as you *if* it); but you know that there are damned souls as well as tragedies. Recollect that it is not a political play, though it may look like it; it is strictly historical: read the history and judge.

Ada's picture is her mother's: I am glad of it—the mother made a good daughter. Send me Gifford's opinion, and never mind the Archbishop. I can neither send you away, nor give you a hundred pistoles, nor a better taste. I send you a tragedy, and you ask for 'facetious epistles'; a little like your predecessor, who advised Dr. Prideaux to 'put some more humour into his Life of Mahomet'.[2]

The drawings for *Juan*[3] are superb: the brush has beat the poetry. In the annexed proof of *Marino Faliero*, the half line —'The law, my Prince' must be stopped thus —— as the Doge interrupts Bertuccio Faliero.

Bankes is a wonderful fellow; there is hardly one of my School

[1] Lamartine in his poem 'L'Homme—à Lord Byron' had addressed Byron as 'chantre des enfers'.
[2] *The True Nature of Imposture fully displayed in the Life of Mahomet*, by Humphrey Prideaux (afterwards Dean of Norwich), 1697.
[3] By Richard Westall, published in 1820.

and College cotemporaries that has not turned out more or less celebrated. Peel, Palmerstone, Bankes, Hobhouse, Tavistock, Bob Mills, Douglas Kinnaird, etc., etc., have all of them talked and been talked of.

Then there is your Galley Knight,[1] and all that—; but I believe that (except Milman perhaps) I am still the youngest of the fifteen hundred first of living poets, as W^m *worth is the oldest. Galley Knight is some Seasons my Senior: pretty Galley! so '*amiable*!!' You Goose, you—such fellows should be flung into Fleet Ditch. I would rather be a Galley Slave than a Galley Knight—so utterly do I despise the middling mountebank's mediocrity in everything but his Income.

We are here going to fight a little, next month, if the Huns don't cross the Po, and probably if they do: I can't say more now. If anything happens, you have matter for a posthumous work, and Moore has my memoirs in MSS.; so pray be civil. Depend upon it, there will be savage work, if once they begin here. The French courage proceeds from vanity, the German from phlegm, the Turkish from fanaticism and opium, the Spanish from pride, the English from coolness, the Dutch from obstinacy, the Russian from insensibility, but the *Italian* from *anger*; so you 'll see that they will spare nothing.

What you say of Lady Caroline Lamb's 'Juan' at the Masquerade [2] don't surprise me: I only wonder that she went so far as 'the *Theatre*' for '*the Devils*', having them so much more natural at home; or if they were busy, she might have borrowed the *, her Mother's—Lady Bessborough to wit—the * * of the last half Century.

Yours,

B.

158. TO RICHARD BELGRAVE HOPPNER

Ravenna, Septr 10th, 1820.

MY DEAR HOPPNER,

Ecco Advocate Fossati's letter. No paper has nor will be signed. Pray *draw* on me for the Napoleons, for I have no mode of remitting them otherwise; Missiaglia would empower some one here to receive them for you, as it is not a *piazza bancale*.

---

[1] Henry Gally Knight. See page 177.
[2] On 1 August, Lady Caroline Lamb appeared at a masquerade at Almack's in the character of Don Juan, and as a climax had herself carried off by devils.

I regret that you have such a bad opinion of Shiloh;[1] you used to have a good one. Surely he has talent and honour, but is crazy against religion and morality. His tragedy[2] is sad work; but the subject renders it so. His *Islam*[3] had much poetry. You seem lately to have got some notion against him.

Clare writes me the most insolent letters about Allegra; see what a man gets by taking care of natural children! Were it not for the poor little child's sake, I am almost tempted to send her back to her atheistical mother, but that would be too bad; you cannot conceive the excess of her insolence, and I know not why, for I have been at great care and expense,— taking a house in the country on purpose for her. She has *two* maids and every possible attention. If Clare thinks that she shall ever interfere with the child's morals or education, she mistakes; she never shall. The girl shall be a Christian and a married woman, if possible. As to seeing her, she may see her —under proper restrictions; but she is not to throw every thing into confusion with her Bedlam behaviour. To express it delicately, I think Madame Clare is a damned bitch. What think you?

Yours ever and truly,

B^N

159. TO JOHN MURRAY

Ravenna, Sept. 11, 1820.

DEAR MURRAY,

Here is another historical *note* for you. I want to be as near truth as the Drama can be.

Last post I sent you a note fierce as Faliero himself, in answer to a trashy tourist, who pretends that he could have been introduced to me. Let me have a proof of it, that I may cut its lava into some shape.

What Gifford says is very consolatory (of the first act). 'English, sterling *genuine English*', is a desideratum amongst you, and I am glad that I have got so much left; though heaven knows how I retain it: I *hear* none but from my Valet, and his is *Nottinghamshire*: and I *see* none but in your new publications, and theirs is *no* language at all, but jargon. Even your 'New

---

[1] Shelley, who had been accused by a discharged servant of misconduct with Claire Clairmont.
[2] *The Cenci*, 1819.
[3] *The Revolt of Islam*, published in 1818.

Jerusalem' is terribly stilted and affected, with '*very, very*'— so soft and pamby.

Oh! if ever I *do* come amongst you again, I will give you such a *Baviad and Mæviad*! not as *good* as the old, but even *better merited*. There never was such a *Set* as your *ragamuffins* (I mean *not* yours only, but every body's). What with the Cockneys, and the Lakers, and the *followers* of Scott, and Moore, and Byron, you are in the very uttermost decline and degradation of literature. I can't think of it without all the remorse of a murderer. I wish that Johnson were alive again to crush them!

I have as yet only had the first and second acts, and no opinion upon the second.

160. TO JOHN MURRAY

Ravenna, 9bre 4°, 1820.

I have received from Mr. Galignani the enclosed letters, duplicates and receipts, which will explain themselves.[1] As the poems are your property by purchase, right, and justice, *all matters of publication*, etc., etc., *are for you to decide upon*. I know not how far my compliance with Mr. G.'s request might be legal, and I doubt that it would not be honest. In case you choose to arrange with him, I enclose the permits to *you*, and in so doing I wash my hands of the business altogether. I sign them merely to enable you to exert the power you justly possess more properly. I will have nothing to do with it further, except, in my answer to Mr. Galignani, to state that the letters, etc., etc., are sent to you, and the causes thereof.

If you can check those foreign Pirates, do; if not, put the permissive papers in the fire: *I* can have no view nor object whatever, but to secure to you your property.

Yours,
BYRON.

P.S.—There will be shortly '*the Devil to pay*' here; and, as there is no saying that I may not form an *Item in his bill*, I shall not now write at greater length: *you* have *not answered* my late letters; and you have acted foolishly, as you will find out some day.

P.S.—I have read part of the *Quarterly* just arrived: Mr.

[1] See next letter.

Bowles [1] shall be answered; he is not *quite* correct in his statement about *E[nglish] B[ards] and S[cotch] R[eviewers]*. They support Pope, I see, in the *Quarterly*. Let them continue to do so: it is a Sin, and a Shame, and a *damnation* to think that *Pope!!* should require it—but he does. Those miserable mountebanks of the day, the poets, disgrace themselves and deny God, in running down Pope, the most *faultless* of Poets, and almost of men.

The *Edinburgh* praises Jack Keats or Ketch,[2] or whatever his names are: why, his is the * of Poetry—something like the pleasure an Italian fiddler extracted out of being suspended daily by a Street Walker in Drury Lane. This went on for some weeks: at last the Girl went to get a pint of Gin—met another, chatted too long, and Cornelli was *hanged outright before she returned*. Such like is the trash they praise, and such will be the end of the * * poesy of this miserable Self-polluter of the human Mind.

W. Scott's *Monastery* just arrived: many thanks for that Grand Desideratum of the last Six Months.

P.S.—You have cut up old Edgeworth,[3] it seems, amongst you. You are right: he was a bore. I met the whole batch—Mr., Mrs., and Miss—at a blue breakfast of Lady Davy's in Blue Square; and he proved but bad, in taste and tact and decent breeding. He began by saying that *Parr* (Dr. Parr) had attacked him, and that he (the father of Miss E.) had *cut him up in* his answer. Now, Parr would have annihilated him; and if he had not, why tell *us* (a long story) *who* wanted to breakfast? I saw them different times in different parties, and I thought him a very tiresome coarse old Irish half-and-half Gentleman, and her a pleasant reserved old woman—* * * * * * * * * * * *

161. TO THOMAS MOORE

Ravenna, November 5, 1820.

Thanks for your letter, which hath come somewhat costively; but better late than never. Of it anon. Mr. Galignani, of the

---

[1] William Lisle Bowles, in his *Invariable Principles of Poetry*, 1819, had corrected Byron's mistake about his poem, *The Spirit of Discovery*, in line 360 of *English Bards, and Scotch Reviewers*. Bowles's remark was quoted in a *Quarterly Review* article on Pope.

[2] Keats had recently published *Lamia, Isabella, The Eve of St. Agnes, and other Poems*.

[3] R. L. Edgeworth, father of Maria Edgeworth, the Irish novelist. They were in London in 1813. See Byron's Diary of 19 January, 1821.

Press, hath, it seems, been supplanted and sub-pirated by another Parisian publisher, who has audaciously printed an edition of L. B.'s works, at the ultra-liberal price of ten francs and (as Galignani piteously observes) eight francs only for booksellers! *horresco referens*. Think of a man's *whole* works producing so little!

Galignani sends me, post haste, a permission *for him, from me*, to publish, etc., etc., which *permit* I have signed and sent to Mr. Murray of Albemarle Street. Will you explain to G. *that I* have no right to dispose of Murray's works without his leave? and therefore I must refer him to M. to get the permit out of his claws—no easy matter, I suspect. I have written to G. to say as much; but a word of mouth from a 'great brother author' would convince him that I could not honestly have complied with his wish, though I might legally. What I could do I have done, viz. signed the warrant and sent it to Murray. Let the dogs divide the carcass, if it is killed to their liking.

I am glad of your epigram. It is odd that we should both let our wits run away with our sentiments; for I am sure that we are both Queen's men at bottom.[1] But there is no resisting a clinch—it is so clever! Apropos of that—we have a 'diphthong' also in this part of the world—not a *Greek*, but a *Spanish* one—do you understand me?—which is about to blow up the whole alphabet. It was first pronounced at Naples, and is spreading; but we are nearer the barbarians, who are in great force on the Po, and will pass it, with the first legitimate pretext.

There will be the devil to pay, and there is no saying who will or who will not be set down in his bill. If 'honour should come unlooked for'[2] to any of your acquaintance, make a Melody of it, that his ghost, like poor Yorick's, may have the satisfaction of being plaintively pitied—or still more nobly commemorated, like 'Oh breathe not his name'.[3] In case you should not think him worth it, here is a Chant for you instead—

> When a man hath no freedom to fight for at home,
> Let him combat for that of his neighbours;
> Let him think of the glories of Greece and of Rome,
> And get knock'd on the head for his labours.

---

[1] Byron refers to the divorce proceedings against Queen Caroline, who had returned to England on the death of George III. On 10 November, in consequence of public feeling, the charges were withdrawn.

[2] *Henry IV*, Part I, v, iii, 63.   [3] Moore's *Irish Melodies*.

K 931

To do good to mankind is the chivalrous plan,
   And is always as nobly requited;
Then battle for freedom wherever you can,
   And, if not shot or hang'd, you 'll get knighted.

So you have gotten the letter of 'Epigrams'—I am glad of it.
You will not be so, for I shall send you more. Here is one I
wrote for the endorsement of 'the Deed of Separation' in 1816;
but the lawyers objected to it, as superfluous. It was written
as we were getting up the signing and sealing. * * has the
original.

Endorsement to the Deed of Separation, in the April of 1816

A year ago you swore, fond she!
   'To love, to honour', and so forth:
Such was the vow you pledged to me,
   And here 's exactly what 'tis worth.

For the anniversary of January 2, 1821, I have a small
grateful anticipation, which, in case of accident, I add—

To Penelope, January 2, 1821

This day, of all our days, has done
   The worst for me and you:—
'Tis just *six* years since we were *one*,
   And *five* since we were *two*.

Pray excuse all this nonsense; for I must talk nonsense just
now, for fear of wandering to more serious topics, which, in the
present state of things, is not safe by a foreign post.

I told you in my last, that I had been going on with the
'Memoirs', and have got as far as twelve more sheets. But I
suspect they will be interrupted. In that case I will send them
on by post, though I feel remorse at making a friend pay so
much for postage, for we can't frank here beyond the frontier.

I shall be glad to hear of the event of the Queen's concern.
As to the ultimate effect, the most inevitable one to you and me
(if they and we live so long) will be that the Miss Moores and
Miss Byrons will present us with a great variety of grandchildren
by different fathers.

Pray, where did you get hold of Goethe's Florentine husband-
killing story? Upon such matters, in general, I may say,
with Beau Clincher, in reply to Errand's wife—

'Oh the villain, he hath murdered my poor Timothy!

'*Clincher*. Damn your Timothy!—I tell you, woman, your husband has *murdered me*—he has carried away my fine jubilee clothes.' [1]

So Bowles has been telling a story, too ('t is in the *Quarterly*), about the woods of 'Madeira', and so forth. I shall be at Bowles again, if he is not quiet. He mis-states, or mistakes, in a point or two. The paper is finished, and so is the letter.

Yours, etc.

162. TO JOHN MURRAY

R[avenn]a, 9bre. 9°, 1820.

DEAR MORAY,

The talent you approve of is an amiable one, and as you say might prove 'a national Service', but unfortunately I must be angry with a man before I draw his real portrait; and I can't deal in '*generals*', so that I trust never to have provocation enough to make a *Gallery*. If '*the* person' had not by many little dirty sneaking traits provoked it, I should have been silent, though I *had observed* him. Here follows an alteration. Put—

> Devil with *such* delight in damning,
> That if at the resurrection
> Unto him the free selection
> Of his future could be given,
> 'Twould be rather Hell than Heaven.

That is to say, if these two new lines do not too much lengthen out and weaken the amiability of the original thought and expression. You have a discretionary power about showing: I should think that Croker and D'Israeli would not disrelish a sight of these light little humorous things, and may be indulged now and then.

D'Israeli wrote the article on Spence:[2] I know him by the mark in his mouth. I am glad that the *Quarterly* has had so much Classical honesty as to insert it: it is good and true.

Hobhouse writes me a facetious letter about my *indolence* and love of Slumber. It becomes him: he is in active life; he writes pamphlets against Canning, to which he does not put

---

[1] Farquhar, *The Constant Couple, or A Trip to the Jubilee*, IV, i.
[2] i.e. the article on Pope, as a review of Joseph Spence's *Anecdotes of Books and Men*, in July 1820. See page 266.

his name; he gets into Newgate and into Parliament—both honourable places of refuge; and he 'greatly daring dines'[1] at all the taverns (why don't he set up a *tap* room at once), and then writes to quiz his laziness.

Why, I do like one or two vices, to be sure; but I can back a horse and fire a pistol 'without winking or blinking' like Major Sturgeon;[2] I have fed at times for two months together on *sheer biscuit and water* (without metaphor); I can get over seventy or eighty miles a day *riding* post, and *swim five* at a Stretch, taking a *piece* before and after, as at Venice, in 1818, or at least I *could do*, and have done it ONCE, and I never was ten minutes in my life over a *solitary* dinner.

Now, my friend Hobhouse, when we were wayfaring men, used to complain grievously of hard beds and sharp insects, while I slept like a top, and to awaken me with his swearing at them: he used to damn his dinners daily, both quality and cookery and quantity, and reproach me for a sort of 'brutal' indifference, as he called it, to these particulars; and now he writes me facetious sneerings because I *do not* get up early in a morning, when there is no occasion—if there were, *he* knows that I was always *out* of bed before him, though it is true that my ablutions detained me longer in dressing than his noble contempt of that 'oriental scrupulosity' permitted.

Then he is still sore about '*the ballad*'[3]—he!! why, he lampooned me at Brighton, in 1808, about Jackson the boxer and bold Webster, etc.: in 1809, he turned the death of my friend E[d] *Long* into ridicule and rhyme, because his name was susceptible of a *pun*; and, although he saw that I was distressed at it, before I left England in 1816, he wrote rhymes upon *D. Kinnaird, you*, and *myself*; and at Venice he parodied the lines 'Though the day of my destiny's over'[4] in a comfortable quizzing way: and now he harps on my ballad about his election! Pray tell him all this, for I will have no underhand work with my 'old Cronies'. If he can deny the facts, let him. I maintain that he is more *carnivorously* and *carnally sensual* than I am, though I am bad enough too for that matter; but not in eating and haranguing at the Crown and Anchor, where I never was but twice—and those were at 'Whores' Hops' when I was a younker in my teens; and, Egad, I think them the most respect-

---

[1] Pope, *Dunciad*, IV, 318.
[2] In Foote's *Mayor of Garratt*, I, i.
[3] The verses with the burden, 'My boy Hobbie O', which were sent to Murray on 25 March, and had since got into print.
[4] 'Dear *Byron* this humbug give over', etc.

able meetings of the two. But he is a little wroth that I would not come over to the *Queen's* trial: *lazy*, quotha! it is so true that he should be ashamed of asserting it. He counsels me not to 'get into a Scrape'; but, as Beau Clincher says, 'How melancholy are Newgate reflections!' [1] To be sure, his advice is worth following; for experience teacheth: he has been in a dozen within these last two years. *I pronounce me the more temperate of the two.*

Have you gotten *The Hints* yet?

I know Henry Matthews: he is the image, to the very voice, of his brother Charles, only darker: his *laugh* his in particular. The first time I ever met him was in Scrope Davies's rooms after his brother's death, and I nearly dropped, thinking that it was his Ghost. I have also dined with him in his rooms at King's College. Hobhouse once purposed a similar memoir; but I am afraid that the letters of Charles's correspondence with me (which are at Whitton with my other papers) would hardly do for the public: for our lives were not over strict, and our letters somewhat lax upon most subjects.

His Superiority over all his cotemporaries was quite indisputable and acknowledged: none of us ever thought of being *at all near* Matthews; and yet there were some high men of his standing—Bankes, Bob Milnes, Hobhouse, Bailey, and many others—without numbering the *mere Academical* men, of whom we hear little out of the University, and whom he beat *hollow* on *their own* Ground.

His gaining the Downing Fellowship was the completest thing of the kind ever known. He carried off both declamation prizes: in short, he did whatever he chose. He was three or four years my Senior, but I lived a good deal with him latterly, and with his friends. He wrote to me the very day of his death (I believe), or at least a day before, if not the very day. He meant to have stood for the University Membership. He was a very odd and humourous fellow besides, and spared nobody: for instance, walking out in Newstead Garden, he stopped at Boatswain's monument inscribed 'Here lies Boatswain, a Dog', etc., and then observing a *blank* marble tablet on the other side, 'So (says he) there is room for another friend, and I propose that the Inscription be "Here lies H—bh—se, a Pig"', etc. You may as well not let *this* transpire to the worthy member, lest he regard neither his dead friend nor his living one, with his wonted Suavity.

[1] *The Constant Couple*, **v**, ii.

Rose's *lines* must be at his own option: *I* can have no objection to their publication. Pray salute him from me.

Mr. Keats, whose poetry you enquire after, appears to me what I have already said: such writing is a sort of mental * * * *_* * * * * * * * his *Imagination*. I don't mean he is *indecent*, but viciously soliciting his own ideas into a state, which is neither poetry nor anything else but a Bedlam vision produced by raw pork and opium. Barry Cornwall would write well, if he would let himself. Croly [1] is superior to many, but seems to think himself inferior to Nobody.

Last week I sent you a correspondence with Galignani, and some documents on your property. You have now, I think, an opportunity of *checking*, or at least *limiting*, those *French re-publications*. You may let all your authors publish what they please *against me* or *mine*: a publisher is not, and cannot be, responsible for all the works that issue from his printer's.

The 'White Lady of Avenel' [2] is not quite so good as a *real well-authenticated* ('Donna bianca') *While Lady* of *Colalto*, or spectre in the Marca Trivigiana, who has been repeatedly seen: there is a man (a huntsman) now alive who saw her also. Hoppner could tell you all about her, and so can Rose perhaps. I myself have *no doubt* of the fact, historical and spectral. She always appeared on particular occasions, before the deaths of the family, etc., etc. I heard Me Benzoni say, that she knew a Gentleman who had seen her cross his room at Colalto Castle. Hoppner saw and spoke with the Huntsman who met her at the Chase, and never *hunted* afterwards. She was a Girl attendant, who, one day dressing the hair of a Countess Colalto, was seen by her mistress to smile upon her husband in the Glass. The Countess had her shut up in the wall at the Castle, like Constance de Beverley. [3] Ever after, she haunted them and all the Colaltos. She is described as very beautiful and fair. It is well authenticated.

Yours,

B.

---

[1] The Rev. George Croly, a miscellaneous writer. His chief poems are modelled on Byron.

[2] In Scott's *Monastery*.

[3] *Marmion*, Canto ii, stanzas xx–xxxiii.

163. TO JOHN MURRAY

Ravenna, 9bre 19, 1820.

DEAR MURRAY,

What you said of the late Charles Skinner Matthews has set me to my recollections; but I have not been able to turn up any thing which would do for the purposed Memoir of his brother,—even if he had previously done enough during his life to sanction the introduction of anecdotes so merely personal. He was, however, a very extraordinary man, and would have been a great one. No one ever succeeded in a more surpassing degree than he did as far as he went. He was indolent, too; but whenever he stripped, he overthrew all antagonists. His conquests will be found registered at Cambridge, particularly his *Downing* one, which was hotly and highly contested, and yet easily *won*. Hobhouse was his most intimate friend, and can tell you more of him than any man. William Bankes also a great deal. I myself recollect more of his oddities than of his academical qualities, for we lived most together at a very idle period of *my* life. When I went up to Trinity, in 1805, at the age of seventeen and a half, I was miserable and untoward to a degree. I was wretched at leaving Harrow, to which I had become attached during the two last years of my stay there; wretched at going to Cambridge instead of Oxford (there were no rooms vacant at Christchurch); wretched from some private domestic circumstances of different kinds, and consequently about as unsocial as a wolf taken from the troop. So that, although I knew Matthews, and met him often *then* at Bankes's, (who was my collegiate pastor, and master, and patron,) and at Rhode's, Milnes's, Price's, Dick's, Macnamara's, Farrell's, Gally Knight's, and others of that *set* of contemporaries, yet I was neither intimate with him nor with any one else, except my old schoolfellow Edward Long (with whom I used to pass the day in riding and swimming), and William Bankes, who was good-naturedly tolerant of my ferocities.

It was not till 1807, after I had been upwards of a year away from Cambridge, to which I had returned again to *reside* for my degree, that I became one of Matthews's familiars, by means of Hobhouse, who, after hating me for two years, because I wore a *white hat*, and a *grey* coat, and rode a *grey* horse (as he says himself), took me into his good graces because I had written some poetry. I had always lived a good deal, and got drunk occasionally, in their company—but now we became really friends in a morning. Matthews, however, was not at this period resident in College. I met *him* chiefly in London, and at uncertain periods at Cambridge. Hobhouse, in the mean time, did great things: he founded the Cambridge 'Whig Club' (which he seems to have forgotten), and the 'Amicable Society', which was dissolved in consequence of the members constantly quarrelling, and made himself very popular with 'us youth', and no less formidable to all tutors, professors, and heads of Colleges. William Bankes was gone; while he stayed, he ruled the roast—or rather the *roasting*—and was father of all mischiefs.

Matthews and I, meeting in London, and elsewhere became great cronies. He was not good tempered—nor am I—but with a little tact his temper was manageable, and I thought him so superior a man, that I was willing to sacrifice something to his humours, which were often, at the same time, amusing and provoking. What became of his *papers* (and he certainly had many), at the time of his death, was never known. I mention this by the way, fearing to skip it over, and *as* he *wrote* remarkably well, both in Latin and English. We went down to Newstead together, where I had got a famous cellar, and *Monks'* dresses from a masquerade warehouse. We were a company of some seven or eight, with an occasional neighbour or so for visitors, and used to sit up late in our friars' dresses, drinking burgundy, claret, champagne, and what not, out of the *skull-cup*, and all sorts of glasses, and buffooning all round the house, in our conventual garments. Matthews always denominated me 'the Abbot', and never called me by any other name in his good humours, to the day of his death. The harmony of these our symposia was somewhat interrupted, a few days after our assembling, by Matthews's threatening to throw Hobhouse out of a *window*, in consequence of I know not what commerce of jokes ending in this epigram. Hobhouse came to me and said, that 'his respect and regard for me as host would not permit him to call out any of my guests, and that he should go to town next morning'. He did. It was in vain that I represented to him that the window was not high, and that the turf under it was particularly soft. Away he went.

Matthews and myself had travelled down from London together, talking all the way incessantly upon one single topic. When we got to Loughborough, I know not what chasm had made us diverge for a moment to some other subject, at which he was indignant. 'Come,' said he, 'don't let us break through

—let us go on as we began, to our journey's end'; and so he continued, and was as entertaining as ever to the very end. He had previously occupied, during my year's absence from Cambridge, my rooms in Trinity, with the furniture; and Jones,[1] the tutor, in his odd way, had said, on putting him in, 'Mr. Matthews, I recommend to your attention not to damage any of the moveables, for Lord Byron, Sir, is a young man of *tumultuous passions*'. Matthews was delighted with this; and whenever anybody came to visit him, begged them to handle the very door with caution; and used to repeat Jones's admonition in his tone and manner. There was a large mirror in the room, on which he remarked, 'that he thought his friends were grown uncommonly assiduous in coming to *see him*, but he soon discovered that they only came to *see themselves*'. Jones's phrase of '*tumultuous passions*', and the whole scene, had put him into such good humour, that I verily believe that I owed to it a portion of his good graces.

When at Newstead, somebody by accident rubbed against one of his white silk stockings, one day before dinner; of course the gentleman apologised. 'Sir,' answered Matthews, 'it may be all very well for you, who have a great many silk stockings, to dirty other people's; but to me, who have only this *one pair*, which I have put on in honour of the Abbot here, no apology can compensate for such carelessness; besides, the expense of washing.' He had the same sort of droll sardonic way about every thing. A wild Irishman, named Farrell, one evening began to say something at a large supper at Cambridge, Matthews roared out 'Silence!' and then, pointing to Farrell, cried out, in the words of the oracle, '*Orson is endowed with reason*'. You may easily suppose that Orson lost what reason he had acquired, on hearing this compliment. When Hobhouse published his volume of poems, the *Miscellany* (which Matthews *would* call the '*Miss-sell-any*'), all that could be drawn from him was, that the preface was 'extremely like *Walsh*'.[2] Hobhouse thought this at first a compliment; but we never could make out what it was, for all we know of *Walsh* is his Ode to King William,[3] and Pope's epithet of '*knowing Walsh*'.[4] When the Newstead party broke up for London, Hobhouse and Matthews, who were

---

[1] The Rev. Thomas Jones, Senior Tutor.

[2] William Walsh (1663–1708), critic and poet. 'The only thing remarkable about Walsh's preface is that Dr. Johnson praises it as "very judicious", but is, at the same time, silent respecting the poems to which it is prefixed' (Moore).

[3] Probably his *Golden Age Restored*. [4] *Prologue to the Satires*, 136.

the greatest friends possible, agreed, for a whim, to *walk together* to town. They quarrelled by the way, and actually walked the latter half of the journey, occasionally passing and repassing, without speaking. When Matthews had got to Highgate, he had spent all his money but three-pence halfpenny, and determined to spend that also in a pint of beer, which I believe he was drinking before a public-house, as Hobhouse passed him (still without speaking) for the last time on their route. They were reconciled in London again.

One of Matthews's passions was 'the fancy'; and he sparred uncommonly well. But he always got beaten in rows, or combats with the bare fist. In swimming, too, he swam well; but with *effort* and *labour*, and *too high* out of the water; so that Scrope Davies and myself, of whom he was therein somewhat emulous, always told him that he would be drowned if ever he came to a difficult pass in the water. He was so; but surely Scrope and myself would have been most heartily glad that

> 'the Dean had lived,
> And our prediction proved a lie'.[1]

His head was uncommonly handsome, very like what *Pope's* was in his youth.

His voice, and laugh, and features, are strongly resembled by his brother Henry's, if Henry be *he* of *King's College*. His passion for boxing was so great, that he actually wanted me to match him with Dogherty [2] (whom I had backed and made the match for against Tom Belcher [3]), and I saw them spar together at my own lodgings with the gloves on. As he was bent upon it, I would have backed Dogherty to please him, but the match went off. It was of course to have been a private fight, in a private room.

On one occasion, being too late to go home and dress, he was equipped by a friend (Mr. Baillie, I believe,) in a magnificently fashionable and somewhat exaggerated shirt and neckcloth. He proceeded to the Opera, and took his station in Fop's Alley. During the interval between the opera and the ballet, an acquaintance took his station by him and saluted him: 'Come round,' said Matthews, 'come round.'—'Why should I come round?' said the other; 'you have only to turn your head—I am close by you.'—'That is exactly what I cannot do,' said Matthews; 'don't you see the state I am in?' pointing

---

[1] Cf. Swift, *On the Death of Dr. Swift*, 131–2.
[2] Dan Dogherty, Irish champion 1806–11.
[3] Younger brother of Jem Belcher, the champion.

to his buckram shirt collar and inflexible cravat,—and there he stood with his head always in the same perpendicular position during the whole spectacle.

One evening, after dining together, as we were going to the Opera, I happened to have a spare Opera ticket (as subscriber to a box), and presented it to Matthews. 'Now, sir,' said he to Hobhouse afterwards, 'this I call *courteous* in the Abbot—another man would never have thought that I might do better with half a guinea than throw it to a door-keeper;—but here is a man not only asks me to dinner, but gives me a ticket for the theatre.' These were only his oddities, for no man was more liberal, or more honourable in all his doings and dealings, than Matthews. He gave Hobhouse and me, before we set out for Constantinople, a most splendid entertainment, to which we did ample justice. One of his fancies was dining at all sorts of out-of-the-way places. Somebody popped upon him in I know not what coffee-house in the Strand—and what do you think was the attraction? Why, that he paid a shilling (I think) to *dine with his hat on*. This he called his '*hat* house', and used to boast of the comfort of being covered at meal times.

When Sir Henry Smith was expelled from Cambridge for a row with a tradesman named 'Hiron', Matthews solaced himself with shouting under Hiron's windows every evening,

> 'Ah me! what perils do environ
> The man who meddles with *hot Hiron*!'[1]

He was also of that band of profane scoffers who, under the auspices of * * * *, used to rouse Lort Mansel (late Bishop of Bristol) from his slumbers in the lodge of Trinity; and when he appeared at the window foaming with wrath, and crying out, 'I know you, gentlemen, I know you!' were wont to reply, 'We beseech thee to hear us, good *Lort*!'—'Good *Lort* deliver us!' (Lort was his Christian name.) As he was very free in his speculations upon all kinds of subjects, although by no means either dissolute or intemperate in his conduct, and as I was no less independent, our conversation and correspondence used to alarm our friend Hobhouse to a considerable degree.

You must be almost tired of my packets, which will have cost a mint of postage.

Salute Gifford and all my friends.

Yours,

B.

---

[1] Butler, *Hudibras*, Part I, Canto III, 1–2, where the last words of the couplet are 'cold iron'.

164. TO JOHN MURRAY

Ravenna, Decr 9th, 1820.

Dear Murray,

I intended to have written to you at some length by this post, but as the Military Commandant [1] is now lying dead in my house, on Fletcher's bed, I have other things to think of.

He was shot at 8 o'Clock this evening about two hundred paces from our door. I was putting on my great Coat to pay a visit to the Countess G., when I heard a shot, and on going into the hall, found all my servants on the balcony exclaiming that 'a Man was murdered'. As it is the custom here to let people fight it through, they wanted to hinder me from going out; but I ran down into the Street: Tita, the bravest of them, followed me; and we made our way to the Commandant, who was lying on his back, with five wounds, of which three in the body—one in the heart. There were about him Diego, his Adjutant, crying like a Child; a priest howling; a Surgeon who dared not touch him; two or three confused and frightened Soldiers; one or two of the boldest of the mob; and the Street dark as pitch, with the people flying in all directions. As Diego could only cry and wring his hands, and the Priest could only pray, and nobody seemed able or willing to do anything except exclaim, shake and stare, I made my Servant and one of the mob take up the body; sent off Diego crying to the Cardinal, the Soldiers for the Guard; and had the Commandant conveyed up Stairs to my own quarters. But he was quite gone. I made the Surgeon examine him, and examined him myself. He had bled inwardly, and very little external blood was apparent. One of the Slugs had gone quite through—all but the Skin: I felt it myself. Two more shots in the body, one in a finger, and another in the arm. His face was not at all disfigured: he seems asleep, but is growing livid. The Assassin has not been taken; but the gun was found—a gun filed down to half the barrel. [2]

He said nothing but *O Dio !* and *O Gesu* two or three times.

The house was filled at last with Soldiers, officers, police, and military; but they are clearing away—all but the Sentinels, and the body is to be removed tomorrow. It seems that, if I had not had him taken into my house, he might have lain in

---

[1] By name Del Pinto.

[2] This incident is introduced into *Don Juan*, Canto v, stanzas xxxiii-xxxix.

the Streets till morning; as here nobody meddles with such things, for fear of the consequences—either of public suspicion, or private revenge on the part of the Slayers. They may do as they please: I shall never be deterred from a duty of humanity by all the assassins of Italy, and that is a wide word.

He was a brave officer, but an unpopular man. The whole town is in confusion.

You may judge better of things here by this detail, than by anything which I could add on the Subject: communicate this letter to Hobhouse and Douglas K^d, and believe me

Yours ever truly,

B.

P.S.—The poor Man's wife is not yet aware of his death: they are to break it to her in the morning.

The Lieutenant, who is watching the body, is smoking with the greatest *Sangfroid*: a strange people.

165. TO THOMAS MOORE

Ravenna, Dec. 25, 1820.

You will or ought to have received the packet and letters which I remitted to your address a fortnight ago (or it may be more days), and I shall be glad of an answer, as, in these times and places, packets per post are in some risk of not reaching their destination.

I have been thinking of a project for you and me, in case we both get to London again, which (if a Neapolitan war don't suscitate) may be calculated as possible for one of us about the spring of 1821. I presume that you, too, will be back by that time, or never; but on that you will give me some index. The project, then, is for you and me to set up jointly a *newspaper*—nothing more nor less—weekly, or so, with some improvement or modifications upon the plan of the present scoundrels, who degrade that department,—but a *newspaper*, which we will edite in due form, and, nevertheless, with some attention.

There must always be in it a piece of poesy from one or other of us *two*, leaving room, however, for such dilettanti rhymers as may be deemed worthy of appearing in the same column: but *this* must be a *sine qua non*; and also as much prose as we can compass. We will take an *office*—our names *not* announced, but suspected—and, by the blessing of Providence, give the age some new lights upon policy, poesy, biography, criticism, morality, theology, and all other *ism*, *ality*, and *ology* whatsoever.

Why, man, if we were to take to this in good earnest, your debts would be paid off in a twelvemonth, and, by dint of a little diligence and practice, I doubt not that we could distance the common-place blackguards who have so long disgraced common sense and the common reader. They have no merit but practice and impudence, both of which we may acquire; and, as for talent and culture, the devil's in 't if such proofs as we have given of both can't furnish out something better than the 'funeral baked meats' which have coldly set forth the breakfast table of all Great Britain for so many years. Now, what think you? Let me know; and recollect that, if we take to such an enterprise, we must do so in good earnest. Here is a hint,—do you make it a plan. We will modify it into as literary and classical a concern as you please, only let us put out our powers upon it, and it will most likely succeed. But you must *live* in London, and I also, to bring it to bear, and *we must keep it a secret*.

As for the living in London, I would make that not difficult to you (if you would allow me), until we could see whether one means or other (the success of the plan, for instance) would not make it quite easy for you, as well as your family; and, in any case, we should have some fun, composing, correcting, supposing, inspecting, and supping together over our lucubrations. If you think this worth a thought, let me know, and I will begin to lay in a small literary capital of composition for the occasion.

Yours ever affectionately,

B.

P.S.—If you thought of a middle plan between a *Spectator* and a newspaper, why not?—only not on a *Sunday*. Not that Sunday is not an excellent day, but it is engaged already. We will call it the 'Tenda Rossa',[1] the name Tassoni[2] gave an answer of his in a controversy, in allusion to the delicate hint of Timour the Lame, to his enemies, by a 'Tenda' of that colour, before he gave battle. Or we will call it *Gli*, or *I Carbonari*,[3] if it so please you—or any other name full of 'pastime and prodigality',[4] which you may prefer. * * * Let me have an answer. I conclude poetically, with the bellman, 'A merry Christmas to you!'

---

[1] 'Red tent.'   [2] Alessandro Tassoni (1565–1635), poet.
[3] In reference to the Italian society of nationalists.
[4] Farquhar, *The Recruiting Officer*, v, i.

166. TO JOHN MURRAY

Ravenna, J. 4th, 1821.

Dᴿ. Mʸ.,

I write to you in considerable surprise, that, since the first days of November, I have never had a line from you. It is so incomprehensible, that I can only account for it by supposing some accident. I have written to you at least ten letters, to none of which I have had a word of answer: one of them was on your own affairs—a proposal of Galignani, relative to your publications, which I referred to you (as was proper), for your own decision.

Last week I sent (addressed to Mr. D. Kinnaird) two packets containing the 5ᵗʰ Canto of *D. J.* I wish to know what you mean to do?[1] anything or nothing.

Of the State of this country I can only say, that, besides the assassination of the Commandant of the 7ᵗʰ (of which I gave you an account, as I took him up, and he died in my house) that there have been *six* murders committed within twenty miles—three last night.

Yours very truly,

B.

P.S.—Have you gotten *the Hints*, that I may alter parts and portions?

I just see, by the papers of Galignani, that there is a new tragedy of great expectation, by Barry Cornwall:[2] of what I have read of his works I liked the *Dramatic Sketches*, but thought his *Sicilian Story* and *Marcian Colonna*, in rhyme, quite spoilt by I know not what affectation of Wordsworth, and Hunt, and Moore, and Myself, all mixed up into a kind of Chaos. I think him very likely to produce a good tragedy, if he keep to a natural style, and not play tricks to form Harlequinades for an audience. As he (B. C. is not his *true* name) was a schoolfellow of mine, I take more than common interest in his success, and shall be glad to hear of it speedily. If I had been aware that he was in that line, I should have spoken of him in the preface to M[arino] F[aliero]: he will do a World's wonder if he produce a great tragedy. I am, however, persuaded, that this is not to be done by following the old dramatists, who are full of gross faults, pardoned only for the beauty of their language; but by writing

[1] i.e. whether or not he would continue to publish the poem anonymously and without imprint.
[2] *The Duke of Mirandola.*

naturally and *regularly*, and producing *regular* tragedies, like the *Greeks*; but not in *imitation*,—merely the outline of their conduct, adapted to our own times and circumstances, and of course *no* chorus.

You will laugh, and say, 'why don't *you* do so?' I have, you see, tried a Sketch in *Marino Faliero*; but many people think my talent '*essentially undramatic*', and I am not at all clear that they are not right. If *Marino Faliero* don't fall, in the perusal, I shall, perhaps, try again (but not for the Stage); and, as I think that *love* is not the principal passion for tragedy (and yet most of ours turn upon it), you will not find me a popular writer. Unless it is Love, *furious*, *criminal*, and *hapless*, it ought not to make a tragic subject: when it is melting and maudlin, it *does*, but it ought not to do; it is then for the Gallery and second price boxes.

If you want to have a notion of what I am trying, take up a *translation* of any of the *Greek* tragedians. If I said the original, it would be an impudent presumption of mine; but the translations are so inferior to the originals, that I think I may risk it. Then judge of the 'simplicity of plot, etc.', and do not judge me by your mad old dramatists, which is like drinking Usquebaugh and then proving a fountain: yet after all, I suppose that you do not mean that spirits is a nobler element than a clear spring bubbling in the sun; and this I take to be the difference between the Greeks and those turbid mountebanks—always excepting B. Jonson, who was a Scholar and a Classic. Or, take up a translation of Alfieri, and try the interest, etc., of these my new attempts in the old line, by *him* in *English*. And then tell me fairly your opinion. But don't measure me by YOUR OWN *old* or *new* tailor's yards. Nothing so easy as intricate confusion of plot, and rant. Mrs. Centlivre,[1] in comedy, has *ten times the bustle of Congreve*; but are they to be compared? and yet she drove Congreve from the theatre.

167. TO THOMAS MOORE

Ravenna, January 22, 1821.

Pray get well. I do not like your complaint. So, let me have a line to say you are up and doing again. To-day I am thirty-three years of age.

[1] Susanna Centlivre (*c.* 1680–1723), authoress of nineteen plays.

> Through life's road, so dim and dirty,
> I have dragged to three-and-thirty.
> What *have* these years left to me?
> Nothing—except thirty-three.

Have you heard that the 'Braziers' Company' have, or mean to present an address at Brandenburgh House, 'in armour', and with all possible variety and splendour of brazen apparel?

> The Braziers, it seems, are preparing to pass
> An address, and present it themselves all in brass—
> A superfluous pageant—for, by the Lord Harry,
> They 'll find where they 're going much more than they carry.

There 's an Ode for you, is it not?—worthy

> Of Wordsworth, the grand metaquizzical poet,
> A man of vast merit, though few people know it;
> The perusal of whom (as I told *you* at Mestri)
> I owe, in great part, to my passion for pastry.

Mestri and Fusina are the 'trajects, or common ferries',[1] to Venice; but it was from Fusina that you and I embarked, though 'the wicked necessity of rhyming'[2] has made me press Mestri into the voyage.

So, you have had a book dedicated to you? I am glad of it, and shall be very happy to see the volume.

I am in a peck of troubles about a tragedy[3] of mine, which is fit only for the (* * * *) closet, and which it seems that the managers, assuming a *right* over published poetry, are determined to enact, whether I will or no, with their own alterations by Mr. Dibdin,[4] I presume. I have written to Murray, to the Lord Chamberlain, and to others, to interfere and preserve me from such an exhibition. I want neither the impertinence of their hisses, nor the insolence of their applause. I write only for the *reader*, and care for nothing but the *silent* approbation of those who close one's book with good humour and quiet contentment.

Now, if you would also write to our friend Perry, to beg of him to mediate with Harris and Elliston[5] to *forbear* this intent, you will greatly oblige me. The play is quite unfit for the stage,

---

[1] *The Merchant of Venice*, III, iv, 53.
[2] Cf. Milton, Preface to *Paradise Lost*, 1668.
[3] *Marino Faliero*.   [4] Thomas John Dibdin, the actor and dramatist.
[5] Managers of Drury Lane Theatre.

as a single glance will show them, and, I hope, *has* shown them;
and, if it were ever so fit, I will never have any thing to do
willingly with the theatres.

Yours ever, in haste, etc.

168. TO JOHN MURRAY

Ravenna, February 16, 1821.

DEAR MORAY,

In the month of March will arrive from Barcelona Signor
Curioni,[1] engaged for the Opera. He is an acquaintance of
mine, and a gentlemanly young man, high in his profession.
I must request your personal kindness and patronage in his
favour. Pray introduce him to such of the theatrical people,
Editors of Papers, and others, as may be useful to him in his
profession, publicly and privately.

He is accompanied by the Signora Arpalice Taruscelli, a
Venetian lady of great beauty and celebrity, and a particular
friend of mine: your natural gallantry will I am sure induce you
to pay her proper attention. Tell Israeli that, as he is fond of
literary anecdotes, she can tell him some of your acquaintance
abroad. I presume that he speaks Italian. Do not neglect
this request, but do them and me this favour in their behalf.
I shall write to some others to aid you in assisting them with
your countenance.

I agree to your request of leaving in abeyance the terms for
the three *D. J.s*, till you can ascertain the effect of publication.
If I refuse to alter, you have a claim to so much courtesy in
return. I had let you off your proposal about the price of the
Cantos, last year (the 3rd and 4th always to reckon as *one* only),
and I do not call upon you to renew it. You have therefore no
occasion to fight so shy of such subjects, as I am not conscious
of having given you occasion.

The 5th is so far from being the last of *D. J.*, that it is hardly
the beginning. I meant to take him the tour of Europe, with
a proper mixture of siege, battle, and adventure, and to make
him finish as *Anacharsis Cloots* [2] in the French revolution. To
how many cantos this may extend, I know not, nor whether
(even if I live) I shall complete it; but this was my notion: I
meant to have made him a *Cavalier Servente* in Italy, and a

---

[1] Alberico Curioni. He remained in London till 1832.
[2] Baron Jean Baptiste ('Anacharsis') Clootz, who was beheaded in 1794.

cause for a divorce in England, and a Sentimental 'Werther-faced man'[1] in Germany, so as to show the different ridicules of the society in each of those countries, and to have displayed him gradually *gâté* and *blasé* as he grew older, as is natural. But I had not quite fixed whether to make him end in Hell, or in an unhappy marriage, not knowing which would be the severest. The Spanish tradition says Hell: but it is probably only an Allegory of the other state. You are now in possession of my notions on the subject.

You say *The Doge* will not be popular: did I ever write for *popularity*? I defy you to show a work of mine (except a tale or two) of a popular style or complexion. It appears to me that there is room for a different style of the drama; neither a servile following of the old drama, which is a grossly erroneous one, nor yet *too French*, like those who succeeded the older writers. It appears to me, that good English, and a severer approach to the rules, might combine something not dishonourable to our literature. I have also attempted to make a play without love. And there are neither rings, nor mistakes, nor starts, nor outrageous ranting villains, nor melodrame, in it. All this will prevent it's popularity, but does not persuade me that it is *therefore* faulty. Whatever faults it has will arise from deficiency in the conduct, rather than in the conception, which is simple and severe.

So *you epigrammatize* upon *my epigram*? I will *pay you* for *that*, mind if I don't, some day. I never let any one off in the long run (*who first begins*): remember *Sam*,[2] and see if I don't do you as good a turn. You unnatural publisher! what! quiz your own authors! You are a paper Cannibal.

In the letter on Bowles[3] (which I sent by Tuesday's post) after the words '*attempts had been made*' (alluding to the re-publication of *English Bards*), add the words '*in Ireland*'; for I believe that Cawthorn did not begin his attempts till after I had left England the second time. Pray attend to this. Let me know what you and your Squad think of the letter on Bowles.

I did not think the second *Seal* so bad: surely it is far better than the Saracen's head with which you have sealed your *last letter*; the larger, in *profile*, was surely much better than that.

So Foscolo says he will get you a *seal cut* better in Italy:

---

[1] Moore, *The Fudge Family in Paris*, Letter V.
[2] Referring to his lines on Rogers, written in September 1820, and beginning: 'Nose and chin would shame a knocker'.
[3] *A Letter to [John Murray], Esqre., on the Rev. W. L. Bowles's Strictures on the Life and Writings of Pope*, published in March 1821.

he means a *throat*—that is the only thing they do dexterously. The Arts—all but Canova's, and Morghen's,[1] and *Ovid's*[2] (I don't *mean poetry*),—are as low as need be: look at the Seal which I gave to Wm Bankes, and own it. How came George Bankes to quote *English Bards* in the House of Commons? All the World keep flinging that poem in my face.

Belzoni *is* a grand traveller, and his English is very prettily broken.[3]

As for News, the Barbarians are marching on Naples, and if they lose a single battle, all Italy will be up. It will be like the Spanish war, if they have any bottom.

Letters opened!—to be sure they are, and that's the reason why I always put in my opinion of the German Austrian Scoundrels: there is not an Italian who loathes them more than I do; and whatever I could do to scour Italy and the earth of their infamous oppression, would be done *con amore*.

Yours, ever and truly,

B.

Recollect that the *Hints*[4] must be printed with the *Latin*, otherwise there is no sense.

169. TO RICHARD BELGRAVE HOPPNER

Ravenna, April 3, 1821.

Thanks for the translation.[5] I have sent you some books, which I do not know whether you have read or no—you need not return them, in any case. I enclose you also a letter from Pisa. I have neither spared trouble nor expense in the care of the child;[6] and as she was now four years old complete, and quite above the control of the servants—and as a *man* living without any woman at the head of his house cannot much attend to a nursery—I had no resource but to place her for a time (at a high pension too) in the convent of Bagna-Cavalli (twelve miles off), where the air is good, and where she will, at least, have her learning advanced, and her morals and religion

---

[1] Raphael Morghen (1758–1835), the famous Italian engraver.

[2] i.e. his *Ars Amatoria*.

[3] The reference is to Giovanni Battista Belzoni's *Narrative of the Operations and Recent Discoveries within the Pyramids, Temples, Tombs, and Excavations in Egypt and Nubia*, published by Murray in 1820.

[4] *Hints from Horace*, which remained unpublished till 1831.

[5] A translation, for which Byron had asked, of the German version of *Manfred*.

[6] Allegra.

inculcated. I had also another reason;—things were and are in such a state here, that I had no reason to look upon my own personal safety as particularly insurable; and I thought the infant best out of harm's way, for the present.

It is also fit that I should add that I by no means intended, nor intend, to give a *natural* child an *English* education, because with the disadvantages of her birth, her after-settlement would be doubly difficult. Abroad, with a fair foreign education and a portion of five or six thousand pounds, she might and may marry very respectably. In England such a dowry would be a pittance, while elsewhere it is a fortune. It is, besides, my wish that she should be a Roman Catholic, which I look upon as the best religion, as it is assuredly the oldest of the various branches of Christianity. I have now explained my notions as to the *place* where she now is—it is the best I could find for the present; but I have no prejudices in its favour.

I do not speak of politics, because it seems a hopeless subject, as long as those scoundrels are to be permitted to bully states out of their independence. Believe me,

Yours ever and truly.

P.S.—There is a report here of a change in France; [1] but with what truth is not yet known.

P.S.—My respects to Mrs. H. I *have* the 'best opinion' of her countrywomen; [2] and at my time of life, (three and thirty, 22d January, 1821), that is to say, after the life I have led, a *good* opinion is the only rational one which a man should entertain of the whole sex—up to *thirty*, the worst possible opinion a man can have of them in *general*, the better for himself. Afterwards, it is a matter of no importance to *them*, nor to him either, *what opinion* he entertains—his day is over, or at least, should be.

You see how sober I am become.

170. TO PERCY BYSSHE SHELLEY

Ravenna, April 26, 1821.

The child continues doing well, and the accounts are regular and favourable. It is gratifying to me that you and Mrs. Shelley do not disapprove of the step which I have taken, which is merely temporary.

[1] The elections of 1821, resulting in the resignation of Richelieu.
[2] Mrs. Hoppner was a Swiss.

I am very sorry to hear what you say of Keats [1]—is it *actually* true? I did not think criticism had been so killing. Though I differ from you essentially in your estimate of his performances, I so much abhor all unnecessary pain, that I would rather he had been seated on the highest peak of Parnassus than have perished in such a manner. Poor fellow! though with such inordinate self-love he would probably have not been very happy. I read the review of *Endymion* in the *Quarterly*. It was severe,—but surely not so severe as many reviews in that and other journals upon others.

I recollect the effect on me of the *Edinburgh* on my first poem; [2] it was rage, and resistance, and redress—but not despondency nor despair. I grant that those are not amiable feelings; but, in this world of bustle and broil, and especially in the career of writing, a man should calculate upon his powers of *resistance* before he goes into the arena.

> 'Expect not life from pain nor danger free,
> Nor deem the doom of man reversed for thee.' [3]

You know my opinion of *that second-hand* school of poetry. You also know my high opinion of your own poetry,—because it is of *no* school. I read *Cenci*—but, besides that I think the *subject* essentially *un*dramatic, I am not an admirer of our old dramatists *as models*. I deny that the English have hitherto had a drama at all. Your *Cenci*, however, was a work of power and poetry. As to *my* drama, pray revenge yourself upon it, by being as free as I have been with yours.

I have not yet got your *Prometheus*,[4] which I long to see. I have heard nothing of mine, and do not know that it is yet published. I have published a pamphlet on the Pope controversy, which you will not like. Had I known that Keats was dead—or that he was alive and so sensitive—I should have omitted some remarks upon his poetry, to which I was provoked by his *attack* upon *Pope*,[5] and my disapprobation of *his own* style of writing.

You want me to undertake a great poem—I have not the inclination nor the power. As I grow older, the indifference —*not* to life, for we love it by instinct—but to the stimuli of life,

---

[1] On 23 February 1821, Keats had died at Rome of consumption. The attack on his *Endymion* in the *Quarterly Review* of September 1818 was said to have hastened his malady.

[2] i.e. *Hours of Idleness*.

[3] Johnson, *The Vanity of Human Wishes*, 155–6.

[4] *Prometheus Unbound, a Lyrical Drama*, 1820.

[5] In 'Sleep and Poetry,' 193–206. Byron's reference to Keats is in the *Second Letter to John Murray*.

increases. Besides, this late failure of the Italians [1] has latterly disappointed me for many reasons,—some public, some personal. My respects to Mrs. S.

Yours ever,

B.

P.S.—Could not you and I contrive to meet this summer? Could not you take a run here *alone*?

171. TO THOMAS MOORE

Ravenna, April 28, 1821.

You cannot have been more disappointed than myself, nor so much deceived. I have been so at some personal risk also, which is not yet done away with. However, no time nor circumstances shall alter my tone nor my feelings of indignation against tyranny triumphant. The present business has been as much a work of treachery as of cowardice,—though both may have done their part. If ever you and I meet again, I will have a talk with you upon the subject. At present, for obvious reasons, I can write but little, as all letters are opened. In *mine* they shall always find *my* sentiments, but nothing that can lead to the oppression of others.

You will please to recollect that the Neapolitans are now nowhere more execrated than in Italy, and not blame a whole people for the vices of a province. That would be like condemning Great Britain because they plunder wrecks in Cornwall.

And now let us be literary;—a sad falling off, but it is always a consolation. If 'Othello's occupation be gone', let us take to the next best; and, if we cannot contribute to make mankind more free and wise, we may amuse ourselves and those who like it. What are you writing? I have been scribbling at intervals, and Murray will be publishing about now.

Lady Noel has, as you say, been dangerously ill; but it may console you to learn that she is dangerously well again.

I have written a sheet or two more of Memoranda for you; and I kept a little Journal for about a month or two, till I had filled the paper-book. I then left it off, as things grew busy, and, afterwards, too gloomy to set down without a painful feeling. This I should be glad to send you, if I had an opportunity; but a volume, however small, don't go well by such posts as exist in this Inquisition of a country.

I have no news. As a very pretty woman said to me a few

[1] An attempted insurrection of the Carbonari at Ravenna. One result was the banishment of the entire Gamba family.

nights ago, with the tears in her eyes, as she sat at the harpsichord, 'Alas! the Italians must now return to making operas'. I fear *that* and maccaroni are their forte, and 'motley their only wear'.[1] However, there are some high spirits among them still. Pray write.

And believe me, etc.

172. TO FRANCIS HODGSON

DEAR HODGSON,   Ravenna, May 12, 1821.

At length your two poems[2] have been sent. I have read them over (with the notes) with great pleasure. I receive your compliments kindly and your censures temperately, which I suppose is all that can be expected among poets. Your poem is, however, excellent, and if not popular only proves that there is a *fortune* in *fame* as in every thing else in this world. Much, too, depends upon a publisher, and much upon luck; and the number of writers is such, that as the mind of a reader can only contain a certain quantum of poetry and poet's glories, he is sometimes saturated, and allows many good dishes to go away untouched (as happens at great dinners), and this not from fastidiousness but fulness.

You will have seen from my pamphlet on Bowles that our opinions are not very different. Indeed, my modesty would naturally *look* at least bashfully on being termed the 'first of living minstrels'[3] (by a brother of the art) if both our estimates of 'living minstrels' in general did not leaven the praise to a sober compliment. It is something like the priority in a retreat. There is but one of your tests which is not infallible: Translation. There are three or four *French* translations, and several German and Italian which I have seen. Moore wrote to me from Paris months ago that 'the French had caught the contagion of Byronism to the highest pitch' and has written since to say that nothing was ever like their 'entusymusy' (you remember Braham) on the subject, even through the 'slaver of a prose translation': these are his words. The Paris translation is also very inferior to the Geneva one, which is very fair, although in prose also, so you see that your test of 'translateable or not' is not so sound as could be wished. It is no pleasure, however, you may suppose, to be criticised through such a translation,

---

[1] *As You Like It*, II, vii, 34.
[2] Most likely *Childe Harold's Monitor* and *Sæculo Mastix, or the Lash of the Age we live in*.
[3] In *Childe Harold's Monitor*.

or indeed through any. I give up *Beppo*, though you know that
it is no more than an imitation of Pulci and of a style common
and esteemed in Italy. I have just published a drama, which is
at least good English, I presume, for Gifford lays great stress
on the purity of its diction.

I have been latterly employed a good deal more on politics
than on anything else, for the Neapolitan treachery and desertion
have spoilt all our hopes here, as well as our preparations. The
whole country was ready. Of course I should not have sate
still with my hands in my breeches' pockets. In fact they were
full; that is to say, the hands. I cannot explain further now,
for obvious reasons, as all letters of all people are opened.
Some day or other we may have a talk over that and other
matters. In the mean time there did not want a great deal of
my having to finish like Lara.

Are you doing nothing? I have scribbled a good deal in the
early part of last year, most of which scrawls will now be published, and part is, I believe, actually printed. Do you mean
to sit still about Pope? If you do, it will be the first time.
I have got such a headache from a cold and swelled face, that
I must take a gallop into the forest and jumble it into torpor.
My horses are waiting. So good-bye to you.

Yours ever,
BYRON.

Two hours after the Ave Maria, the Italian date of twilight.

DEAR HODGSON,

I have taken my canter, and am better of my headache.
I have also dined, and turned over your notes. In answer to
your note of page 90 [1] I must remark from *Aristotle* and *Rymer*,
that the *hero* of tragedy and (I add *meo periculo*) a tragic poem
must *be guilty*, to excite '*terror and pity*', the end of tragic poetry.
But hear not *me*, but my betters. 'The pity which the poet is
to labour for is *for* the criminal. The terror is likewise in the
punishment of the said criminal, who, if he be represented too
great an offender, will *not be pitied*; if altogether *innocent* his
punishment will be unjust'.[2] In the Greek Tragedy innocence
is unhappy often, and the offender escapes. I must also ask
you is *Achilles* a *good* character? or is even Æneas anything but
a successful runaway? It is for Turnus men feel and not for

---

[1] '. . . The long series of depraved heroes . . . who have formed the
prominent object in our more popular literature for many years, cannot
but have had the worst effect on the minds of the young. . . .'
[2] Johnson, *Life of Dryden*.

the Trojan.   Who is the hero of *Paradise Lost*?   Why Satan,—
and Macbeth, and Richard, and Othello, Pierre, and Lothario,
and Zanga?   If you talk so, I shall 'cut you up like a gourd',
as the Mamelukes say.   But never mind, go on with it.

173. TO THOMAS MOORE

May 14, 1821.

If any part of the letter to Bowles has (unintentionally, as
far as I remember the contents) vexed you, you are fully
avenged; for I see by an Italian paper that, notwithstanding
all my remonstrances through all my friends (and yourself among
the rest), the managers persisted in attempting the tragedy,
and that it has been 'unanimously hissed!!' This is the consolatory phrase of the Milan paper (which detests me cordially,
and abuses me, on all occasions, as a Liberal,) with the addition,
that *I* 'brought the play out' of my own good will.

All this is vexatious enough, and seems a sort of dramatic
Calvinism—predestined damnation, without a sinner's own fault.
I took all the pains poor mortal could to prevent this inevitable
catastrophe—partly by appeals of all kinds, up to the Lord
Chamberlain, and partly to the fellows themselves.   But, as
remonstrance was vain, complaint is useless.   I do not understand it—for Murray's letter of the 24th, and all his preceding
ones, gave me the strongest hopes that there would be no
representation.   As yet, I know nothing but the fact, which
I presume to be true, as the date is Paris, and the 30th.   They
must have been in a *hell* of a hurry for this damnation, since
I did not even know that it was published; and, without its
being first published, the histrions could not have got hold of it.
Any one might have seen, at a glance, that it was utterly
impracticable for the stage; and this little accident will by no
means enhance its merit in the closet.

Well, patience is a virtue, and, I suppose, practice will make
it perfect.   Since last year (spring, that is) I have lost a lawsuit
of great importance, on Rochdale collieries—have occasioned a
divorce—have had my poesy disparaged by Murray and the
critics—my fortune refused to be placed on an advantageous
settlement (in Ireland) by the trustees;—my life threatened last
month (they put about a paper here to excite an attempt at my
assassination, on account of politics, and a notion which the
priests disseminated that I was in a league against the Germans,)
—and, finally, my mother-in-law recovered last fortnight, and

my play was damned last week! These are like 'the eight-and-twenty misfortunes of Harlequin'.[1] But they must be borne. If I give in, it shall be after keeping up a spirit at least. I should not have cared so much about it, if our southern neighbours had not bungled us all out of freedom for these five hundred years to come.

Did you know John Keats? They say that he was killed by a review of him in the *Quarterly*—if he be dead, which I really don't know. I don't understand that *yielding* sensitiveness. What I feel (as at this present) is an immense rage for eight-and-forty hours, and then, as usual—unless this time it should last longer. I must get on horseback to quiet me.

Yours, etc.

Francis I wrote, after the battle of Pavia, 'All is lost except our honour'. A hissed author may reverse it—'*Nothing* is lost, except our honour'. But the horses are waiting, and the paper full. I wrote last week to you.

174. TO JOHN MURRAY

Rᵃ May 25ᵗʰ 1821.

MR. MORAY,

Since I wrote the enclosed a week ago, and for some weeks before, I have not had a line from you. Now I should be glad to know upon what principle of common or *un*common feeling, you leave me without any information but what I derive from garbled gazettes in English, and abusive ones in Italian (the Germans hating me as a *Coal-heaver*),[2] while all this kick up has been going on about the play? You SHABBY fellow!!! Were it not for two letters from Douglas Kinnaird, I should have been as ignorant as you are negligent.

I send you an Elegy as follows:—

> Behold the blessings of a lucky lot!
> My play *is damned*, and Lady Noel *not*.

So, I hear Bowles has been abusing Hobhouse:[3] if that's the case, he has broken the truce, like Morillo's successor, and I will cut him out, as Cochrane did the Esmeralda.[4]

---

[1] Narrated in *Le disgratie d'Arlecchino : viz. Harlequin's Misfortunes*,1726.
[2] i.e. a carbonaro.
[3] In his second *Letter to the Right Honourable Lord Byron*, 1821. Hobhouse was the author of the original lines attacking Bowles in *English Bards, and Scotch Reviewers*.
[4] On 5 November 1820, Lord Cochrane, commanding the Chilian navy, cut out the Spanish frigate *Esmeralda* under the batteries of Callao.

Since I wrote the enclosed packet, I have completed (but not copied out) four acts of a new tragedy. When I have finished the fifth, I will copy it out. It is on the subject of *Sardanapalus*,[1] the last king of the Assyrians. The words *Queen* and *pavilion* occur, but it is not an allusion to his Britanic Majesty, as you may tremulously (for the admiralty custom) imagine. This you will one day see (if I finish it), as I have made Sardanapalus *brave*, (though voluptuous, as history represents him,) and also as *amiable* as my poor powers could render him. So that it could neither be truth nor satire on any living monarch. I have strictly preserved all the unities hitherto, and mean to continue them in the fifth, if possible; but *not for the Stage*. Yours, in haste and hatred, you scrubby correspondent!

B.

175. TO THOMAS MOORE

Ravenna, June 22, 1821.

Your dwarf of a letter came yesterday. That is right;— keep to your *magnum opus*—magnoperate away. Now, if we were but together a little to combine our *Journal of Trevoux!* [2] But it is useless to sigh, and yet very natural,—for I think you and I draw better together, in the social line, than any two other living authors.

I forgot to ask you, if you had seen your own panegyric in the correspondence of Mrs. Waterhouse and Colonel Berkeley? [3] To be sure, *their* moral is not quite exact; but *your passion* is fully effective; and all poetry of the *Asiatic* kind—I mean Asiatic, as the Romans called 'Asiatic oratory', and not because the scenery is Oriental—must be tried by that test only. I am not quite sure that I shall allow the Miss Byrons (legitimate or illegitimate) to read *Lalla Rookh*—in the first place, on account of this said *passion*; and, in the second, that they mayn't discover that there was a better poet than papa.

You say nothing of politics—but, alas! what can be said?

> The world is a bundle of hay,
>   Mankind are the asses who pull,
> Each tugs it a different way,—
>   And the greatest of all is John Bull!

---

[1] Published with *The Two Foscari* and *Cain* in December 1821.
[2] Alluding to the Jesuit literary journal, *Mémoires de Trévoux*, founded in 1701.
[3] Produced in an action brought by John Waterhouse for the seduction of his wife.

How do you call your new project?[1] I have sent Murray a new tragedy, ycleped *Sardanapalus*, writ according to Aristotle —all, save the chorus—I could not reconcile me to that. I have begun another, and am in the second act;—so you see I saunter on as usual.

Bowles's answers have reached me; but I can't go on disputing for ever,—particularly in a polite manner. I suppose he will take being *silent* for *silenced*. He has been so civil that I can't find it in my liver to be facetious with him,—else I had a savage joke or two at his service.

.   .   .   .   .

I can't send you the little journal, because it is in boards, and I can't trust it per post. Don't suppose it is any thing particular; but it will show the *intentions* of the natives at that time—and one or two other things, chiefly personal, like the former one.

So, Longman don't *bite*.—It was my wish to have made that work of use. Could you not raise a sum upon it (however small), reserving the power of redeeming it, on repayment?

Are you in Paris, or a villaging? If you are *in* the city, you will never resist the Anglo-invasion you speak of. I do not see an Englishman in half a year, and, when I do, I turn my horse's head the other way. The fact, which you will find in the last note to the Doge, has given me a good excuse for quite dropping the least connection with travellers.

I do not recollect the speech you speak of, but suspect it is not the Doge's, but one of Israel Bertuccio to Calendaro. I hope you think that Elliston behaved shamefully—it is my only consolation. I made the Milanese fellows contradict their lie, which they did with the grace of people used to it.

Yours, etc.,

B.

176. TO THOMAS MOORE

Ravenna, July 5, 1821.

How could you suppose that I ever would allow any thing that *could* be said on your account to weigh with *me*? I only regret that Bowles had not *said* that you were the writer of that note,[2] until afterwards, when out he comes with it, in a private

---

[1] *Alciphron*, which was not published till 1839.
[2] A complimentary note from Moore which Bowles had used, suppressing the signature. Byron's facetiousness was aroused at the expense of 'the gentleman in asterisks'.

letter to Murray, which Murray sends to me. D——n the
controversy!

> 'D——n Twizzle,
>   D——n the bell,
> And d——n the fool who rung it—Well!
> From all such plagues I 'll quickly be delivered.' [1]

I have had a friend of your Mr. Irving's—a very pretty lad—
a Mr. Coolidge,[2] of Boston—only somewhat too full of poesy
and 'entusymusy'. I was very civil to him during his few
hours' stay, and talked with him much of Irving, whose writings
are my delight. But I suspect that he did not take quite so
much to me, from his having expected to meet a misanthropical
gentleman, in wolf-skin breeches, and answering in fierce monosyllables, instead of a man of this world. I can never get people
to understand that poetry is the expression of *excited passion*,
and that there is no such thing as a life of passion any more
than a continuous earthquake, or an eternal fever. Besides,
who would ever *shave* themselves in such a state?

I have had a curious letter to-day from a girl in England
(I never saw her), who says she is given over of a decline, but
could not go out of the world without thanking me for the delight
which my poesy for several years, etc., etc., etc. It is signed
simply N. N. A. and has not a word of 'cant' or preachment in
it upon *any* opinions. She merely says that she is dying, and
that as I had contributed so highly to her existing pleasure,
she thought that she might say so, begging me to *burn* her
letter—which, by the way, I can *not* do, as I look upon such a
letter in such circumstances as better than a diploma from
Gottingen. I once had a letter from Drontheim in *Norway*
(but not from a dying woman), in verse, on the same score of
gratulation. These are the things which make one at times
believe one's self a poet. But if I must believe that * * * * *,
and such fellows, are poets also, it is better to be out of the
corps.

I am now in the fifth act of *Foscari*, being the third tragedy in
twelve months, besides *proses*; so you perceive that I am not
at all idle. And are you, too, busy? I doubt that your life
at Paris draws too much upon your time, which is a pity. Can't
you divide your day, so as to combine both? I have had plenty
of all sorts of worldly business on my hands last year, and yet

---

[1] 'The Elder Brother', in *Broad Grins*, by George Colman the Younger,
1811.
[2] An account of this visit is given in Byron's *Detached Thoughts*, 25.

it is not so difficult to give a few hours to the *Muses*. This sentence is so like * * * * that——

Ever, etc.

If we were together, I should publish both my plays (periodically) in our *joint* journal. It should be our plan to publish all our best things in that way.

177. TO JOHN MURRAY

R*ª* July 6*th* 1821.

DEAR SIR,

In agreement with a wish expressed by Mr. Hobhouse, it is my determination to omit the Stanza upon the *horse* of Semiramis in the fifth Canto of *Don Juan*.[1] I mention this in case you are, or intend to be, the publisher of the remaining Cantos.

By yesterday's post, I ought, in point of time, to have had an acknowledgement of the arrival of the MSS. of *Sardanapalus*. If it *has* arrived, and you have delayed the few lines necessary for this, I can only say that you are keeping two people in hot water—the postmaster here, because the packet was insured, and myself, because I had but that one copy.

I am in the *fifth* act of a play on the subject of the Foscaris, father and son: Foscolo can tell you their story.

I am, yours, etc.,

B.

P.S.—At the particular request of the Contessa G. I have promised *not* to continue *Don Juan*. You will therefore look upon these 3 cantos as the last of that poem. She had read the two first in the French translation, and never ceased beseeching me to write no more of it. The reason of this is not at first obvious to a superficial observer of FOREIGN manners; but it arises from the wish of all women to exalt the *sentiment* of the passions, and to keep up the illusion which is their empire. Now *Don Juan* strips off this illusion, and laughs at that and most other things. I never knew a woman who did *not* protect *Rousseau*, nor one who did not dislike de Grammont, Gil Blas, and all the *comedy* of the passions, when brought out naturally. But 'King's blood must keep word', as Sergeant Bothwell says.[2]

Write, you Scamp!

Your parcel of *extracts* never came and never will: you should

---

[1] Stanza lxi.   [2] *Old Mortality*, chap. vi.

have sent it by the post; but you are growing a sad fellow, and some fine day we shall have to dissolve partnership.

Send some Soda powders.

178. TO JOHN MURRAY

DEAR SIR,   R. July 30th, 1821.

Enclosed is the best account of the Doge Faliero, which was only sent to me from an old MSS. the other day. Get it translated, and append it as a note to the next edition. You will perhaps be pleased to see that my conceptions of his character were correct, though I regret not having met with this extract before. You will perceive that he himself said exactly what he is made to say, about the Bishop of Treviso.[1] You will see also that he spoke very little, and those only words 'of rage and disdain',[2] *after* his arrest, which is the case in the play, except when he breaks out at the close of Act fifth. But his speech to the Conspirators is better in the MSS. than in the play: I wish that I had met with it in time. Do not forget this note, with a translation.

In a former note to the *Juans*, speaking of Voltaire, I have quoted his famous 'Zaire, tu pleures', which is an error; it should be 'Zaire, *vous pleurez*':[3] recollect this; and recollect also that your *want* of *recollection* has permitted you to publish the note on the Kelso traveller, which *I had positively desired you not*, for proof of which I refer you to my letters. I presume that you are able to lay your hand upon these letters, as you are accused publicly, in a pamphlet, of showing them about.

I wait your acknowledgement of the packets containing *The Foscaris*, notes, etc., etc.: now your Coronation[4] is over, perhaps you will find time. I have also written to Mr. Kinnaird, to say that I expect the two tragedies to be published speedily, and to inform him that I am willing to make any abatement, on your statement of loss liable to be incurred by publishing at an improper season.

I am so busy here about these poor proscribed exiles, who are scattered about, and with trying to get some of them recalled, that I have hardly time or patience to write a short preface, which will be proper for the two plays. However, I will make it out, on receiving the next proofs.

Yours ever and truly,

B.

---

[1] *Marino Faliero*, i, ii.   [2] Cf. *Christabel*, Part II, 416–17.
[3] *Zaïre*, iv, ii.   [4] George IV was crowned on 19 July 1821.

P.S.—Please to append the letter about *the Hellespont* as a note to your next opportunity of the verses on Leander, etc., etc., etc., in *Childe Harold*. Don't forget it amidst your multitudinous avocations, which I think of celebrating in a dithyrambic ode to Albemarle Street.

Are you aware that Shelley has written an elegy on Keats, and accuses the *Quarterly* of killing him?

'Who killed John Keats?'
'I,' says the Quarterly,
So savage and Tartarly;
''Twas one of my feats.'

'Who shot the arrow?'
'The poet-priest Milman
(So ready to kill man),
Or Southey or Barrow.'

You know very well that I did not approve of Keats's poetry, or principles of poetry, or of his abuse of Pope; but, as he is dead, omit *all* that is said *about him* in any *MSS.* of mine, or publication. His *Hyperion* is a fine monument, and will keep his name. I do not envy the man who wrote the article: your review people have no more right to kill than any other foot pads. However, he who would die of an article in a review would probably have died of something else equally trivial.[1] The same thing nearly happened to Kirke White, who afterwards died of a consumption.

179. TO JOHN MURRAY

Ravenna, August 10, 1821.

DEAR SIR,

Your conduct to Mr. Moore is certainly very handsome;[2] and I would not say so if I could help it, for you are not at present by any means in my good graces.

With regard to additions, etc., there is a Journal which I kept in 1814 which you may ask him for; also a Journal which you must get from Mrs. Leigh, of my journey in the Alps, which contains all the germs of *Manfred*. I have also kept a small Diary here for a few months last winter, which I would send you,

---

[1] See *Don Juan*, Canto XI, stanza lx.
[2] Murray had offered Moore two thousand guineas for Byron's Memoirs, on condition that in the event of survivorship he would edit them.

and any continuation. You would find easy access to all my papers and letters, and do *not neglect this* (in case of accidents) on account of the mass of confusion in which they are; for out of that chaos of papers you will find some curious ones of mine and others, if not lost or destroyed. If circumstances, however (which is almost impossible), made me ever consent to a publication in my lifetime, you would in that case, I suppose, make Moore some advance, in proportion to the likelihood or non-likelihood of success. You are both sure to survive me, however.

You must also have from Mr. Moore the correspondence between me and Lady B., to whom I offered the sight of all which regards herself in these papers. This is important. He has *her* letter, and a copy of my answer. I would rather Moore edited me than another.

I sent you Valpy's letter to decide for yourself, and Stockdale's to amuse you. *I* am always loyal with you, as I was in Galignani's affair,[1] and *you* with me—now and then.

I return you Moore's letter, which is very creditable to him, and you, and me.

Yours ever,

B.

180. TO JOHN MURRAY

Rᵃ August 31ˢᵗ 1821.

DEAR SIR,

I have received the *Juans*,[2] which are printed so *carelessly*, especially the 5ᵗʰ Canto, as to be disgraceful to me, and not creditable to you. It really must be *gone over again* with the *Manuscript*, the errors are so gross—words added—changed—so as to make cacophony and nonsense. You have been careless of this poem because some of your Synod don't approve of it; but I tell you, it will be long before you see any thing half so good as poetry or writing. Upon what principle have you omitted the *note* on Bacon and Voltaire? and one of the concluding stanzas sent as an addition? because it ended, I suppose, with—

> And do not link two virtuous souls for life
> Into that *moral Centaur*, man and wife?

Now, I must say, once for all, that I will not permit any human being to take such liberties with my writings because I am absent. I desire the omissions to be replaced (except the stanza on

---

[1] See page 265.
[2] Cantos III, IV, and V, published together in August 1821.

Semiramis)—particularly the stanza upon the Turkish marriages; and I request that the whole be carefully *gone over* with the MSS.

I never saw such stuff as is printed:—Gulleyaz instead of Gulbeyaz, etc. Are you aware that Gul*b*eyaz is a real name, and the other nonsense? I copied the *Cantos* out carefully, so that there is *no* excuse, as the Printer reads or at least *prints*, the MSS. of the plays without error.

If you have no feeling for your own reputation, pray have some little for mine. I have read over the poem carefully, and I tell you, *it is poetry*. Your little envious knot of parson-poets may say what they please: time will show that I am not in this instance mistaken.

Desire my friend Hobhouse to correct the press, especially of the last Canto, from the Manuscript as it is: it is enough to drive one out of one's senses, to see the infernal torture of words from the original. For instance the line—

And *pair* their rhymes as Venus yokes her doves—

is printed—

And *praise* their rhymes, etc.

Also '*precarious*' for '*precocious*'; and this line, stanza 133.—

*And this strong extreme effect to tire no long*er.

Now do turn to the Manuscript and see if I ever wrote such a *line*: it is *not verse*.

No wonder the poem should fail (which, however, it *won't*, you will see) with such things allowed to creep about it. Replace what is omitted, and correct what is so shamefully misprinted, and let the poem have fair play; and I fear nothing.

I see in the last two Numbers of the *Quarterly* a strong itching to assail me (see the review of the '*Etonian*'): let it, and see if they shan't have enough of it. I don't allude to Gifford, who has always been my friend, and whom I do not consider as responsible for the articles written by others.

But if I do not give Mr. Milman, and others of the crew, something that shall occupy their dreams! I have *not* begun with *the* Quarterers; but let them look to it. As for *Milman* (*you* well know I have not been unfair to his poetry ever), but I have lately had some information of his critical proceedings in the *Quarterly*, which may bring that on him which he will be sorry for. I happen to know *that* of him, which would annihilate him, when he pretends to preach *morality*—*not* that *he* is immoral,

* *

You will publish the plays when ready. I am in such a humour about this printing of *Don Juan* so inaccurately, that I must close this.

Yours ever,

B.

P.S.—I presume that you have *not* lost the *stanza* to which I allude? it was sent afterwards: look over my letters and find it.

The *Notes* you can't have lost—you acknowledged them: they included eight or nine corrections of Bacon's mistakes in the apophthegms.

And now I ask once more if such liberties, taken in a man's absence, are fair or praise-worthy? As for *you*, you have no opinions of your own, and never had, but are blown about by the last thing said to you, no matter by whom.

DEAR SIR,

The enclosed letter is written in bad humour, but not without provocation. However, let it (that is, the bad humour) go for little; but I must request your serious attention to the abuses of the printer, which ought never to have been permitted. You forget that all the fools in London (the chief purchasers of your publications) will condemn in me the stupidity of your printer. For instance, in the Notes to Canto fifth, 'the *Adriatic* shore of the Bosphorus', instead of the *Asiatic ! !* All this may seem little to you—so fine a gentleman with your ministerial connections; but it is serious to me, who am thousands of miles off, and have no opportunity of not proving myself the fool your printer makes me, except your pleasure and leisure, forsooth.

The Gods prosper you, and forgive you, for I won't.

B.

181. TO JOHN MURRAY

Ravenna, September 12th 1821.

DEAR SIR,

By Tuesday's post, I forwarded, in three packets, the drama of '*Cain*', in three acts, of which I request the acknowledgement when arrived. To the last speech of *Eve*, in the last act (i.e. where she curses Cain), add these three lines to the concluding one—

> May the Grass wither from thy foot! the Woods
> Deny thee shelter! Earth a home! the Dust
> A Grave! the Sun his light! and Heaven her God!

There's as pretty a piece of Imprecation for you, when joined to the lines already sent, as you may wish to meet with in the course of your business. But don't forget the addition of the above three lines, which are clinchers to Eve's speech.

Let me know what Gifford thinks (if the play arrives in safety); for I have a good opinion of the piece, as poetry: it is in my gay metaphysical style, and in the *Manfred* line.

You must at least commend my facility and variety, when you consider what I have done within the last fifteen months, with my head, too, full of other and of mundane matters. But no doubt you will avoid saying any good of it, for fear I should raise the price upon you: that's right—stick to business! Let me know what your other ragamuffins are writing, for I suppose you don't like starting too many of your Vagabonds at once. You may give them the start, for any thing I care.

If this arrives in time to be added to the other two dramas, publish them *together*: if not, publish it separately, in the *same* form, to tally for the purchasers. Let me have a proof of the whole speedily. It is longer than *Manfred*.

Why don't you publish my *Pulci*? the best thing I ever wrote, with the Italian to it. I wish I was alongside of you: nothing is ever done in a man's absence; every body runs counter, because they *can*. If ever I *do* return to England, (which I shan't though,) I will write a poem to which *English Bards*, etc., shall be New Milk, in comparison. Your present literary world of mountebanks stands in need of such an Avatar; but I am not yet quite bilious enough: a season or two more, and a provocation or two, will wind me up to the point, and then, have at the whole set!

I have no patience with the sort of trash you send me out by way of books; except Scott's novels, and three or four other things, I never saw such work or works. Campbell is lecturing, Moore idling, Southey twaddling, Wordsworth driveling, Coleridge muddling, Joanna Baillie piddling, Bowles quibbling, squabbling, and sniveling. Milman will *do*, if he don't cant too much, nor imitate Southey: the fellow has poesy in him; but he is envious, and unhappy, as all the envious are. Still he is among the best of the day. Barry Cornwall will do better by and bye, I dare say, if he don't get spoilt by green tea, and the praises of Pentonville and Paradise Row. The pity of these men is, that they never lived either in *high life*, nor in *solitude*: there is no medium for the knowledge of the *busy* or the *still* world. If admitted into high life for a season, it is merely as *spectators*—they form no part of the Mechanism thereof. Now Moore and I, the one by circumstances, and the other by birth, happened to be free of the corporation, and to have entered into its pulses and passions, *quarum partes fuimus.* Both of us have learnt by this much which nothing else could have taught us.

Yours,

B.

P.S.—I saw one of your brethren, another of the Allied Sovereigns of Grub-Street, the other day, viz.: Mawman the Great,[1] by whom I sent due homage to your imperial self. To-morrow's post may perhaps bring a letter from you; but you are the most ungrateful and ungracious of correspondents. But there is some excuse for you, with your perpetual levee of politicians, parson-scribblers, and loungers: some day I will give you a *poetical* Catalogue of them.

The post is come: no letter, but never mind.

How is Mrs. Murray, and Gifford? Better? Say *well*.

My Compliments to Mr. Heber upon his Election.[2]

182. TO THOMAS MOORE

Ravenna, September 19, 1821.

I am in all the sweat, dust, and blasphemy of an universal packing of all my things, furniture, etc., for Pisa, whither I go for the winter. The cause has been the exile of all my fellow Carbonics, and, amongst them, of the whole family of Madame G.; who, you know, was divorced from her husband last week, 'on account of P.P. clerk of this parish',[3] and who is obliged to join her father and relatives, now in exile there, to avoid being shut up in a monastery, because the Pope's decree of separation required her to reside in *casa paterna*, or else, for decorum's sake, in a convent. As I could not say with Hamlet, 'Get thee to a nunnery', I am preparing to follow them.

It is awful work, this love, and prevents all a man's projects of good or glory. I wanted to go to Greece lately (as every thing seems up here) with her brother,[4] who is a very fine, brave fellow (I have seen him put to the proof), and wild about liberty. But the tears of a woman who has left her husband for a man,

[1] J. Mawman, a publisher.
[2] On 24 August, Richard Heber was elected to Parliament for the University of Oxford.
[3] Alluding to Pope's *Memoirs of P.P., Clerk of this Parish.*
[4] Count Pietro Gamba.

and the weakness of one's own heart, are paramount to these projects, and I can hardly indulge them.

We were divided in choice between Switzerland and Tuscany, and I gave my vote for Pisa, as nearer the Mediterranean, which I love for the sake of the shores which it washes, and for my young recollections of 1809. Switzerland is a curst, selfish, swinish country of brutes, placed in the most romantic region of the world. I never could bear the inhabitants, and still less their English visitors; for which reason, after writing for some information about houses, upon hearing that there was a colony of English all over the cantons of Genèva, etc., I immediately gave up the thought, and persuaded the Gambas to do the same.

By the last post I sent you 'The Irish Avatar',—what think you? The last line—'a name never spoke but with curses or jeers'—must run either 'a name only uttered with curses or jeers', or, 'a wretch never named but with curses or jeers'. Be*case* as *how*, 'spoke' is not grammar, except in the House of Commons; and I doubt whether we can say 'a name *spoken*', for *mentioned*. I have some doubts, too, about 'repay',—'and for murder repay with a shout and a smile'. Should it not be 'and for murder repay him with shouts and a smile', or '*reward* him with shouts and a smile'?

So, pray put your poetical pen through the MS. and take the least bad of the emendations. Also, if there be any further breaking of Priscian's head, will you apply a plaster? I wrote in the greatest hurry and fury, and sent it to you the day after; so, doubtless, there will be some awful constructions, and a rather lawless conscription of rhythmus.

With respect to what Anna Seward calls 'the liberty of transcript',—when complaining of Miss Matilda Muggleton, the accomplished daughter of a choral vicar of Worcester Cathedral, who had abused the said 'liberty of transcript', by inserting in the *Malvern Mercury* Miss Seward's 'Elegy on the South Pole', as her *own* production, with her *own* signature, two years after having taken a copy, by permission of the authoress— with regard, I say, to the 'liberty of transcript', I by no means oppose an occasional copy to the benevolent few, provided it does not degenerate into such licentiousness of Verb and Noun as may tend to 'disparage my parts of speech' [1] by the carelessness of the transcribblers.

I do not think that there is much danger of the 'King's Press being abused' upon the occasion, if the publishers of journals

[1] Mrs. Malaprop, in *The Rivals*, III, iii.

have any regard for their remaining liberty of person. It is as pretty a piece of invective as ever put publisher in the way to 'Botany'. Therefore, if *they* meddle with it, it is at *their* peril. As for myself, I will answer any jontleman — though I by no means recognise a 'right of search' into an unpublished production and unavowed poem. The same applies to things published *sans* consent. I hope you like, at least the concluding lines of the *Pome*?

What are you doing, and where are you? in England? Nail Murray—nail him to his own counter, till he shells out the thirteens. Since I wrote to you, I have sent him another tragedy—*Cain* by name—making three in MS. now in his hands, or in the printer's. It is in the *Manfred* metaphysical style, and full of some Titanic declamation;—Lucifer being one of the *dram. pers.*, who takes Cain a voyage among the stars, and afterwards to 'Hades', where he shows him the phantoms of a former world, and its inhabitants. I have gone upon the notion of Cuvier,[1] that the world has been destroyed three or four times, and was inhabited by mammoths, behemoths, and what not; but *not* by man till the Mosaic period, as, indeed, is proved by the strata of bones found;—those of all unknown animals, and known, being dug out, but none of mankind. I have, therefore, supposed Cain to be shown, in the *rational* Preadamites, beings endowed with a higher intelligence than man, but totally unlike him in form, and with much greater strength of mind and person. You may suppose the small talk which takes place between him and Lucifer upon these matters is not quite canonical.

The consequence is, that Cain comes back and kills Abel in a fit of dissatisfaction, partly with the politics of Paradise, which had driven them all out of it, and partly because (as it is written in Genesis) Abel's sacrifice was the more acceptable to the Deity. I trust that the Rhapsody has arrived—it is in three acts, and entitled '*A Mystery*', according to the former Christian custom, and in honour of what it probably will remain to the reader.

Yours, etc.

183. TO JOHN MURRAY

DEAR MURRAY, Rᵃ Septʳ 20ᵗʰ 1821.

You need not send '*The Blues*',[2] which is a mere buffoonery, never meant for publication.

---

[1] *Discours sur les révolutions de la surface du globe.*
[2] *The Blues : a Literary Eclogue*, published in No. III of *The Liberal*.

The papers to which I allude,[1] in case of Survivorship, are collections of letters, etc., since I was sixteen years old, contained in the trunks in the care of Mr. Hobhouse. This collection is at least doubled by those I have now here; all received since my last Ostracism. To these I should wish the Editor to have access, *not* for the purpose of *abusing confidences*, nor of *hurting* the feelings of correspondents living, or the memories of the dead; but there are things which would do neither, that I have left unnoticed or unexplained, and which (like all such things) Time only can permit to be noticed or explained, though some are to my credit. The task will, of course, require delicacy; but that will not be wanting, if Moore and Hobhouse survive me, and, I may add, yourself; and that you may all three do so, is, I assure you, my very sincere wish. I am not sure that long life is desirable for one of my temper and constitutional depression of Spirits, which of course I suppress in society; but which breaks out when alone, and in my writings, in spite of myself. It has been deepened, perhaps, by some long past events (I do not allude to my marriage, etc.—on the contrary, *that* raised them by the persecution giving a fillip to my Spirits); but I call it constitutional, as I have reason to think it. You know, or you do *not* know, that my maternal Grandfather [2] (a very clever man, and amiable, I am told) was strongly suspected of Suicide (he was found drowned in the Avon at Bath), and that another very near relative of the same branch took poison, and was merely saved by antidotes. For the first of these events there was no apparent cause, as he was rich, respected, and of considerable intellectual resources, hardly forty years of age, and not at all addicted to any unhinging vice. It was, however, but a strong suspicion, owing to the manner of his death and to his melancholy temper. The *second had* a cause, but it does not become me to touch upon it; it happened when I was far too young to be aware of it, and I never heard of it till after the death of that relative, many years afterwards. I think, then, that I may call this dejection *constitutional*. I had always been told that in *temper* I more resembled my maternal Grandfather than any of my *father's* family—that is, in the gloomier part of his temper, for he was what you call a good natured man, and I am not.

The Journal here I sent by Mawman to Moore the other day; but as it is a mere diary, only *parts* of it would ever do for publication. The other Journal, of the tour in 1816, I should

---

[1] See page 299.   [2] George Gordon, who died in 1779.

think Augusta might let you have a copy of; but her nerves
have been in such a state since 1815, that there is no knowing.
Lady Byron's people, and L^y Caroline Lamb's people, and a
parcel of that set, got about her and frightened her with all
sorts of hints and menaces, so that she has never since been
able to write to *me* a *clear common letter*, and is so full of mysteries
and miseries, that I can only sympathize, without always
understanding her.   All my loves, too, make a point of calling
upon her, which puts her into a flutter (no difficult matter);
and, the year before last I think, Lady F[rances] W[edderburn]
W[ebster] marched in upon her, and Lady O[xford], a few years
ago, spoke to her at a party; and these and such like calamities
have made her afraid of her shadow.   It is a very odd fancy
that they all take to her: it was only six months ago, that I had
some difficulty in preventing the Countess G. from invading her
with an Italian letter.   I should like to have seen Augusta's
face, with an Etruscan Epistle, and all its Meridional style of
issimas, and other superlatives, before her.

I am much mortified that Gifford don't take to my new
dramas: to be sure, they are as opposite to the English drama
as one thing can be to another; but I have a notion that, if
understood, they will in time find favour (though *not* on the
stage) with the reader.   The Simplicity of plot is intentional,
and the avoidance of *rant* also, as also the compression of the
Speeches in the more severe situations.   What I seek to show
in *The Foscaris* is the *suppressed* passion, rather than the rant
of the present day.   For that matter—

> 'Nay, if thou 'lt mouth,
> I 'll rant as well as thou '— [1]

would not be difficult, as I think I have shown in my younger
productions—*not dramatic* ones, to be sure.   But, as I said
before, I am mortified that Gifford don't like them; but I see
no remedy, our notions on the subject being so different.   How
is he? well, I hope: let me know.   I regret his demur the more
that he has been always my grand patron, and I know no praise
which would compensate me in my own mind for his censure.
I do not mind *reviews*, as I can work them at their own weapons.

Yours ever and truly,

B.

P.S.—By the way, on our next settlement (which will take
place with Mr. Kinnaird), you will please to deduct the various

<hr>

[1] *Hamlet*, v, i, 306-7.

sums for *books*, packages *received* and *sent*, the *bust*, tooth-powder, etc., etc., expended by you on my account.

Hobhouse, in his preface to '*Rimini*', will probably be better able to explain my dramatic system, than I could do, as he is well acquainted with the whole thing. It is more upon the Alfieri School than the English.

I hope that we shall not have Mr. Rogers here: there is a mean minuteness in his mind and tittle-tattle that I dislike, ever since I *found him out* (which was but slowly); bésides he is not a good man: why don't he go to bed? What does he do travelling?

The Journal of 1814 I dare say Moore will give, or a copy.

Has *Cain* (the dramatic third attempt), arrived yet? Let me know.

Address to me at *Pisa*, whither I am going. The reason is, that all my Italian friends here have been exiled, and are met there for the present; and I go to join them, as agreed upon, for the Winter.

184. TO JOHN MURRAY

Ravenna, September 24. 1821.

DEAR MURRAY,

I have been thinking over our late correspondence, and wish to propose to you the following articles for our future:—

1stly That you shall write to me of yourself, of the health, wealth, and welfare of all friends; but of *me* (*quoad me*) little or nothing.

2dly That you shall send me Soda powders, tooth-powder, tooth-brushes, or any such anti-odontalgic or chemical articles, as heretofore, *ad libitum*, upon being re-imbursed for the same.

3dly That you shall *not* send me any modern, or (as they are called) *new*, publications in *English whatsoever*, save and excepting any writing, prose or verse, of (or reasonably presumed to be of) Walter Scott, Crabbe, Moore, Campbell, Rogers, Gifford, Joanna Baillie, *Irving* (the American), Hogg, Wilson (*Isle of Palms* Man), or *any* especial *single* work of fancy which is thought to be of considerable merit; *Voyages* and *travels*, provided that they are *neither in Greece, Spain, Asia Minor, Albania, nor Italy*, will be welcome: having travelled the countries mentioned, I know that what is said of them can convey nothing further which I desire to know about them. No other English works whatsoever.

4thly That you send me *no periodical works* whatsoever—*no*

Edinburgh, *Quarterly*, *Monthly*, nor any Review, Magazine, Newspaper, English or foreign, of any description.

5^{thly} That you send me *no* opinions whatsoever, either *good*, *bad*, or *indifferent*, of yourself, or your friends, or others, concerning any work, or works, of mine, past, present, or to come.

6^{thly} That all negotiations in matters of business between you and me pass through the medium of the Honble Douglas Kinnaird, my friend and trustee, or Mr. Hobhouse, as *Alter Ego*, and tantamount to myself during my absence, or presence.

Some of these propositions may at first seem strange, but they are founded. The quantity of trash I have received as books is incalculable, and neither amused nor instructed. Reviews and Magazines are at the best but ephemeral and superficial reading: *who thinks* of the *grand article* of *last year* in any *given review*? in the next place, if they regard *myself*, they tend to increase *Egotism*; if favourable, I do not deny that the praise *elates*, and if unfavourable, that the abuse *irritates*—the latter may conduct me to inflict a species of Satire, which would neither do good to you nor to your friends: *they* may smile *now*, and so may *you*; but if I took you all in hand, it would not be difficult to cut you up like gourds. I did as much by as powerful people at nineteen years old, and I know little as yet, in three and thirty, which should prevent me from making all your ribs Gridirons for your hearts, if such were my propensity. But it is *not*. Therefore let me hear none of your provocations. If any thing occurs so very *gross* as to require my notice, I shall hear it from my personal friends. For the rest, I merely request to be left in ignorance.

The same applies to opinions, *good*, *bad*, or *indifferent*, of persons in conversation or correspondence: these do not *interrupt*, but they *soil* the *current* of my *Mind*. I am sensitive enough, but *not* till I am *touched;* and *here* I am beyond the touch of the short arms of literary England, except the few feelers of the Polypus that crawl over the Channel in the way of Extract.

All these precautions *in* England would be useless: the libeller or the flatterer would there reach me in spite of all; but in Italy we know little of literary England, and think less, except what reaches us through some garbled and brief extract in some miserable Gazette. For *two years* (excepting two or three articles cut out and sent to *you*, by the post) I never read a newspaper which was not forced upon me by some accident, and know, upon the whole, as little of England as you all do of Italy, and God knows *that* is little enough, with all your travels, etc., etc.,

etc. The English travellers *know Italy* as *you* know Guernsey: how much is *that*?

If any thing occurs so violently gross or personal as to require notice, Mr. D's Kinnaird will let me *know*; but of *praise* I desire to hear *nothing*.

You will say, 'to what tends all this?' I will answer THAT;—to keep my mind *free and unbiassed* by all paltry and personal irritabilities of praise or censure;—to let my Genius take its natural direction, while my feelings are like the dead, who know nothing and feel nothing of all or aught that is said or done in their regard.

If you can observe these conditions, you will spare yourself and others some pain: let me not be worked upon to rise up; for if I do, it will not be for a little: if you can *not* observe these conditions, we shall cease to be correspondents, but *not friends*; for I shall always be

Yours ever and truly,

BYRON.

P.S.—I have taken these resolutions not from any irritation against *you* or *yours*, but simply upon reflection that all reading, either praise or censure, of myself has done me harm. When I was in Switzerland and Greece, I was out of the way of hearing either, and *how I wrote there!* In Italy I am out of the way of it too; but latterly, partly through my fault, and partly through your kindness in wishing to send me the *newest* and most periodical publications, I have had a crowd of reviews, etc., thrust upon me, which have bored me with their jargon, of one kind or another, and taken off my attention from greater objects. You have also sent me a parcel of trash of poetry, for no reason that I can conceive, unless to provoke me to write a new *English Bards*. Now *this* I wish to avoid; for if ever I *do*, it will be a strong production; and I desire peace, as long as the fools will keep their nonsense out of my way.

185. TO THOMAS MOORE

September—no—October 1, 1821.

I have written to you lately, both in prose and verse, at great length, to Paris and London. I presume that Mrs. Moore, or whoever is your Paris deputy, will forward my packets to you in London.

I am setting off for Pisa, if a slight incipient intermittent

fever do not prevent me.   I fear it is not strong enough to give
Murray much chance of realising his thirteens again.   I hardly
should regret it, I think, provided you raised your price upon
him—as what Lady Holderness (my sister's grandmother, a
Dutchwoman) used to call Augusta, her *Residee Legatoo*—so as
to provide for us all: *my* bones with a splendid and *larmoyante*
edition, and you with double what is extractable during
my lifetime.

I have a strong presentiment that (bating some out of the
way accident) you will survive me.   The difference of eight
years, or whatever it is, between our ages, is nothing.   I do not
feel (nor am, indeed, anxious to feel) the principle of life in me
tend to longevity.   My father and mother died, the one at
thirty-five or six, and the other at forty-five; and Dr. Rush, or
somebody else, says that nobody lives long, without having
one parent, at least, an old stager.

I *should*, to be sure, like to see out my eternal mother-in-law,
not so much for her heritage, but from my natural antipathy.
But the indulgence of this natural desire is too much to expect
from the Providence who presides over old women.   I bore you
with all this about lives, because it has been put in my way by
a calculation of insurances which Murray has sent me.   I *really
think* you should have more, if I evaporate within a reasonable
time.

I wonder if my *Cain* has got safe to England.   I have written
since about sixty stanzas of a poem, in octave stanzas, (in the
Pulci style, which the fools in England think was invented by
Whistlecraft—it is as old as the hills in Italy,) called *The Vision
of Judgment*,[1] by Quevedo Redivivus, with this motto—

> 'A Daniel come to *judgment*, yea, a Daniel:
>   I thank thee, Jew, for teaching me that word'.[2]

In this it is my intent to put the said George's Apotheosis in
a Whig point of view, not forgetting the Poet Laureate for his
preface and his other demerits.

I am just got to the pass where Saint Peter, hearing that the
royal defunct had opposed Catholic Emancipation, rises up, and,
interrupting Satan's oration, declares *he* will change places with
Cerberus sooner than let him into heaven, while *he* has the
keys thereof.

---

[1] Published in 1822 in the first number of *The Liberal: Verse and Prose
from the South*.   Quevedo is Francisco Gomez de Quevedo Villegas (1580–
1645), the Spanish satirist.
[2] *The Merchant of Venice*, IV, i, 340–1.

I must go and ride, though rather feverish and chilly. It is the ague season; but the agues do me rather good than harm. The feel after the *fit* is as if one had got rid of one's body for good and all.

The gods go with you!—Address to Pisa.

Ever yours.

P.S.—Since I came back, I feel better, though I stayed out too late for this malaria season, under the thin crescent of a very young moon, and got off my horse to walk in an avenue with a Signora for an hour. I thought of you and

> 'When at eve thou rovest
> By the star thou lovest'.[1]

But it was not in a romantic mood, as I should have been once; and yet it was a *new* woman, (that is, new to me,) and, of course, expected to be made love to. But I merely made a few commonplace speeches. I feel, as your poor friend Curran[2] said, before his death, 'a mountain of lead upon my heart', which I believe to be constitutional, and that nothing will remove it but the same remedy.

186. TO SAMUEL ROGERS

Ravenna, Oct. 21st 1821.

DEAR ROGERS,

I shall be (the Gods willing) in Bologna on Saturday next. This is a curious answer to your letter; but I have taken a house in Pisa for the winter, to which all my chattels—furniture, horses, carriages, and live stock—are already removed, and I am preparing to follow.

The cause of this removal is, shortly, the exile or proscription of all my friends' relations and connections here into Tuscany, on account of our late politics; and where they go, I accompany them. I merely remained till now to settle some arrangements about my daughter, and to give time for my furniture, etc., to precede me. I have not here a seat or a bed hardly, except some *jury* chairs, and tables, and a mattrass for the week to come.

If you will go on with me to Pisa, I can lodge you for as long as you like; (they write that the house, the Palazzo Lanfranchi, is spacious: it is on the Arno;) and I have four carriages, and as many saddle-horses (such as they are in these parts), with all

---

[1] The beginning of the second stanza of Moore's 'Go where glory waits thee', in the *Irish Melodies*.

[2] See page 236.

other conveniences at your command, as also their owner. If you can't do this, we may, at least, cross the Apennines together; or if you are going by another road, we shall meet at Bologna, I hope.   I address this to the post-office (as you desire), and you will probably find me at the Albergo di *San Marco*. If you arrive first, wait till I come up, which will be (barring accidents) on Saturday or Sunday at farthest.

I presume you are alone in your voyages.   Moore is in London *incog.* according to my latest advices from those climates.

It is better than a lustre (five years and six months and some days, more or less) since we met; and like the man from Tadcaster in the farce *Love Laughs at Locksmiths* [1] whose acquaintances, including the cat and the terrier, 'who caught a halfpenny in his mouth', were all 'gone dead', but too many of our acquaintances have taken the same path.   Lady Melbourne, Grattan, Sheridan, Curran, etc., etc.—without reckoning the οἱ πολλοι—almost every body of much name of the old school. But 'so am not I, said the foolish fat scullion'; [2] therefore let us make the most of our remainder.

Let me find two lines from you at 'the Hostel or Inn'.

Yours ever, etc.,

B.

187. TO JOHN MURRAY

Pisa, November 3, 1821.

Dear Moray,

The two passages [3] cannot be altered without making Lucifer talk like the Bishop of Lincoln—which would not be in the character of the former.   The notion is from Cuvier (that of the *old Worlds*), as I have explained in an additional note to the preface.   The other passage is also in character: if *nonsense*— so much the better, because then it can do no harm, and the sillier Satan is made, the safer for every body.   As to 'alarms', etc., do you really think such things ever led any body astray? Are these people more impious than Milton's Satan? or the Prometheus of Æschylus? or even than the Sadducees of your envious parson, the *Fall of Jerusalem* fabricator? [4]   Are not Adam, Eve, Adah, and Abel, as pious as the Catechism?

Gifford is too wise a man to think that such things can have any *serious* effect: *who* was ever altered by a poem?   I beg leave

---

[1] By George Colman the Younger.
[2] In *Tristram Shandy*, Book v, chap. vii.
[3] In *Cain*.   [4] The Rev. Henry Hart Milman.

to observe, that there is no creed nor personal hypothesis of mine in all this: but I was obliged to make Cain and Lucifer talk consistently, and surely this has always been permitted to poesy. Cain is a proud man: if Lucifer promised him kingdoms, etc., it would *elate* him: the object of the Demon is to *depress* him still further in his own estimation than he was before, by showing him infinite things and his own abasement, till he falls into the frame of mind that leads to the Catastrophe, from mere *internal* irritation, *not* premeditation, or envy of *Abel* (which would have made him contemptible), but from the rage and fury against the inadequacy of his state to his conceptions, and which discharges itself rather against Life, and the Author of Life, than the mere living.

His subsequent remorse is the natural effect of looking on his sudden deed. Had the *deed* been *premeditated*, his repentance would have been tardier.

The three last MS. lines of Eve's curse are replaced from *memory* on the proofs, but incorrectly (for I keep no copies). Either keep *these three*, or *replace* them with the *other three*, whichever are thought the least bad by Mr. Gifford. There is no occasion for a *revise*; it is only losing time.

Either dedicate it to Walter Scott, or, if you think he would like the dedication of *The Foscaris* better, put the dedication to *The Foscaris*. Ask him which.[1]

Your first note was queer enough; but your two other letters, with Moore's and Gifford's opinions, set all right again. I told you before that I can never *recast* any thing. I am like the Tiger: if I miss the first spring, I go growling back to my Jungle again; but if I *do hit*, it is crushing. Now for Mr. Mawman, I received him civilly as *your* friend, and he spoke of you in a friendly manner. As one of the squadron of Scribblers I could not but pay due reverence to a commissioned officer.

I gave him that book with the inscription to show to *you*, that you might correct the errors. With the rest I can have nothing to do; but he has served you very *right*. You have played the stepmother to D[on] J[uan] throughout, either ashamed or afraid, or negligent, to your own loss and nobody's credit. Who ever heard before of a *publisher's not* putting *his* name? The reasons for *my anonyme* I stated; they were family ones entirely. Some travelling Englishmen whom I met the other day at Bologna told me, that you affect to wish to be considered as *not* having anything to do with that work, which,

[1] He accepted the dedication of *Cain*.

by the way, is sad half and half dealing—for you will be a long time before you publish a better poem.

You seem hurt at the words '*the publisher*'. *What!* you—who won't put your name on the title page—would have had me stick J. M. Esqre on the blank leaf. No, Murray! you are an excellent fellow, a little variable and somewhat of the opinion of every body you talk with (particularly the last person you see), but a good fellow for all that; yet nevertheless I can't tell you that I think you have acted very gallantly by that persecuted book—which has made its way entirely by *itself*, without the light of your countenance, or any kind of encouragement—critical—or bibliopolar. You disparaged the last three cantos to me, and kept them back above a year; but I have heard from England that (notwithstanding the errors of the press) they are well thought of; for instance, by American Irving, which last is a feather in my (fool's) cap.

You have received my letter (open) through Mr. Kinnaird, and so, pray, send me no more reviews of any kind. I will read no more of evil or good in that line. Walter Scott has not read a review of *himself* for *thirteen years*.

The bust [1] is not *my* property, but *Hobhouse's*. I addressed it to you as an Admiralty man, great at the Custom house. Pray deduct the expences of the same, and all others.

Yours ever,
BYRON.

188. TO LADY BYRON

(To the care of the Hon. Mrs. Leigh, London.) [2]

Pisa, November 17, 1821.

I have to acknowledge the receipt of 'Ada's hair', which is very soft and pretty, and nearly as dark already as mine was at twelve years old, if I may judge from what I recollect of some in Augusta's possession, taken at that age. But it don't curl,—perhaps from its being let grow.

I also thank you for the inscription of the date and name, and I will tell you why;—I believe that they are the only two or three words of your hand-writing in my possession. For your letters I returned; and except the two words, or rather the one

[1] By Thorwaldsen.
[2] 'The letter which I enclose I was prevented from sending by my despair of its doing any good. I was perfectly sincere when I wrote it, and am so still.' (Byron, in a letter to Lady Blessington, 6 May, 1823.)

word, 'Household', written twice in an old account book, I have no other. I burnt your last note, for two reasons:—firstly, it was written in a style not very agreeable; and, secondly, I wished to take your word without documents, which are the wordly resources of suspicious people.

I suppose that this note will reach you somewhere about Ada's birthday—the 10th of December, I believe. She will then be six, so that in about twelve more I shall have some chance of meeting her;—perhaps sooner, if I am obliged to go to England by business or otherwise. Recollect, however, one thing, either in distance or nearness;—every day which keeps us asunder should, after so long a period, rather soften our mutual feelings, which must always have one rallying-point as long as our child exists, which I presume we both hope will be long after either of her parents.

The time which has elapsed since the separation has been considerably more than the whole brief period of our union, and the not much longer one of our prior acquaintance. We both made a bitter mistake; but now it is over, and irrevocably so. For, at thirty-three on my part, and a few years less on yours, though it is no very extended period of life, still it is one when the habits and thought are generally so formed as to admit of no modification; and as we could not agree when younger, we should with difficulty do so now.

I say all this, because I own to you, that, notwithstanding every thing, I considered our re-union as not impossible for more than a year after the separation;—but then I gave up the hope entirely and for ever. But this very impossibility of re-union seems to me at least a reason why, on all the few points of discussion which can arise between us, we should preserve the courtesies of life, and as much of its kindness as people who are never to meet may preserve perhaps more easily than nearer connections. For my own part, I am violent, but not malignant; for only fresh provocations can awaken my resentments. To you, who are colder and more concentrated, I would just hint, that you may sometimes mistake the depth of a cold anger for dignity, and a worse feeling for duty. I assure you that I bear you *now* (whatever I may have done) no resentment whatever. Remember, that *if you have injured me* in aught, this forgiveness is something; and that, if I have *injured you*, it is something more still, if it be true, as the moralists say, that the most offending are the least forgiving.

Whether the offence has been solely on my side, or reciprocal, or on yours chiefly, I have ceased to reflect upon any but two things—viz. that you are the mother of my child, and that we shall never meet again. I think if you also consider the two corresponding points with reference to myself, it will be better for all three.

Yours ever,

NOEL [1] BYRON.

189. TO THE HON. DOUGLAS KINNAIRD

MY DEAR KINNAIRD,   Pisa, November 20, 1821.

I ought to have answered your letter long ago, but I am but just subsiding into my new residence, after all the bore and bustle of changing. The traveller can 'take his ease in his inn', but those who are settled in a place, and must move with bag and baggage, are (as I suppose you know by experience) necessarily more tardy in their arrangements.

I have a very good spacious house, upon the Arno, and have nothing to complain of, except that it is less quiet than my house in Ravenna.—And so you are at Rome?—I am glad you have got rid of the gout;—the tumour, if not of podagrous origin, will subside of itself.

At Bologna I met with Rogers, and we crossed the Apennines together—probably you have got him at Rome by this time. I took him to visit our old friend the sexton, at the Certosa, (where you and I met with Bianchetti), who looked at him very *hard*, and seemed well disposed to keep him back in his skull-room. The said sexton, by the way, brought out his two daughters, to renew our acquaintance; one of them is very pretty, and the other sufficiently so. He talked pathetically of the venality of the age, in which young virgins could not be espoused without a *dower*: so that, if you are disposed to portion them in your way to Milan, you have an opportunity of exercising your benevolence.

I was obliged to set out the next day with [Rogers]; remained with him a day at Florence, and then came on alone to Pisa, where I found all my friends in good health and plight. [Rogers] looks a little black still about being called 'venerable',[2] but he did not mention it. It was at his own request that I met him in the City of Sausages: he is not a bad traveller, but bilious.

---

[1] On the death of his mother-in-law on 28 January 1822, Byron, by royal licence, assumed the name of Noel.

[2] An epithet used of Rogers in Byron's first letter on Bowles.

As to *Don Juan*, it is not impossible that he might have visited the city which you recommend to his inspection; but these costermonger days are unfavourable to all liberal extension of morality. As to his author, he can hardly come on to Rome again for the present; but some day or other probably may. You ask after Bowles? but he has been so extremely civil, that I could not, without appearing overbearing and insolent, continue the controversy; for I could not answer without saying something sharp, and therefore it is better to be silent.

If Lord Clare [1] and Lord Sligo are at Rome, and are of your acquaintance, will you tell them both, with my best remembrances, that I will answer their letters soon.

I find my old friends have got a notion (founded, I suppose, on an angry note of mine to a poem), that I receive nobody, and renew no old acquaintance. They are very much mistaken —I only desire no *new* ones. The silly note, (which, by the way, I desired Murray to suppress before publication), was caused by a really impudent assertion of an anonymous traveller, who said, that he, or she, had frequently declined an introduction to me. Now I never in my life proposed, and rarely would accept, an English introduction since I came abroad.

Let me hear from you whenever you think it is not a bore to do so, and believe me,

Ever and truly yours,
BYRON.

190. TO JOHN MURRAY

DEAR SIR,
Pisa, December 4, 1821.

By extracts in the English papers,—in your holy Ally, Galignani's *Messenger*,—I perceive that 'the two greatest examples of human vanity in the present age' are, firstly, 'the ex-Emperor Napoleon', and secondly, 'his Lordship, etc., the noble poet', meaning your humble servant, 'poor guiltless I'.[2]

Poor Napoleon! he little dreamed to what 'vile comparisons' the turn of the Wheel would reduce him! I cannot help thinking, however, that had our learned brother of the newspaper office seen my very moderate answer to the very scurrile epistle of my radical patron, John Hobhouse, M.P.,[3] he would

---

[1] John Fitzgibbon, second Earl of Clare, his 'dearest' Harrow friend.

[2] Pope, *Prologue to the Satires*, 281.

[3] Hobhouse, who was primarily annoyed at the miscarriage of Thorwaldsen's bust of Byron, had also 'launched . . . into a most violent invective upon the subject of *Cain*', and taken Byron to task for the writing and gift of his Memoirs.

have thought the thermometer of my 'Vanity' reduced to a very decent temperature. By the way you do not happen to know whether Mrs. Fry had commenced her reform of the prisoners at the time when Mr. Hobhouse was in Newgate? there are some of his phrases, and much of his style (in that same letter), which led me to suspect that either she had not, or that he had profited less than the others by her instructions. Last week I sent back the deed of Mr. Moore signed and witnessed. It was inclosed to Mr. Kinnaird with a request to forward it to you. I have also transmitted to him my opinions upon your proposition, etc., etc., but addressed them to himself.

I have got here into a famous old feudal palazzo, on the Arno, large enough for a garrison, with dungeons below and cells in the walls, and so full of *Ghosts*, that the learned Fletcher (my valet) has begged leave to change his room, and then refused to occupy his *new* room, because there were more ghosts there than in the other. It is quite true that there are most extraordinary noises (as in all old buildings), which have terrified the servants so as to incommode me extremely. There is one place where people were evidently *walled up*; for there is but one possible passage, *broken* through the wall, and then meant to be closed again upon the inmate. The house belonged to the Lanfranchi family, (the same mentioned by Ugolino in his dream, as his persecutor with Sismondi,) and has had a fierce owner or two in its time. The staircase, etc., is said to have been built by Michel Agnolo [*sic*]. It is not yet cold enough for a fire. What a climate!

I am, however, bothered about these spectres, (as they say the last occupants were, too,) of whom I have as yet seen nothing, nor, indeed, heard (*myself*); but all the other ears have been regaled by all kinds of supernatural sounds. The first night I thought I heard an odd noise, but it has not been repeated. I have now been here more than a month.

Yours,

BYRON.

P.S.—Pray send me two or three dozen of '*Acton's corn-rubbers*' in a parcel by the post—*packed dry* and well—if you can.

I have received safely the parcel containing the Seal—the *E. Review*—and some pamphlets, etc. The others are I presume upon their way.

Are there not designs from *Faust*? Send me some, and a translation of it,—if such there is. Also of Goethe's life if such there be; if not—the original German.

191. TO JOHN MURRAY

Pisa, Fy 8th 1822.

DEAR SIR,

Attacks upon me were to be expected; but I perceive one upon *you* [1] in the papers, which I confess that I did not expect. How, or in what manner, *you* can be considered responsible for what *I* publish, I am at a loss to conceive.

If *Cain* be 'blasphemous', *Paradise Lost* is blasphemous; and the very words of the Oxford Gentleman, 'Evil, be thou my Good', are from that very poem, from the mouth of Satan; and is there anything more in that of Lucifer in the Mystery? *Cain* is nothing more than a drama, not a piece of argument: if Lucifer and Cain speak as the first Murderer and the first Rebel may be supposed to speak, surely all the rest of the personages talk also according to their characters—and the stronger passions have ever been permitted to the drama.

I have even avoided introducing the Deity, as in Scripture, (though Milton does, and not very wisely either); but have adopted his Angel as sent to Cain instead, on purpose to avoid shocking any feelings on the subject by falling short of what all uninspired men must fall short in, viz. giving an adequate notion of the effect of the presence of Jehovah. The Old Mysteries introduced him liberally enough, and all this is avoided in the New one.

The Attempt to *bully you*, because they think it won't succeed with me, seems to me as atrocious an attempt as ever disgraced the times. What? when Gibbon's, Hume's, Priestley's, and Drummond's publishers have been allowed to rest in peace for seventy years, are *you* to be singled out for a work of *fiction*, not of history or argument? there must be something at the bottom of this—some private enemy of your own: it is otherwise incredible.

I can only say, *Me, me, adsum qui feci*; [2] that any proceedings directed against you, I beg, may be transferred to me, who am willing, and *ought*, to endure them all; that if you have lost money by the publication, I will refund any or all of the Copyright; that I desire you will say, that both *you* and *Mr. Gifford* remonstrated against the publication, as also Mr. Hobhouse; that *I* alone occasioned it, and I alone am the person who, either legally or otherwise, should bear the burthen. If they prosecute, I will come to England—that is, if, by meeting it in

[1] The *Remonstrance* of 'Oxoniensis'. [2] Virgil, *Æneid*, IX, 427.

my own person, I can save yours. Let me know: you shan't suffer for me, if I can help it. Make any use of this letter which you please.

Yours ever,
BYRON.

P.S.—You will now perceive that it was as well for you, that I have decided upon changing my publisher; though *that* was not my motive, but dissatisfaction at one or two things in your conduct, of no great moment perhaps even then. But now, all such things disappear in my regret at having been unintentionally the means of getting you into a scrape. Be assured that no momentary irritation (at real or supposed omissions or commissions) shall ever prevent me from doing you justice when you deserve it, or that I will allow you (if I can avoid it), to participate in any odium or persecution, which ought to fall on me only. I had been laughing with some of my correspondents at the rumours, etc., till I saw this assault upon *you*; and I should at that too, if I did not think that it may perhaps hurt your feelings or your business.

When you re-publish (if you do so) *The Foscari*, etc., etc., to the note upon Southey add Mr. Southey's *answer* (which was in the papers): this is but fair play; and I do not desire it out of an affected contempt. What my rejoinder to him will be, is another concern, and is not for publication. Let me have your answer: remember me to Gifford, and do not forget to state that both you and he objected to publishing *Cain* in its present form. As for what the Clergyman says of *Don Juan*, you have brought it upon yourself by your absurd half and half prudery, which, I always foresaw, would bother you at last. An author's *not* putting his name, is nothing—it has been always the custom to publish a thousand anonymous things; but *who* ever heard before of a *publisher's* affecting such a Masquerade as yours was? However, now, you may put my name to the *Juans*, if you like it, though it is of the latest to be of use to you. I always stated to you, that *my* only objection was, in case of the law deciding against you, that they would annihilate my guardianship of the Child. But now (as you really seem in a damned scrape), they may do what they like with me, so that I can get you out of it; but, cheer up: though I have 'led my ragamuffins where they are well peppered',[1] I will stick by them as long as they will keep the field.

[1] *Henry IV*, Part I, v, iii, 36.

I write to you about all this row of bad passions and absurdities with the *Summer* Moon (for here our Winter is clearer than your Dog days) lighting the winding Arno, with all her buildings and bridges, so quiet and still: what Nothings we are! before the least of these Stars!

192. TO THOMAS MOORE

Pisa, March 4, 1822.

Since I wrote the enclosed,[1] I have waited another post, and now have your answer acknowledging the arrival of the packet [2] —a troublesome one, I fear, to you in more ways than one, both from weight external and internal.

The unpublished things in your hands, in Douglas K.'s, and Mr. John Murray's, are, *Heaven and Earth*, a lyrical kind of Drama upon the Deluge, etc.;—*Werner, now with you;*—a translation of the First Canto of the *Morgante Maggiore;—ditto* of an Episode in Dante;—some stanzas to the Po, June 1st, 1819; —*Hints from Horace*, written in 1811, but a good deal, *since*, to be omitted;—several prose things, which may, perhaps, as well remain unpublished;—*The Vision*, etc., of Quevedo Redivivus, in verse.

Here you see is 'more matter for a May morning';[3] but how much of this can be published is for consideration. The Quevedo (one of my best in that line) has appalled the Row already, and must take its chance at Paris, if at all. The new Mystery is less speculative than *Cain*, and very pious; besides, it is chiefly lyrical. The *Morgante* is the *best* translation that ever was or will be made; and the rest are—whatever you please to think them.

I am sorry you think *Werner* even *approaching* to any fitness for the stage, which, with my notions upon it, is very far from my present object. With regard to the publication, I have already explained that I have no exorbitant expectations of either fame or profit in the present instances; but wish them published because they are written, which is the common feeling of all scribblers.

With respect to 'Religion', can I never convince you that *I* have no such opinions as the characters in that drama, which seems to have frightened every body? Yet *they* are nothing to the expressions in Goethe's *Faust* (which are ten times hardier), and not a whit more bold than those of Milton's Satan. My

---

[1] A letter of 1 March.   [2] Containing *Werner*.
[3] *Twelfth Night*, III, iv, 156.

ideas of a character may run away with me: like all imaginative men, I, of course, embody myself with the character while I *draw* it, but not a moment after the pen is from off the paper.

I am no enemy to religion, but the contrary. As a proof, I am educating my natural daughter a strict Catholic in a convent of Romagna; for I think people can never have *enough* of religion, if they are to have any. I incline, myself, very much to the Catholic doctrines; but if I am to write a drama, I must make my characters speak as I conceive them likely to argue.

As to poor Shelley, who is another bugbear to you and the world, he is, to my knowledge, the *least* selfish and the mildest of men—a man who has made more sacrifices of his fortune and feelings for others than any I ever heard of. With his speculative opinions I have nothing in common, nor desire to have.

The truth is, my dear Moore, you live near the *stove* of society, where you are unavoidably influenced by its heat and its vapours. I did so once—and too much—and enough to give a colour to my whole future existence. As my success in society was *not* inconsiderable, I am surely not a prejudiced judge upon the subject, unless in its favour; but I think it, as now constituted, *fatal* to all great original undertakings of every kind. I never courted it *then*, when I was young and high in blood, and one of its 'curled darlings'; and do you think I would do so *now*, when I am living in a clearer atmosphere? One thing *only* might lead me back to it, and that is, to try once more if I could do any good in *politics*; but *not* in the petty politics I see now preying upon our miserable country.

Do not let me be misunderstood, however. If you speak your *own* opinions, they ever had, and will have, the greatest weight with *me*. But if you merely *echo* the *monde*, (and it is difficult not to do so, being in its favour and its ferment,) I can only regret that you should ever repeat any thing to which I cannot pay attention.

But I am prosing. The gods go with you, and as much immortality of all kinds as may suit your present and all other existence.

Yours, etc.

193. TO PERCY BYSSHE SHELLEY
April 23, 1822.

The blow [1] was stunning and unexpected; for I thought the danger over, by the long interval between her stated ameliora-

---
[1] Allegra died of fever at Bagnacavallo, 22 April.

tion and the arrival of the express. But I have borne up against it as I best can, and so far successfully, that I can go about the usual business of life with the same appearance of composure, and even greater. There is nothing to prevent your coming to-morrow; but, perhaps, to-day, and yester-evening, it was better not to have met. I do not know that I have any thing to reproach in my conduct, and certainly nothing in my feelings and intentions towards the dead. But it is a moment when we are apt to think that, if this or that had been done, such event might have been prevented,—though every day and hour shows us that they are the most natural and inevitable. I suppose that Time will do his usual work—Death has done his.

Yours ever,

N. B.

194. TO SIR WALTER SCOTT

Pisa, May 4, 1822.

MY DEAR SIR WALTER,

Your account of your family is very pleasing: would that I 'could answer this comfort with the like!'[1] but I have just lost my natural daughter, Allegra, by a fever. The only con-solation, save time, is the reflection that she is either at rest or happy; for her few years (only five) prevented her from having incurred any sin, except what we inherit from Adam.

'Whom the gods love die young.'

I need not say that your letters are particularly welcome, when they do not tax your time and patience; and now that our correspondence is resumed, I trust it will continue.

I have lately had some anxiety, rather than trouble, about an awkward affair here, which you may perhaps have heard of; but our minister has behaved very handsomely, and the Tuscan Government as well as it is possible for such a government to behave, which is not saying much for the latter. Some other English and Scots, and myself, had a brawl with a dragoon, who insulted one of the party, and whom we mistook for an officer, as he was medalled and well mounted, etc.; but he turned out to be a sergeant-major. He called out the guard at the gates to arrest us (we being unarmed); upon which I and another (an Italian) rode through the said guard; but they succeeded in detaining others of the party. I rode to my house, and sent my secretary to give an account of the attempted and illegal

---

[1] *Macbeth*, IV, iii, 192–3.

arrest to the authorities, and then, without dismounting, rode back towards the gates, which are near my present mansion. Half-way I met my man vapouring away and threatening to draw upon me (who had a cane in my hand, and no other arms). I, still believing him an officer, demanded his name and address, and gave him my hand and glove thereupon. A servant of mine thrust in between us (totally without orders), but let him go on my command. He then rode off at full speed; but about forty paces further was stabbed, and very dangerously (so as to be in peril), by some *Callum Beg* [1] or other of my people (for I have some rough-handed folks about me), I need hardly say without my direction or approval. The said dragoon had been sabring our unarmed countrymen, however, at the *gate*, *after they were in arrest*, and held by the guards, and wounded one, Captain Hay, very severely. However he got his paiks [2]— having acted like an assassin, and being treated like one. *Who* wounded him, though it was done before thousands of people, they have never been able to ascertain, or prove, nor even the *weapon*; some said a *pistol*, an *air-gun*, a stiletto, a sword, a lance, a pitchfork, and what not. They have arrested and examined servants and people of all descriptions, but can make out nothing. Mr. Dawkins, our minister, assures me that no suspicion is entertained of the man who wounded him having been instigated by me, or any of the party. I enclose you copies of the depositions of those with us, and Dr. Craufurd, a canny Scot (*not* an acquaintance), who saw the latter part of the affair. They are in Italian.

These are the only literary matters in which I have been engaged since the publication and row about *Cain*;—but Mr. Murray has several things of mine in his obstetrical hands. Another *Mystery*—a *Vision*—a Drama—and the like. But you *won't* tell me what *you* are doing—however, I shall find you out, write what you will. You say that I should like your son-in-law—it would be very difficult for me to dislike any one connected with you; but I have no doubt that his own qualities are all that you describe.

I am sorry you don't like Lord Orford's new work. [3] My aristocracy, which is very fierce, makes him a favourite of mine. Recollect that those 'little factions' comprised Lord Chatham and Fox, the father; and that *we* live in gigantic and exaggerated

---

[1] *Waverley*, chap. lviii.   [2] A phrase from *Rob Roy*.
[3] *Memoirs of the Last Ten Years of the Reign of George II*, edited by Lord Holland.

near it as convenient I could wish Allegra to be buried, and on the wall a marble tablet placed, with these words: [1]

In memory of
Allegra,
daughter of G. G. Lord Byron,
who died at Bagnacavallo,
in Italy, April 20th, 1822,
aged five years and three months.

'I shall go to her, but she shall not return to me.'   *2nd Samuel*, xii, 23.

The funeral I wish to be as private as is consistent with decency; and I could hope that Henry Drury will, perhaps, read the service over her. If he should decline it, it can be done by the usual Minister for the time being. I do not know that I need add more just now.

I will now turn to other subjects. Since I came here, I have been invited by the Americans on board of their Squadron, where I was received with all the kindness which I could wish, and with *more ceremony* than I am fond of. I found them finer ships than your own of the same class, well manned and officered. A number of American gentlemen also were on board at the time, and some ladies. As I was taking leave, an American lady asked me for a *rose* which I wore, for the purpose, she said, of sending to America something which I had about me, as a memorial. I need not add, that I felt the compliment properly. Captain Chauncey [2] showed me an American and very pretty edition of my poems, and offered me a passage to the United States, if I would go there. Commodore Jones was also not less kind and attentive. I have since received the enclosed letter, desiring me to sit for my picture for some Americans. It is singular that, in the same year that Lady Noel leaves by will an interdiction for my daughter to see her father's portrait for many years, the individuals of a nation, not remarkable for their liking to the English in particular, nor for flattering men in general, request me to sit for my 'pourtraicture', as Baron Bradwardine calls it. [3] I am also told of considerable literary honours in Germany. Goethe, I am told, is my professed patron and protector. At Leipsic, this year, the highest prize

---

[1] Byron's desires were not carried into effect. Objection was raised to the burial of a natural child in the church, and she was interred at the entrance, without memorial.

[2] Isaac Chauncey.   [3] *Waverley*, chap. xiii.

was proposed for a translation of two Cantos of *Childe Harold*. I am not sure that this was at *Leipsic*, but Mr. Bancroft [1] was my authority—a good German Scholar (a young American), and an acquaintance of Goethe's.

Goethe and the Germans are particularly fond of *Don Juan*, which they judge of as a work of Art. I had heard something like this before through Baron Lutzerode.[2] The translations have been very frequent of several of the works, and Goethe made a comparison between *Faust* and *Manfred*.

All this is some compensation for your English native brutality, so fully displayed this year (I mean *not your* individually) to its brightest extent.

I forgot to mention a little anecdote of a different kind. I went over the *Constitution* (the Commodore's flag ship), and saw, among other things worthy of remark, a little boy *born* on board of her by a sailor's wife. They had christened him 'Constitution Jones'. I, of course, approved the name; and the woman added, 'Ah, Sir, if he turns out but half as good as his name!'

> Yours ever and truly,
>
> N. B.

197. TO JOHN MURRAY

Pisa, July 8th 1822.

DEAR SIR,

Last week I returned you the packet of proofs. You had, perhaps, better not publish in the same volume the *Po* and *Rimini* translation.[3]

I have consigned a letter to Mr. John Hunt [4] for the *Vision of Judgement*, which you will hand over to him. Also the *Pulci*, original and Italian, and any *prose* tracts of mine; for Mr. Leigh Hunt is arrived here, and thinks of commencing a periodical work, to which I shall contribute. I do not propose to you to be the publisher, because I know that you are unfriends; but all things in your care, except the volume now in the press, and the MSS. purchased of Mr. Moore, can be given for this

---

[1] George Bancroft, afterwards the historian of the United States.
[2] The translator of *Cain*.
[3] *Stanzas to the Po* and *Francesca of Rimini*.
[4] Brother of Leigh Hunt, printer, publisher, and co-proprietor of *The Examiner* and *The Liberal*.

purpose, according as they are wanted; and I expect that you will show fair play, though with no very good will on your part.

With regard to what you say about your 'want of memory', I can only remark, that you inserted the note to *Marino Faliero* against my positive revocation, and that you omitted the dedication of *Sardanapalus* to Goethe (place it before the volume now in the press), both of which were things not very agreeable to me, and which I could wish to be avoided in future, as they might be with a very little care, or a simple Memorandum in your pocket book.

It is not impossible that I may have three or four cantos of *D. Juan*[1] ready by autumn, or a little later, as I obtained a permission from my Dictatress to continue it,—*provided always* it was to be more guarded and decorous and sentimental in the continuation than in the commencement. How far these Conditions have been fulfilled may be seen, perhaps, by and bye; but the Embargo was only taken off upon these stipulations. You can answer at your leisure.

Yours ever,

N. B.

198. TO JOHN MURRAY

Pisa, August 3d 1822.

DEAR SIR,

I have received your scrap with H. D[rury]'s letter enclosed. It is just like him: always kind and ready to oblige his old friends.

Will you have the goodness to *send immediately* to Mr. Douglas Kinnaird, and inform him that I have *not* received the *remittances*, *due* to me from the funds a month and more ago, and *promised by him to be sent by every post*, which omission is of great inconvenience to me, and indeed inexcusable as well as unintelligible. As I have written to *him* repeatedly, I suppose that *his* or *my* letters have miscarried.

I presume you have heard that Mr. Shelley and Capt. Williams were lost on the 7th Ulto in their passage from Leghorn to Spezia in their own open boat.[2] You may imagine the state of their families: I never saw such a scene, nor wish to see such another. You were all brutally mistaken about Shelley, who was,

---

[1] The later cantos were published by John Hunt, in 1823.
[2] Shelley was returning after a visit to Leigh Hunt.

without exception, the *best* and least selfish man I ever knew.   I
never knew one who was not a beast in comparison.

Yours ever,

N. B.

199. TO THOMAS MOORE

Pisa, August 27, 1822.

It is boring to trouble you with 'such small gear'; [1] but it
must be owned that I should be glad if you would enquire
whether my Irish subscription ever reached the committee [2] in
Paris from Leghorn.   My reasons, like Vellum's, 'are three-
fold': [3]—First, I doubt the accuracy of all almoners, or remitters
of benevolent cash; second, I do suspect that the said Committee, having in part served its time to time-serving, may have
kept back the acknowledgment of an obnoxious politician's
name in their lists; and third, I feel pretty sure that I shall one
day be twitted by the government scribes for having been a
professor of love for Ireland, and not coming forward with the
others in her distresses.

It is not, as you may opine, that I am ambitious of having
my name in the papers, as I can have that any day in the week
gratis.   All I want is to know if the Reverend Thomas Hall
did or did not remit my subscription (200 scudi of Tuscany, or
about a thousand francs, more or less,) to the Committee
at Paris.

The other day, at Viareggio, I thought proper to swim off to
my schooner (the Bolivar) in the offing, and thence to shore
again—about three miles, or better, in all.   As it was at midday, under a broiling sun, the consequence has been a feverish
attack, and my whole skin's coming off, after going through the
process of one large continuous blister, raised by the sun and
sea together.   I have suffered much pain; not being able to
lie on my back, or even side; for my shoulders and arms were
equally St. Bartholomewed.   But it is over,—and I have got
a new skin, and am as glossy as a snake in its new suit.

We have been burning the bodies of Shelley and Williams on
the sea-shore, to render them fit for removal and regular inter-
ment.   You can have no idea what an extraordinary effect such
a funeral pile has, on a desolate shore, with mountains in the
background and the sea before, and the singular appearance the

---

[1] Cf. *King Lear*, III, iv, 144.
[2] A committee formed in Paris to raise funds for the Irish poor.
[3] Addison, *The Drummer*, II, i.

salt and frankincense gave to the flame. All of Shelley was consumed, except his *heart*, which would not take the flame, and is now preserved in spirits of wine.

Your old acquaintance Londonderry has quietly died at North Cray![1] and the virtuous De Witt was torn in pieces by the populace! What a lucky * * the Irishman has been in his life and end. In him your Irish Franklin *est mort!*

Leigh Hunt is sweating articles for his new Journal; and both he and I think it somewhat shabby in *you* not to contribute. Will you become one of the *properrioters?* 'Do, and we go snacks'.[2] I recommend you to think twice before you respond in the negative.

I have nearly (*quite three*) four new cantos of *Don Juan* ready. I obtained permission from the female Censor Morum of *my* morals to continue it, provided it were immaculate; so I have been as decent as need be. There is a deal of war—a siege, and all that, in the style, graphical and technical, of the shipwreck in Canto Second, which 'took', as they say in the Row.

Yours, etc.

P.S.—That * * * Galignani has about ten lies in one paragraph. It was not a Bible that was found in Shelley's pocket, but John Keats's poems. However, it would not have been strange, for he was a great admirer of Scripture as a composition. *I* did not send my bust to the academy of New York; but I sat for my picture to young West, an American artist, at the request of some members of that Academy to *him* that he would take my portrait,—for the Academy, I believe.

I had, and still have, thoughts of South America, but am fluctuating between it and Greece. I should have gone, long ago, to one of them, but for my liaison with the Countess G.; for love, in these days, is little compatible with glory. *She* would be delighted to go too; but I do not choose to expose her to a long voyage, and a residence in an unsettled country, where I shall probably take a part of some sort.

200. TO MARY SHELLEY

6th October, 1822.

The sofa—which I regret is *not* of your furniture—it was purchased by me at Pisa since you left it.[3]

[1] On 12 August. Byron did not know that he had suicided.
[2] Pope, *Prologue to the Satires*, 66.
[3] Byron and his Countess, Mrs. Shelley and the Hunts, had now removed to two houses in Genoa.

It is convenient for my room, though of little value (about 12 pauls), and I offered to send another (now sent) in its stead. I preferred retaining the purchased furniture, but always intended that you should have as good or better in its place. I have a particular dislike to any thing of Shelley's being within the same walls with Mrs. Hunt's children. They are dirtier and more mischievous than Yahoos. What they can't destroy with their filth they will with their fingers. I presume you received ninety and odd crowns from the wreck of the *Don Juan*, and also the price of the boat purchased by Captain R.,[1] if not, you will have *both*. Hunt has these in hand.

With regard to any difficulties about money, I can only repeat that I will be your banker till this state of things is cleared up, and you can see what is to be done; so there is little to hinder you on that score. I was confined for four days to my bed at Lerici. Poor Hunt, with his six little blackguards, are coming slowly up; as usual he turned back once—was there ever such a *kraal* out of the Hottentot country.

N. B.

201. TO LADY ———

Albaro, November 10, 1822.

* * * * * *

The Chevalier persisted in declaring himself an ill-used gentleman, and describing you as a kind of cold Calypso, who lead astray people of an amatory disposition without giving them any sort of compensation, contenting yourself, it seems, with only making *one* fool instead of two, which is the more approved method of proceeding on such occasions. For my part, I think you are quite right; and be assured from me that a woman (as society is constituted in England) who gives any advantage to a man may expect a lover, but will sooner or later find a tyrant; and this is not the man's fault either, perhaps, but is the necessary and natural result of the circumstances of society, which, in fact, tyrannise over the man equally with the woman; that is to say, if either of them have any feeling or honour.

You can write to me at your leisure and inclination. I have always laid it down as a maxim, and found it justified by experience, that a man and a woman make far better friendships than can exist between two of the same sex; but *these*

[1] Captain Daniel Roberts bought the *Ariel*, or *Don Juan*, when it was recovered.

with this condition, that they never have made, or are to make, love with each other. Lovers may, and, indeed, generally *are* enemies, but they never can be friends; because there must always be a spice of jealousy and a something of self in all their speculations.

Indeed, I rather look upon love altogether as a sort of hostile transaction, very necessary to make or to break matches, and keep the world going, but by no means a sinecure to the parties concerned.

Now, as my love perils are, I believe, pretty well over, and yours, by all accounts, are never to begin, we shall be the best friends imaginable, as far as both are concerned; and with this advantage, that we may both fall to loving right and left through all our acquaintance, without either sullenness or sorrow from that amiable passion, which are its inseparable attendants.

Believe me, etc.,

N. B.

202. TO [MARY SHELLEY]

[December, 1822.]

*   *   *   *   *   *

I presume that you, at least, know enough of me to be sure that I could have no intention to insult Hunt's poverty.[1] On the contrary, I honour him for it; for I know what it is, having been as much embarrassed as ever he was, without perceiving aught in it to diminish an honourable man's self-respect. If you mean to say that, had he been a wealthy man, I would have joined in this Journal, I answer in the negative. * * * I engaged in the Journal from good-will towards him, added to respect for his character, literary and personal; and no less for his political courage, as well as regret for his present circumstances: I did this in the hope that he might, with the same aid from literary friends of literary contributions (which is requisite for all journals of a mixed nature), render himself independent.

*   *   *   *   *

I have always treated him, in our personal intercourse, with such scrupulous delicacy, that I have forborne intruding advice which I thought might be disagreeable, lest he should impute it to what is called 'taking advantage of a man's situation'.

---

[1] An indiscreet remark of Byron's, in a letter to Murray, as to the assistance afforded by him to Leigh Hunt in Italy, had been reported to Hunt.

As to friendship, it is a propensity in which my genius is very limited. I do not know the *male* human being, except Lord Clare, the friend of my infancy, for whom I feel any thing that deserves the name. All my others are men-of-the-world friendships. I did not even feel it for Shelley, however much I admired and esteemed him; so that you see not even vanity could bribe me into it, for, of all men, Shelley thought highest of my talents,—and, perhaps, of my disposition.

I will do my duty by my intimates, upon the principle of doing as you would be done by. I have done so, I trust, in most instances. I may be pleased with their conversation— rejoice in their success—be glad to do them service, or to receive their counsel and assistance in return. But as for friends and friendship, I have (as I already said) named the only remaining male for whom I feel any thing of the kind, excepting, perhaps, Thomas Moore. I have had, and may have still, a thousand friends, as they are called, in *life*, who are like one's partners in the waltz of this world—not much remembered when the ball is over, though very pleasant for the time. Habit, business, and companionship in pleasure or in pain, are links of a similar kind, and the same faith in politics is another. * * *

203. TO JOHN MURRAY

Genoa, 10bre 25º, 1822.

I had sent you back the *Quarterly*, without perusal, having resolved to read no more reviews, good, bad, or indifferent; but 'who can control his fate?'[1] Galignani, to whom my English studies are confined, has forwarded a copy of at least one half of it,[2] in his indefatigable Catch-penny weekly compilation; and as, 'like Honour, it came unlooked for', I have looked through it. I must say that, upon the *whole*, that is, the whole of the *half* which I have read (for the other half is to be the Segment of Gal.'s next week's Circular), it is extremely handsome, and any thing but unkind or unfair. As I take the good in good part, I must not, nor will not, quarrel with the bad: what the Writer says of *Don Juan* is harsh, but it is inevitable. He must follow, or at least not directly oppose, the opinion of a prevailing, and yet not very firmly seated, party: a review may and will direct or 'turn awry' the Currents of opinion,[3] but it must not directly oppose them. *Don Juan* will be known by

---

[1] *Othello*, v, ii, 265.   [2] A review of Byron's dramas.
[3] See *Hamlet*, III, i, 187.

and bye, for what it is intended,—a *Satire* on *abuses* of the present states of Society, and not an eulogy of vice: it may be now and then voluptuous: I can't help that. Ariosto is worse; Smollett (see Lord Strutwell in vol. 2ᵈ of R[oderick] R[andom]) ten times worse; and Fielding no better. No Girl will ever be seduced by reading *D. J.*—no, no; she will go to Little's poems and Rousseau's romans for that, or even to the immaculate De Staël: they will encourage her, and not the Don, who laughs at that, and—and—most other things. But never mind —Ça ira!

And now to a less agreeable topic, of which *pars magna es* —you Murray of Albemarle Sᵗ and the other Murray of Bridge Street [1]—'Arcades Ambo' ('*Murrays both*') 'et *cant*-are pares': ye, I say, between you, are the Causes of the prosecution of John Hunt, Esqʳᵉ on account of the *Vision*,[2] You, by sending him an incorrect copy, and the other, by his function. Egad, but H.'s Counsel will lay it on you with a trowel for your ter-giversifying as to the MSS., etc., whereby poor H. (and, for anything I know, myself—I am willing enough) is likely to be impounded.

Now, do you see what you and your friends do by your injudicious rudeness?—actually cement a sort of connection which you strove to prevent, and which, had the H.'s *prospered*, would not in all probability have continued. As it is, I will not quit them in their adversity, though it should cost me character, fame, money, and the usual et cetera.

My original motives I already explained (in the letter which you thought proper to show): [3] they are the *true* ones, and I abide by them, as I tell you, and I told Lᵈ Hᵗ when he questioned me on the subject of that letter. He was violently hurt, and never will forgive me at bottom; but I can't help that. I never meant to make a parade of it; but if he chose to question me, I could only answer the plain truth: and I confess I did not see anything in the letter to hurt him, unless I said he was 'a *bore*', which I don't remember. Had their Journal gone on well, and I could have aided to make it better for them, I should then have left them, after my safe pilotage off a lee shore, to make a prosperous voyage by themselves. As it is, I can't, and would not, if I could, leave them amidst the breakers.

As to any community of feeling, thought, or opinion, between

---

[1] Charles Murray, attorney to the Constitutional Association.
[2] *The Vision of Judgment*, published in the first number of *The Liberal*.
[3] See page 335.

L. H. and me, there is little or none: we meet rarely, hardly ever; but I think him a good principled and able man, and must do as I would be done by. I do not know what world he has lived in, but I have lived in three or four; and none of them like his Keats and Kangaroo *terra incognita*. Alas! poor Shelley! how he would have laughed had he lived, and how we used to laugh now and then, at various things, which are grave in the Suburbs!

You are all mistaken about Shelley. You do not know how mild, how tolerant, how good he was in Society; and as perfect a Gentleman as ever crossed a drawing-room, when he liked, and where he liked.

I have some thoughts of taking a run down to Naples (*solus*, or, at most, *cum solâ*) this Spring, and writing, when I have studied the Country, a fifth and sixth Canto of *Ch^e Harolde*: but this is merely an idea for the present, and I have other excursions and voyages in my mind. The busts are finished: are you worthy of them?

Yours, etc.,
N. B.

P.S.—Mrs. Shelley is residing with the Hunts at some distance from me: I see them very seldom, and generally on account of their business. Mrs. S., I believe, will go to England in the Spring.[1]

Count Gamba's family, the father and Son and daughter, are residing with me by Mr. Hill's [2] (the minister's) recommendation, as a safer asylum from the political persecutions than they could have in another residence; but they occupy one part of a large house, and I the other, and our establishments are quite separate.

Since I have read the Q[*uarterly*], I shall erase two or three passages in the latter 6 or 7 Cantos, in which I had lightly stroked over two or three of your authors; but I will not return evil for good. I liked what I read of the article much.

Mr. J. Hunt is most likely the publisher of the new Cantos; with what prospects of success I know not, nor does it very much matter, as far as I am concerned; but I hope that it may be of use to him, for he is a stiff, sturdy, conscientious man, and I like him: he is such a one as Prynne or Pym might be. I bear you no ill will for declining the *D. J.'s*, but I cannot commend your conduct to the H.'s.

---

[1] She left Genoa on 5 July 1823.
[2] William Noel-Hill, British Envoy to Sardinia.

Have you aided Madame de Yossy, as I requested? I sent her 300 francs. Recommend her, will you, to the Literary F., or to some benevolence within your Circles.

204. TO JOHN HUNT

Genoa, Mh. 17ᵗʰ 1823.

SIR,

Your brother will have forwarded by the post a corrected proof of *The Blues* for some ensuing number of the journal; but I should think that yᵉ Pulci translation had better be preferred for the immediate number, as *The Blues* will only tend further to indispose a portion of your readers.

I still retain my opinion that my connection with the work will tend to any thing but its success. Such I thought from the first, when I suggested that it would have been better to have made a kind of literary appendix to the *Examiner*; the other expedient was hazardous, and has failed hitherto accordingly; and it appears that the two pieces of my contribution have precipitated that failure more than any other. It was a pity to print such a quantity, especially as you might have been aware of my general unpopularity, and the universal run of the period against my productions, since the publication of Mr. Murray's last volume. My talent (if I have any) does not lie in the kinds of composition which is [*sic*] most acceptable to periodical readers. By this time you are probably convinced of this fact. The Journal, if continued (as I see no reason why it should not be), will find much more efficacious assistance in the present and other contributors than in myself. Perhaps also, you should, for the present, reduce the number printed to two thousand, and raise it gradually if necessary. It is not so much against *you* as against me that the hatred is directed; and, I confess, I would rather withstand it *alone*, and grapple with it as I may. Mr. Murray, partly from pique, for he is a Mortal—mortal as his publications, though a bookseller—has done more harm than you are fully aware of, or I either; and you will perceive this probably on my first separate publication, no less than in those connected with *The Liberal*. He has the Clergy, and the Government, and the public with him; I do not much embarrass myself about them when *alone*; but I do not wish to drag others down also. I take this to be the fact, for I do not recollect that so much odium was directed against your family and friends, till your brother, unfortunately for himself, came in literary contact with myself. I will not, however, quit *The Liberal* without mature consideration, though I feel persuaded that it would be for your advantage that I should do so. Time and Truth may probably do away this hostility, or, at least, its effect; but, in the interim, you are the sufferer. Every publication of mine has latterly failed; I am not discouraged by this, because writing and composition are habits of my mind, with which Success and Publication are objects of remoter reference—*not causes* but *effects*, like those of any other pursuit. I have had enough both of praise and abuse to deprive them of their novelty, but I continue to compose for the same reason that I ride, or read, or bathe, or travel—it is a habit.

I want sadly *Peveril of the Peak*, which has not yet arrived here, and I will thank you much for a copy; I shall direct Mr. Kinnaird to reimburse you for the price. It will be useless to forward *The Liberal*, the insertion of which will only prevent the arrival of any other books in the same parcel. That work is strictly prohibited, and the packet which came by sea was extracted with the greatest difficulty. Never send by sea, it is a loss of four months; by land, a fortnight is sufficient.

Yours ever,

N. B.

205. TO THOMAS MOORE

Genoa, April 2, 1823.

I have just seen some friends of yours, who paid me a visit yesterday, which, in honour of them and of you, I returned to-day;—as I reserve my bear-skin and teeth, and paws and claws, for our enemies.

I have also seen Henry Fox, Lord Holland's son, whom I had not looked upon since I left him a pretty, mild boy, without a neck-cloth, in a jacket, and in delicate health, seven long years agone, at the period of mine eclipse—the third, I believe, as I have generally one every two or three years. I think that he has the softest and most amiable expression of countenance I ever saw, and manners correspondent. If to those he can add hereditary talents, he will keep the name of Fox in all its freshness for half a century more, I hope. I speak from a transient glimpse—but I love still to yield to such impressions; for I have ever found that those I liked longest and best, I took to at first sight; and I always liked that boy—perhaps, in part, from some resemblance in the less fortunate part of our destinies

—I mean, to avoid mistakes, his lameness. But there is this difference, that *he* appears a halting angel, who has tripped against a star; whilst I am *Le Diable Boiteux*,—a soubriquet, which I marvel that, amongst their various *nominis umbræ*, the Orthodox have not hit upon.

Your other allies, whom I have found very agreeable personages, are Milor Blessington and *épouse*,[1] travelling with a very handsome companion, in the shape of a 'French Count' (to use Farquhar's phrase in the *Beaux Stratagem* [2]), who has all the air of a *Cupidon déchaîné*, and is one of the few specimens I have seen of our ideal of a Frenchman *before* the Revolution—an old friend with a new face, upon whose like I never thought that we should look again. Miladi seems highly literary, to which, and your honour's acquaintance with the family, I attribute the pleasure of having seen them. She is also very pretty, even in a morning,—a species of beauty on which the sun of Italy does not shine so frequently as the chandelier. Certainly, Englishwomen wear better than their continental neighbours of the same sex. Mountjoy seems very good-natured, but is much tamed, since I recollect him in all the glory of gems and snuffboxes, and uniforms, and theatricals, and speeches in our house —'I mean, of peers',—(I must refer you to Pope [3]—whom you don't read and won't appreciate—for that quotation, which you must allow to be poetical,) and sitting to Stroelling, the painter, (do you remember our visit, with Leckie, to the German?) to be depicted as one of the heroes of Agincourt, 'with his long sword, saddle, bridle, Whack fal de',[4] etc., etc.

I have been unwell—caught a cold and inflammation, which menaced a conflagration, after dining with our ambassador, Monsieur Hill,—not owing to the dinner, but my carriage broke down in the way home, and I had to walk some miles, up hill partly, after hot rooms, in a very bleak, windy evening, and over hotted, or over-colded myself. I have not been so robustious as formerly, ever since the last summer, when I fell ill after a long swim in the Mediterranean, and have never been

---

[1] The Earl of Blessington (see page 256) married Marguerite Farmer, the widowed daughter of a small Irish landowner, on 16 February 1818. Her *Journal of the Conversations with Lord Byron*, which was kept during this visit, first appeared in the *New Monthly Magazine*, July 1832–December 1833.

[2] Count Bellair, 'a French officer'. The reference is to Alfred Guillaume Gabriel D'Orsay, son of one of Napoleon's generals, and an artist.

[3] 'On receiving from the Right Hon. the Lady Frances Shirley a standish and two pens'.

[4] *The Bold Dragoon.*

quite right up to this present writing. I am thin,—perhaps thinner than you saw me, when I was nearly transparent, in 1812,—and am obliged to be moderate of my mouth; which, nevertheless, won't prevent me (the gods willing) from dining with your friends the day after to-morrow.

They give me a very good account of you, and of your nearly Emprisoned *Angels*.[1] But why did you change your title?— you will regret this some day. The bigots are not to be conciliated; and, if they were—are they worth it? I suspect that I am a more orthodox Christian than you are; and, whenever I see a real Christian, either in practice or in theory, (for I never yet found the man who could produce either, when put to the proof,) I am his disciple. But, till then, I cannot truckle to tithe-mongers,—nor can I imagine what has made *you* circumcise your Seraphs.

I have been far more persecuted than you, as you may judge by my present decadence,—for I take it that I am as low in popularity and bookselling as any writer can be. At least, so my friends assure me—blessings on their benevolence! This they attribute to Hunt; but they are wrong—it must be, partly at least, owing to myself; be it so. As to Hunt, I prefer *not* having turned him to starve in the streets to any personal honour which might have accrued from such genuine philanthropy. I really act upon principle in this matter, for we have nothing much in common; and I cannot describe to you the despairing sensation of trying to do something for a man who seems incapable or unwilling to do anything further for himself,—at least, to the purpose. It is like pulling a man out of a river who directly throws himself in again. For the last three or four years Shelley assisted, and had once actually extricated him. I have since his demise,—and even before,—done what I could: but it is not in my power to make this permanent. I want Hunt to return to England, for which I would furnish him with the means in comfort; and his situation *there*, on the whole, is bettered, by the payment of a portion of his debts, etc.; and he would be on the spot to continue his Journal, or Journals, with his brother, who seems a sensible, plain, sturdy, and enduring person. * *

[1] Moore's *Loves of the Angels*, published in December 1822.

206. TO JOHN CAM HOBHOUSE

MY DEAR H.,   Genoa, April 7th, 1823.

I saw Capt. Blaquiere, and the Greek companion of his
mission,[1] on Saturday. Of course I entered very sincerely into
the object of their journey, and have even offered to go up to
the Levant in July, if the Greek provisional government think
that I could be of any use. It is not that I could pretend to
anything in a military capacity. I have not the presumption of
the philosopher at Ephesus [2] who lectured before Hannibal on
the art of war; nor is it much that an individual foreigner can
do in any other way, but perhaps as a reporter of the actual
state of things there, or in carrying on any correspondence
between them and their western friends, I might be of use; at
any rate, I would try. Capt. Blaquiere (who is to write to you)
wishes to have me named as a member of the committee in
England. I fairly told him that my name, in its present unpopularity there, would probably do more harm than good; but
of this you can judge, and certainly without offence to me, for
I have no wish either to *shine*, or to appear officious; in the meantime, he is to correspond with me. I gave him a letter to Ld.
Sidney Osborne [3] at Corfu; but a mere letter of introduction, as
Osborne will be hampered by his office in any political point of
view. There are some obstacles, too, to my own going up to
the Levant, which will occur to you.

My health, though pretty good, is not quite the same as when
it subdued the Olympian malaria in 1810; and the unsettled
state of my lawsuit with Mr. Deardon [4] and the affairs still in
Hanson's hands tend to keep me nearer home.

Also you may imagine that the 'absurd womankind', as
Monkbarns [5] calls them, are by no means favourable to such
an enterprise. Madame Guiccioli is of course, and naturally
enough, opposed to my quitting her, though but for a few months;
and as she had influence enough to prevent my return to England in 1819, she may be not less successful in detaining me from
Greece in 1823. Her brother, Count Gamba the younger, who

[1] In January 1823, a committee was formed in London to aid the Greeks
in their war of independence. Edward Blaquiere volunteered to return
with the Greek agent, Andreas Luriottis, to collect information. Knowing
Byron's sympathy with Greece, they had called to enlist his aid.
[2] Phormio. See Cicero, *De Oratore*, II, 18.
[3] Lord Sidney Godolphin Osborne, who was acting as Treasurer and
Secretary to the Senate at Corfu.
[4] James Dearden, lessee of Byron's coal-pits at Rochdale.
[5] *The Antiquary*.

is a very fine, spirited young fellow—as Blaquiere will tell you—
is of a very different opinion, and ever since the ruin of Italian
hopes in 1820, has been eager to go to Spain, or to Greece, and
very desirous to accompany me to one or other of those countries;
or at any rate to go himself. I wish you had seen him, you
would have found a very different person from the usual run
of young Italians.

With regard to my peculium. I am pretty well off; I have
still a surplus of three thousand pounds of last year's income;
a thousand pounds in Exchequer bills in England, and by this
time, as also in July, there ought to be further monies paid to
my account in Kinnaird's bank.

From literary matters I know not if anything will be produced;
but even out of my own, K[innair]d will, I suppose, furnish me
with a further credit if I should require it, since all my receipts
will pass through his hands.

You must be aware that it would not do to go without means
into a country where means are so much wanted; and that I
should not like to be an incumbrance, go where I would. Now
I wish to know whether *there* or (if that should not take place)
here I can do anything, by correspondence or otherwise, to
forward the objects of the well-wishers of the Hellenic struggle.
Will *you* state this to them, and desire them to command me,
if they think it could be of any service? Of course, I must in
no way interfere with Blaquiere, so as to give him umbrage;
or to any other person. I have great doubts, not of my own
inclination, but from the circumstances already stated, whether
I shall be able to go up myself, as I fain would do; but Blaquiere
seemed to think that I might be of some use even *here,* though
what he did not specify. If there were any things which you
wished to have forwarded to the Greeks—as surgeon's medicines,
powder, and swivels, etc., of which they tell me that they are
in want—you would find me ready to follow any directions, and,
what is more to the purpose, to contribute my own share to
the expense.

Will you let me hear from you, at any rate, your opinion; and
believe me,

Ever yours,
N. B.

P.S.—You may show this letter to D[ouglas] K[innair]d, or
to anyone you please, including such members of the committee as you think proper, and explain to them that I shall
confine myself to following their directions, if they give me any

instructions. My uncertainty as to whether *I* can so manage as to go *personally* prevents me from being more explicit (I hear that strangers are not very welcome to the Greeks, from jealousy), except as far as regards anything I might be able to do *here*, by obtaining good information, or affording assistance.

207. TO JOHN BOWRING [1]

Genoa, May 12, 1823.

SIR,

I have great pleasure in acknowledging your letter, and the honour which the Committee have done me:—I shall endeavour to deserve their confidence by every means in my power. My first wish is to go up into the Levant in person, where I might be enabled to advance, if not the cause, at least the means of obtaining information which the Committee might be desirous of acting upon; and my former residence in the country, my familiarity with the Italian language, (which is there universally spoken, or at least to the same extent as French in the more polished parts of the Continent,) and my *not* total ignorance of the Romaic, would afford me some advantages of experience. To this project the only objection is of a domestic nature, and I shall try to get over it;—if I fail in this, I must do what I can where I am; but it will be always a source of regret to me, to think that I might perhaps have done more for the cause on the spot.

Our last information of Captain Blaquiere is from Ancona, where he embarked with a fair wind for Corfu, on the 15th ult.; he is now probably at his destination. My last letter *from* him personally was dated Rome; he had been refused a passport through the Neapolitan territory, and returned to strike up through Romagna for Ancona:—little time, however, appears to have been lost by the delay.

The principal material wanted by the Greeks appears to be, first, a park of field artillery—light, and fit for mountain-service; secondly, gunpowder; thirdly, hospital or medical stores. The readiest mode of transmission is, I hear, by Idra, addressed to Mr. Negri,[2] the minister. I meant to send up a certain quantity of the two latter—no great deal—but enough for an individual to show his good wishes for the Greek success,—but am pausing,

[1] A writer and linguist, afterwards distinguished in public life and knighted, who was acting as secretary to the Greek Committee.

[2] Theodore Negris, formerly Ottoman deputy-ambassador at Paris.

because, in case I should go myself, I can take them with me. I do not want to limit my own contribution to this merely, but more especially, if I can get to Greece myself, I should devote whatever resources I can muster of my own, to advancing the great object. I am in correspondence with Signor Nicolas Karrellas (well known to Mr. Hobhouse), who is now at Pisa; but his latest advice merely stated, that the Greeks are at present employed in organising their *internal* government, and the details of its administration: this would seem to indicate *security*, but the war is however far from being terminated.

The Turks are an obstinate race, as all former wars have proved them, and will return to the charge for years to come, even if beaten, as it is to be hoped they will be. But in no case can the labours of the Committee be said to be in vain; for in the event even of the Greeks being subdued, and dispersed, the funds which could be employed in succouring and gathering together the remnant, so as to alleviate in part their distresses, and enable them to find or make a country (as so many emigrants of other nations have been compelled to do), would 'bless both those who gave and those who took',[1] as the bounty both of justice and of mercy.

With regard to the formation of a brigade, (which Mr. Hobhouse hints at in his short letter of this day's receipt, enclosing the one to which I have the honour to reply,) I would presume to suggest—but merely as an opinion, resulting rather from the melancholy experience of the brigades embarked in the Columbian service[2] than from any experiment yet fairly tried in GREECE,—that the attention of the Committee had better perhaps be directed to the employment of *officers* of experience than the enrolment of *raw British* soldiers, which latter are apt to be unruly, and not very serviceable, in irregular warfare by the side of foreigners. A small body of good officers, especially artillery; an engineer, with quantity (such as the Committee might deem requisite) of stores of the nature which Captain Blaquiere indicated as most wanted, would, I should conceive, be a highly useful accession. Officers, also, who had previously served in the Mediterranean would be preferable, as some knowledge of Italian is nearly indispensable.

It would also be as well that they should be aware, that they are not going 'to rough it on a beef-steak and bottle of port', —but that Greece—never, of late years, very plentifully stocked

---

[1] *The Merchant of Venice*, IV, i, 185.
[2] In 1819, when the Republic of Colombia was formed under Bolivar.

for a *mess*—is at present the country of all kinds of *privations*. This remark may seem superfluous; but I have been led to it, by observing that many *foreign* officers, Italian, French, and even Germans (but *fewer* of the *latter*), have returned in disgust, imagining either that they were going up to make a party of pleasure, or to enjoy full pay, speedy promotion, and a very moderate degree of duty. They complain, too, of having been ill received by the Government or inhabitants; but numbers of these complainants were mere adventurers, attracted by a hope of command and plunder, and disappointed of both. Those Greeks I have seen strenuously deny the charge of inhospitality, and declare that they shared their pittance to the last crum with their foreign volunteers.

I need not suggest to the Committee the very great advantage which must accrue to Great Britain from the success of the Greeks, and their probable commercial relations with England in consequence; because I feel persuaded that the first object of the Committee is their EMANCIPATION, without any interested views. But the consideration might weigh with the English people in general, in their present passion for every kind of speculation,—they need not cross the American seas for one much better worth their while, and nearer home. The resources even for an emigrant population, in the Greek islands alone, are rarely to be paralleled; and the cheapness of every kind of, not *only necessary*, but *luxury*, (that is to say, *luxury* of *nature*,) fruits, wine, oil, etc., in a state of peace, are far beyond those of the Cape and Van Dieman's Land, and the other places of refuge which the English people are searching for over the waters.

I beg that the Committee will command me in any and every way. If I am favoured with any instructions, I shall endeavour to obey them to the letter, whether conformable to my own private opinion or not. I beg leave to add, personally, my respect for the gentleman whom I have the honour of addressing,

And am, Sir, your obliged, etc.

P.S.—The best refutation of Gell [1] will be the active exertions of the Committee;—I am too warm a controversialist; and I suspect that if Mr. Hobhouse have taken him in hand, there will be little occasion for me to 'encumber him with help'.[2] If I go up into the country, I will endeavour to transmit as accurate and impartial an account as circumstances will permit.

[1] Sir William Gell, in his *Narrative of a Journey in the Morea*, 1823, had asserted that Russian rule would be beneficial to the Greeks.
[2] Dr. Johnson's Letter to Lord Chesterfield.

I shall write to Mr. Karrellas. I expect intelligence from Captain Blaquiere, who has promised me some early intimation from the seat of the Provisional Government. I gave him a letter of introduction to Lord Sidney Osborne, at Corfu; but as Lord S. is in the government service, of course his reception could only be a *cautious* one.

208. TO THE HON. DOUGLAS KINNAIRD

MY DEAR DOUGLAS,   Genoa, May 21st, 1823.

I am doing all I can to get away, but I have all kinds of obstacles thrown in my way by the 'absurd womankind', who seems determined on sacrificing herself in every way, and preventing me from doing any good, and all without reason; for her relations, and her husband (who is moving the Pope and the Government here to get her to live with him again) and everybody, are earnest with her to return to Ravenna.[1] She wants to go up to Greece too! forsooth, a precious place to go to at present! Of course the idea is ridiculous, as everything must there be sacrificed to seeing her out of harm's way. It is a case too, in which interest does not enter, and therefore hard to deal with; for I have no kind of control in that way, and if she makes a scene (and she has a turn that way) we shall have another romance, and tale of ill usage, and abandonment, and Lady Carolining, and Lady Byroning, and Glenarvoning, all cut and dry. There never was a man who gave up so much to women, and all I have gained by it has been the character of treating them harshly. However I shall do what I can, and have hopes; for her father has been recalled from his political exile; but with this proviso, that he do not return without his daughter. If I left a woman for another woman, she might have cause to complain, but really when a man merely wishes to go on a great duty, for a good cause, this selfishness on the part of the 'feminie' is rather too much.

                                                 Ever yrs.,
                                                     N. B.

209. TO HENRI BEYLE [2]

SIR,   Genoa, May 29, 1823.

At present, that I know to whom I am indebted for a very flattering mention in the *Rome, Naples, and Florence*, in 1817,

[1] The order for the banishment of the Gambas had been repealed in April 1823.

[2] Henri-Marie Beyle (1783–1842), the essayist and novelist, better known as the Comte de Stendhal.

by Mons. Stendhal, it is fit that I should return my thanks
(however undesired or undesirable) to Mons. Beyle, with whom
I had the honour of being acquainted at Milan, in 1816. You
only did me too much honour in what you were pleased to say
in that work; but it has hardly given me less pleasure than the
praise itself, to become at length aware (which I have done by
mere accident) that I am indebted for it to one of whose good
opinion I was really ambitious. So many changes have taken
place since that period in the Milan circle, that I hardly
dare recur to it;—some dead, some banished, and some in
the Austrian dungeons.—Poor Pellico![1] I trust that, in his
iron solitude, his Muse is consoling him in part—one day to
delight us again, when both she and her Poet are restored to
freedom.

Of your works I have only seen *Rome*, etc., the Lives of Haydn
and Mozart, and the *brochure* on Racine and Shakespeare. The
Histoire de la Peinture I have not yet the good fortune to
possess.

There is one part of your observations in the pamphlet which
I shall venture to remark upon;—it regards Walter Scott.
You say that 'his character is little worthy of enthusiasm',
at the same time that you mention his productions in the manner
they deserve. I have known Walter Scott long and well, and
in occasional situations which call forth the *real* character—and
I can assure you that his character *is* worthy of admiration—
that of all men he is the most *open*, the most *honourable*, the
most *amiable*. With his politics I have nothing to do: they
differ from mine, which renders it difficult for me to speak of
them. But he is *perfectly sincere* in them: and Sincerity may be
humble, but she cannot be servile. I pray you, therefore, to
correct or soften that passage. You may, perhaps, attribute
this officiousness of mine to a false affectation of *candour*, as
I happen to be a writer also. Attribute it to what motive you
please, but *believe* the *truth*. I say that Walter Scott is as nearly
a thorough good man as man can be, because I *know* it by
experience to be the case.

If you do me the honour of an answer, may I request a speedy
one?—because it is possible (though not yet decided) that
circumstances may conduct me once more to Greece. My
present address is Genoa, where an answer will reach me in a
short time, or be forwarded to me wherever I may be.

[1] Silvio Pellico (1788-1854), the dramatist, had been imprisoned in 1820
for his political activities.

I beg you to believe me, with a lively recollection of our brief acquaintance, and the hope of one day renewing it,

Your ever obliged

And obedient humble servant,

NOEL BYRON.

210. TO EDWARD JOHN TRELAWNY [1]

June 15, 1823.

MY DEAR T.,

You must have heard that I am going to Greece. Why do you not come to me? I want your aid, and am exceedingly anxious to see you. Pray come, for I am at last determined to go to Greece; it is the only place I was ever contented in. I am serious, and did not write before, as I might have given you a journey for nothing; they all say I can be of use in Greece. I do not know how, nor do they; but at all events let us go.

Yours, etc., truly,

N. BYRON.

211. TO JOHN BOWRING

July 7, 1823.

We sail on the 12th for Greece.—I have had a letter from Mr. Blaquiere, too long for present transcription, but very satisfactory. The Greek Government expects me without delay.

In conformity to the desires of Mr. B. and other correspondents in Greece, I have to suggest, with all deference to the Committee, that a remittance of even '*ten thousand pounds only*' (Mr. B.'s expression) would be of the greatest service to the Greek Government at present. I have also to recommend strongly the attempt of a loan, for which there will be offered a sufficient security by deputies now on their way to England. In the meantime, I hope that the Committee will be enabled to do something effectual.

For my own part, I mean to carry up, in cash or credits, above eight, and nearly nine thousand pounds sterling, which I am enabled to do by funds I have in Italy, and credits in England. Of this sum I must necessarily reserve a portion for the subsistence of myself and suite; the rest I am willing to apply in the

[1] Author, adventurer, and friend of Shelley. Byron had met him at Pisa in 1821, and at the time of Shelley's death he was skipper of Byron's yacht, the *Bolivar*.

manner which seems most likely to be useful to the cause—having of course some guarantee or assurance, that it will not be misapplied to any individual speculation.

If I remain in Greece, which will mainly depend upon the presumed probable utility of my presence there, and of the opinion of the Greeks themselves as to its propriety—in short, if I am welcome to them, I shall continue, during my residence at least, to apply such portions of my income, present and future, as may forward the object—that is to say, what I can spare for that purpose. Privations I can, or at least could once, bear—abstinence I am accustomed to—and as to fatigue, I was once a tolerable traveller. What I may be now, I cannot tell—but I will try.

I await the commands of the Committee.—Address to Genoa —the letters will be forwarded to me, wherever I may be, by my bankers, Messrs. Webb and Barry. It would have given me pleasure to have had some more *defined* instructions before I went; but these, of course, rest at the option of the Committee. I have the honour to be,

Your obedient, etc.

P.S.—Great anxiety is expressed for a printing press and types, etc. I have not the time to provide them, but recommend this to the notice of the Committee. I presume the types must, partly at least, be *Greek*: they wish to publish papers, and perhaps a Journal, probably in Romaic, with Italian translations.

212. TO J. J. COULMANN [1]

Genoa, July 12(?), 1823.

MY DEAR SIR,

Your letter, and what accompanied it, have given me the greatest pleasure. The glory and the works of the writers who have deigned to give me these volumes, bearing their names, were not unknown to me, but still it is more flattering to receive them from the authors themselves. I beg you to present my thanks to each of them in particular; and to add, how proud I am of their good opinion, and how charmed I shall be to cultivate their acquaintance, if ever the occasion should occur. The productions of M. Jouy [2] have long been familiar to me. Who

---

[1] A Frenchman who had sought Byron's acquaintance. The letter is a retranslation of Coulmann's French version.

[2] Victor Joseph Etienne de Jouy (1764–1836), author of *L'Hermite de la Chaussée d'Antin; Sylla, tragédie*, and other works.

has not read and applauded *The Hermit* and *Sylla*? But I cannot accept what it has pleased your friends to call their *homage*, because there is no sovereign in the republic of letters; and even if there were, I have never had the pretension or the power to become a usurper.

I have also to return you thanks for having honoured me with your own compositions; I thought you too young, and probably too amiable, to be an author. As to the Essay,[1] etc., I am obliged to you for the present, although I had already seen it joined to the last edition of the translation. I have nothing to object to it, with regard to what concerns myself personally, though naturally there are some of the facts in it discoloured, and several errors into which the author has been led by the accounts of others. I allude to facts, and not criticisms. But the same author has cruelly calumniated my father and my grand-uncle, but more especially the former. So far from being 'brutal', he was, according to the testimony of all those who knew him, of an extremely amiable and lively (*enjoué*) character, but careless (*insouciant*) and dissipated. He had, consequently, the reputation of a good officer, and showed himself such in the Guards, in America. The facts themselves refute the assertion. It is not by 'brutality' that a young Officer in the Guards seduces and carries off a Marchioness, and marries two heiresses. It is true that he was a very handsome man, which goes a great way. His first wife (Lady Conyers and Marchioness of Carmarthen) did not die of grief, but of a malady which she caught by having imprudently insisted upon accompanying my father to a hunt, before she was completely recovered from the accouchement which gave birth to my sister Augusta.

His second wife, my respected mother, had, I assure you, too proud a spirit to bear the ill-usage of any man, no matter who he might be; and this she would have soon proved. I should add, that he lived a long time in Paris, and was in habits of intimacy with the old Marshal Biron, Commandant of the French Guards; who, from the similitude of names, and Norman origin of our family, supposed that there was some distant relationship between us. He died some years before the age of forty, and whatever may have been his faults, they were certainly not those of harshness and grossness (*dureté et grossièreté*). If the notice should reach England, I am certain that

---

[1] *Essai sur le génie et le caractère de Lord Byron*, by Amédée Pichot, in the French translation of Byron's works.

the passage relative to my father will give much more pain to my sister (the wife of Colonel Leigh, attached to the Court of the late Queen, *not* Caroline, but Charlotte, wife of George III), even than to me; and this she does not deserve, for there is not a more angelic being upon earth. Augusta and I have always loved the memory of our father as much as we loved each other, and this at least forms a presumption that the stain of harshness was not applicable to it. If he dissipated his fortune, that concerns us alone, for we are his heirs; and till we reproach him with it, I know no one else who has a right to do so. As to Lord Byron, who killed Mr. Chaworth in a duel, so far from retiring from the world, he made the tour of Europe, and was appointed Master of the Staghounds after that event, and did not give up society until his son had offended him by marrying in a manner contrary to his duty. So far from feeling any remorse for having killed Mr. Chaworth, who was a fire-eater (*spadassin*), and celebrated for his quarrelsome disposition, he always kept the sword which he used upon that occasion in his bed-chamber, where it still was *when he died.*. It is singular enough, that when very young, I formed a strong attachment for the grand-niece and heiress of Mr. Chaworth,[1] who stood in the same degree of relationship as myself to Lord Byron; and at one time it was thought that the two families would have been united in us. She was two years older than me, and we were very much together in our youth. She married a man of an ancient and respectable family; but her marriage was not a happier one than my own. Her conduct, however, was irreproachable, but there was no sympathy between their characters, and a separation took place. I had not seen her for many years. When an occasion offered, I was upon the point, with her consent, of paying her a visit, when my sister, who has always had more influence over me than anyone else, persuaded me not to do it. 'For,' said she, 'if you go, you will fall in love again, and then there will be a scene; one step will lead to another, *et cela fera un éclat*', etc. I was guided by these reasons, and shortly after I married; with what success it is useless to say. Mrs. C. some time after, being separated from her husband, became insane; but she has since recovered her reason, and is, I believe, reconciled to her husband. This is a long letter, and principally about my family, but it is the fault of M. Pichot, my benevolent biographer. He may say of me whatever of good or evil pleases him, but I desire that he should

[1] Mary Chaworth, afterwards Mrs. Musters.

speak of my relations only as they deserve. If you could find an occasion of making him, as well as M. Nodier, rectify the facts relative to my father, and publish them, you would do me a great service, for I cannot bear to have him unjustly spoken of. I must conclude abruptly, for I have occupied you too long. Believe me to be very much honoured by your esteem, and always your obliged and obedient servant,

NOEL BYRON.

P.S.—The tenth or twelfth of this month I shall embark for Greece. Should I return, I shall pass through Paris, and shall be much flattered in meeting you and your friends. Should I not return, give me as affectionate a place in your memory as possible.

213. TO JOHANN WOLFGANG VON GOETHE

Leghorn, July 24, 1823.

ILLUSTRIOUS SIR,

I cannot thank you as you ought to be thanked for the lines [1] which my young friend, Mr. Sterling, sent me of yours; and it would but ill become me to pretend to exchange verses with him who, for fifty years, has been the undisputed sovereign of European literature. You must therefore accept my most sincere acknowledgments in prose—and in hasty prose too; for I am at present on my voyage to Greece once more, and surrounded by hurry and bustle, which hardly allow a moment even to gratitude and admiration to express themselves.

I sailed from Genoa some days ago, was driven back by a gale of wind, and have since sailed again and arrived here, 'Leghorn', this morning, to receive on board some Greek passengers for their struggling country.

Here also I found your lines and Mr. Sterling's letter; and I could not have had a more favourable omen, a more agreeable surprise, than a word of Goethe, written by his own hand.

I am returning to Greece, to see if I can be of any little use there: if ever I come back, I will pay a visit to Weimar, to offer the sincere homage of one of the many millions of your admirers. I have the honour to be, ever and most respectfully, y[our]

Obliged adm[irer] and se[rvant],

NOEL BYRON.

[1] On Byron, sent with a letter acknowledging the dedication to himself of *Werner*.

214. TO JOHN CAM HOBHOUSE

Metaxata,[1] September 11th, 1823.

MY DEAR HOBHOUSE,

This letter will be delivered by Captain Scott, of the 'Hercules', who brought me up into these parts, and has behaved very well. He is a fine tough old tar, and has been a great amusement during our voyage; he is moreover brother to two of your constituents, and as such to be treated with all due respect, also some grog with which he regularly rounds off most hours of the four and twenty. He is a character I assure you, as you will perceive at a single glance.

I have received your, and the committee's letters, to both of which this will serve for present answer. I will endeavour to do my duty by the committee, and the cause.

On our arrival here, early in August, we found the opposite coast blockaded by the Turkish fleet. All kind of reports in circulation about divisions amongst the Greeks themselves— the Greek fleet not out (and it is not out yet as far as I know)— Blaquiere gone home again; or at least on his way there, and no communications for me from the Morea or elsewhere. Under these circumstances, added to the disinclination of Captain Scott (naturally enough) to risk his vessel among the blockaders, or their vicinity, without being insured for the full value of his *bastimento*, I resolved to remain here for a favourable opportunity of passing over; and also to collect, if possible, something like positive information.

In the meantime, I made a tour over the hills here in our old style, and then crossed over to Ithaca, which as a pendant to the Troad, a former Greek traveller would like to see. I was much gratified by both; and we have, moreover, been treated in the kindest manner by all the authorities, military and civil, from Colonel Napier,[2] the resident (whose name and fame you are aware of), the officers of the 8th, and in short by all our own countrymen.

Their hospitality both here and in Ithaca was indeed rather impressive: for dinners kill a weakly-stomached gentleman. They also insisted on lodging us, but I would not so far abuse their good nature, and am here in a very pretty village, between the mountains and the sea, waiting what Napoleon calls the 'March of Events'. The events, however, keep their march somewhat secret, but it appears nearly certain that there be

[1] In Cephalonia, which was under British protection.
[2] Colonel Charles Napier, the future conqueror of Scinde.

divisions; and that Mavrocordato [1] is *out* (some say *in* again) which were a pity, since he is the only civilised person (*on dit*) amongst the liberators.

The Turkish fleet has sailed, leaving fifteen Algerine vessels to cruise in the Gulph.

Mr. Brown [2] and Mr. Trelawny are since then gone over in a boat, to a part of the coast out of blockade, with letters from me to the Greek government at Tripolitza; and to collect information. There is little risk for small boats; but it is otherwise with larger vessels, which cannot slide in everywhere, as the Mussulmans are not very particular. Count Gamba, a young man about twenty-three, is here with me, and is very popular amongst the English; and is, I assure you, a fine fellow in all respects. I have written to apprize the Greek government of the probable approach of the vessel indicated by the committee; and prepare them to receive its continents. I wrote soon after my arrival, to Marco Bozzari, in Acarnania, and at a considerable expense sent the letter by a small boat which ran through the blockade. He answered, desiring me to come over, and stated that he meant to give battle to the Turks next day (after the date of his epistle), which he did, and was killed, but his party gained the victory; and he behaved most gallantly, by all accounts, till mortally wounded. This was very vexatious on all accounts, as well for the general loss of the individual, for I was particularly recommended to him (the chief of the Suliotes), and I cannot have the same confidence in his successor, who is less known.

I took forty Suliotes [3] here into pay; got their arms (through Colonel Napier's intercession with General Adam), and sent them to join their countrymen a few days ago, when the blockade was partly done away with. They have cost me a tolerable number in dollars, and the price of their passage (somewhat high), etc., but it was thought best that I should wait for directions from Tripolitza, before I fixed on the place where I ought to proceed with the approbation of the Greek Government.

I have also spent some hundred dollars in assisting the Greek refugees in Ithaca, and providing for a Moriote family, who were in great distress.

The Turks are in force in Acarnania, but you cannot depend

---

[1] Prince Alexander Mavrocordatos, whom Byron had known at Pisa, was leader of the Western Greeks.

[2] Hamilton Browne, a former official in the Ionian Isles.

[3] A military caste of Albanians.

upon any *accounts*. The report of the day is contradicted on
the morrow. Great divisions and difficulties exist; and several
foreigners have come away in disgust, as usual. It is at present
my intention to remain *here*, or *there*, as long as I see a prospect
of advantage to the cause; but I must not conceal from you,
and the committee, that the Greeks appear in more danger from
their own divisions than from the attacks of the enemy. There
is a talk of treachery, and all sorts of parties amongst them;
a jealousy of strangers, and a desire of nothing but *money*.
All improvements in tactics they decline, and are not very kind,
it is said, to the foreign officers, etc., in their service.

I give you this as report, but certainly I cannot say much
for those I have seen here; the slave is not yet improved by his
Saturnalia. As you are aware what they were before, I need
say little on the subject.

Pray write and say how you are. I am better for my voyage,
and stood the hot sun on the hills of this island, and of Ithaca,
like a dial.

Ever yours, most truly,

N. B.

September 14th, 1823.

P.S.—I have sent over to Messolonghi some medical stores
for the wounded there. Metaxa (the commandant of the town)
is very pressing that I should go over there; but I must first
have an answer from the Tripolitza government, and also keep
a look out for the arrival of the committee's vessel. When
these things are settled, I may as well be in one place as another
I suppose, though I have as little cunning in fortifying a besieged
town as 'honour hath skill in surgery'.[1]

Colonel Napier told me yesterday that there is a story in the
island Corfu, etc., 'that he and I had a quarrel about *arms* on
board my vessel, that it was seized after some resistance or
opposition, etc., etc., etc.', in short, a damned lie; which I
merely mention that you may contradict, and laugh at it, if
you hear anything of the kind. Napier says if his commission
could be saved to him that he would go over too. You know
he is a famous soldier, one of Sir John Moore's 'Well done, my
Majors!' left for dead at Corunna, and all alive and martial at
this moment. He is besides an excellent fellow, greatly liked,
and a thorough Liberal. He wishes me to state to the committee, *quietly*, recollect, his wish to have some communication

[1] *Henry IV*, Part I, v, i, 134.

with them. He would be just the man for a *Chef*, if it could be managed.

215. TO THE HON. AUGUSTA LEIGH

Cephalonia, 8bre 12th 1823.

MY DEAREST AUGUSTA,

Your three letters on the subject of Ada's indisposition have made me very anxious to hear further of her amelioration. I have been subject to the same complaint, but not at so early an age, nor in so great a degree. Besides, it never affected my eyes but rather my hearing, and that only partially and slightly and for a short time. I had dreadful and almost periodical headaches till I was fourteen, and sometimes since; but abstinence and a habit of bathing my head in cold water every morning cured me, I think, at least I have been less molested since that period . . . Let me know how she is. I need not say how *very* anxious I am (at this distance particularly) to hear of her welfare.

You ask why I came up amongst the Greeks? It was stated to me that my so doing might tend to their advantage in some measure in their present struggle for independence, both as an individual and as a member for the Committee now in England. How far this may be realized I cannot pretend to anticipate, but I am willing to do what I can. They have at length found leisure to quarrel among themselves, after repelling their other enemies, and it is no very easy part that I may have to play to avoid appearing partial to one or other of their factions. They have turned out Mavrocordato, who was the only *Washington* or *Kosciusko* kind of man amongst them, and they have not yet sent their deputies to London to treat for a loan, nor in short done themselves so much good as they might have done. I have written to Mr. Hobhouse three several times with a budget of documents on the subject, from which he can extract all the present information for the Committee. I have written to their Govt. at Tripolizza and Salamis, and am waiting for instructions *where* to proceed, for things are in such a state amongst them, that it is difficult to conjecture where one could be useful to them, if at all. However, I have some hopes that they will see their own interest sufficiently not to quarrel till they have received their national independence, and then they can fight it out among them in a domestic manner—and welcome. You may suppose that I have something to *think* of at least, for you can have no idea what an intriguing cunning unquiet generation they are, and as emissaries of all parties come to me at present, and I must act impartially, it makes me exclaim, as Julian did at his military exercises, 'Oh! Plato, what a task for a Philosopher!' [1]

However, *you* won't think much of *my philosophy*; nor do I, *entre nous*.

If you think this epistle or any part of it worth transmitting to L^y B. you can send her a copy, as I suppose . . . she cannot be altogether indifferent as to my 'whereabouts' and *what*abouts.

I am at present in a very pretty village (Metaxata in Cephalonia) between the mountains and the Sea, with a view of Zante and the Morea, waiting for some more decisive intelligence from the provisional Gov^t in Salamis.—— But here come some visitors.

I was interrupted yesterday by Col. Napier and the Captain of a King's ship now in the harbour. Col. N. is Resident or Governor here and has been extremely kind and hospitable, as indeed have been all the English here. When their visit was over a Greek arrived on business about this eternal siege of Mesalonghi (on the Coast of Acarnania or Etolia) and some convoys of provisions which we want to throw in; and after this was discussed, I got on horseback (I brought up my horses with me on board and troublesome neighbours they were in blowing weather) and rode to Argostoli and back; and then I had one of my *thunder* headaches (*you* know how my head acts like a barometer when there is electricity in the air) and I could not resume till this morning. Since my arrival in August I made a tour to Ithaca (which you will take to be Ireland, but if you look into Pope's *Odyssey*, you will discover to be the antient name of the Isle of Wight) and also over some parts of Cephalonia.

We are pretty well in health, the Gods be thanked!

* * * * *

There is a clever but eccentric man here, a Dr. Kennedy,[2] who is very pious and tries in good earnest to make converts; but his Christianity is a queer one, for he says that the priesthood of the Church of England are no more Christians than 'Mahound or Termagant' [3] are. He has made some converts, I suspect rather to the beauty of his wife (who is pretty as well

---

[1] Gibbon, *Decline and Fall of the Roman Empire*, chap. xix.
[2] James Kennedy, of the Army Medical Service, stationed at Corfu.
[3] i.e. Mahomet and Termagant a supposed Mohammedan deity.

as pious) than of his theology. I like what I have seen of him, of *her* I know nothing, nor desire to know, having other things to think about. *He* says that the dozen shocks of an Earthquake we had the other day are a sign of his doctrine, or a judgement on his audience, but this opinion has not acquired proselytes. One of the shocks was so prolonged that, though not very heavy, we thought the house would come down, and as we have a staircase to dismount *out* of the house (the buildings here are different from ours), it was judged expedient by the inmates (all *men* please to recollect, as if there had been females we must have helped them out or broken our heads for company) to make an expeditious retreat into the court-yard. *Who* was *first* out of the door I know not, but when I got to the bottom of the stairs I found several arrived before me, which could only have happened by their jumping out of the windows or down *over* or from the stairs (which had no balustrade or bannisters) rather than in the regular way of descent. The scene was ludicrous enough, but we had several more slight shocks in the night but stuck quietly to our beds, for it would have been no use moving, as the house would have been down first, had it been to come down at all.

There was no great damage done in the Island (except an old house or two cracking in the middle), but the soldiers on parade were lifted up as a boat is by the tide, and you could have seen the whole line waving (though no one was in motion) by the heaving of the ground on which they were drawn up. You can't complain of this being a brief letter.

I wish you would obtain from Lady B. some account of Ada's disposition, habits, studies, moral tendencies, and temper, as well as of her personal appearance, for except from the miniature drawn five years ago (and she is now double that age nearly) I have no idea of even her aspect. When I am advised on these points, I can form some notion of her character and what way her dispositions or indispositions ought to be treated [, and though I will never interfere with or thwart her mother, yet I may perhaps be permitted to suggest, as she (Lady B.) is not obliged to follow my notions unless she likes—which is not very likely. Is the girl imaginative?] [1] At *her* present age I have an idea that I had many feelings and notions which people would not believe if I stated them *now*, and therefore I may as well keep them to myself. Is she social or solitary, taciturn or talkative,

---

[1] Supplied from the fragment of the letter printed in Lady Lovelace's edition of Lord Lovelace's *Astarte*, 1921.

fond of reading or otherwise? And what is her *tic?*—I mean her foible. Is she passionate? I hope that the Gods have made her anything save *poetical*—it is enough to have one such fool in a family. You can answer all this at your leisure: address to *Genoa* as usual, the letters will be forwarded better by my Correspondents there.

Yours ever,

N. B.

P.S.—Tell Douglas K^d I have only just got his letter of August 19th, and not only approve of his accepting a sum not under ten or twelve thousand pounds for the property in question, but also of his getting as much as can be gotten above that price.

216. TO THE HON. DOUGLAS KINNAIRD

Cephalonia, 8bre 29th, 1823.

MY DEAR DOUGLAS,

I have sent to Hobhouse various documents and dispatches, from which he can furnish the proper information to the committee. The Greek government have invited me to Napoli di Romania, and I expect to proceed there in November. You had better address to me by Genoa (to Messrs. Webb and Barry). My letters reach me sooner through that channel, as vessels sail frequently.

I shall take your advice about the reverend care of my purse and person, as far as is consistent with propriety. The former has not yet suffered much, having only been lightened of about a thousand dollars, partly an aid to the Suliotes, and partly to some of the refugees, and also some expenses for sending boats with dispatches, etc., and the latter is for the present in tolerable plight.

You, gentlemen of the committee, must exert yourselves, and I will second you as well as I can; but your newspaper accounts are highly exaggerated, for neither Turks nor Greeks have done much this year. I shall continue to state things to you all exactly as they are, or appear to me, and the best way *not* to despond is perhaps to commence with not being over-sanguine. The cause is good, and I think eventually *safe* (if the Holy Alliance leave the Greeks to themselves), and I am inclined to believe that the committee may be of essential service in forwarding supplies, or monies, and obtaining a loan for the Independents; but there is still a good deal to be done, and more than is imagined in your part of the world, for proof (or at least assertions) of which I refer you to high authorities amongst the Greeks themselves, transmitted to me by Hobhouse. Ld. Sidney Osborne came over yesterday from Corfu to meet me; and I dine with the Government Resident, Col. Napier, to-day to meet him. He came up (i.e. Ld. S.) to Metaxata, where I now am, yesterday, and we had a luncheon, and some talk together. I then rode back with him towards Argostoli.

He is in good preservation, and as clever and *insouciant* as ever. He tells me that Alvanley is at length 'rectus in curia' with his creditors, and in possession of his long expected uncle's property. Tell him that I have discovered a text in St. Paul's Epistle to the Romans, Chapter X, of such unimpeachable veracity, that I have been converted into a firm believer of all the rest. It is this (vide Chapter X) '*For there is no difference between the* JEW *and the* GREEK', these are the literal words, and what is more to the purpose, the literal truth. Some of their bankers tried to make me pay interest for *my own money* in my *own possession*, which I came to spend, for their cause, too! and this I think equals or beats the tribes of Israel, unless perhaps the *ten*, who are still supposed to exist in the heart of Asia. But I 'sorted them I trow',[1] having the staff for the present in my own hands.

Believe me truly your affectionate,

N. B.

P.S.—I hope you have retained the best counsel for the H[unt]s;[2] have you received the 12th Co. of D. J. sent on the 14th 10bre 1822? I do not know what security we can have for H[unt]'s accounting for the profits but he has a property in the *Examiner*. A fair account of profit or loss would perhaps be the better way, supposing it to be accurately stated.

I have had a letter from my sister, wishing me *not* to leave anything by my will to *her* children!! I do not know if I mentioned to you a similar circumstance; when Allegra died I was going to leave the five thousand pounds which I had originally bequeathed to that infant to Madame La Comtesse Guiccioli, which she declined in the most positive, and indeed, displeased terms, declaring that she should consider such a bequest as not only an injustice to my daughter by Lady B., and to my sister's family, but as a posthumous insult to herself,

---

[1] *The Antiquary*, chap. xiv.
[2] In the prosecution for publishing Byron's *Vision of Judgment*. Hunt was eventually fined.

and persisted so, that I have been obliged to leave my will as it was. Is not this odd? *Two women* of different countries concurring upon the same point! It is true Madame G. has her separate allowance (by the Pope's decree) from her husband, and will have a considerable jointure at his demise, but it is not unhandsome conduct nevertheless.

217. TO JOHN BOWRING

9bre 29, 1823.

This letter will be presented to you by Mr. Hamilton Browne, who precedes or accompanies the Greek deputies. He is both capable and desirous of rendering any service to the cause, and information to the Committee. He has already been of considerable advantage to both, of my own knowledge. Lord Archibald Hamilton, to whom he is related, will add a weightier recommendation than mine.

Corinth [1] is taken, and a Turkish squadron said to be beaten in the Archipelago. The public progress of the Greeks is considerable, but their internal dissensions still continue. On arriving at the seat of Government, I shall endeavour to mitigate or extinguish them—though neither is an easy task. I have remained here till now, partly in expectation of the squadron in relief of Messolonghi, partly of Mr. Parry's [2] detachment, and partly to receive from Malta or Zante the sum of four thousand pounds sterling, which I have advanced for the payment of the expected squadron. The bills are negotiating, and will be cashed in a short time, as they would have been immediately in any other mart; but the miserable Ionian merchants have little money, and no great credit, and are besides *politically shy* on this occasion; for although I had letters of Messrs. Webb (one of the strongest houses of the Mediterranean), and also of Messrs. Ransom, there is no business to be done on *fair* terms except through English merchants. These,[3] however, have proved both able and willing,—and upright as usual.

Colonel Stanhope [4] has arrived, and will proceed immediately;

---

[1] The Greeks recovered Corinth on 16 September.

[2] William Parry, a former firemaster of the Navy, was engaged by the Greek Committee as artilleryman and mechanic, and arrived in February 1824.

[3] Messrs. Samuel Barff and Charles Hancock, bankers, of Zante and Argostoli.

[4] Colonel the Hon. Leicester Stanhope, afterwards fifth Earl of Harrington, who had offered his services to the Greek Committee.

he shall have my co-operation in all his endeavours: but, from every thing that I can learn, the formation of a brigade at present will be extremely difficult, to say the least of it. With regard to the reception of foreigners,—at least of foreign officers, —I refer you to a passage in Prince Mavrocordato's recent letter, a copy of which is enclosed in my packet sent to the Deputies. It is my intention to proceed by sea to Napoli di Romania as soon as I have arranged this business for the Greeks themselves—I mean the advance of two hundred thousand piastres for their fleet.

My time here has not been entirely lost,—as you will perceive by some former documents that any advantage from my *then* proceeding to the Morea was doubtful. We have at last moved the Deputies, and I have made a strong remonstrance on their divisions to Mavrocordato, which, I understand, was forwarded by the Legislative to the Prince. With a loan they *may* do much, which is all that *I*, for particular reasons, can say on the subject.

I regret to hear from Colonel Stanhope, that the Committee have exhausted their funds. Is it supposed that a brigade can be formed without them? or that three thousand pounds would be sufficient? It is true that money will go farther in Greece than in most countries; but the regular force must be rendered a *national concern*, and paid from a national fund; and neither individuals nor committees, at least with the usual means of such as now exist, will find the experiment practicable.

I beg once more to recommend my friend, Mr. Hamilton Browne, to whom I have also personal obligations, for his exertions in the common cause, and have the honour to be

Yours very truly.

218. TO THE GENERAL GOVERNMENT OF GREECE

Cephalonia, November 30, 1823.

The affair of the Loan, the expectation so long and vainly indulged of the arrival of the Greek fleet, and the danger to which Messolonghi is still exposed, have detained me here, and will detain me till some of them are removed. But when the money shall be advanced for the fleet, I will start for the Morea; not knowing, however, of what use my presence can be in the present state of things. We have heard some rumours of new dissensions, nay, of the existence of a civil war. With all my heart I pray that these reports may be false or exaggerated, for I can imagine no calamity more serious than this; and I must frankly confess that unless union and order are established, all hopes of a Loan will be vain; and all the assistance which the Greeks could expect from abroad — and assistance neither trifling nor worthless — will be suspended or destroyed; and, what is worse, the great powers of Europe, of whom no one was an enemy to Greece, but seemed to favour her establishment of an independent power, will be persuaded that the Greeks are unable to govern themselves, and will, perhaps, themselves undertake to settle your disorders in such a way as to blast the brightest hopes of yourselves and of your friends.

Allow me to add, once for all,—I desire the well-being of Greece, and nothing else; I will do all I can to secure it; but I cannot consent, I never will consent, that the English public, or English individuals, should be deceived as to the real state of Greek affairs. The rest, Gentlemen, depends on you. You have fought gloriously;—act honourably towards your fellow-citizens and the world, and it will then no more be said, as has been repeated for two thousand years with the Roman historians, that Philopœmen was the last of the Grecians.[1] Let not calumny itself (and it is difficult, I own, to guard against it in so arduous a struggle) compare the patriot Greek, when resting from his labours, to the Turkish pacha, whom his victories have exterminated.

I pray you to accept these my sentiments as a sincere proof of my attachment to your real interests, and to believe that I am, and always shall be,

Yours, etc.

219. TO THE HON. DOUGLAS KINNAIRD

Cephalonia, December 23, 1823.

MY DEAR [DOUGLAS],

I shall be as saving of my purse and person as you recommend: but you know that it is as well to be in readiness with one or both in the event of either being required.

I presume that some agreement has been concluded with Mr. Murray about *Werner*. Although the copyright should only be worth two or three hundred pounds, I will tell you what can be done with them. For three hundred pounds I

---

[1] Plutarch, *Philopœmen*, cap. i.

can maintain in Greece, at more than the *fullest pay* of the Provisional Government, rations included, one hundred armed men for *three months*. You may judge of this when I tell you, that the four thousand pounds advanced by me to the Greeks is likely to set a fleet and an army in motion for some months.

A Greek vessel has arrived from the squadron to convey me to Missolonghi, where Mavrocordato now is, and has assumed the command, so that I expect to embark immediately. Still address, however, to Cephalonia, through Messrs. Webb and Barry of Genoa, as usual; and get together all the means and credit of mine you can, to face the war establishment, for it is 'in for a penny, in for a pound', and I must do all that I can for the ancients.

I have been labouring to reconcile these parties, and there is *now* some hope of succeeding. Their public affairs go on well. The Turks have retreated from Acarnania without a battle, after a few fruitless attempts on Anatoliko. Corinth is taken, and the Greeks have gained a battle in the Archipelago. The squadron here, too, has taken a Turkish corvette with some money and a cargo. In short, if they can obtain a Loan, I am of opinion that matters will assume and preserve a steady and favourable aspect for their independence.

In the mean time I stand paymaster, and what not; and lucky it is that, from the nature of the warfare and of the country, the resources even of an individual can be of a partial and temporary service.

Colonel Stanhope is at Messolonghi. Probably we shall attempt Patras next. The Suliotes, who are friends of mine, seem anxious to have me with them, and so is Mavrocordato. If I can but succeed in reconciling the two parties (and I have left no stone unturned), it will be something; and if not, we must go over to the Morea with the Western Greeks—who are the bravest, and at present the strongest, having beaten back the Turks—and try the effect of a little *physical* advice, should they persist in rejecting *moral* persuasion.

Once more recommending to you the reinforcement of my strong box and credit from all lawful sources and resources of mine to their practicable extent—for, after all, it is better playing at nations than gaming at Almack's or Newmarket—and requesting you to write to me as often as you can,

I remain ever yours,

N. B.

220. TO THOMAS MOORE

Cephalonia, December 27, 1823.

I received a letter from you some time ago. I have been too much employed latterly to write as I could wish, and even now must write in haste.

I embark for Missolonghi to join Mavrocordato in four-and-twenty hours. The state of parties (but it were a long story) has kept me here till *now*; but now that Mavrocordato (their Washington, or their Kosciusko) is employed again, I can act with a *safe conscience*. I carry money to pay the squadron, etc., and I have influence with the Suliotes, *supposed* sufficient to keep them in harmony with some of the dissentients;—for there are plenty of differences, but trifling.

It is imagined that we shall attempt either Patras or the castles on the Straits; and it seems, by most accounts, that the Greeks, at any rate the Suliotes, who are in affinity with me of 'bread and salt',—expect that I should march with them, and —be it even so! If any thing in the way of fever, fatigue, famine, or otherwise, should cut short the middle age of a brother warbler,—like Garcilasso de la Vega,[1] Kleist,[2] Körner,[3] Joukoffsky [4] (a Russian nightingale—see Bowring's *Anthology*), or Thersander,[5] or,—or somebody else—but never mind—I pray you to remember me in your 'smiles and wine'.[6]

I have hopes that the cause will triumph; but whether it does or no, still 'honour must be minded as strictly as milk diet'. I trust to observe both.

Ever, etc.

221. TO COLONEL THE HON. LEICESTER STANHOPE

Scrofes (or some such name), on board a
Cephaloniote Mistico,[7] Dec. 31, 1823.

MY DEAR STANHOPE,

We are just arrived here, that is, part of my people and I, with some things, etc., and which it may be as well not to specify

[1] Garcilaso de la Vega (1503–36), the Spanish poet, died of wounds received in battle.
[2] Ewald Christian von Kleist (1715–59) died after battle.
[3] Karl Theodor Körner (1791–1813) was killed in a skirmish.
[4] Vasili Andreevitch Zhukovsky (1783–1852), author of the *Minstrel in the Russian Camp*, which was translated in Bowring's *Specimens of the Russian Poets*. Byron must have been under the impression that he perished in the Battle of the Tarutino, 1812.
[5] Thersander was killed in the attack on Troy.
[6] Moore, *Irish Melodies*, 'The Legacy'.
[7] A long, sharp, swift boat, with both sails and oars, and one or more guns.

in a letter (which has a risk of being intercepted, perhaps); —but Gamba, and my horses, negro, steward, and the press, and all the Committee things, also some eight thousand dollars of mine, (but never mind, we have more left, do you understand?) are taken by the Turkish frigates, and my party and myself, in another boat, have had a narrow escape last night (being close under their stern and hailed, but we would not answer, and bore away), as well as this morning. Here we are, with sun and clearing weather, within a pretty little port enough; but whether our Turkish friends may not send in their boats and take us out (for we have no arms except two carbines and some pistols, and I suspect, not more than four fighting people on board), is another question, especially if we remain long here, since we are blocked out of Messolonghi by the direct entrance.

You had better send my friend George Drake (Draco), and a body of Suliotes, to escort us by land or by the canals, with all convenient speed. Gamba and our Bombard [1] are taken into Patras, I suppose; and we must take a turn at the Turks to get them out: but where the devil is the fleet gone?—the Greek, I mean; leaving us to get in without the least intimation to take heed that the Moslems were out again.

Make my respects to Mavrocordato, and say that I am here at his disposal. I am uneasy at being here: not so much on my own account as on that of a Greek boy with me, for you know what his fate would be; and I would sooner cut him in pieces, and myself too, than have him taken out by those barbarians. We are all very well.

N. B.

The Bombard was twelve miles out when taken; at least, so it appeared to us (if taken she actually be, for it is not certain); and we had to escape from another vessel that stood right between us and the port.

222. TO HENRY MUIR [2]

Dragomestri, January 2, 1824.

MY DEAR MUIR,

I wish you many returns of the season, and happiness therewithal. Gamba and the Bombard (there is a strong reason to believe) are carried into Patras by a Turkish frigate, which we saw chase them at dawn on the 31st: we had been close under

---

[1] Bomb-vessel.   [2] Dr. Henry Muir, the health officer of Argostoli.

the stern in the night, believing her a Greek till within pistol shot, and only escaped by a miracle of all the Saints (our captain says), and truly I am of his opinion, for we should never have got away of ourselves. They were signalising their consort with lights, and had illuminated the ship between decks, and were shouting like a mob;—but then why did they not fire? Perhaps they took us for a Greek brûlot, and were afraid of kindling us—they had no colours flying even at dawn nor after.

At daybreak my boat was on the coast, but the wind unfavourable for *the port*;—a large vessel with the wind in her favour standing between us and the Gulf, and another in chase of the Bombard about twelve miles off, or so. Soon after they stood (i.e. the Bombard and frigate) apparently towards Patras, and, a Zantiote boat making signals to us from the shore to get away, away we went before the wind, and ran into a creek called Scrofes, I believe, where I landed Luke [1] and another (as Luke's life was in most danger), with some money for themselves, and a letter for Stanhope, and sent them up the country to Messolonghi, where they would be in safety, as the place where we were could be assailed by armed boats in a moment, and Gamba had all our arms except two carbines, a fowling-piece, and some pistols.

In less than an hour the vessel in chase neared us, and we dashed out again, and showing our stern (our boat sails very well), got in before night to Dragomestri, where we now are. But where is the Greek fleet? I don't know—do you? I told our master of the boat that I was inclined to think the two large vessels (there were none else in sight) Greeks. But he answered, 'They are too large—why don't they show their colours?' and his account was confirmed, be it true or false, by several boats which we met or passed, as we could not at any rate have got in with that wind without beating about for a long time; and as there was much property, and some lives to risk (the boy's especially) without any means of defence, it was necessary to let our boatmen have their own way.

I despatched yesterday another messenger to Messolonghi for an escort, but we have yet no answer. We are here (those of my boat) for the fifth day without taking our clothes off, and sleeping on deck in all weathers, but are all very well, and in good spirits. It is to be supposed that the Government will send, for their own sakes, an escort, as I have 16,000 dollars on board, the greater part for their service. I had (besides personal

[1] The Greek boy.

property to the amount of about 5000 more) 8000 dollars in specie of my own, without reckoning the Committee's stores; so that the Turks will have a good thing of it, if the prize be good.

I regret the detention of Gamba, etc., but the rest we can make up again; so tell Hancock to set my bills into cash as soon as possible, and Corgialegno to prepare the remainder of my credit with Messrs. Webb to be turned into monies. I shall remain here, unless something extraordinary occurs, till Mavrocordato sends, and then go on, and act according to circumstances. My respects to the two colonels, and remembrances to all friends. Tell 'Ultima Analise'[1] that his friend Raidi[2] did not make his appearance with the brig, though I think that he might as well have spoken with us in or off Zante, to give us a gentle hint of what we had to expect.

> Yours ever affectionately,
>
> N. B.

P.S.—Excuse my scrawl on account of the pen and the frosty morning at daybreak. I write in haste, a boat starting for Kalamo. I do not know whether the detention of the Bombard (if she be detained, for I cannot swear to it, and I can only judge from appearances, and what all these fellows say), be an affair of the Government, and neutrality, and, etc.—but she was stopped at least twelve miles distant from any port, and had all her papers regular from Zante for Kalamo and we also. I did not land at Zante, being anxious to lose as little time as possible; but Sir F. S.[3] came off to invite me, etc., and every body was as kind as could be, even in Cephalonia.

223. TO CHARLES HANCOCK [4]

Messolonghi, January 13, 1824.

DEAR SIR,

Many thanks for yours of the fifth; ditto to Muir for his. You will have heard that Gamba and my vessel got out of the hands of the Turks safe and intact; nobody knows well how or why, for there is a mystery in the story somewhat melodramatic. Captain Valsamachi has, I take it, spun a long yarn by this

---

[1] A nickname for Count Delladecima, from his habit of using the phrase on all occasions.
[2] Possibly Praidi, Mavrocordatos' secretary.
[3] Sir Frederick Stoven, British Resident at Zante.
[4] Of Messrs. Barff and Hancock. See page 363.

time in Argostoli. I attribute their release entirely to Saint Dionysius, of Zante, and the Madonna of the Rock, near Cephalonia.[1]

The adventures of my separate bark were also not finished at Dragomestri: we were convoyed out by some Greek gunboats, and found the *Leonidas*, brig-of-war at sea to look after us. But blowing weather coming on, we were driven on the rocks *twice* in the passage of the Scrofes, and the dollars had another narrow escape. Two thirds of the crew got ashore over the bowsprit: the rocks were rugged enough, but water very deep close in-shore, so that she was, after much swearing and some exertion, got off again, and away we went with a third of our crew, leaving the rest on a desolate island, where they might have been now, had not one of the gun-boats taken them off, for we were in no condition to take them off again.

Tell Muir that Dr. Bruno [2] did not show much fight on the occasion; for besides stripping to his flannel waistcoat, and running about like a rat in an emergency, when I was talking to a Greek boy (the brother of the Greek girls in Argostoli), and telling him the fact that there was no danger for the passengers, whatever there might be for the vessel, and assuring him I could save both him and myself without difficulty (though he can't swim), as the water, though deep, was not very rough— the wind *not* blowing *right* on shore (it was a blunder of the Greeks who missed stays),—the Doctor exclaimed, 'Save *him*, indeed! by G—d! save *me* rather—I'll be first if I can'—a piece of egotism which he pronounced with such emphatic simplicity as to set all who had leisure to hear him laughing, and in a minute after the vessel drove off again after striking twice. She sprang a small leak, but nothing further happened, except that the captain was very nervous afterwards.

To be brief, we had bad weather almost always, though not contrary; slept on deck in the wet generally for seven or eight nights, but never was in better health (I speak personally)— so much so that I actually bathed for a quarter of an hour on the evening of the 4th instant in the sea (to kill the fleas, and others, etc.), and was all the better for it.

We were received at Missolonghi with all kinds of kindness and honours; and the sight of the fleet saluting, etc., and the crowds and different costumes was really picturesque. We

---

[1] The reason was that Valsamarchi had once saved the life of the commander of the Turkish frigate, who carried them to Patras.

[2] Francesco Bruno, Byron's physician.

think of undertaking an expedition soon, and I expect to be ordered with the Suliotes to join the army.

All well at present. We found Gamba already arrived, and every thing in good condition. Remembrance to all friends.

Yours ever,

N. B.

P.S.—You will, I hope, use every exertion to realise the *assets*. For, besides what I have already advanced, I have undertaken to maintain the Suliotes for a year, (and will accompany them either as a Chief, or ——[1] whichever is most agreeable to the Government,) besides sundries. I do not understand Browne's '*letter of credit*'. I neither gave nor ordered a letter of credit that I know of; and though of course, if you have done it, I will be responsible, I was not aware of any thing, except that I would have backed his bills, which you said was unnecessary. As to *orders*—I ordered nothing but some *red cloth* and *oil cloth*, both of which I am ready to receive; but if Gamba has exceeded my commission, *the other things must be sent back, for I cannot permit any thing of the kind, nor will*. The servants' journey will of course be paid for, though *that* is exorbitant. As for Browne's letter, I do not know any thing more than I have said, and I really cannot defray the charges of half Greece and the Frank adventurers besides. Mr. Barff must send us some dollars soon, for the expenses fall on me for the present.

P.S.Al.—Will you tell Saint (Jew) Geronimo Corgialegno that I mean to draw for the balance of my credit with Messrs. Webb and Co. I shall draw for two thousand dollars (that being the amount, more or less); but, to facilitate the business, I shall make the draft payable also at Messrs. Ransom and Co's, Pall-Mall East, London. I believe I already showed you my letters, (but if not, I have them to show,) by which, besides the credits now realising, you will have perceived that I am not limited to any particular amount of credit with my bankers. The Honourable Douglas, my friend and trustee, is a principal partner in that house, and having the direction of my affairs, is aware to what extent my present resources may go, and the letters in question were from him. I can merely say, that within the *current* year, 1824, besides the money already advanced to the Greek Government, and the credits now in your hands and your partner's (Mr. Barff), which are all from

[1] Illegible.

the income of 1823, I have anticipated nothing from that of the present year hitherto. I shall or ought to have at my disposition upwards of an hundred thousand dollars, (including my income, and the purchase-money of a manor lately sold,) and perhaps more, without infringing on my income for 1825, and not including the remaining balance of 1823.

Yours ever,

N. B.

224. TO HIS HIGHNESS YUSUFF PASHA [1]

Missolonghi, January 23, 1824.

HIGHNESS!

A vessel, in which a friend and some domestics of mine were embarked, was detained a few days ago, and released by order of your Highness. I have now to thank you; not for liberating the vessel, which, as carrying a neutral flag, and being under British protection, no one had a right to detain; but for having treated my friends with so much kindness while they were in your hands.

In the hope, therefore, that it may not be altogether displeasing to your Highness, I have requested the governor of this place to release four Turkish prisoners, and he has humanely consented to do so. I lose no time, therefore, in sending them back, in order to make as early a return as I could for your courtesy on the late occasion. These prisoners are liberated without any conditions: but should the circumstance find a place in your recollection, I venture to beg, that your Highness will treat such Greeks as may henceforth fall into your hands with humanity; more especially since the horrors of war are sufficiently great in themselves, without being aggravated by wanton cruelties on either side.

NOEL BYRON.

225. TO CHARLES HANCOCK

Messolonghi, February 5, 1824.

DEAR SIR,

Dr. Muir's letter and yours of the 23d reached me some days ago. Tell Muir that I am glad of his promotion for his sake, and of his remaining near us for our sakes; though I cannot but regret Dr. Kennedy's departure, which accounts for the

[1] Written in Italian and translated by Moore (*Letters and Journals of Lord Byron*).

previous earthquakes and the present English weather in this climate. With all respect to my medical pastor, I have to announce to him, that amongst other fire-brands, our fire-master Parry (just landed) has disembarked an elect blacksmith, entrusted with three hundred and twenty-two Greek Testaments. I have given him all facilities in my power for his works spiritual and temporal; and if he can settle matters as easily with the Greek Archbishop and hierarchy, I trust that neither the heretic nor the supposed sceptic will be accused of intolerance.

By the way, I met with the said Archbishop at Anatolico (where I went by invitation of the Primates a few days ago, and was received with a heavier cannonade than the Turks, probably), for the second time (I had known him here before); and he and P. Mavrocordato, and the Chiefs and Primates and I, all dined together, and I thought the metropolitan the merriest of the party, and a very good Christian for all that. But Gamba (we got wet through on our way back) has been ill with a fever and colic; and Luke (not the Evangelist, but a disciple of mine) has been out of sorts too, and so have others of the people, and I have been very well,—except that I caught cold yesterday, with swearing too much in the rain at the Greeks, who would not bear a hand in landing the Committee stores, and nearly spoiled our combustibles; but I turned out in person, and made such a row as set them in motion, blaspheming at them all from the Government downwards, till they actually did *some* part of what they ought to have done several days before, and this is esteemed, as it deserves to be, a wonder.

Tell Muir, that notwithstanding his remonstrances, which I receive thankfully, it is perhaps best that I should advance with the troops; for if we do not do something soon, we shall only have a third year of defensive operations and another siege, and all that. We hear that the Turks are coming down in force, and sooner than usual: and as these fellows do mind me a little, it is the opinion that I should go—firstly, because they will sooner listen to a foreigner than one of their own people, out of native jealousies: secondly, because the Turks will sooner treat or capitulate (if such occasion should happen) with a Frank than a Greek; and, thirdly, because nobody else seems disposed to take the responsibility—Mavrocordato being very busy here, the foreign military men too young or not of authority enough to be obeyed by the natives, and the Chiefs (as aforesaid) inclined to obey any one except, or rather than, one of their own body. As for me, I am willing to do what I am bidden, and to follow my instructions. I neither seek nor shun that nor any thing else that they may wish me to attempt: as for personal safety, besides that it ought not to be a consideration, I take it that a man is on the whole as safe in one place as another; and, after all, he had better end with a bullet than bark in his body. If we are not taken off with the sword, we are like to march off with an ague in this mud basket; and to conclude with a very bad pun, to the ear rather than to the eye, better *martially* than *marsh-ally*;—the situation of Messolonghi is not unknown to you. The dykes of Holland when broken down are the Deserts of Arabia for dryness, in comparison.

And now for the sinews of war. I thank you and Mr. Barff for your ready answer, which, next to ready money, is a pleasant thing. Besides the assets and balance, and the relics of the Corgialegno correspondence with Leghorn and Genoa, (I sold the dog's flour, tell him, but not at *his* price,) I shall request and require, from the beginning of March ensuing, about five thousand dollars every two months, i.e. about twenty-five thousand within the current year, at regular intervals, independent of the sums now negotiating. I can show you documents to prove that these are considerably *within* my supplies for the year in more ways than one; but I do not like to tell the Greeks *exactly what* I *could* or would advance on an emergency, because, otherwise, they will double and triple their demands (a disposition that they have already sufficiently shown): and though I am willing to do all I can *when* necessary, yet I do not see *why* they should not help a little; for they are not quite so bare as they pretend to be by some accounts.

February 7, 1824.

I have been interrupted by the arrival of Parry, and afterwards by the return of Hesketh,[1] who has not brought an answer to my epistles, which rather surprises me. You will write soon, I suppose. Parry seems a fine rough subject, but will hardly be ready for the field these three weeks: he and I will (I think) be able to draw together,—at least, *I* will not interfere with or contradict him in his own department. He complains grievously of the mercantile and *enthusymusy*, as Braham pronounces enthusiasm, part of the Committee, but greatly praises Gordon and Hume. Gordon *would* have given three or four thousand pounds and come out *himself*, but Kennedy or

[1] A young Englishman in the Greek service.

somebody else disgusted him, and thus they have spoiled part of their subscription and cramped their operations. Parry says Blaquiere is a humbug, to which I say nothing. He sorely laments the printing and civilising expenses, and wishes that there was not a Sunday-school in the world, or *any* school *here* at present, save and except always an academy for artilleryship.

He complained also of the cold, a little to my surprise; firstly, because, there being no chimneys, I have used myself to do without other warmth than the animal heat and one's cloak, in these parts; and, secondly, because I should as soon have expected to hear a volcano sneeze, as a firemaster (who is to burn a whole fleet) exclaim against the atmosphere. I fully expected that his very approach would have scorched up the town like the burning-glasses of Archimedes.[1]

Well, it seems that I am to be Commander-in-Chief, and the post is by no means a sinecure, for we are not what Major Sturgeon calls 'a set of the most amicable officers'.[2] Whether we shall have 'a boxing bout between Captain Sheers and the Colonel', I cannot tell; but, between Suliote chiefs, German barons, English volunteers, and adventurers of all nations, we are likely to form as goodly an allied army as ever quarrelled beneath the same banner.

February 8, 1824.

Interrupted again by business yesterday, and it is time to conclude my letter. I drew some time since on Mr. Barff for a thousand dollars, to complete some money wanted by the Government. The said Government got cash on that bill *here*, and at a profit; but the very same fellow who gave it to them, after proposing to give me money for other bills on Barff to the amount of thirteen hundred dollars, either could not, or thought better of it. I had written to Barff advising him, but had afterwards to write to tell him of the fellow's having not come up to time. You must really send me the balance soon. I have the artillerists and my Suliotes to pay, and Heaven knows what besides; and as every thing depends upon punctuality, all our operations will be at a stand-still unless you use despatch. I shall send to Mr. Barff or to you further bills on England for three thousand pounds, to be negotiated as speedily as you can. I have already stated here and formerly the sums I can com-

---

[1] Alluding to the tradition that Archimedes destroyed the Roman fleet in Syracuse by means of burning-glasses.
[2] Foote's *Mayor of Garratt*, i.

mand at home within the year,—without including my credits, or the bills already negotiated or negotiating, or Corgialegno's balance of Messrs. Webb's letter,—and my letters from my friends (received by Mr. Parry's vessel) confirm what I already stated. How much I may require in the course of the year I can't tell, but I will take care that it shall not exceed the means to supply it.

Yours ever,
N. B.

P.S.—I have had, by desire of a Mr. *Gerosstati*, to draw on Demetrius Delladecima (is it our friend *in ultima analise?*) to pay the Committee expenses. I really do not understand what the Committee mean by some of their proceedings. Parry and I get on well *hitherto*: how long this may last, Heaven knows, but I hope it will, for a good deal for the Greek service depends upon it; but he has already had some *miffs* with Col. S[tanhope], and I do all I can to keep the peace amongst them. However, Parry is a fine fellow, extremely active, and of strong, sound, practical talent, by all accounts. Enclosed are bills for three thousand pounds, drawn in the mode directed (i.e. parcelled out in smaller bills). A good opportunity occurring for Cephalonia to send letters on, I avail myself of it. Remembrances to Stevens and all friends. Also my compliments and every thing kind to the colonels and officers.

February 9, 1824.

P.S.—2d or 3d. I have reason to expect a person from England directed with papers (on business) for me to sign, somewhere in the Islands, by and by: if such should arrive, would you forward him to me by a safe conveyance, as the papers regard a transaction with regard to the adjustment of a lawsuit, and a sum of several thousand pounds, which I, or my bankers and trustees for me, may have to receive (in England) in consequence. The time of the probable arrival I cannot state, but the date of my letters is the 2d. Nov., and I suppose that he ought to arrive soon.

226. TO THE HON. DOUGLAS KINNAIRD (?)

MY DEAR [DOUGLAS], *Missolonghi, February 21, 1824.*

I have received yours of the 2d of November. It is essential that the money should be paid, as I have drawn for it all, and

more too, to help the Greeks. Parry is here, and he and I agree
very well; and all is going on hopefully for the present,
considering circumstances.

We shall have work this year, for the Turks are coming down
in force; and, as for me, I must stand by the cause. I shall
shortly march (according to orders) against Lepanto, with two
thousand men. I have been here some time, after some narrow
escapes from the Turks, and also from being shipwrecked.
We were twice upon the rocks; but this you will have heard,
truly or falsely, through other channels, and I do not wish to
bore you with a long story.

So far I have succeeded in supporting the Government of
Western Greece, which would otherwise have been dissolved.
If you have received the eleven thousand and odd pounds,
these, with what I have in hand, and my income for the current
year, to say nothing of contingencies, will, or might, enable me
to keep the 'sinews of war' properly strung. If the deputies
be honest fellows, and obtain the loan, they will repay the
4000l. as agreed upon; and even then I shall save little, or indeed
less than little, since I am maintaining nearly the whole machine
—in this place, at least—at my own cost. But let the Greeks
only succeed, and I don't care for myself.

I have been very seriously unwell,[1] but am getting better, and
can ride about again; so pray quiet our friends on that score.

It is not true that I ever *did, will, would, could,* or *should*
write a satire against Gifford, or a hair of his head. I always
considered him as my literary father, and myself as his 'prodigal
son'; and if I have allowed his 'fatted calf' to grow to an ox
before he kills it on my return, it is only because I prefer beef
to veal.

Yours ever,
N. B.

227. TO THE HON. AUGUSTA LEIGH [2]

Missolonghi, [Monday] Feby 23^d 1824.

MY DEAREST AUGUSTA,

I received a few days ago yours and Lady B.'s report of
Ada's health, with other letters from England for which I ought
to be and am (I hope) sufficiently thankful, as they were of
great comfort and I wanted some, having been recently unwell,
but am now much better. So that you need not be alarmed.

---

[1] On 15 February Byron had had an epileptic seizure.
[2] An unfinished letter found on Byron's writing-table after his death.

You will have heard of our journeys and escapes, and so forth, perhaps with some exaggeration; but it is all very well now, and I have been for some time in Greece, which is in as good a state as could be expected considering circumstances. But I will not plague you with politics, wars, or *earthquakes*, though we had another very smart one three nights ago, which produced a scene ridiculous enough, as no damage was done except to those who stuck fast in the scuffle to get first out of the doors or windows, amongst whom some recent importations, fresh from England, who had been used to quieter elements, were rather squeezed in the press for precedence.

I have been obtaining the release of about nine and twenty Turkish prisoners—men, women, and children—and have sent them at my own expense home to their friends, but one, a pretty little girl of nine years of age named Hato or Hatagèe, has expressed a strong wish to remain with me, or under my care, and I have nearly determined to adopt her. If I thought that Lady B. would let her come to England as a Companion to Ada—(they are about the same age), we could easily provide for her; if not, I can send her to Italy for education. She is very lively and quick, and with great black oriental eyes, and Asiatic features. All her brothers were killed in the Revolution; her mother wishes to return to her husband who is at Prevesa, but says that she would rather entrust the child to me in the present state of the Country. Her extreme youth and sex have hitherto saved her life, but there is no saying what might occur in the course of the *war* (and of *such* a war), and I shall probably commit her to the charge of some English lady in the islands for the present. The Child herself has the same wish, and seems to have a decided character for her age. You can mention this matter if you think it worth while. I merely wish her to be respectably educated and treated, and, if my years and all things be considered, I presume, it would be difficult to conceive me to have any other views.

With regard to Ada's health, I am glad to hear that it is so much better. But I think it right that Lady B. should be informed, and guard against it accordingly, that her description of much of her indisposition and tendencies very nearly resemble my *own* at a similar age, except that I was much more impetuous. Her preference of *prose* (strange as it may seem) *was* and indeed *is* mine (for I hate *reading* verse, and always did), and I never invented anything but '*boats—ships*' and generally relating to the Ocean. I showed the report to Col. Stanhope, who was struck with the resemblance of *parts* of it to the *paternal* line even *now*. But it is also fit, though unpleasant, that I should mention that my recent attack, and a very severe one, had a strong appearance of *epilepsy*. *Why*—I know not, for it is late in life—its first appearance at thirty-six—and, as far as I *know*, it is not *hereditary*, and it is that it may not *become* so, that you should tell Lady B. to take some precautions in the case of Ada. My attack has not yet returned, and I am fighting it off with abstinence and exercise, and thus far with success; if merely casual, it is all very well.

228. TO JOHN MURRAY

Messolonghi, February 25, 1824.

I have heard from Mr. Douglas Kinnaird that you state 'a report of a satire on Mr. Gifford having arrived from Italy, *said* to be written by *me !* but that *you* do not believe it'. I dare say you do not, nor any body else, I should think. Whoever asserts that I am the author or abetter of anything of the kind on Gifford lies in his throat. I always regarded him as my literary father, and myself as his prodigal son; if any such composition exists, it is none of mine. *You* know as well as any body upon *whom* I have or have not written; and *you* also know whether they do or did not deserve that same. And so much for such matters.

You will perhaps be anxious to hear some news from this part of Greece (which is the most liable to invasion); but you will hear enough through public and private channels. I will, however, give you the events of a week, mingling my own private peculiar with the public; for we are here jumbled a little together at present.

On Sunday (the 15th, I believe,) I had a strong and sudden convulsive attack, which left me speechless, though not motionless—for some strong men could not hold me; but whether it was epilepsy, catalepsy, cachexy, or apoplexy, or what other *exy* or *epsy*, the doctors have not decided; or whether it was spasmodic or nervous, etc.; but it was very unpleasant, and nearly carried me off, and all that. On Monday, they put leeches to my temples, no difficult matter, but the blood could not be stopped till eleven at night (they had gone too near the temporal artery for my temporal safety), and neither styptic nor caustic would cauterise the orifice till after a hundred attempts.

On Tuesday, a Turkish brig of war ran on shore. On Wednesday, great preparations being made to attack her, though protected by her consorts, the Turks burned her and retired to Patras. On Thursday a quarrel ensued between the Suliotes and the Frank guard at the arsenal: a Swedish officer [1] was killed, and a Suliote severely wounded, and a general fight expected, and with some difficulty prevented. On Friday, the officer was buried; and Captain Parry's English artificers mutinied, under pretence that their lives were in danger, and are for quitting the country:—they may.

On Saturday we had the smartest shock of an earthquake which I remember, (and I have felt thirty, slight or smart, at different periods; they are common in the Mediterranean,) and the whole army discharged their arms, upon the same principle that savages beat drums, or howl, during an eclipse of the moon: —it was a rare scene altogether—if you had but seen the English Johnnies, who had never been out of a cockney workshop before!—or will again, if they can help it—and on Sunday we heard that the Vizier is come down to Larissa, with one hundred and odd thousand men.

In coming here, I had two escapes; one from the Turks, (*one* of my vessels was taken, but afterwards released,) and the other from shipwreck. We drove twice on the rocks near the Scrofes (Islands near the coast).

I have obtained from the Greeks the release of eight-and-twenty Turkish prisoners, men, women, and children, and sent them to Patras and Prevesa at my own charges. One little girl of nine years old, who prefers remaining with me, I shall (if I live) send, with her mother, probably, to Italy, or to England, and adopt her. Her name is Hato, or Hatagèe. She is a very pretty lively child. All her brothers were killed by the Greeks, and she herself and her mother merely spared by special favour and owing to her extreme youth, she being then but five or six years old.

My health is now better, and I ride about again. My office here is no sinecure, so many parties and difficulties of every kind; but I will do what I can. Prince Mavrocordato is an excellent person, and does all in his power; but his situation is perplexing in the extreme. Still we have great hopes of the success of the contest. You will hear, however, more of public news from plenty of quarters: for I have little time to write.

Believe me, yours, etc., etc.

N. Bn.

[1] Lieutenant Sass.

229. TO THOMAS MOORE

Messolonghi, Western Greece, March 4, 1824.

MY DEAR MOORE,

Your reproach is unfounded—I have received two letters from you, and answered both previous to leaving Cephalonia. I have not been 'quiet' in an Ionian island, but much occupied with business, as the Greek deputies (if arrived) can tell you. Neither have I continued *Don Juan*, nor any other poem. You go, as usual, I presume, by some newspaper report or other.

When the proper moment to be of some use arrived, I came here; and am told that my arrival (with some other circumstances) *has* been of, at least, temporary advantage to the cause. I had a narrow escape from the Turks, and another from shipwreck, on my passage. On the 15th (or 16th) of February, I had an attack of apoplexy, or epilepsy,—the physicians have not exactly decided which, but the alternative is agreeable. My constitution, therefore, remains between the two opinions, like Mahomet's sarcophagus between the magnets.[1] All that I can say is, that they nearly bled me to death, by placing the leeches too near the temporal artery, so that the blood could with difficulty be stopped, even with caustic. I am supposed to be getting better, slowly, however. But my homilies will, I presume, for the future, be like the Archbishop of Granada's—in this case, 'I order you a hundred ducats from my treasurer, and wish you a little more taste.'[2]

For public matters I refer you to Colonel Stanhope's and Capt. Parry's reports,—and to all other reports whatsoever. There is plenty to do—war without, and tumult within—they 'kill a man a week', like Bob Acres in the country.[3] Parry's artificers have gone away in alarm, on account of a dispute in which some of the natives and foreigners were engaged, and a Swede was killed, and a Suliote wounded. In the middle of their fright there was a strong shock of an earthquake; so, between that and the sword, they boomed off in a hurry, in despite of all dissuasions to the contrary. A Turkish brig ran ashore, etc., etc., etc.[4]

You, I presume, are either publishing or meditating that

---

[1] According to the legend Mahomet's coffin, of iron, hangs in the air between two lodestones.
[2] See page 5.   [3] *The Rivals*, IV, i.
[4] Incidents already described in the letters are here omitted by Moore.

same. Let me hear from and of you, and believe me, in all
events,

Ever and affectionately yours,

N. B.

P.S.—Tell Mr. Murray that I wrote to him the other day,
and hope that he has received, or will receive, the letter.

230. TO JAMES KENNEDY

Messolonghi, March 4, 1824.

My dear Doctor,

I have to thank you for your two very kind letters, both
received at the same time, and one long after its date. I am
not unaware of the precarious state of my health, nor am, nor
have been, deceived on that subject. But it is proper that I
should remain in Greece; and it were better to die doing something than nothing. My presence here has been supposed so
far useful as to have prevented confusion from becoming worse
confounded, at least for the present. Should I become, or be
deemed useless or superfluous, I am ready to retire; but in the
interim I am not to consider personal consequences; the rest is
in the hands of Providence,—as indeed are all things. I shall,
however, observe your instructions, and indeed did so, as far
as regards abstinence, for some time past.

Besides the tracts, etc., which you have sent for distribution,
one of the English artificers, (hight Brownbill, a tinman,) left
to my charge a number of Greek Testaments, which I will
endeavour to distribute properly. The Greeks complain that
the translation is not correct, nor in *good* Romaic: Bambas can
decide on that point. I am trying to reconcile the clergy to
the distribution, which (without due regard to their hierarchy)
they might contrive to impede or neutralise in the effect, from
their power over their people. Mr. Brownbill has gone to the
Islands, having some apprehension for his life, (not from the
priests, however,) and apparently preferring rather to be a saint
than a martyr, although his apprehensions of becoming the
latter were probably unfounded. All the English artificers
accompanied him, thinking themselves in danger on account of
some troubles here, which have apparently subsided.

I have been interrupted by a visit from Prince Mavrocordato
and others since I began this letter, and must close it hastily,
for the boat is announced as ready to sail. Your future convert,

Hato, or Hatagée, appears to me lively, and intelligent, and promising, and possesses an interesting countenance. With regard to her disposition I can say little, but Millingen,[1] who has the mother (who is a middle-aged woman of good character) in his house as a domestic (although their family was in good worldly circumstances previous to the Revolution), speaks well of both, and he is to be relied on. As far as I know, I have only seen the child a few times with her mother, and what I have seen is favourable, or I should not take so much interest in her behalf. If she turns out well, my idea would be to send her to my daughter in England (if not to respectable persons in Italy), and so to provide for her as to enable her to live with reputation either singly or in marriage, if she arrive at maturity. I will make proper arrangements about her expenses through Messrs. Barff and Hancock, and the rest I leave to your discretion and to Mrs. K.'s, with a great sense of obligation for your kindness in undertaking her temporary superintendence.

Of public matters here, I have little to add to what you will already have heard. We are going on as well as we can, and with the hope and the endeavour to do better. Believe me,

Ever and truly, etc.,

N. B.

231. TO THE HON. DOUGLAS KINNAIRD

Messalonghi, March 30th 1824.

My dear Douglas,

Signor Zaimi,[2] the third Greek Deputy, will present this to you; and in his behalf I bespeak good hospitality and usual kindness. The other Deputies here can, could or should have presented an introductory epistle to you, as well as to others, on their arrival. The same letter enclosed also a copy of the paper signed by themselves and drawn up in their own way—on my advancing 4000*l*. Sterling to the Greek Gov^t, which was (by their own express wish) to be repaid in the event of their obtaining a national loan in London, which it should seem that they have accomplished. I have also to apprize you that I have cashed for P. Mavrocordato bills to the amount of 550*l*. Sterling, which bills are drawn on Mr. Bowring and directed to you. P. Mavrocordato says that SS. Orlando and Luriotti

---

[1] Dr. Julius Millingen, who had come out with an introduction to Byron. In January 1824 he opened a dispensary at Missolonghi.
[2] Andreas Zaimes.

have assets to supply the needful to the said Mr. Bowring, a fact which you will duly ascertain, or otherwise the 550*l.* Sterling, monies advanced by me on the specified bills may be in some sort likely to hitch in their progress to payment.

The Greek Cause up to this present writing hath cost me of mine own monies about thirty thousand Spanish dollars *advanced*, without counting my own contingent expences of every kind. It is true, however, that every thing would have been at a standstill in Messalonghi if I had not done so. Part of this money, more particularly the 4000*l.* advanced, and guaranteed by the G^k Deputies is, or ought to be, repaid. To this you will look, but I shall still spend it in the Cause, for I have some hundred men under my command, regularly paid and pretty men enough.

I have written to you repeatedly, imploring you to sell out of the Funds while they are high, and to take four per cent.— or any per cent.—on landed security for the monies.

I have also been, and am, anxious to hear how you have succeeded with Rochdale, the Kirkby Arrears, the new publications, the settling of lawsuits, etc., etc., etc., and always concluding by a request for all possible credits to the extent of my resources, for I must do the thing handsomely.

I have been very unwell, but am supposed to be better, and almost every body else has been ill too—Parry and all, tho' he is a sort of hardworking Hercules. We have had strange weather and strange incidents—natural, moral, physical, martial and political, all which you will hear of perhaps, truly or falsely, from other quarters—I can't gossip just now. I am called to a Congress at Salona with P. Mavrocordato to meet Ulysses and the Eastern Chiefs on State affairs, and on the opening Campaign. What the result is likely to be I cannot say. The General Gov^t have assured me the direction of this province, or to join them in the Morea. I am willing to do anything that may be useful.

We were to have besieged Lepanto, but the Suliotes did not like the service 'against Stone walls', and have had a row besides with some foreigners, in which blood was spilt on both sides, so that that scheme was postponed. Capt Parry is doing all that circumstances will permit in his department, and indeed in many others, for he does *all* that is done here, without any aid except the Committee's and mine, for the G^k local Gov^t have not a *sou*, *they* say, and are in debt besides. I have two hundred and twenty five regulars and irregulars in my pay—and had five hundred of the latter, but when they quarrelled amongst themselves, and tried to heighten their pretensions besides, I boomed them off; and by dint of so doing, and turning restive when fair means would not do, the rest are reduced to very good order, and the *regulars* have all along behaved very well, upon the whole—as well as any other troops anywhere. Six Guns belong to this auxiliary Corps of Artillery, which, by the way, is the only *regularly paid* corps in Greece. The Gov.ᵗ only give them rations—and those reluctantly: they have mutinied twice on account of bad bread, and really with cause, for it was quite unmasticable; but we have gotten a new Commissary, and a Baker, instead of the Bricklayer who furnished the former loaves, apparently,—and with not very good bricks neither. Yesterday there was a Court Martial on a man for stealing; the German Officers wanted to flog, but I positively prohibited anything of the kind: the culprit was dismissed the service—publicly, and conducted through the town to the Police Office to have him punished according to the Civil law. Same day, one amicable officer challenged two others; I had the parties put under arrest until the affair was accommodated: if there is any more challenging, I will call them all out and wafer one half of them.

Matters, however, go on very tolerably, and we expect them to mend still further now that the Greeks have got their loan, and may be organized. Believe me,

Ever yours and truly,

N. B.

232. TO CHARLES F. BARRY [1]

Dear Barry,　　　　　　　　　　　　　　April 9th [2] 1824.

The Account up to 11th July was 40,541, etc., Genoese livres in my favour: since then I have had a letter of Credit of Messrs. Webb for 60,000 Genoese livres, for which I have drawn; but how the account stands *exactly*, you do not state. The balance will of course be replaced by my London Correspondent, referring more particularly to the Hon.ble Douglas Kinnaird, who is also my Agent and trustee, as well as banker, and a friend besides since we were at College together—which is favourable to business, as it gives confidence, or ought to do so.

I had hoped that you had obtained the price of the Schooner [3]

---

[1] Of Messrs. Webb and Barry, Byron's bankers at Genoa and Leghorn.
[2] On this day, through exposure to wet, Byron contracted the fever of which he died ten days later.
[3] The *Bolivar*.

from Ld Blessington: you must really tell him that I must make the affair public, and take other steps which will be agreeable to neither, unless he speedily pays the money, so long due, and contracted by his own headstrong wish to purchase. You *know* how fairly I treated him in the whole affair.

Every thing except the best (i.e. the Green travelling Chariot) may be disposed of, and that speedily, as it will assist to balance our accompt. As the Greeks have gotten their loan, they may as well repay mine, which they no longer require: and I request you to forward a copy of the agreement to Mr. Kinnaird, and direct him from me to claim the money from the Deputies. They were welcome to it in their difficulties, and also for good and all, supposing that they had not got out of them; but, as it is, they can afford repayment, and I assure you that, besides *this*, they have had many 'a strong and long pull' at my purse, which has been (and still is) disbursing pretty freely in their cause: besides, I shall have to *re-expend* the same monies, having some hundred men under orders, at my own expense, for the Gk. Government and National service.

Of all their proceedings here, health, politics, plans, acts, and deeds, etc.--good or otherwise, Gamba or others will tell you—truly or not truly, according to their habits.

Yours ever,
N. B^n.

INDEX TO THE INTRODUCTION
AND NOTES

INDEX OF CORRESPONDENTS

(The numbers are those of the letters)

MADE AT THE
TEMPLE PRESS LETCHWORTH
IN GREAT BRITAIN